The Analysis of Film

Raymond Bellour

Edited by Constance Penley

INDIANA UNIVERSITY PRESS

Bloomington and Indianapolis

This book is a publication of

Indiana University Press
601 North Morton Street
Bloomington, IN 47404-3797 USA

http://www.indiana.edu/~iupress

Telephone orders 800-842-6796
Fax orders 812-855-7931
Orders by e-mail iuporder@indiana.edu
First reprinted in paperback in 2001
© 2000 by Indiana University Press

The paper used in this publication meets the minimum requirements of American National Standard for Information Sciences—
Permanence of Paper for Printed Library Materials, ANSI Z39.48-
1984.

Manufactured in the United States of America

Library of Congress Cataloging-in-Publication Data

Bellour, Raymond.
  [Analyse du film. English]
  The analysis of film/Raymond Bellour; edited by Constance
Penley.
    p.   cm.
  Includes bibliographical references and index.
  ISBN 0-253-33700-3 (alk. paper)—ISBN 0-253-21364-9 (pbk.:
alk. paper)
    1. Hitchcock, Alfred, 1899– 2. Motion pictures—Production
and direction. 3. Cinematography.   I. Penley, Constance, 1948–
II. Title.

PN1998.3.H58 B4513 2000
791.43'0233'092—dc21
                                                          99-045486
        2   3   4   5   05   04   03   02   01

To

THIERRY KUNTZEL

CHRISTIAN METZ

CONTENTS

PREFACE

Constance Penley

Raymond Bellour's approach to scholarship and writing has been astonishingly consistent over many years, especially given the broad range of nineteenth- and twentieth-century images and texts that he has worked on, including film, photography, video, novels, interviews, diaries, and critical editions of writers from the Brontës to Michaux. He typically advances knowledge by following his own fascinations rather than the protocols of a set research program. He tends not to adopt technical languages wholesale but rather to borrow and recombine terms and concepts for the needs of the task at hand. He warrants his arguments through art as much as science. He refuses to claim as definitive even his most exhaustive analyses. He relishes collaboration, as can be seen in the work he has done over the years with friends and colleages, most notably Christian Metz, Thierry Kuntzel, and Serge Daney. Although never anyone's disciple, he created his own "book of others" (*Le livre des autres*) by inerviewing and writing about many of France's most important thinkers, Merleau-Ponty and Blanchot from the fifties; then the "structuralists," Barthes, Lacan, Lévi-Strauss, and Foucault; later and very importantly Deleuze; and always certain historians, in particular Ariès. Finally, he understood the importance of situated knowledge long before it became *de rigueur* in academic discourse, as can be seen in the frank acknowledgment of his implication in the Western, male-dominated stories and structures his work attempts to analyze.

The Analysis of Film is based largely on *L'analyse du film*, first published in 1979 and reprinted in 1995.[1] It brings together Bellour's now classical analyses of classical Hollywood film, in a volume that consists of at least three books. The first book presents his pioneering methods for the close analysis of film. The second examines the work of Alfred Hitchcock, one of the greatest formal innovators in the history of cinema. The third offers original insights that are informed by a lifetime of research on American cinema.

There is yet a fourth, more virtual, book that appears when reading Bellour's extensive comments on the role of the woman in Western representation alongside the lively feminist engagement with his film analyses. Feminist film scholar Judith Mayne, writing in 1990, claimed that "much feminist work of the last decade or so has been a response to the assumptions inherent in both [Laura] Mulvey's and Bellour's work."[2] Even feminists who found his conclusions about female subjectivity in Hollywood film to be too pessimistic or totalizing nonetheless believed that his approach offered a powerful model of how to write about the complexities of film meaning and narrative, shot by shot, sequence by sequence, while addressing larger social and psychological issues of subjectivity, desire, and identification in Western culture.[3]

A key feature of *The Analysis of Film* is the appearance for the first time in English of "Symbolic Blockage," Bellour's magisterial, monograph-length study of *North by Northwest*, which brilliantly demonstrates the intricate ways in which the multiple mirroring and interlocking systems of the film — micro- and macro-textual, hermeneutic, symbolic — resolve themselves in an Oedipally fueled fantasy of nation and couple so typical of American cinema. This study complements a new chapter, "To Alternate/To Narrate" (chapter 8), on D. W. Griffith's *The Lonedale Operator*, which was written after the publication of *L'analyse du film*. This 1980 study is included here because it shows so convincingly that the dynamics of alternation and the repetition-resolution effect that Bellour discovered to be the heartbeat of Hollywood narrative film were already there in nascent form at the beginning of cinema. The stakes of the argument of "To Alternate/To Narrate" can best be understood by placing the essay in its original context, Bellour's two-volume, still definitive collection on American cinema, *Le cinéma américain: Analyses de film* (1980), which brought together the best of French and Anglo-American analyses of American films and their history.[4] Bellour's contribution to the study of American film stretches back to at least 1966, the year in which his edited collection *Le Western* appeared. As Janet Bergstrom pointed out in her 1979 interview with him, while other contributors to that volume chose to write about such elements of the genre as "Indian attack," "sheriff's office," "fistfight," "gambler," or "ranch," Bellour chose "woman." Bergstrom also notes that even in this very early study of American cinema, Bellour closely links "an analysis of the woman's symbolic position as crucial in determining the narrative structure, the system of fictional representation carried over from the nineteenth-century novel, and enunciation as the *principe producteur* of the narrative."[5]

Four short but seminal essays from *L'analyse du film* are regrettably missing here for reasons of space. (Bellour's introduction has been modified slightly to reflect these omissions and the addition of one new essay.) Even though they are from what the author refers to as his "pre-analytic" period, the degree to which these early essays prefigure — conceptually and practically — all of his later approaches to analyzing the system of classical Hollywood cinema, and beyond that, other national cinemas and other media as well, is striking. These four essays also show his early predilection for the work of directors who "embody the very possibility of cinema" and who state and restate through their direction — the mise-en-scène — the "primacy of vision," as Bellour puts it in "On Fritz Lang," the only one of the essays published in English.[6] In "Le monde et la distance," "Sur Fritz Lang," "Sur l'espace cinématographique," and "Ce que savait Hitchcock," it is clear that he was already concerned, from the mid-sixties on, with the necessity of understanding the minimal signifying elements of filmic narration (camera distance, framing, movements within the frame, etc.), enunciation and the director's role in enunciation, and the whole range of repetitions, oppositions, and variations between and across levels that gradually produce the film's volume and meaning.[7]

It was no simple auteurism that attracted Bellour first to Lang and then

Hitchcock in these early essays. Although he admired the way both directors sustained an original filmmaking practice across very different film cultures and indus-
tries, he was more drawn to them because they were directors who self-consciously
reflected on cinema and often staged within their films a mise-en-scène of cinematic
vision. It is notable that Bellour entitled the last of the four essays "Ce que savait
Hitchcock." By making reference to "What Maisie Knew," Henry James's most sublime staging of the way desire and fear are bound up in the act of seeing/knowing,
Bellour is insisting that Hitchcock's films, too, be seen in all of their equally sublime
complexity of affect and vision. Throughout his career of writing about film, of
ceaselessly experimenting with how to write about film, Bellour finds his inspiration
and his method in the films of directors who are also researchers carrying out experiments with the forms and address of cinema. Rather than trying to grid "the system"
of "classical American cinema," his analytic practice attempts to learn from and
with directors who are trying to creatively expand the possibilities of cinema (and,
later, video and other mixed media forms).

These four essays, especially the last one, opened up two directions for the
analysis of film. The first, more "structural," approach was pursued in all of the
following studies by Bellour that were eventually collected in *L'analyse du film*.
Bellour would later follow up on the second approach to film analysis, one that goes
beyond structuralist concerns to focus more on figuration, the body, and emotion,
as well as the different logics of other photographic and digital media. This second
approach appears mainly in the essays collected in two volumes, *L'entre-image: Photo, cinéma, vidéo* (1990) and *L'entre-images 2: Mots, images* (1999).[8] Many of Bellour's ideas about the "passages" or movements between images that have accumulated at the convergence of three arts—photography, video, and cinema—are
summed up in English in the special issue of *Camera Obscura* that he edited with
Elisabeth Lyon in 1990.[9] "Unspeakable Images" addresses the artistic, philosophi-
cal, and sociological consequences of the fact that video has become the agent of all
the new passages between images, creating images that are hard to speak about ("unspeakable"), and precipitating new relations between images and between images
and words. During this period Bellour's chosen texts for analysis are increasingly art
videos (especially the work of theorist-turned-videomaker Thierry Kuntzel, Gary
Hill, and Bill Viola) and work created for television such as Jean-Luc Godard's
France Tour Détour Deux Enfants, Histoire(s) du cinéma, and *Puissance de la parole*.
He still writes about films but for the most part only films by the more experimental
filmmakers who are known for mixing different kinds of images, still and moving,
analog and nonanalog, or cinema and television: Chantal Akerman, Akira Kuro-
sawa, Roberto Rossellini, Samuel Beckett, Ridley Scott, Jean-Marie Straub, Danièle
Huillet, and always Chris Marker. These filmmakers are among the "heroes" listed
on the back cover of *L'entre-image 2*, along with the videomakers that he admires as
well as artists, writers, and theorists who have inspired him, ranging from Christian
Boltanski to Gilles Deleuze, and from Christian Metz to Maurice Sendak.

What are the consequences for film analysis of this new attention to the logics
of other media, and especially to the changes wrought by the advent of video? In
1985, in a move that seemed surprising only at first, Bellour sounded the death knell

for film analysis, pronouncing it "an art without a future." Going even further, as if that were possible, he claimed that "there are no longer, or should no longer be, any analyses of films." How, in one short article entitled "Analysis in Flames," did the arch-practitioner of film analysis become its fiery executioner?[10] Rather than asking how, it may be more useful to ask why. In so doing it becomes clear that Bellour wanted to kill off only what film analysis had become, to then be able to see if it were possible to breathe life back into that textual and theoretical corpse.

It is not for nothing that the title of this book is *The Analysis of Film* and not the more definitive *Film Analysis*. As with the title of the 1979 French edition, *L'analyse du film*, Bellour is always trying to resist that moment when the critical practice of the close study of film becomes a theoretical genre, a "legitimate" discipline with fixed methods and authoritative boundaries. "Analysis in Flames" suggests that we have come to this perhaps inevitable moment of institutionalization but urges us to not give up the ghost. We should instead replace those now-rigid methods and boundaries with "gestures," by which Bellour seems to mean new creative strategies that could open up the illusory science of film analysis to a wider world of images and to relations between and among images and texts.

These gestures paradoxically derive from the problems and possibilities of film analysis itself. Sounding a bit like Stan Brakhage at his most Romantic, Bellour calls for "a cleansed eye . . . an eye at last freely fascinated," while invoking the "magic gesture par excellence," the stopping of films. In "A Bit of History," the introduction to the present volume (again, the same anti-definitive tactic, "A Bit of" not "The" or even "A"), Bellour reminds us of that revelatory moment in the late sixties and early seventies when film critics first took the film off the projector and onto the editing table to be able to view it shot by shot, stopping and starting it according to the needs of the analysis rather than the rhythms of "normal" viewing time. This simple move opened up a world of discoveries about the language, semiotics, and rhetoric of film.

While always attentive to the unquotable irreducibility of film, the difficulty of verbally translating even one stopped image—the topic of his 1975 essay, "The Unattainable Text" (chapter 1)—Bellour nonetheless urges us to take advantage of all the new technological ways to stop the image, which started, of course, with the VCR. The almost infinite possibilities we now have to freeze the frame allow us to turn film analysis into creative play, whether in the shared pleasures of domestic cinephilia or pedagogical fun in the classroom.

Bellour believes that the difficulty of writing about film that can be stopped and started and stopped again served to push film analysts to learn how to write in a way that would match this new form of creative play with the image. He praises Serge Daney for being among the first film critics to discover how to write so that pauses in the sentence would correspond with freeze frames that are projected into the reader's mind. Daney's mental incorporation of this film theoretical tactic shows well the interaction that can take place between theory and criticism. Insisting on the collective creativity of this activity, Bellour claims (or hopes) that increasing numbers of writers and readers are learning how to freeze images and then make them move in another way. Volume 2 of *L'entre-images* takes this writerly experiment very far. In the short preface to that volume he acknowledges that there are always too many images, or never enough, in a book in which it is not so much a matter of illustrating the film but trying to create a substitute for the "improbable body of moving images." After having taken the gamble of too many images in volume 1, he decides to do without them in volume 2 in an attempt to approximate in writing the indeterminate and fleeting relation between word and image.

Bellour's real point in "Analysis in Flames" is not that we have to quit doing film analysis but rather the analysis of the whole film. He has always been self-reflective about the madness in his method, in recognizing from early on the film analyst's desire to touch the body of the film, to embrace it by enumerating, transcribing, and charting its every signifying element, a desire whose crazy brilliance most revealed itself in "Symbolic Blockage." But what if film analysis has naturally dissolved into cinematic theory? If so then we do not need to analyze a whole film for the sake of analyzing a whole film, but only those parts of it that can contribute to solving a theoretical problem. In each particular case, "the strategy should comply with the stakes of the analysis" (p. 55), a strategy determined by an internal calculation that also takes into consideration the material means of conducting the analysis.

But it is Bellour's understanding of the degree to which film, like all other representational media, has been absorbed into video and new media that most thoroughly deconstructs the discipline of film analysis, a discipline that taught us how to write about images. Now we can do research on cinema history and theory by quoting images rather than trying to turn images into language. Bellour cites the French television series "Cinéastes de notre temps" as an early example of the rich possibilities opened up by the lavish use of film frames and clips for quotation. More recent examples are Lauren Rabinovitz's and Greg Easley's The *Rebecca* Project, Steven Mamber's CD-ROM analysis of *The Birds*, and Henry Jenkins's Virtual Screening Room pilot project, all contributing to what is soon to be an explosion of such analytic innovations. On a utopian note, Bellour says that these new creative strategies for analyzing film can advance not only the theory of cinema but also filmmaking itself, an idea since realized in Godard's *Histoire(s) du cinéma*.

After killing off the grand film analysis project of writing about the system of a whole film, Bellour returned to just such a project in 1992 in an article in *Trafic*, a cinema journal that he founded with Serge Daney and a few others in 1991 with the aim of developing new theoretical propositions and new ways of writing about film and other media in the "post-cinema" landscape. "Le film qu'on accompagne" [The film that one accompanies], like all articles in *Trafic*, uses no frame enlargements, publicity stills, or video grabs—no images whatever except a small token icon on the journal's plain brown cover—is an attempt to challenge the writer to find the language to write about image regimes that are increasingly complex and difficult to describe.[11] It is as if, in recognition of the limits of a "still" to function either as an adequate scholarly citation or a poetic evocation of the film, it is better to rely on the magic of dark marks on a white page to create (recreate) the film's images and affects in the reader's mind. Rather than merely offering a new belle-lettrism of the cinema, *Trafic*'s borrowing of the fiction-effect for media criticism represents one of today's most inspired responses to the question of how to create the language that would ensure a critical purchase on new media technologies and cultures. For all of Bellour's enthusiasm for using images to analyze images, he does not propose that we should let up on the effort to develop the artful science of writing about those always unattainable images. In an earlier time, this would have been a call for a "struggle on two fronts."

"Le film qu'on accompagne" offers a close analysis of the shots and sequences of Ritwik Ghatak's 1960 film *The Hidden Star* (*Meghe Dhaka Tara*). In his earlier film analyses, the ones included in this book, Bellour attempted to describe and explain the dizzying abstraction of the signifying work of the film in the interaction of its most micro elements with its most macro levels. But here he focuses on the interior figuration of the shot and the emotional relation to elements in it. Identifying *The Hidden Star* as a "classical" film but with "modern" ruptures, Bellour shows how the shot serves the development of the action, the story, but is also composed as much in relation to its own interior as to the following shot. "This provokes an emotion rarely attained, that depends on the pure force of each instant, on the singular disequilibrium that it induces and that is going to travel, and build, from one end of the film to the other." Although this new and seemingly simpler focus on the shot itself and the emotion that it provokes appears to contrast with Bellour's earlier emphasis on the dazzling complexity of the build-up of textual "volume," it resembles those first analyses in one key respect: it, too, takes its analytical methods from the ground up, from the nature of the text itself. Bellour's close analysis of *The Hidden Star* reveals and responds to *this* film's system by demonstrating, for example, how Ghatak sets up a modulation and a disequilibrium between open and full spaces that in just three shots echoes the historic and personal disequilibrium that is the emotional basis of the film: the partition of Bengal. All of Ghatak's films, Bellour says, are marked by an exile that he turned into "a system of mise-en-scène" based on loss, shock, separation. This film's system calls for a method of analysis that can respond to the emotion organized by the mise-en-scène. It is not so much a film that one critiques or analyzes after the fact but a film that one accompanies.

Here, in an essay that loops back to Bellour's seemingly relinquished desire to analyze the signifying system of a whole film, he returns to precisely that kind of project but only when he has fashioned a strategy that complies with "the stakes of the analysis." He not only gives unprecedented attention to the interior of the shot in its modulation of affective relations, he also puts a new focus on the role of music and sound in the film insofar as the emotional structure of the film is entirely bound up with the way the ragas of Indian melodrama interact with the shots, sounds, and changing mise-en-scène. But even though Bellour is now focusing on different elements of the film than he did in his earlier analyses (showing that the categories of his earlier film analyses were never meant to be simply "gridded" over other films), one strategy remains the same, a signature stylistic and rhetorical choice that has major implications for how we conceive the work of film theory and history. Whether he is writing about Ghatak's film from 1960, a classical American film, one of Godard's television shows, or the latest Bill Viola video installation, he is not so much concerned with establishing the *system* of those different media forms (as demanded by an approach to film analysis with a more scientific superego) but with trying to follow the creation of the textual *volume* of works that are constantly experimenting with both issues of representation and the "contract" between medium and spectator/audience. In this sense, all of Bellour's analyses have tended to "accompany" the text, producing a second textual volume, theoretically infinite, that mirrors, critiques, and builds on an "original" text chosen for its own creative experimentation. One theoretical and historical irony, at least in an American context, is that Bellour's "creative writing" on film has produced some of the most substantive scholarly discoveries about the signifying and narrative system of classical cinema and the history of its forms and institutional modes. In this scientistic and positivistic moment of the development of "film studies" as a proper academic discipline, there is a great deal to be learned from an analytical practice that chooses its objects of study on the basis of a passion for the medium, a passion shared with a director determined to challenge what we think about "the" image, relations between and among images, narration, the relation of the spectator to the screen, and the way that representation is bound up with culture, history, memory. Godard, of course, in his ethical and political "passages" between and among images, has been a constant figure for Bellour's writing and thinking on these issues.[12]

A final lesson for film studies can be found in Bellour's own passages between and among images, which is the limitation of studying cinema in artistic, theoretical, social, or technological isolation. In an essay called "Cinema and . . . ," which Bellour originally wrote as a paper for a conference examining the legacy of Christian Metz's work, he argues for "the force, at once simple and unexpected, which consists of saying *cinema and . . .* : and thus accepting all the consequences."[13]

✳   ✳   ✳

Many people over many years have helped to create the English language version of Raymond Bellour's collected analyses of film. First, Bertrand Augst, who not only translated Bellour but also introduced hundreds of students to his work by establishing the American University Center for the Study of Film in Paris and inviting him to teach there. Bertrand, as always, generously (and with great humor and patience) responded to my requests for help with every phase of this book.

The founding *Camera Obscura* editors all studied with Bellour in what is more informally known as the "Paris Film Program" and went on to publish translations of his work in some of the earliest, most formative issues of the journal. Janet Bergstrom's 1979 interview with Bellour in *Camera Obscura* (3–4) and her accompanying essay, "Enunciation and Sexual Difference," set the tone for the way feminists engaged, critiqued, and built on contemporary film theory's ideas about the structuring role of sexual difference in classical Hollywood film and its spectators. Much later, in 1990, Elisabeth Lyon co-edited with Bellour a special issue of *Camera Obscura* (24) on "Unspeakable Images." In that issue they and the contributors explored a range of images—film, photography, video—whose meanings are unsayable, not reducible to linguistic meaning. I remain very grateful, after all these years, to Janet and Liz for their help in elucidating Bellour's ideas and words.

The work of the translators for this volume deserves special recognition: Ben Brewster for "System of a Fragment" and "The Unattainable Text"; Diana Matias for "The Obvious and the Code" and "To Segment/To Analyze"; Bertrand Augst and Hilary Radner for "To Enunciate"; Nancy Huston for "Psychosis, Neurosis, Perversion"; and Inge Pruks for "To Alternate/To Narrate." The late Mary Quaintance took on the challenge of translating the monograph-length "Symbolic Blockage." The grace and intelligence she brought to translating this chapter also shines through in her rendering of the introduction, "A Bit of History."

Catherine Nesci, a friend and colleague at the University of California, Santa Barbara, who is a great admirer of Bellour's work on nineteenth-century literature, jumped into twentieth-century film to help me with several last questions about the translation. I am also grateful to Catherine for putting me in touch with Roxanne Lapidus, the managing editor of *Substance*, who ironed out some of the final wrinkles. I appreciate her deftness and speed.

Ben Brewster and Lea Jacobs volunteered for the huge job of checking the film termi-nology in the translation of "Symbolic Blockage" as well as for creating electronic versions of the chapter's numerous tables.

Allan Langdale saved the day by helping me put the manuscript into electronic form.

I could not have finished the manuscript without the aid of my research assistant Aubrey Anable, who brought her considerable editing skills, honed as a *Camera Obscura* intern, to the project and who was also willing to learn the art of making frame enlargements so that I did not have to re-learn it. Juan Monroy, another hardworking *Camera Obscura* intern, gave crucial help at the end.

The work of Melanie Richter-Bernburg, manuscript editor at Indiana University Press, was invaluable.

Joan Catapano, senior editor at Indiana University Press, deserves the thanks of the entire film community for keeping up the Press's commitment to translate and publish the most important works of classical and contemporary film theory.

I am grateful to the journals that granted permission to reprint the translations: *Screen, Camera Obscura,* and *Australian Journal of Screen Theory. Quarterly Review of Film Studies* published a translation by Maureen Turim of an earlier version of "To Segment/ To Ana-lyze." Rick Altman commissioned Diana Matias to translate a later version for his collection *Genre: The Musical,* which is the one reprinted here. And many thanks to the British Film Institute for permission to reprint "System of a Fragment," which previously existed only as a BFI Education Department pamphlet entitled *"The Birds:* Analysis of a Sequence."

Notes

1. *L'analyse du film* (Paris: Editions Albatros, 1979; 2nd ed., Paris: Calmann-Lévy, 1995).

2. Judith Mayne, *The Woman at the Keyhole: Feminism and Women's Cinema* (Bloomington: Indiana University Press, 1990). Mayne's survey includes a discussion of the work of Mary Ann Doane, Tania Modleski, Teresa de Lauretis, and Lucy Fischer, among others.

3. Feminist work that engaged with Bellour's methods and theories includes: "The Lady Doesn't Vanish," introduction to *Feminism and Film Theory,* ed. Constance Penley (New York and London: Routledge and BFI Publishing, 1988); also in that volume see Janet Bergstrom's important early essay on Bellour's work, "Enunciation and Sexual Difference," and an excerpt from her 1979 in-depth interview with Bellour, "Alternation, Segmentation, Hypnosis," in which he answers questions about his pessimistic stance toward the possibili-ties of female agency and subjectivity in film and film spectatorship (for the full text of the interview see *Camera Obscura* 3–4 [1979]); Jacqueline Rose, "Paranoia and Film System"; and (for the most critical response) Joan Copjec's *"India Song/Son Nom de Venise dans Calcutta Désert: The Compulsion to Repeat."* See also, Sandy Flitterman, "Woman, Desire, and the Look: Feminism and the Enunciative Apparatus in Cinema," *Ciné-tracts* 2.1 (Fall 1978); Constance Penley, "A Certain Refusal of Difference: Feminism and Film Theory" and "Feminism, Film Theory, and the Bachelor Machines," in *The Future of an Illusion: Film, Feminism, and Psychoanalysis* (Minneapolis: Minnesota University Press, 1989); Tania Modleski, *The Women Who Knew Too Much: Hitchcock and Feminist Theory* (New York: Methuen, 1988); Judith Mayne, *The Woman at the Keyhole* (see note 2); Kaja Silverman, *The Acoustic Mirror: The Female Voice in Psychoanalysis and Cinema* (Bloomington: Indiana University Press, 1988), pp. 202–12; Patrice Petro, "Rematerializing the Vanishing 'Lady': Feminism, Hitchcock, and Interpretation" and Barbara Klinger, *"Psycho:* The Institutional-ization of Female Sexuality," in *A Hitchcock Reader,* ed. Marshall Deutelbaum and Leland

Poague (Ames: Iowa State University Press, 1986); Donald Grieg, "The Sexual Differentiation of the Hitchcock Text," *Screen* 28.1 (Winter 1987). Perhaps the most sympathetic critique of the limits and possibilities of Bellour's work for feminist film criticism is David Rodowick's *The Difficulty of Difference: Psychoanalysis, Sexual Difference and Film Theory* (New York: Routledge, 1991), especially the chapter "Analysis Interminable." More recent queer readings of Hitchcock have also productively engaged with Bellour's analyses: two good examples are Sabrina Barton, "Crisscross: Paranoia and Projection in *Strangers on a Train*," and Lucretia Knapp, "The Queer Voice in *Marnie*," both in *Out in Culture: Gay, Lesbian, and Queer Essays on Popular Culture*, ed. Corey K. Creekmur and Alexander Doty (Durham: Duke University Press, 1995).

4. *Le cinéma américain: Analyses de film* (two volumes), ed. Raymond Bellour (Paris: Flammarion, 1980). Besides "To Alternate/To Narrate," Bellour's other contributions to the two volumes are: "Symboliques" (on *The Westerner* [William Wyler, 1941]) and "*The Mystery of the Wax Museum* (Michael Curtiz, 1933); for a long discussion in English of his work on *The Westerner* see the excerpt from Janet Bergstrom's interview, "Desire and Law in the Western," *Feminism and Film Theory*, pp. 90–93); and "L'instant du code" (on Eastman Kodak advertisements published in *The Film Daily* in the 1950s). Other contributors to these stellar volumes on American cinema include Stephen Heath, Noel Burch, Jacques Aumont, Jean Douchet, Jonathan Rosenbaum, the *Cahiers du cinéma* collective, Thierry Kuntzel, Ron Levaco, Jean-Louis Leutrat, Alan Williams, Nick Browne, Marie-Claire Ropars, Michel Marie, Bernard Eisenschitz, Marc Vernet, Fina Bathrick, David Rodowick, Maureen Turim, Philippe Venault, and Pierre Baudry, among others.

5. For the full reference to Janet Bergstrom's interview with Raymond Bellour, see note 3.

6. "On Fritz Lang," Raymond Bellour, *Substance* 9 (1974): 25–34.

7. The four articles from *L'analyse du film* that do not appear in *The Analysis of Film* are "Le monde et la distance," originally in *Dictionnaire du cinéma* (Paris: Editions Universitaires, 1966); "Sur Fritz Lang," originally in *Critique* 226 (March 1966), reprinted in Raymond Bellour, *Le livre des autres* (Paris: L'Herne, 1971); "Remarques sur l'espace cinématographique," originally in *Sciences de l'art* 4 (1967); and Ce que savait Hitchcock," *Cahiers du cinéma* 190 (May 1967), reprinted in *Le livre des autres*.

8. Raymond Bellour, *L'entre-images: Photo, cinéma, vidéo* (Paris: La Différence, 1990), and "*L'entre-images 2: Mots, images* (Paris: P.O.L. Trafic, 1999).

9. "Unspeakable Images," special issue of *Camera Obscura* 24 (1991), ed. Elisabeth Lyon and Raymond Bellour. Bellour's contributions were "The Power of Words, the Power of Images" (his part of the introduction, trans. Elisabeth Lyon); "The Film Stilled" (a critique of Deleuze through a look at films that are interrupted or temporarily stopped, for example, *La jetée, The Man with the Movie Camera, The Crazy Ray, The 400 Blows*, many of Godard's films, *Persona*, and especially the little-known film of Roberto Rossellini, *The Machine for Killing Bad People* (trans. Alison Rowe with Elisabeth Lyon); and "The Letter goes on . . . ," an essay on Shuntaro Tanikawa and Shuji Terayama's *Video Letter* (trans. Alison Rowe with Elisabeth Lyon).

10. Raymond Bellour, "Analysis in Flames," *Diacritics* (Spring 1985); originally "L'analyse flambée," *Carte Semiotiche* 1 (September 1985).

11. Raymond Bellour, "Le film qu'on accompagne," *Trafic* 4 (Fall 1992).

12. Bellour has written a great deal about Godard's work in both volumes of *L'entre-images*. His writing on Godard that has appeared in English includes *Jean-Luc Godard: Son + Image*, a catalog that he edited with Mary Lea Bandy for a 1992 Museum of Modern Art

exhibition, which includes his essay "(Not) Just An Other Filmmaker"; his contribution to *Camera Obscura* 8–9–10, special issue on Godard, "I am an Image"; and his discussion of Godard's *Puissance de la parole* in "Cinema and . . . " (see note 13).

13. Raymond Bellour, "Cinema and . . . ," *Semiotica* 112–1/2 (1996): 207–29.

The Analysis of Film

A Bit of History

A book is all the more definitely the product of a series of subtractions when it presents itself as the sum of a finite number of elements. That is more true of this book than it is of many others, for reasons that result in part from its object. In it, in fact, at least three books can be found: first, a book on Hitchcock—a real but fragmentary book that must be gleaned haphazardly from four studies; second, a sketch of a study on classical American cinema; third, and this is the main point, a sort of history that has no value but that of its own example, a history in progress of a subdiscipline with a singularly equivocal status: the analysis of film.

These words, which I have chosen as title, suppose the existence of a proper activity that would consist, does consist, in analyzing films, just as we analyze texts or paintings. In this sense the analysis of film clearly has a place in the general development (especially in France, for a good number of years now) of what we call textual analysis. Let us call it the analysis of texts so as not to institutionalize it too quickly, and also to see what tradition it is inscribed in, even if it displaces its terms: the return of exegesis, which Foucault has shown to be historically linked to the concern for the formalization and expansion of literature as such at the very beginning of the nineteenth century.[1] We must see that today it is a question of a paradoxical movement, very unitary and profoundly divergent. Unitary, for it bespeaks a new attention to the multiple operations for which the text is the occasion and the site: an irreversible attention, one that modifies our relation to the body, to the effect of any text. But this movement is also profoundly divergent: first, in proportion to the very multiplicity of textual operations; second, and above all, because of the diversity of strategies, often irreconcilable strategies, in which the text finds itself caught up (from, e.g., its utopic expansion in Barthes to its newer function as "archeological" utterance in Foucault, and, in between, all the accumulated scholarship gathered under the name of "poetics"). Without always realizing it, the analysis of film can't help finding itself, has found itself, forcibly caught up from the beginning in the shifting diversity of these strategies. And still it is not caught up, may never be fully or as fully caught up in it, or at least not with the same exemplarity as the analysis of literary texts. There are two reasons for this: one, which has already become secondary, results from the historical discrepancy between the development of theoretical work on the literary (pictorial, etc.) object and on the cinematic object; the other, which is fundamental and which is one reason for the first, results from the very nature of the cinema's signifier. That is why the analysis of film had trouble at first in constituting itself as such; that is why today it already has trouble and no doubt will always have trouble detaching from itself.

My background is criticism, which explains, above all, this fascinated familiarity with films—a profound and uncontrolled desire directed toward an institution: cinema. The simplest and most common critical act, that of the "critique" or review, supposes a distance, an initial murder of the object. But it is a minimal distance, in which the body of the object is fractured only to be immediately restored to its addressee in the form of an imaginary whole, just as it is restored to the transmitter who feeds on this intimacy. In contrast, any true detailed analysis carries the murder of the object to its extreme: through an inevitable reversal, it goes so far as to institute itself as a new body in which the maximum intimacy with the object becomes the condition of a certain process of knowledge. It is no doubt impossible to demarcate an exact boundary between analysis and the critical act, which never stops displacing itself and breaking itself down, from simple nomination to fragmentary abstraction. Nevertheless, in the case of cinema (much more clearly than in that of the book), a demarcation is created that depends on whether one violates the law of continuity that is its principle. Whether, that is, one makes the *frozen image* the condition of one's discourse. This is still only to sketch a partial boundary; but it already seems to me to hold some weight, to have a strong if relative value in the task of delimitation.

I remember a friend telling me a long time ago that he had seen critics from *Positif* (extremely important people to the adolescents that we were) taking notes in the dark during the projection of a film. This struck me as something quite extraordinary, on the order of a transgression and a power. Now I can see what this power was, or wanted to be; I can see the impotence played out in it, and what took shelter in it. To take notes during a projection is in fact nothing less than a denegation: it is a way of freezing the image without violating the law of continuity. To be sure, there are many justifications for this strange practice. First, there is the overriding law of continuity that forbids us to watch a movie the way we read a book, by stopping and starting, by going back and rereading, by taking notes if we wish—by reading, in short, as a free reader or a professional reader without having to violate its order from the outset. Then there is everything that reinforces this law, everything that made and continues to make it so difficult to transgress: the lack of individual (or semi-collective) ownership of the means of projection (projectors and above all prints of films freely at one's disposal). Hence, when critical investment is limited, too general, or too partial (when the interest is in a few shots in a film, a single figure here and there), there is still this recourse to the notebook and the ballpoint pen (some even come equipped with a light to help battle the darkness proper to the mechanical fascination of the cinematic apparatus). I spent years this way, when the analysis of film was still in its prehistory (it was one of the forms of its prehistory), years in this strange limbo made even stranger by its obstinacy: years in the dark, my eyes fixed very much on the screen and not the page, trying to capture with a practiced but fatally inept and always insufficient hand the skeleton of this polyvalent succession of elements that almost always constitutes a film. I jotted down dialogue, action, and especially shot sequence, along with their primary relevance. I jotted down "everything," as nearly as I could: filling notebooks to the point of absurdity, retranscribing them on cards when they weren't too illegible or too erratic. I always got the impression that something, the essence, was still eluding me, that I had come up empty-handed. One day I even managed, after several successive viewings, to jot down the essence of a long sequence: a simple enough sequence in that it was almost devoid of dialogue and edited in clearly marked units but complex in its high number of shots — 72 shots, I believe, in a fragment of Hitchcock's *The Birds* that I was soon to learn included 82. But a vertigo and a hysterical trembling remained: the vertigo of not being sure of my text, and with it, hidden by the relative impossibility of doing so, a different kind of profound vertigo determined by what the implications would be if I were someday able to be sure of it.

It was in 1966 that I wrote or published, among other things, the four articles that make up the second section of the French version of this book that are not included here: "Le monde et la distance," "Sur Fritz Lang,"[2] "Sur l'espace cinématographique," and "Ce que savait Hitchcock." There was one more article, "Pour une stylistique du film,"[3] which I did not reprint in the original book because it was too general, said nothing that the others did not say in trying to assume their object, and above all said nothing that I have not said more felicitously since. In a sense, it was a synthesis of the others and presented itself as a program for a kind of activity or sub-discipline with half-determined contours.

Today all this strikes me as very improbable, given how quickly things have changed. If someone recognized the uncertain but imperious need to analyze films, what, in all that has been written about cinema, did he or she put to use? There was, of course, the considerable mass of theoretical and critical writings, contemporary and otherwise — already an infinite number of texts; and still, in the end, there was not much. At its highest point of theoretical elaboration — in Bazin's articles, or of acuity — in articles by Godard, Truffaut, Rohmer, and Rivette, film criticism continued to maintain a relation of external intimacy with its objects, an essential but insufficient relation. It sometimes cut to the quick of filmic textuality: one thinks of Bazin's classical analyses of the sequence shot (in Welles or Wyler), or of the art film or the Western; one thinks of some intuition of Godard on the work of cinema — of color, scope, framing, etc. — in the films of Nicholas Ray, or of some scene in Anthony Mann's *The Last Frontier* so precisely rearranged by Rohmer.[4] And above all one thinks of that fragment of a Truffaut text in which, to demonstrate Hitchcock's *auteur* quality, he devotes himself to an impressive gloss of the number "two" in *Shadow of a Doubt*, elaborately etching the skeleton for what is certainly one of the first analyses of film.[5] All of these are irreplaceable achievements in theorized cinephilia, which has literally invented a mode of impassioned and critical familiarity toward films.

One also thinks of a book from another quarter, like Jean Mitry's book on Eisenstein.[6] One cannot help being struck by its semi-systematic descriptions, which try to subordinate the filmic material to a set of organizing principles. But although this approach is very diverse, used on many films and many segments or fragments,[7] one immediately senses its limitations. For Mitry, it is only a matter of reorganizing and prolonging the analyses that Eisenstein himself provided of his films in his theoretical writings. The singularity of this attempt at reading arises from the exceptional situation of a director more "conscious" of the determinations that rule the organi-zation of his works. There is, in short, no textual unconscious, no displacement of the reading.[8]

In this regard we would have to ask ourselves about the way in which the "politique des auteurs," as practiced in *Cahiers du cinéma* or elsewhere (on very different grounds, with much less imagination and cultural creativity) has ended up promoting and limiting a meticulous approach to films. Directed at singularities, it promotes it with the differentiations, the disjunctions, the refinements that it pro-duces. But it also limits it, with the relation of adequation and obviousness that it tends to establish between the work and its *auteur* through a kind of manifest circu-larity that tries to make the singularity of the filmic text coincide with what the *auteur* thinks and says about it, or what he or she is made to say. This partly explains the development of a systematic approach to interviewing by the *Cahiers* editors, which is meant to provide, virtually, something like the obligatory counterpart of Eisenstein's writings for each filmmaker. These interviews, of course, are an attempt to inform and verify hypotheses, to make connections that are often quite sugges-tive; but through a strange boomerang effect, they also end up reducing the role of analysis by bringing it into the partial light of a more or less explicit phenomenology of making and seeing, joined and folded onto each other. In fact, this amounts to going through the same process in relation to the films themselves that Metz spelled out in relation to the institution and to the cinema as object: he explains quite well how the idealist theory of cinema, which contributed so much to his understanding of cinema, only did so at the price of a "lure of the ego" that is its "blind spot."[9]

Hence a remarkable consequence, which results from the semi-distance (not too far, not too close) that is maintained from the film object. The approach is always more precise when one remains at the level of theme, of scenario, of what in the image most belongs to the narrative; it always risks, at least, being singular, as-tonishingly partial; and it also risks imprecision as soon as it is applied to the smallest elements of the filmic fabric, especially those displaying the highest degree of cin-ematic specificity. That is why historical, critical, theoretical discourse, punctuated by remarkable flashes, is also, at that time, constantly punctuated by errors as soon as it is a question of films.[10] All of these errors result more or less from the overvalu-ation of memory and from the undervaluation of what has become obvious—that, like everything else, film never stops saying something other than what one thinks it says, and that, above all, it says it differently than one, always too easily, would make it say it. Many of these errors result from the floundering that comes with general description when it does not recognize the willful imprecision to which it is con-signed by generality: this is the case in the narrative of *Monsieur Verdoux* sketched by Mitry in his *Tout Chaplin*.[11] Because they want too precisely to include "image," that is, not amalgamated narrative but rather distinctive series of shots (segments on train wheels, which very subtly punctuate and divide the narrative), they most often situate them in their imprecise place in respect to the diegesis in which they are inscribed. Other, finer errors come from a will to analyze that does not provide itself with the means to realize a desire it does not recognize. I am thinking, for example, of an error that very much shocked me, for it retrospectively shook my faith in the power of truth in texts and cast suspicion on all previous propositions: a claim made by Bazin (who was, moreover, intellectual conscience itself) in his unpublished writings on Renoir. There he explained the profound singularity of *The River* by the fact that the film was composed exclusively of stationary shots.[12] Struck by this singularity, since I was interested in relations of movement and fixity, I went (by chance, it was showing) to see the film again. It had (among a very large number of stationary shots, it is true) no less than fifteen to twenty shots that were clearly moving, including the last, which closed the film with a very long, very slow traveling shot of the river. That day, I better understood how I could have transformed two stationary shots in the wedding sequence in *Brigadoon* into a wonderful camera movement that I had literally dreamed. I have seen what happens to film writing when one writes from memory or with the help of a few notes taken in the theater—when one wants to avoid the very costly, perhaps too costly penalty for freezing the image.[13]

For it is very much toward this still obscure, potential, indeterminate necessity of a generalized change in filmic attention that, in their floundering, their limitations and their very errors, the history, criticism, and theory of cinema have been moving since the fifties. Let us listen again to Truffaut in the article on Hitchcock, where we see the outline for his great book of interviews: "The homage that one can pay to an author or film-maker is to attempt to know and understand his book or his film as well as he does himself."[14] And to Godard, ten years later: "One could imagine the critique of a film as the text and its dialogue, with photos and a few words of commentary: together they would form a kind of critique, an analysis of the film."[15] Through this wish for an apparatus in which the filmmaker's desire speaks in the voice of the critic, the slow and ineluctable pressure is sketched for a new relation between the absent text of the film and the language that doubles it. That is what, like others (I think especially of Noël Burch and Marie-Claire Ropars),[16] I experienced in my pre-analytic approaches. Without yet knowing that the new precision (which little by little will take the place of the generous and relative imprecision from which it was born) would soon take on something truly other by instituting a threshold or a rupture in the apparent development of a continuity of knowledge: the rupture of a specific passion, which, when exercised, will profoundly modify the relation between the observer and his or her object.[17]

In this shifting landscape whose history may someday be told, this is where we would have to place the works of Lotte Eisner as well as filmology's contributions. Eisner's work addresses fundamental problems of composition, at the joint levels of narrative and image, and inscribes them in the global development of a cultural space and logic. This approach has only become deeper since her articles in *La revue du cinéma*[18]—through the two successive editions of *L'écran démoniaque*,[19] in her fine book on Murnau,[20] and up to her last book on Fritz Lang.[21] She is singular in that, using the privileged example of great German cinema, she very precisely subordinates the history of cinema to theoretical and methodological achievements in the history of art and the history of ideas. Even if her rather classical analysis maintains a certain textual indeterminacy in regard to films, it also brings out an uncommon precision, which touches the subtlest aspects of the image (framing, lighting, movement, distribution of masses, etc.) and refers its organization to that of the cultural components of which it forms the substratum.[22]

If filmology, for its part, has not shown much interest in films, it has significantly contributed to the shift in film theory's center of gravity by determining it in relation to certain "scientific" achievements, and, despite the generality of its stakes, has sometimes wound up touching several levels of textual singularity[23]—and above all reviving a concern for method, which will have more or less long term direct effects on the analysis of film, thanks to a progressive displacement at work from filmology toward semiology. A bit symbolically, we might think of a series of interventions (articles and interviews) by Barthes starting in the sixties.[24] In them we can see quite well that to pose in strict terms the problem of signification, in cinema as in other fields, is immediately, if only potentially, to touch on the problem of the units that produce it and the materiality of the text that they hierarchize; in the questions arising from the two interviews, we can also see an indication of the change that will soon strike film criticism at its highest level and consequently give rise to analysis.[25]

One book stands out in those years, devoted, significantly, to a single film: *Hiroshima mon amour*.[26] The rupture that surrounds this film repeats the effect that *Citizen Kane*, for example, had on the development of cinematic forms twenty years before. Two things are remarkable about this book, a collaborative effort supervised by Raymond Raver. Most of the collaborators are strangers to cinematic criticism; they come from elsewhere in that vast informal field that ranges from literary criticism to the multiplicity of the humanities.[27] The final shots of the film appear as an appendix, like the sign of a work that wants to restore literality to the film. Doubtless, no true circulation is established between this document and the studies, even the most analytic studies, that justifies its publication. But a distinct pressure exerts itself here and there; it attests that because of this catalyst (an exceptional film, owing to the conjunction of an explicitly "formalist" director and a writer), something in the relation to the cinema-object is moving. This is what lies behind the following lines by Raymond Raver, which, with a sort of positive naiveté, introduce the question that this attentive book does not yet answer but whose imminence it does mark: "Is there a method that would allow us to push analysis to the level of the signifying *detail*? How are we to bring to light the network of signifying details and take the analysis down to the smallest possible unit? Are the fiction film and the language that expresses it reducible to a single method of approach? Which one? How?"[28]

Another sign, contemporary with this same concern, is the trend toward publishing filmic "texts." Michel Marie, who has sketched the history of this phenomenon,[29] reminds us that, as early as the twenties, a Delluc or a Gance published more or less detailed descriptions of his films. More strikingly, for this time the text was established by third parties from what were already prints, Italian publishers after 1945 established very exact shot breakdowns for certain classical films. From 1961 on this discontinued tradition will be systematically developed in France in *L'avant-scène cinéma*, at the price of an interesting imprecision: the "text" of the film, scrupulously drawn from watching it on a viewing table, is in most cases retranscribed in a semi-literary way, without strict demarcations of shots, which ends up miring the film in a too "technical" description and restoring it to an ambiguous form of legibility. The implication is, and this is quite true, that a pure shooting script is in a certain sense unreadable, and that a book can never take the place of a film as anything but a heightened illustration substituted for description, as can be seen since that time in the confused attempts of American publishing ("The Film Classics Library") or the much more precise efforts of French publishing (André Balland). This also emphasizes that the strategy in no way offers in book form a mnemonic and museographic restitution of the illusory, defective object that all films are; in seizing upon the viewing table for support, the strategy does not attempt to describe "objectively" (a word which really has no meaning, even if it could be useful) but rather to open up a clearing that is necessarily particular, determined by the subjective singularity of an operation or an analytic treatment. For this to have happened, there would have had to be a decision that was not a decision, if it were not for someone who obscurely saw it at the crossroads of a series of determinations: a decision drawn from the winds of the times, the overflowing pressure of structuralism—which is responsible for, among many things, the birth of a semiology of cinema.

Let us try to be exact. The first semiology, that of Metz's "Cinéma: langue ou langage?" (1964),[30] seemed to exclude, or at least to omit, what was not yet called film analysis. With a justified concern for generality, a desire to shield the theory of cinema from the more or less contradictory imprecisions for which it had up to that point been the stage, and with the restriction of its frame of reference to structural linguistics, nothing in the semiologic rupture (if not for a fundamental concern for precision and method) proved to be of a nature to really support a desire for analysis, to respond as much to the ineluctable particularity of the object as to the signifying multiplicity for which it seemed it had to be the site. Far from knowing, any more than Metz knew at the time, that film analysis was quite simply the other textual side of a semiology or a semiotics in which psychoanalysis would play a determining role, I tried to delimit a realm that essentially tended to constitute itself as a more elaborated form of criticism. Hence the term "stylistics," borrowed from Spitzer, which I articulated in relation to the four historical attitudes enumerated by Metz in the approach to the cinematic fact (criticism, history, theory of cinema, and filmology) and to semiology itself, as Metz enunciated what semiology owed to each of these postures and what distinguished it from them. It will be apparent that with the term stylistics I was calling for a study of styles: first and foremost, in the direct tradition of *Cahiers du cinéma* and of a large part of criticism, for a deeper, more detailed, more rigorous study of the great film *auteurs*. This was to pay off the debt to my formation, to my very access to the objects—while in fact, even if it was still externally, in this text I was throwing down very fragile bases for what could or should be the structural analysis of film. (It has become clear that these two tendencies, far from being contradictory, could only be complementary; just as on another axis nothing could possibly oppose history and analysis. It is never more than a question of orders of magnitude, whose status must be recognized without inferring too much about what they specify or, above all, about what they exclude.)

I no longer regret (I have regretted it) not using that attractive term/program "structural analysis" at the time. Better yet, I am happy today to amputate its qualifier to give this book its title. Not so much because structuralism would be dated now (it is and it is not) as because of that tendency, sadly inherent to intellectual life, which uses denomination as a subtle but trenchant and often illusory game of delimitation and exclusion. But, under the impetus of Lévi-Strauss and Barthes, that certainly was my game at the time. "An intrinsic esthetic of film defined as a work in a universe of works," "the autonomous system of the film," "the film considered from the viewpoint of its formal and semantic unity," "a singular system," "the film as a singular work," "a totalitarian and systematic object," "the system that permits the film's readability," "the systematic reality of the work," "the film as system": these expressions from throughout my 1966 article, "Pour une stylistique du film,"[31] show that it was indeed this same notion of "textual system," later expanded by Metz in *Langage et cinéma*,[32] that paradoxically led me to keep a distance from the nascent semiology to which I nevertheless felt very close. It was quite simply the problem of the plurality of codes, of their diversity and multiple relations—of their "work," Thierry Kuntzel will say, spelling it out in relation to the dream-work[33]—that was in suspense. Curiously, it is in this very suspense that the first systematic analysis of a film watched on a viewing table, shot by shot, or rather segment by segment, was born: the syntagmatic analysis of the image track of *Adieu Philippine*, which was meant to illustrate the code of montage then at the heart of Metz's preoccupations.[34] Its condition of possibility then resulted from the following principle: put only a single code into play (even if others are outlined in the course of the commentary, in keeping with the ineluctable tendency of textual expansion), and describe it exhaustively instead of determining its mode of operation.[35] It is for this reason, I believe, that this work on *Adieu Philippine* seemed to me at the time to be an obstacle to what I was hoping for from analysis rather than a help to it. That was not at all what I felt before such and such a film by one of the *auteurs* that I was working on (Lang, Hitchcock, Minnelli), before such and such a fragment or segment whose multiple organization obsessed me without my yet knowing how to set it forth in its relative autonomy.

I remember a remarkable hesitation that has since always amused me. Sensing that there was more than one point of connection in our divergent preoccupations, Metz and I decided (this was in the spring of 1967) to work on a piece of film with the intention of eventually presenting it together at the Pesaro Film Festival. Mixing criteria, tastes, and possibilities, we ended up finding a print of *Suspicion*. We finally settled, I no longer know why, on the train scene—the meeting of the diegetic couple (Cary Grant and Joan Fontaine). We watched it several times. Nothing. No desire for analysis. No desire for anything. There was a sort of denseness before the object. *Suspicion* was not a bad object—far from it, if we think of the use to which it has been put since by Stephen Heath.[36] Perhaps we were simply resisting the fact that we found ourselves facing the object together, even if that is what we wanted: it is profoundly difficult, sometimes, for desire to apprehend itself. Moreover, I think we were looking for two different though absolutely linked things. Metz was looking for a concept (that of textual system), which had no need of any film because it had to account for all films, and which could never be inferred from a fragment of film alone, even if it was indeed its problematic site. I, on the other hand, hoped in some obscure way that the "desire of the film" would be concentrated in every fragment, without knowing what to do, given a certain level of detail, with the "too much" of an entire film or the "not enough" of each of its moments. I think, finally, that neither one of us managed to truly stop the film; in the absence of an as yet unspecified exigency, this, too, was denseness, resulting from the excessive identification still accorded an object that in return seemed too impoverished to respond to our desire for work.

Curiously, it was having to keep my distance from the object that finally allowed me to accede to it. I had just suffered a great disappointment: *Notorious*, on which I had accumulated many notes "in the theater," was pulled out of circulation by RKO. At the very moment that it became necessary, it was impossible to get a print on which, this time no doubt, I would have known much better where to stop, and known what I wanted to verify, since I had already preformed my object. Point of view; alternations; repetitions—in single scenes and between two scenes; gradual hiercharization of symmetry and dissymmetry; concentration on close-ups, of faces and of objects, caught up in multiple networks of symbolization; braiding together motifs for a synthetic effect of resolution that prescribes for the film a rigorous orchestration; assigning a sort of integrative logic to the movement that carried it from its beginning toward its end: all of this is what I felt was being played out in this film that fate had stolen from me. At the time, I did not question myself at all about the reasons for these successive thefts. If it was a matter of showing that there was "system" in film, why did I not simply rent a copy of a French, Italian, Soviet, or even an American film from the ciné-clubs? Why did I not take up once again the much more accessible material of my earlier critical work (on Astruc, on Resnais)? Since then I have better understood what constitutes, at least for me, a desire for analysis. Even if it must permit us to infer general propositions (I would say especially if it must permit it), this desire is profoundly singular. It is only after having found the object and taken it on that we can lightly say to ourselves: but it could just as well have been such and such another. From this transparent and enigmatic singularity is born the fear of the object, which is only the other side of its allure. It is heightened even more in the choice of the film object, which further compels two specific transgressions that clearly reinforce each other: a material transgression (the viewing table, the print, etc.) and a fantasmatic transgression (the attempt to violate the apparatus). In short, only a certain configuration could at the time sustain to its utmost my desire for analysis.

A stroke of good luck allowed me to obtain from Truffaut, for lack of a print, the final shot breakdown of *The Birds*, established from the print owned by the distributor. I was able to verify that the film fragment whose logic I had sketched out in an earlier text ("Le monde et la distance")[37] did not have 71 or 72 shots but 82. I had a "text," with an already high imaginary investment, guaranteed (so I believed at least) by the unimpeachable objectivity of a professional accounting.[38] I think I was happy to avoid freezing the image by thus effecting it, a bit magically, in a piece: it was as if the film were denied, in the fullness of its continuity and the weight of its inexhaustible phenomenality; and I had less trouble detaching myself from it so that I could construct it, reconstruct it, at whim from what seemed to me to be its most interior form—let us say its "unconscious." For quite a long time, three things stopped me. It seemed to me excessive to submit this volatile material whose time I had suspended to such a minute breakdown. I no doubt rediscovered this time in a manner both real and displaced, in the analytic movement of expansion; the excess of the combinative, produced from a finite number of elements, guaranteed the fascination and the violent condensed emotion that I felt before this film fragment. A modest Mallarmé reassured on all sides by the objectivity of the multiple models constituted by the human sciences, I had, however, the sense that I was accomplishing something like "an act of madness."[39] The second difficulty resulted from the writing itself: it was necessary to accept the fatal abstraction of a construction stripped of all signifying familiarity with its object. I understood that the impossibility of citation, except by the fallacious means of making a "*découpage*" using frame enlargements, involved a particular, essentially unsuccessful strategy—but one that also led from there to a singular *jouissance*, in face of this present-absent body of the film that incessantly ebbs and flows through the analysis. Finally, I was worried about the status of this fragment, even though its boundaries seemed indisputable: how was I to legitimate it in relation to the film as a whole from which these 82 shots had been excerpted? What meaning was I to assign to this absolutely astonishing systematic closure, which seemed to hold up a mirror to the whole film and to fit the whole within the part? How was I to understand it in relation to the notions of *oeuvre* and *auteur*, of enunciation and subject, or, more broadly, of the classical model, of American cinema? In short, I asked myself some of the many questions that were beginning insistently to form toward the film taken as the object of a preoccupation one could call *close*, sustained by two demands: one for a greater material intimacy, the other for a greater conceptual precision.

In ten years, the analysis of film thus lives out a first period of its history, obsessed by the theory of cinema being developed in it. This theory is produced by the insistence of its foci and also envelops it, as if from outside, with a subtle and progressive movement. I see two reasons for this productive tension: first, the relative autonomy of analyses, which must give themselves the proof of their possibility and sustain the paradox of their own work, as soon as they are truly precise; second, as if in opposition, the buoying up with large successive blocks that one finds in Metz's work, and its exteriority to all textual investment. (But at the same time this tension could have been experienced in a completely different mode, and in a sense eluded, through a much more polemical and global enveloping of all the terms, a more implicit circulation between levels, in all the considerable work of *Cahiers du cinéma*.) On the one hand, then, Metz's theoretical outpost is articulated, amplified, and comes to think filmic analysis as a dimension internal to it. Certain articles— "Propositions méthodologiques pour l'analyse du film," 1968; "Démarcations et ponctuations dans le film de diégèse," 1971–1972[40]—overtly inscribe the course of semiology in the perspective of textual singularity. In a parallel but more fundamental way, the notion of "textual system" is elaborated in two periods, a notion at once rigorous and fluctuating (its virtual force results from its fluctuating rigor). The first period: in *Langage et cinéma* (1971), under the impetus of a semiology that still gave priority to the linguistic, founded on a series of productive oppositions (film/cinema, filmic writing/cinematic language, specific/nonspecific codes, group of films/ class of films, etc.), the film object finds itself constituted as the site of a combination and perpetual displacement of codes, of a singular and irreducible but still determinable complexity.[41] The second period, which itself is subdivided into two stages: in "Le signifiant imaginaire" [translated as "The Imaginary Signifier"]

(1975),[42] a fundamental interrogation of the nature of the cinema's signifier, this complexity is illuminated by putting psychoanalytic processes and instances into perspective through a retrospective overview of the works variously inspired by psychoanalyis, particularly filmic analyses; in "Métaphore/Métonymie ou le référent imaginaire" [translated as "Metaphor/Metonymy, or the Imaginary Referent"] (1977),[43] under the pretext of much vaster stakes (articulation among linguistics, rhetoric, psychoanalysis), it is the very fabric, the internal composition of the textual system that ends up being theoretically innervated, even though it is no longer really in question. Turning back upon itself, the semiology of cinema "psychoanalyzes" itself and thus assumes in its generality the signifying plurality that, given its singularity, the analysis of film in certain of its outposts could not help recognizing from the very first moment.

During this same period textual approaches are also multiplying, first in France and then abroad, especially in Italy (one thinks of, among others, Gianfranco Bettetini's highly developed attempts), in England (Stephen Heath, Peter Wollen, Kari Hanet, etc.), and in the United States (Nick Browne, Alan Williams, David Bordwell, the *Camera Obscura* collective, etc.). These approaches, certainly diverse, all maintain a relation to semiology, then to the semio-psychoanalysis that is elaborated and owes them, by force of things, a part of itself; this relation also sees itself as more or less supple, according to the inclination, the "genius" and the more or less acknowledged goals of their authors. A preliminary inventory of these works has already been undertaken[44] and their history has begun to be established.[45] This is not my project. In a few words and without hoping for too much, I would simply like to try to dissipate a misunderstanding that has weighed and continues to weigh on the field of cinematic theory. Through Metz's work, it affects the semiology of cinema and rebounds to affect the analysis of film—which is its flip side and participates in its definition.

This misunderstanding is a projective image: that of "semiology" as science. It similarly but also inversely affects those who mean to apply it, as such, in particular to the analysis of films, and to those who wish to escape it, whether by exceeding and transgressing it or by opposing it. As if all of that were not a sadly dated debate, imaginarily devoted to a discipline that no longer exists today except in bad books, and that never truly existed except in its first incarnations as pure methodological space, as programmatic overture to a work or as a merely virtual study. As if semiology, in Metz, Barthes, Kristeva, and so many others, had not almost from its origin ceased to transform itself in its self-relation to the point of estrangement from the fictive image of a science of the transparency of the sign. As if, progressively informed by everything to which it held up the mirror of its models (psychoanalysis, Marxism, history, anthropology, and all the ways of thinking that arise from them), an unrecognizable and dispersed semiology did not in all domains simply become confounded with the intellectual inquiry of these last years and with the very ways of thinking meant to contest it, which become assimilated to it as semiology is displaced and metamorphized in them. The rest is purely a philosophers' debate, the acid, excessive, and mundane crystallization of differences. What seems important is that modes of thought and writings emerge from this rare melting pot of initiatives, methods, and musings. Faced with objects and the institutions that permit them (here films and cinema), these thoughts and writings end up contributing, each according to its mode but with perhaps a bit more precision than before (which history would show to be the contribution of semiology as such), to one of the most fundamental critical tasks of this period: the logic and history of representations.

In discussing the fragment from *The Birds,* I said that only a certain configuration could at that time sustain my desire for analysis. Of course, I did not understand that until later, and only bit by bit, at the cost of necessary excursions outside of cinema (my work on poetry, the Brontës, Alexandre Dumas).[46] These allowed me to better conceive the historical position of the objects I had given myself—a set of classical American films, including several Hitchcock films—and of my own history in them, as a subject inscribed in the cultural structures whose setting they delimit. I may regret it, but it is so: no begging the question, no intellectual leftism can be of any help. Godard said it: "children of Karl Marx and Coca-Cola." Let us also say: grandchildren of Sigmund Freud and the camera. We can only advance at the cost of dissociation from and rejection of certain images; and we can only separate ourselves, really, from what we have at least understood.

This configuration is founded on the relation of narcissistic doubling between man and woman. From the end of the eighteenth century and throughout the nineteenth, from which we are barely emerging, this doubling rules the two sexes' relations of desire. From it psychoanalysis is born—first Freudian, then Lacanian—using the univocal model of Oedipus and castration to organize conflict and sexual difference around the restricted scene of the nuclear family.[47] Thus one finds this configuration in most Western films, especially in classical American cinema, which (as has often been remarked) seems to have given itself the object of leading back through the great novelistic heritage of the nineteenth century and everything in it that continues to compel us.

It is the logic of this narcissistic doubling that I have tried to circumscribe through the seven close analyses included in this book. Thus I have sketched a kind of working draft of the narrative space-time, the enunciative determination and the socio-historic reality of American cinema. A subject of desire, historical through and through, finds itself defined through a systematic arrangement determined by a series of constraints; these constraints, which gain their force from being shifting and regulated at once, aim to produce a certain effect by inscribing the diegetic couple in the fiction. I have called this effect "symbolic blockage." By this I mean to suggest, first, that the movement that opens the film is the same that permits it to close, according to a program in which contingency is offered as the condition of the more or less rigorous necessity for a determinant relation between repetition and its resolution; second, that through a skillfully orchestrated hierarchization and according to an effect of continuous echo, this movement is propagated as much at the level of the global destiny of the narrative, of its massive and manifest design, as it is at the level of the infinite detail of each of its components; and, finally, that this extreme formalization is not content until it almost infinitely—but according to a very determined schema of sexual difference reorganized upon the model of the dominant representation of a single sex—reflects the mirror image of the diegetic couple devoted to the final reconciliation of desire and the law, or to their impossible conjunction (or again, through subtle splits, to the pressure of these two forces conjugated as one). Symbolic blockage: how the desire of the Western subject finds itself caught up, regulated by the double insistence of the narrative and the image, the narrative in images, according to a properly infinite process of expansion of the same, of repetition subordinated to its resolution.

For a long time, I wished to concentrate this desire for analysis on a single film. On *Notorious* first, then on *The Birds*—a bit in the way Barthes at a certain moment preferred to take extreme pains to undo the meaning of one narrative, the meaning of all (classical) narratives. I am not quite sure why I finally renounced this wish. No doubt my project was not really the same as that of *S/Z* (not to mention the considerable difference between a film and a literary text). In fact it was not so much the dispersed plurality of signifieds and their ascent to a prevailing order of the signifier that appeared to me to be my object; it was, rather, a certain relation of systematic nesting among the narrative's different dimensional orders, at their double level of expression and content, united by the determinant and historically determined pressure of the psychoanalytic signifier. It may also have been of greater demonstrative value to distribute this material across several films, even if two-thirds of them ended up being by the same *auteur*, Hitchcock, whose work allows me to more narrowly circumscribe the subject put into play by classical fiction and the institution that makes it possible. Whatever the reason, I would like these six studies to be read according to two complementary points of view: as, on the one hand, various approaches to one and the same film; and, on the other, as approaches to that immense, undefinable, and yet so suggestive "group" of films constituted by classical American cinema.

The first point of view makes it possible to deepen the empirical but also abstract notion of textual system as I have tried to situate it, notably in the final pages of my long study of *North by Northwest*. Ideally, in fact, each of the six films put into play could be the object of six joint studies. The first four, in particular, are articulated fairly distinctly through their respective levels of analysis. The first (*The Birds*) attempts to show the value of the textual logic of a fragment, that is, of an indeterminate piece of the filmic chain (82 shots), delimited only by the insistence of what can be formulated by analysis. The second *(The Big Sleep)* repeats this operation with a segment, that is, a textually predetermined fragment of the filmic chain, a specific narrative unit that offers the particular interest of constituting a sort of basic segment (12 shots), simple yet already complex, whose exemplarity makes all its worth. The third *(North by Northwest)* takes on the much more difficult task of measuring what is implied by the projective relation between the micro-elementary study of a segment of great textual extension (133 shots) and the analysis of the scenario as a whole. The fourth *(Gigi)* also pursues the textual logic of the film as a whole, but does so on the basis of organic relations between segments, more or less analogous to the relations displayed between shots within segments (if not for the fact that the segmentation has no ultimate meaning beyond the mise-en-abîme that, despite the coherence of its initial principle, makes it pass progressively from the level of the segment to that of the shot—and even to that of the fragment of a shot). The last two studies more or less resume, by overlapping, the levels of analysis proper to one or another of the first four. The fifth *(Marnie)* takes on the placement of the enunciative process in those privileged moments that the first shots or segments so often are in classical films. The sixth *(Psycho)* returns to the film as a whole, according to a free play between the whole and the part facilitated by the previous analyses: it attempts to disengage the great psychic positions that structure the enunciative process through the figuration of characters and their diegetic metamorphoses and that put the voyeuristic apparatus into play to bring this process back to the institution of cinema.

From the superimposable relation of these six levels of analysis (one could, of course, conceive of others), it clearly follows that the classical text is above all a *volume.* In each of these points, it thus undergoes the global pressure of a properly infinite number of relations, which can never be more than partially and projectively grasped and ordered. A volume is never resolved; it is doubled by that other logical, analogical volume that is analysis itself. In this sense the textual system is always virtual, determined by a certain ideality of representation that analysis must tend to. But it is no less definable, and rigorously, as if in proportion to the force that keeps it from ever being grasped by any analytic exhaustion. For through and through, at all micro- and macro-elementary levels of content and expression, it displays the insistence of an order, determined by a set of formal operations, singular and general at once (alternations, ruptures of alternation, condensations, displacements, oppositions, similarities, differences, repetitions, resolutions, etc.), borne along by figurative, narrative, and representational options.[48] The phrase "symbolic blockage" designates the insistence of this order.

The second point of view would imply that these six films could by themselves represent all of American cinema. This proposition, which can only be false, also strikes me as singularly true. In any case, it is unverifiable. Nevertheless, parallel approaches (I am thinking in particular of the works of Thierry Kuntzel, Stephen Heath, and certain of the collective or individual analyses conducted by *Cahiers du cinéma*), a collective volume on American cinema in which I brought together more than twenty French and American contributions,[49] and many experiences pursued through years of teaching have never ceased to confirm for me that, for historical and economic reasons that remain to be spelled out, the classical American cinema of the great studios, from, let us say, Griffith (see chapter 8) to the last great *auteurs* such as Hitchcock and Hawks, has never ceased to constitute itself according to this unitary logic whose possible formulations I have traced. No doubt other films, other *auteurs*, other periods, other genres, other levels of preoccupation (other configurations privileged by analysis) find themselves or could find themselves inflecting the description in a slightly different way. They would thus above all cause very numerous thematic, social, and political determinations to emerge, linked to this or that circuit of representations. In this sense an immense amount of work remains to be done (not to mention properly historic or simply documentary work). But it seems that the configuration determined by the image of the diegetic couple remains absolutely central to the fiction of a cinema powerfully obsessed by the ideology of the family and of marriage, which constitutes its imaginary and symbolic base. And at the level of the textual management of representations, of their mode of distribution and their coherence, I do not think that a diversification of inquiry ends up overly weakening or relativizing what has been done.

It is clear that if I have adhered to the description of a cultural model, to the singular evaluation of a symbolic regime the propositions sketched in these analyses largely exceed the frame defined by this model. Hence the title I have seen fit to give this book—not so much because a method, in the strict sense, is defined in it (in this order of activities, one can never sufficiently mistrust the claim of methods to external and illusory transparency) but because it is about, to the point of obsession, a methodical kind of work. And, further, because among the products of a given time, and among those that arise from the same means of expression, the minute inventory of singularities never fails to bring forth a certain number of similarities, of common features and foundations, on a basis full of divergences and differences.

One cannot help being struck, in fact, by the links that form between analyses once they really put into play what Lévi-Strauss so aptly called "the pregnancy of detail."[50] I am thinking, for example, of the fragment of *Muriel*[51] worked on by Marie-Claire Ropars, or again of her analysis of the opening sequence of *October*.[52] Why does the matricial, enunciative role of the first sequence in *October* so closely evoke the role that Thierry Kuntzel's analyses revealed so well in such dissimilar movies as Lang's *M* or Cooper and Schoedsack's *The Most Dangerous Game?* Why, in spite of the difference in narrative function, do the textual operations of displacement, condensation, alternation, symmetry and dissymmetry never fail to manifest the same types of arrangement and organization between the elements that they display in the classical, particularly the Hollywood film? Why does the very notion of sequence (that is, of a filmic segment circumscribed by criteria of unity of representation and of treatment of the cinematic signifier) have a comparable value of delimitation in films so different in nature and intention? These are some of the questions that arise, to the extent that their objects differ, from analyses that strive to systematically elucidate the modes of structuration of the filmic text.

No doubt this is simply to arrive at that very great banality that consists in assigning the human spirit, following Freud, Lévi-Strauss, or Benveniste, a certain number of laws or structures, a certain mode of functioning whose trace can be found in its multiple products. But in another sense it is to rediscover them in the concreteness of their historical expansion, in the process of understanding the singular inscription that is more or less irreducible to excessive generalizations; it is to profoundly anchor them in relation to the material reality of an art, to the socio-fantasmatic reality of an institution. We could assign two extremes to the analysis of film that would constitute, if you like, its proper territory, its two reversible points of fascination: the singular system from which it arises to constitute, according to a variable extension, its critical doubling, and the mental mechanisms it puts into play according to the proper determinations of figurability prescribed by the visual materiality of the cinema-apparatus. Between these two extremes and in proportion to the plurality of levels that it puts into play, the analysis of film ends up, strictly, contributing as much to the history as to the theory of cinema. To theory—of which, strictly limited to itself, it is like a detached fragment—for it offers sociology, semiology, metapsychology, or any approach to the screen of singularities that leads back to their concepts. To history—for even if their junction is difficult and always somewhat virtual, it helps endow it with formal and stylistic benchmarks that can inform it on two of its complementary scales: that of specific codes, of their evolution, in short of the history of cinematic language, and that of works, of directors, of companies, of periods, of genres, of local and national configurations. The development of Noël Burch's work attests to this, his book on Japanese cinema[53] as much as the research he pursued with Jorge Dana on the genealogy of cinematic language. A similar example is the articulation undertaken by Pierre Sorlin on another axis, around concrete analyses, in the third part of his *Sociologie et cinéma*, "Analyse filmique et histoire sociale."[54] More generally—since 1973, as if in echo to the whole set of French theoretical works, but in a very original mode—it is in *Screen* that one can find the most synthetic image of this imbrication made up of shuttlings between the different levels of theory and analysis put into play by the multiplicity of films in the institution of cinema.

One final point. In "The Unattainable Text," I pointed out the paradox in which filmic analysis finds itself trapped, one that constrains the writer as well as the reader: how does one recapture, reconstruct and reorganize a text that never ceases to slip away? How does one imagine an already imaginary body, double it, in aid of a certain intellection, the possession-dispossession that constitutes the singular stake of every film: the stake of cinema? The force of this paradox has led me to open this collection with a brief attempt to circumscribe it. I would like to point out a few more instances.

The analysis of film is a costly operation. First, as I have mentioned, there is the psychic cost of freezing the image, which has for a long time marked a threshold and which constitutes the preliminary condition of all analysis. We must accept the interruption of its continuity and of the strong fantasy attached to it, accept that we must situate ourselves "neither on the side of motion nor on the side of stillness, but *between* them, in the generation of the projected film by the film-strip, in the negation of this film-strip by the projected film."[55] You are in the dark, in that particular darkness in which light falls from the point in the dream that rouses you; you modulate at whim that immaterial body of which fiction is made in order to escape you. You slowly yield to the fascination of "the other film":[56] that virtual film, global volume and burst instants at once, which all the more continually overflows onto itself in that its "unconscious" is endlessly modeled to the whim of your own. I believe that if it is so difficult to stop a film, it is because it is also difficult, once one has begun, to stop stopping it, and to subordinate this stopping to the ends one has supposed for it.

This displacement of the fantasy is in fact very burdensome and constraining, if one wishes to hold fast to it, detain it, and to subordinate the object, however slightly, to the goals of analysis. One must take notes, transcribe, appropriate, photograph, to try to rediscover, between two mediums and through a strangely fixed mixture of words and images, this between-the-two born so well of the frozen image, of this contradictory movement in relation to which the written text must always be lacking. However detailed and complete it may be, and even if it says more, much more, than the film ever appeared to say, the written text can never capture anything but a kind of elementary skeleton, stripped of flesh from the beginning. Such is the destiny of written analysis, and of its impossible struggle with the heterogeneous body to which it means to submit.

This explains many things. And first of all it explains these very words *"textual analysis,"* which have seen a remarkable fate in the field of cinema studies. They are in fact used much less frequently to designate the work of analysis as practiced on a literary text, a myth or a painting, which tends more often to be qualified by its proper method and its frame of reference (structuralist, generativist, genetic, psychoanalytic, iconologic, etc.) or by the name of the author that inspires it (Lévi-Strauss, Barthes, Deleuze, Derrida, etc., to restrict ourselves to recent, and Parisian, examples). These designations also serve, of course, to characterize this or that filmic analysis; but they are immediately subsumed by the more general and, it seems, more real term of textual analysis. For literary analysis, to restrict ourselves to it, has a history that, without mentioning the classical or medieval tradition, goes back at least as far as the great German philology of the nineteenth century. It thus proceeds through references, disjunctions, and fine differentiations in places where the analysis of film, so much more recent, is more inclined to mix various levels. But above all, literary analysis is "natural," thanks to the signifying osmosis of writing in relation to itself—whereas the analysis of film is the product of a double transgression in which the film is constituted as text and, from there, a text is constituted. It is this specific effort, this act, that is first and foremost designated by the words "textual analysis": an act proper, seemingly closed upon itself by the psychic and material transgressions it implies and the investments it puts into play. The analysis of film is more purely textual, in a sense, because it cannot help sticking to its text, all the more strikingly in that it always undoes it and constructs it. As if in proportion to the proper trouble it has in constituting itself, it thus experiences a profound difficulty in detaching from itself, in leaving the enchanted circle that creates its paradoxical condition, as if it perpetually fell victim to its own body.

That is why, in the same stroke, filmic analyses, even as they multiply, are still relatively rare in a finished state as published text and carried along by a recognizable strategy of word and image, an acknowledged and elaborated form of management of the defect proper to themselves. This implies not only the patience and "genius" of authors but also the concrete editorial possibilities, still so precarious and rarely reconciled, required by the burden and the cost of these operations. It will also be understood that filmic analysis may be, more than a kind of writing, the privileged object of an activity of teaching. Prints, a projector, a screen: the work is elaborated *in vivo*, in the game of this between-the-two with its higher and higher stakes, between mobile and immobile, which supposes no true interruption, no scission of experience. The remarkable thing is that the analytic skeleton seems to draw itself, no longer aspiring to the global, irreducible phenomenality of every film. Thus the text incessantly dislocates itself without ever truly breaking; it drifts with its whole weight, crystallized, at every moment, through the punctiform course of the chains that constitute it and that it pulls along in its movement. A great many analyses (and among the most accomplished) have thus remained at the stage one could call happy. This is not to imply any facility, but rather a failure to subordinate the writing to the fiction, a failure in which the analyses will only have won something on the condition of losing something else. Let us not forget, in this happiness, the dimension belonging to the social part of work, which in the best of cases makes of the seminar, in the sense in which Barthes spoke of it, the real but also utopic site of an exchange. To put it a bit more freely, it is founded on the projective and critical circulation of imaginaries.

It will perhaps be better understood that this material determination has oriented the choice of objects of analysis more profoundly than is often thought. I am thinking in particular of the way in which filmic analysis has somehow seemed to ignore avant-garde cinema and the experimental film (even if it is around one of these films that Thierry Kuntzel has articulated the terms that allow us to conceive this lack,[57] and even if, among some rare attempts, Bernhard Lindemann's book was able to impose the idea of a possible course that takes the reader from Fernand Léger's *Ballet mécanique* to Hollis Frampton's *Zorns Lemma*).[58] I do not aim here to elucidate the foundation of the difficult and ambiguous relations between "semiology" and "avant-garde cinema," but only, if possible, to dissipate an equivocation by unraveling the part that comes back down to the proper materiality of experience. Submitted to the continuity without which there would be no cinematic projection, the avant-garde film, most often through the acceleration and multiplication of visual information, but also and perhaps even more disconcertingly, through the dilation of duration, threatens the realism of representation, the normative administration of the impression of reality. It thus increases the degree of cinematic specificity of its components, in inverse proportion to its relinquishment of narrativity, or at least of narrativity regulated by the reproduction of movement dedicated to the imitation of life. For example, ever since *T-wo-men* was shown at the Toulon Festival, Thierry Kuntzel and I have wanted to work on this film and later, other films of Werner Nekes. Once past the work at the viewing table, in which propositions already elaborated in approaches to classical films were reformulated in other terms, an impossibility forced its way through: how can one convey, other than through coded combinations of variable structures, something of the speed, the speeds, the intensities proper to these operations, which confer on narrativity (since in *T-wo-men* we are talking about a regime bursting with super-narrativity) its irreducible and unreproducible body? How can one say more (when there is more to say) than Nekes himself does in the texts where he so precisely records his serialization procedures? Or indeed, how is one to sustain a discourse that no longer puts these films into play as the signs of an abstract paradigm (that of the virtualities of the avant-garde, of the catalog of operations with which it constitutes the projective space) but rather in their material singularity, their subjective reflexivity?[59]

To this, as to the difficulties proper to all analysis, I see only one real, if partial, response: that of cinema itself. A long time ago, when the question of analysis first began to be posed, I was struck by a series of television broadcasts that constitute, it seems to me, the only significant example of a discourse sustained on cinema by cinema itself: *Cinéastes de notre temps*, produced over several years by Janine Bazin and André S. Labarthe.[60] I came back to it in "The Unattainable Text" to underscore how the obstacle anterior to filmic citation ended up resolving itself, and how from there one could envisage the keener, more precise and much more systematic possibility of a true discourse of film on film. We have reached the point where a preliminary theoretical refinement, very difficult to conceive without the fixity of writing, seems to have given analysis its bases, or at least a sort of intellectual imaginary. This ought to enable a greater freedom of approach from now on, and in particular to offer the fusional doubling of discourse that gives literary analysis an inalienable privilege. The discourse of film on film will probably never, even from afar, effect such osmosis. But we can imagine what irreplaceable things it could contribute at its level: first, of course, the full force of citation; second, a modeling and fortification of filmic operations according to those multiple paradigms of which every text is the stake. A first attempt in this direction has already been made by Thierry Kuntzel: *La rejetée*, a critical-imaginary *montage* of Chris Marker's *La jetée*. Still imperfect, technically, because video technology is not yet what it could be, it does allow a glimpse of what will soon be its definitive version: a second discourse of images and words, in a perpetual mise-en-abîme with itself. And yet this work is on a film that of all films would seem to favor a written analysis, since with the exception of a single shot it is composed of still photos. But if the reduplication of movement (of camera, actor, motifs) appears to be the first postulation of the film on the film, it is in fact secondary to the discourse that orders it, to the arrangements of critical restructuring. And it is within the apparatus itself, through its contrivance, that the work of thought is performed, thus reuniting a bit mythically the conditions of commentary and the objects of its reading.[61] Along with the written text and the situation of teaching, this, I believe, is another path by which the analysis of film can provide itself with a means of existing more freely and multiply inventing itself a language.

I will also add this. In the domain of thinking about cinema (unlike what has happened in many other domains), I have really only been influenced by a small number of people. The first was Alexandre Astruc. To have seen and loved *Une vie* and *Vertigo* in the same week, after having first lived through *Hiroshima mon amour* and the films of Chris Marker, to have immediately had the good fortune to speak often and at length with him about them was truly determinant for a certain approach to filmic fascination. My book on Astruc, contemporaneous with the issues of *Artsept*[62] devoted above all, for me, to Marker and Resnais, was a first effort in the study of an intellection of what must for lack of a better word be called classical cinema. Traces of this can also be found in my articles from 1966 on Lang and Hitchcock. Two people, later on, truly mattered: Christian Metz and Thierry Kuntzel. The first through a general and always very precise incitement to the effects of theory put into play by cinema, as discourse and as institution; the second through a renewed incitement to analytic depth, of which he has provided several irreplaceable examples. They are both much too close to me for me to be able to say more about them than I already have. Or simply this. With the differences implied by age and character, their influence was very quickly felt in complementarity and reciprocity. Far beyond the life of work but with the real and symbolic complicity it implies, it has become friendship. It is hence quite naturally to them that this book is dedicated.

I wish to thank all those who have variously contributed to the realization of this book: Etienne Souriau, who encouraged me to pursue this work in all independence under the auspices of the Centre National de la Recherche Scientifique; Louis Daquin, who allowed me to work regularly on prints of films at the Institut des Hautes Etudes Cinématographiques; François Truffaut, who provided me with indispensable documents on Hitchcock; Marie-José Corajoud and Robert Louit, who translated or revised most of the shot breakdowns and dialogue; Gérard Vaujoie, Daniel Delille, Patrick Brion, Bertrand Augst, Constance Penley and the *Camera Obscura* collective, who helped me to assemble the illustrations and execute the frame enlargements; Dominique Pujebet, who drew the diagrams; *Les éditions du Seuil*, who graciously went along with the idea of the elaborate photographic reproductions for "Symbolic Blockage"; and Marie-Jeanne Noirot, who did the layout when the essay originally appeared in *Communications* 23 (1975); the various reviews or publications in which these articles first appeared, in French and English: *Cahiers du cinéma, Revue d'esthétique, Communications, Ça cinéma, Screen, Quarterly Review of Film Studies, Camera Obscura*, and *Australian Journal of Screen Theory.*

1979
TRANSLATED BY MARY QUAINTANCE

1. The Unattainable Text

That the film is a text, in the sense in which Barthes uses the word, is obvious enough. That as such it might, or should, receive the same kind of attention as has been devoted to the literary text is also obvious. But it is already not quite so obvious. We shall soon see why.

The text of the film is indeed an unattainable text. In saying this, despite the temptation of a play on words, I do not mean to evoke the special difficulties that very often make it impossible to obtain the film in the material sense or find the proper conditions to constitute it into a text, that is, the editing table or the projector with freeze-frame facility. These difficulties are still enormous: they are very often discouraging, and they go a long way toward explaining the comparative backwardness of film studies. However, one can imagine, if still only hypothetically, that one day, at the price of a few changes, the film will find something that is hard to express, a status analogous to that of the book or rather that of the phonograph record with respect to the concert. If film studies are still done then, they will undoubtedly be more numerous, more imaginative, more accurate, and above all more enjoyable than the ones we carry out in fear and trembling, threatened continually with dispossession of the object. And yet, curious as it might seem, the situation of the film analyst, even when he does possess the film, any film, will not change in every particular.

I shall not linger over the indisputable fact that one does not have the text, the "methodological field," the "production," the " traversal," as Barthes puts it, when one has the work, the "fragment of substance."[1] But without going into the theoretical labyrinths opened up by the notion of the text, I shall stress two things. On the one hand the material possession of the work alone permits one full access to the textual fiction, since it alone allows one a full experience of the multiplicity of operations carried out in the work and makes it precisely into a text. On the other, as soon as one studies a work, quotes a fragment of it, one has implicitly taken up a textual perspective, even if feebly and one-dimensionally, even if in a restrictive and regressive fashion, even if one continues to close the text back onto itself although it is, as Barthes has insisted, and before him, Blanchot, the locus of an unbounded openness. That is why it is possible, in a slide that is both justified and somewhat abusive, like all slides, to speak of quoting the text when by text one means work, even if at a later stage one may be driven, as Barthes has been, to think the literary experience from the starting point of an opposition between the work and the text.

In connection with these terms, but without evading them, I should just like to emphasize here a fatal flaw: the text of the film is unattainable because it is an unquotable text. To this extent, and to this extent only, the word text as applied to film is metaphorical; it clearly pinpoints the paradox that inflicts the filmic text and to such a degree only the filmic text.

When one chooses to read, to study a work, to recognize in it the pressure of the text, so close in a sense to what Blanchot has conceptualized as literature, nothing is more immediate, simpler than to quote a word, a phrase, a few lines, a sentence, a page. Omit the quotation marks that signal it and the quotation is invisible; it is quite naturally absorbed into the page. Despite the change of regime it introduces, it does not really break up the reading; it even helps to make description, analysis, a special form of discourse, in the best of cases a new text, by a reduplication whose fascination has been fully felt by modern thought. This effect is obviously peculiar to the literary work, more generally to the written work, and to it alone. It lies in the undivided conformity of the object of study and the means of study, in the absolute material coincidence between language and language. That is why only the written work was able to provide, so to speak, a pretext for a theory of the text, or at least for the first effects of its practice. That is why Barthes so strongly distrusts everything that escapes the written, for the meta-language effect is more tangible there, by definition. Indeed, one speaks the more "about" an object the less one can draw it into the material body of the commentary. At the same time this is obviously to emphasize the absolute privilege of written expression in this conversion of the work into a text. The material reality of a commentary that in its turn comes to have more or less the function of a text constitutes the necessary mediation for this transmutation, which in the last instance would like to appear in the absolute guise of a play. That is to say that in fact it aims for an integral reconciliation between language and language, and between the subject and the subject, receiving from the exteriority of language the absolution that would restore it to its desire. For clarity's sake, one thing should be remembered. This idea arises with the joint emergence of the two concepts literature and science of literature. It arose for the first time, in a still uncertain fashion, with romanticism and the beginnings of literary criticism; a second time at the turn of the century in the first great mutual concussion of literature and the human sciences, in Nietzsche and Mallarmé, Freud and Saussure; a third time today under the internal and external pressure exercised on literature by what Barthes has called "the conjoint action of Marxism, psychoanalysis and structuralism." To sum up, let us say that the science of literature has enabled us to recognize in the work the reality and the utopia of the text; but this movement has no meaning unless it dissolves the science into the body of its object to the extent, in the ideal case, of abolishing any divergence between science and literature, analysis and the work.[2]

It is from the starting point of this both real and mythical level that the apparently quite secondary fact of the possibility of quotation turns out to assign a paradoxical specificity to the cinematic text. The written text is the only one that can be quoted unimpededly and unreservedly. But the filmic text does not have the same differential relations with the written text as the pictorial text, the musical text, the theatrical text (and all the intermediate mixed texts they give rise to). The pictorial text is in fact a quotable text. No doubt the quotation stands out in its heterogeneity, its difference; no doubt there are many material difficulties in its way, difficulties expressing the specifically material loss undergone by the work from the very fact of its reproduction. The format of the book in particular, always reductive, obviously produces an inevitable distortion through the disproportion between the original and its reproduction. But the quotation is on the other hand perfectly satisfactory, allowing a remarkable play on the detail with respect to the whole. From the critical point of view it has one advantage that only painting possesses: one can see and take in the work at one glance. Which literary analysis cannot do, except when it has as its object short poems in which vision and reading are superimposed (e.g., Ruwet's, Lévi-Strauss's and Jakobson's analyses of Baudelaire sonnets). Beyond these, even when it chooses to quote "the whole text" in limit-case experiments like Barthes's in S/Z, it can only rediscover the inevitable linearity of the written.

The musical text, conversely, sets two obstacles in the way of quotation. First, at the level of the score. It is certainly quotable, in whole or in part, like the literary text. But it opposes to language an infinitely greater heterogeneity than that of the picture—that of a specific codification whose extreme technicality marks a break. On the other hand, and much more profoundly (for a society in which everyone could read music is conceivable—was this not the case in the micro-societies of the aristocracy and the bourgeoisie?), the musical text is divided, since the score is not the performance. But sound cannot be quoted. It cannot be described or evoked. In this the musical text is irreducible to the text, even if it is, metaphorically, and in reality, thanks to the plurality of its operations, just as textual as the literary text. With the one difference that it cannot really be experienced except by hearing it— never by analyzing it, subjecting it to a reading, since then one is no longer hearing it, or only hearing it virtually. Finally, one last problem and not the least: the score is fixed but performance changes. Some more or less aleatoric types of modern music that increase this gap between score and performance take the phenomenon to an extreme but do not change its terms. The work is unstable. In a sense this mobility increases even further the degree of textuality of the musical work, since the text, as Barthes has said again and again, is mobility itself. But by a kind of paradox, this mobility cannot be reduced to the language that attempts to grasp it in order to bring it out by duplication. In this the musical text is less textual than are the picto-rial text and above all the literary text, whose mobility is in some sense inversely proportional to the fixity of the work. The possibility of keeping to the letter of the text is in fact the condition of its possibility.

The theatrical text demonstrates the same paradox and the same division, al-though in a different way. On the one hand, the work, the text in the ordinary sense of the term, can be reduced unequivocally to the problematic of the literary text, except that the play more or less inevitably brings with it the absence of its perfor-mance. On the other, the performance creates a mobile text, as open and aleatoric as that of the musical text. A mise-en-scène can be discussed, its principles stated, its novelty, its uniqueness felt; but it cannot really be described or quoted. Its textuality, though indisputable, escapes the text once again through its infinite mobility, the too radical divergence between the text which provides it with a pretext and a material and vocal figurability without any real delimitation. At most, just as the phonograph record has become the fixed memory of the concert, making an end if not of the variety of interpretations, at least of the internal variability of each performance, one might imagine fixing some mise-en-scène, as has been done on all too few occasions, by the only means apt to reproduce it: the film. Pushing aside the problem of the theater, this automatically reinforces the paradoxical uniqueness of the cinema.

Indeed, the film exhibits the peculiarity, remarkable for a spectacle, of being a fixed work. The scenario, the initial shooting script, are indeed not absolutely comparable with the score or the theatrical play. They are pro-texts, as, without being similar, plans and drafts are for the written work, sketches for a picture. Performance, in the film, is annihilated in the same way, to the advantage of the immutability of the work. This immutability, as we have seen, is a paradoxical precondition for the conversion of the work into a text, insofar as, if only by the abuttment it constitutes, it favors the possibility of a voyage through language that unties and reties the many operations by which the work is made into a text. But this movement, which brings the film closer to the picture and the book, is at the same time a broadly contradictory one: indeed, the text of the film never fails to escape the language that constitutes it. In a sense one can no more quote a film than one can a musical work or a theatrical production. However, this is not quite true. The analysis of the film suffers the force of this paradox, which derives from the perfect delimitation of the work but equally from the mixture of materials whose location is the cinema.

Once it is a talking cinema, it conjoins five matters of expression, as Christian Metz has shown: phonetic sound, written titles, musical sound, noises, and the moving photographic image. The first two of these pose no apparent problems for quotation. Nothing is more easily reproduced than the dialogue of a film: publishers know what they are doing when they imply, as they often do, that they are recreating the film for us by printing its dialogue and playing a dubious game with the image to recreate that absolutely illusory thing known as its story. But it is quite obvious that something is lost thereby: written titles belong fully to the written, dialogue both to sound and to the written (it was written before being spoken, and even if it is improvised, it can be transcribed, since it does not change). Thus it undergoes a considerable reduction as soon as it is quoted: it loses tone, intensities, timbres, pitches, everything that constitutes the profound solidity of the voice. The same is true of noises, except that it is much less easy to reduce them to the signified, since this reduction can only be a translation, a kind of paraphrastic evocation. In this respect, what might be called motivated noise, which can always be evoked, more or less, since it indicates the real, should be distinguished from arbitrary noise, which can go so far as to serve as a score, escaping in this way all translatability since it is not even codified as is the musical score (confining ourselves for simplicity's sake to music in which the score is still truly determinant). Note that these are only two extremes, extremes that can be inverted: an arbitrary but simple noise can be delimited, while a motivated but overcomplex one cannot. How in an analysis is one to deal with the noise track of a film like *La mort en ce jardin*, for example, made up solely of the noises of the Amazon forest but so rich that it substitutes more or less for music? The bird calls in *The Birds* can be thought of in the same way; orchestrated by Robert Burks, thanks to the possibilities of electronic sound, they constitute a true score in this film from which music is apparently absent. In short, noise constitutes a greater obstacle to the textuality of the film the more it is one of the major instruments of its textual materiality. Musical sound obviously takes this divergence between text and text to the extreme: given the specifications implied by the phenomenon of combination, which makes film music not a work in itself but an internal dimension of the work, we have here again the problems posed in this respect by musical works. With one difference, and by no means a negligible one. If the division between score and performance, code and sound, remains an integral one, here the musical text is received, thanks to a petrifaction seemingly opposed to its very virtuality, in that immutability of the work which defines the film.

There remains the image, and with it, rightly or wrongly, the essential. First for a historical reason: for thirty years, with the indispensable support of written titles (and not counting the intermittent assistance of a music outside the material specificity of the work), the image represented the film, all films: the cinema. And it did so to such an extent that even today it is too often confused with it, by an excessive simplification the a priori assumptions of which have been unraveled by Christian Metz. The unique situation of the image among the cinema's matters of expression will perhaps allow us, if not to excuse this excess, at least to understand it. The image is indeed located, with respect to the echo it might receive from language, halfway between the semi-transparency of written titles and dialogue and the more or less complete opacity of music and noise. Moreover, it is this which quite logically gives the image as such, as a moving image, the highest degree of cinematic specificity among the matters of expression whose combination, on the other hand, creates many more or less specifically cinematic coordinations. Until very recently, no doubt, this insistence on the specificity of the image was usually a convenient pretext to remove the film from any true critical undertaking and to negotiate, as it were, the image in terms of the scenario, that is, of contents, themes. But over and above its distortions and its inadequacies, which are as negative as they are idealist, this contradiction did confusedly express something absolutely essential: a highly paradoxical relationship between the moving image and the language that seeks to reveal in the film the filmic text itself. This has been clearly seen since the area was turned upside down by the semiology of the cinema and the first true textual analyses. It is no accident that the only code constituted by Christian Metz has been a syntagmatics of the image track and that most analyses have concentrated, with a kind of impatience and quite explicable fascination, on the textual workings of the image, as it were expressing a voluntarily agreed restriction that clearly never ceases to transgress its limit, since that limit is illusory.

This restriction and fascination derive from the paradox introduced by the moving image. On the one hand it spreads in space like a picture; on the other it plunges into time, like a story which its serialization into units approximates more or less to the musical work. In this it is peculiarly unquotable, since the written text cannot restore to it what only the projector can produce: a movement, the illusion of which guarantees the reality. That is why the reproduction even of many stills is only ever able to reveal a kind of radical inability to assume the textuality of the film. However, stills are essential. Indeed they represent an equivalent, arranged each time according to the needs of the reading, to freeze-frames on the editing table, with the absolutely contradictory function of opening up the textuality of the film just at the moment they interrupt its unfolding. In a sense it is really what is done when a reader stops at a sentence in a book to re-read it and reflect on it. But it is not the same movement that is frozen. Continuity is suspended, meaning fragmented; but the material specificity of a means of expression is not interfered with in the same way. The cinema, through the moving image, is the only art of time which, when we go against the principle on which it is based, still turns out to give us something to see, and moreover something alone that allows us to feel its textuality fully: a theatrical play cannot be stopped, unless it has been filmed, nor can a concert; and if a phonograph record is stopped there is simply nothing left to hear. That is why it turns out that despite what it does allow, the phonograph record (or the recording tape), which might seem the magical instrument of musical analysis, only apparently resolves a basic contradiction, that of sound. The frozen frame and the still that reproduces it are simulacra; obviously they never prevent the film from escaping, but paradoxically they allow it to escape as a text. Obviously the language of the analysis is responsible for the rest. It attempts to link together the multiplicity of textual operations between the simulacra of the frozen images like any other analysis. But the analysis of the film thus receives its portion of an inevitability known to no other: not to literary analysis, which constantly makes language return freely to language; nor to the analysis of the picture, which can partly or wholly reestablish its object in the space of the commentary; nor to musical analysis, irreducibly divided between the accuracy of a score and the otherness of a performance; nor to that of theatrical representation, where the same division is at once less complete and less precise. In fact, filmic analysis, if it is to take place at all, must take upon itself this rhythmical as well as figurative and actantial narrative component for which the stills are the simulacra, indispensable but already derisory in comparison with what they represent. Thus it constantly mimics, evokes, describes; in a kind of principled despair it can but try frantically to compete with the object it is attempting to understand. By dint of seeking to capture it and recapture it, it ends up always occupying a point at which its object is perpetually out of reach. That is why filmic analyses, once they begin to be precise, and while, for the reasons I have just suggested, they remain strangely incomplete, are always so long, according to the extent of their coverage, even if analysis is, as we know, always in a sense interminable. That is why they are so difficult, or more accurately, so graceless to read, repetitive, complicated, I shall not say needlessly so, but necessarily so, as the price of their strange perversity. That is why they always seem a little fictional: playing on an absent object, never able, since their aim is to make it present, to adopt the instruments of fiction even though they have to borrow them. The analysis of film never stops filling up a film that never stops running out: it is the Danaids' cask par excellence. This is what makes the text of the film an unattainable text: but it is so surely only at this price.

We might change our point of view completely—though this would be to go much further than intended here—and ask if the filmic text should really be approached in writing at all. I am thinking, *a contrario*, of the wonderful impression I had on two occasions, to cite only these two, when confronted with two quotations in which film was taken as the medium of its own criticism. This was in two broadcasts in the series "Cinéastes de notre temps," one on Max Ophüls and one on Samuel Fuller. The viewer saw, and then resaw, while a voice off emphasized certain features, two of the most extraordinary camera movements in the history of the cinema, in which such movements are by no means uncommon. The first was in the ball in *Le plaisir*, just as the masked figure more and more unsteadily crosses the length of the ballroom, then collapses in a box where, beneath the mask of a young man an old one is revealed; the second, in *Forty Guns*, follows the hero from the hotel he is leaving to the post office to which he goes to send a telegram, and saves for the end of a long dialogue his meeting in a single continuous field with the "forty guns" that race past on horseback on the left side of the frame. Here there is no longer any divergence, no need of narration. A true quotation, in all its obviousness. But this sudden quotability that film allows to film (and in the same way sound to sound) obviously has its other side: will oral language ever be able to say what written language says? And if not, at the price of what changes? Beneath the appearances of an answer *a contrario*, this is a serious question—economic, social, political, profoundly historical—since it touches on the formidable collusion of writing and Western history in which the written alternately or even simultaneously performs a liberating and repressive function. Can or should the work, be it image or sound, in its efforts to accede to the text, that is, to the social utopia of a language without separation, do without the text, free itself from the text?

1975
TRANSLATED BY BEN BREWSTER

2. System of a Fragment*
🔳 (on *The Birds*)

The following pages are an extract from a study in preparation on Hitchcock's work. I offer them to the reader as an essay in systematic analysis, and as such they can claim to organize as large as possible a number of the elements that constitute the cinematic "text" within a limited segment. However, this analysis, although long and detailed, is still incomplete, insofar as it is true that every attempt or temptation of this kind is fated to enter the circle whose terms were so admirably defined by Freud: "die endliche und die unendliche Analyse," the analysis which ends and the analysis which never ends.

Second, I have quite deliberately restricted myself to a vocabulary free of any semiological or linguistic reference. Film, like every object of communication, is undoubtedly a system of signs and can someday expect to obtain the sanction of a codified formalization; but I have preferred to allow it to reveal itself as such in all the wealth of its logical provocativeness, rather than constrained and masked by the sometimes hasty and castrating rhetoric of a premature conceptualization. Hence the rather imprecise word "rhyme," which I have used exclusively to denote very powerful formal homologies and which independently imposed itself, and also the concepts of condensation and displacement that so clearly convey the experience of the material abstraction of film.

Let me add, finally, that from the outset, I did not intend this work to be very conclusive. This is because of the partial nature of its object, which seemed to disallow any too precise closure without further extensions and tests, either where its global object, Hitchcock—and beyond him, the cinematic narrative—or where the operation of the analysis itself were concerned.

However, the reader may perhaps recognize running through it an idea that is directed at an idealism too old not to be formulated. The beautiful has always been held to defy analysis and in the last resort to reduce the work to the romantic indefiniteness of its excesses. But it is precisely the beautiful which analysis meets, in its very possibility, when it brings to light the always shaky, always compound equilibrium of a set of forms and structures which define the work, that object of aesthetic pleasure as the site of a beauty, at the same time as they determine it with complete logical reversibility, as the site of desire.[1]

I. PRELIMINARIES

The analysis of this sequence from *The Birds* aims to demonstrate how meaning emerges in the succession of a story in pictures by the double constraint of repetition and variation, hierarchized according to the logical progression of symmetry and asymmetry. The elements to which the meaning effects relate are marshalled here in a fragment that follows the natural order of the plot, even if they would gain by being articulated in a different way to other similar or dissimilar elements distributed in the field of the whole plot, or better, that web of plots stamped with the name Alfred Hitchcock. On the other hand, the tiny fragments into which it breaks down, which brings Hitchcock so close to Griffith's original lesson, enables us to isolate the elements by the simplest kind of listing—numbering the successive shots. Finally, words and music are almost entirely absent from this sequence: it brings out, in the heart of the sound cinema, the great stylistic and demonstrative virtues of the silent film.

In these ways, this example facilitates analysis, in particular the always conjectural quotation of the cinematic "text." But this simplicity has its obverse. The example is doubly constraining by the rigor of the order of succession and by the large number of shots. It is useful to remember that "sequence" is an approximate term, often descriptive in that art of supple and continuous narrative proper to the classicism of the great American cinema. Thus, although our excerpt has its justification, it also has its arbitrariness. Neither the beginning nor the end can properly be said to constitute this segment of film as a closed and strictly definable unit. The analysis might go beyond them, even to the extent of rediscovering the whole film, by a series of extensions. But, inversely, it is the analysis that determines the autonomy of this segment of film, precisely in the distance it covers and its possibility. Let me add, lastly, that this choice is due to the logical accident of a fascination, not at all to convenience deriving from the retrospective needs of the analysis.

A sequence, then—once the word is merely conventional and reveals itself to be as inadequate to designate a fixed unit of narration as the shot is for a fixed unit of the photography.[2] The arbitrariness of the excerpt as well as the deliberate absence of any linguistic reference prevent me from using the refined categories proposed by Christian Metz to list the syntagmatic units of the continuity of film.[3] Let me simply suggest that it would not be correct to describe this segment as an "ordinary sequence" since, if its consecutiveness does seem unique, it is not discontinuous. As we shall see, it could be called an "alternating narrative syntagm," if the cleavage between the one who sees and his or her vision, which have become a double action, were interpreted as a double temporal consecutiveness; or finally a "scene," if we were to recognize in it the law of one single and continuous consecutiveness. This last is the word that rings the truest: its simplicity suggests to the mind a closed space in which heroes confront one another. And beyond, it touches on the myth that Freud recalled, from the depths of earliest infancy, as the "primal scene."

II. THE SEQUENCE

The text that follows is a complete breakdown of the sequence. It begins with shot 3 because the numbers, for the sake of convenience, follow the purely material division of the copy into reels. The notation accompanying the description of each shot constitutes the series of the most marked pertinences. I have deliberately restricted their number; I have also formulated them as strict oppositions. The opposition static/movement, which denotes the absence or presence of camera movements, is absolutely rigorous. The other two are relative and have to be explained in the light of nuances in the breakdown as well as of those in the interpretation, in particular, the opposition close/distant, which translates the dialectic of the framing and thus marks a relation between one shot and another rather than any fixed units.

I have decided not to bother to indicate the time. The whole sequence lasts six minutes fifteen seconds. It consists almost exclusively of short takes, whose exact lengths are not pertinent in an art which, unlike music, does not proceed according to a rhythmic notation in conventional units.

Simply for differentiation's sake, I have called the wooden structure which gives access to the shore on arrival at the Brenners' house, the "dock," and the one which surrounds the little harbor of Bodega Bay, the "pier."

Analysis forces me and structure invites me to divide the sequence into registerable segments, grouping sometimes a larger sometimes a smaller number of shots. I have called these *groups* or *series*. Most of the series are grouped in two *sets*, which I have called A and B: hence the notation Al, etc. for the series of the first set, B1, etc. for those of the second. Each set is defined by a center, called center A and center B. The initial and final series are simply distinguished by the words "departure" and "arrival." Certain shots, as we shall see, overlap two series: the convenience of the excerpt dictated this, and it will be explained in the commentary. The following schematic summary of the scene will be of some assistance in reading the latter, as well as the breakdown:

SHOT #		
3–12		Departure
12–14	(A0)	Melanie on the boat
15–24	A1	The boat, paddled by Melanie, approaching the dock
25–31	A2	Melanie's progress to the house on the dock
32–36	A3 (Center A)	Melanie in the house
37–43	A4	Melanie toward the boat on the left
44–56	A5–B1	Melanie in the boat
56–60	B2 (Center B)	Melanie in boat; Mitch looking at Melanie
60–71	B3	Melanie in the boat, Mitch in the car
72–84		Arrival

The film is in color. If this does not emerge from a mere reading, that is because I would have had to convert the technical fiction into an accurate description, at the risk of forcing the film into the form of a novel in the attempt to recapture its flesh and bones. This is a first restriction in principle on the power of analysis: it is impossible to force film, which talks life, to reveal directly nothing but structures of the mind.

The film started ten minutes ago. We are in Bodega Bay, a small California town. Melanie Daniels, a young socialite from San Francisco, arrives at Bodega Bay to give Cathy Brenner a pair of the kind of parrots called "lovebirds" for her birthday. She does not know the child, but she met her brother, Mitch Brenner, at a pet shop in San Francisco, and their half-mocking, half-aggressive conversation on that occasion so aroused her interest that she has made the sixty-mile journey from the city.

The scene begins just as Melanie Daniels arrives at the pier in Bodega Bay to take the birds as a surprise to Mitch Brenner's house, which is visible in the distance on the other side of the water.

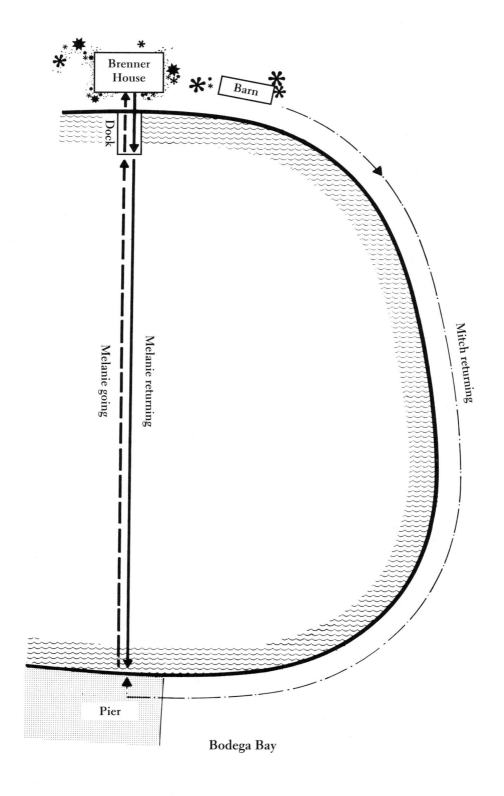

THE SHOTS

3 **FULL SHOT** Melanie drives from background right, around corner and to foreground (sound of seagulls off-screen).		Static	
4 **LONG SHOT** Melanie drives car down slope and out foreground right.		Static	
5 **HIGH-ANGLE LONG PAN SHOT** Melanie parks behind "The Tides" boat rental and gets out of car with birdcage in hand. She moves onto pier and camera pans right with her along it and toward fisherman in background.		Movement	

6 **MEDIUM SHOT**
 Melanie enters foreground left to face fisherman.
     Melanie: Do you have a boat for Miss Daniels?
     Fisherman: Er . . . er . . . yes ma'am. It . . . it's the one right below.
 Melanie starts right.
		Static	

7 **CLOSE SHOT** Fisherman stares at Melanie as she hands him cage and exits down off-screen stairs.		Static	
8 **MEDIUM PAN SHOT** As fisherman helps her, camera pans down with Melanie's descent of ladder and off fisherman.		Movement	
9 **CLOSE SHOT** Fisherman straightens, shakes his head, and starts down off-screen ladder.		Static	
10 **MEDIUM SHOT** Melanie seated in skiff as fisherman moves down ladder and into boat and starts the motor, stepping up onto ladder as Melanie pulls boat out foreground (sound of motorboat).		Static	
11 **CLOSE SHOT** Fisherman on ladder looking after off-screen right Melanie.	Fisherman seeing	Static	Close
12 **HIGH-ANGLE LONG SHOT (POV)** Down to Melanie piloting boat toward background.	Melanie seen	Static	Distant

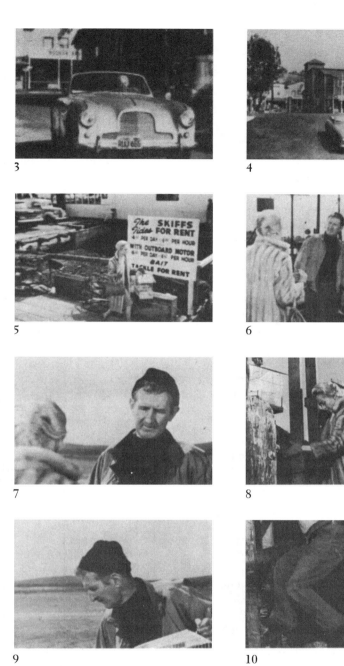

THE SHOTS *(cont.)*

13 LONG SHOT (SIDE ANGLE) Melanie piloting motorboat left to right.	Melanie	Static	Distant
14 HIGH-ANGLE LONG SHOT Down to Melanie driving boat toward foreground, the village in background.	Melanie	Static	Distant
15 MEDIUM SHOT Melanie piloting boat and looking hard off foreground right.	Melanie seeing	Static	Close
16 LONG SHOT (POV) Brenner house. Mitch, Lydia, and Cathy moving toward pickup truck parked in driveway.	Mitch seen	Static	Distant
17 MEDIUM SHOT Melanie piloting boat and watching off- screen right group. She turns and cuts the motor (sound of motorboat out).	Melanie seeing	Static	Distant
18 LONG SHOT (POV) Brenner house. The Brenners move to pickup truck and start to get in.	Mitch seen	Static	Distant
19 MEDIUM SHOT Melanie watching off-screen group (sound of off-screen truck motor).	Melanie seeing	Static	Close
20 LONG SHOT (POV) Brenner house. The pickup driving out left to right, Mitch running down slope left to right (very slight movement or reframing left to right of Mitch).	Mitch seen	Static (½ movement)	Distant
21 CLOSE SHOT Melanie looking at off-screen right to Mitch, then lifting oar and starting to paddle toward foreground.	Melanie seeing	Static	Close
22 LONG SHOT (POV) Brenner house. Mitch opening barn door and going inside (sound of paddle off-screen).	Mitch seen	Static	Distant

13   14

15   16

17   18

19   20

21   22

THE SHOTS (cont.)

23 MEDIUM FULL SHOT Melanie paddling toward foreground and looking off right.	Melanie seeing	Static	Close
24 FULL SHOT (POV) The dock of Brenner house as off-screen Melanie's boat moves toward it, with forward movement.	Dock	Movement	Distant
25 HIGH-ANGLE FULL PAN SHOT Down to Melanie paddling boat to dock, grabbing it and tying boat up, then rising and picking up cage, stepping onto dock, camera panning up with her, and starting up foreground steps, looking off left.	Melanie seeing	Movement	Close
26 LONG FORWARD MOVING SHOT (POV) The Brenner place, the barn door wide open.	Barn	Movement	Distant
27 MEDIUM CLOSE DOLLY SHOT Camera tracks back with Melanie, who smiles as she walks toward foreground looking off left.	Melanie seeing	Movement	Close
28 MOVING SHOT (POV) Camera tracks left and in on the barn area.	Barn	Movement	Distant
29 MEDIUM DOLLY SHOT Camera tracks back with Melanie's smiling advance.	Melanie seeing	Movement	Close
30 FULL FORWARD MOVING SHOT (POV) Camera tracks left and in on the barn area.	Barn	Movement	Distant
31 MEDIUM CLOSE DOLLY SHOT Camera tracks left with Melanie moving up steps to house door, opening it and starting in.	Melanie seeing	Movement	Close
32 DOLLY SHOT Interior of Brenner house. Camera fixed on door as Melanie enters in long shot, then tracks back with her movement to foreground toward living room, where she stops and looks around. Camera pans right with her as she moves into the room, where she puts cage down on a hassock, looks around, then opens her purse and starts to reach inside it.	Melanie	Movement	Distant

23

24

25

26

27

28

29

30

31

32

THE SHOTS (cont.)

33 CLOSE-UP (INSERT) On Melanie's hands as she takes two envelopes from purse. A slight movement left to right leads from her hands to cage, revealing second bird on right; she puts envelope marked "To Cathy" in front of cage and tears up one marked "To Mitchell Brenner," putting torn pieces into her purse and moving off-screen left. (Sound of paper tearing.)	Melanie (her hands)	Static (½ movement)	Close (close-up)
34 FULL PAN SHOT Camera pans left with Melanie to dining room window, where she looks out left.	Melanie seeing	Movement	Distant
35 FULL SHOT (POV) To the open door of barn as curtain is pulled aside foreground.	Barn	Static	Distant
36 LONG PAN SHOT Camera pans right with Melanie to hallway; she runs to background door, looks around and starts out.	Melanie	Movement	Distant
37 MEDIUM CLOSE DOLLY PAN SHOT Melanie comes out of house and camera dollies and pans right with her across porch and down stairs; she starts toward background, looking off left.	Melanie seeing	Movement	Close
38 MOVING FULL SHOT (POV) The barn.	Barn	Movement	Distant
39 HIGH-ANGLE FULL PAN SHOT Camera tilts up as Melanie moves along dock toward background, looking over shoulder foreground left off-screen.	Melanie seeing	Movement	Close
40 MOVING LONG SHOT (POV) The barn.	Barn	Movement	Distant
41 MEDIUM DOLLY SHOT Camera tracks in with Melanie moving toward edge of dock, looking over shoulder off-screen left foreground.	Melanie seeing	Movement	Close
42 MOVING LONG SHOT The house and barn.	House, Barn	Movement	Distant

33 34

35 36

37 38

39 40

41 42

THE SHOTS (*cont.*)

43 HIGH-ANGLE FULL DOLLY PAN Melanie looks off foreground left, camera tracks in and pans down and left with her climb down steps to the boat. She steps down into boat, picks up paddle to shove off, sits and unties the skiff, and pushes off; camera pans left and up with her paddling toward background, looking over her shoulder to foreground left. (Sound of paddling.)	Melanie seeing	Movement	Close
44 LONG SHOT (POV) Mitch moving from barn toward foreground. (Reframing or very slight movement left to right on Mitch.)	Mitch seen	Static (½ movement)	Distant
45 MEDIUM CLOSE SHOT Melanie puts down oar, turns and leans over stern of boat with a smile, looking toward off-screen house.	Melanie seeing	Static	Close
46 LONG SHOT (POV) Mitch moves to door of house, wipes feet on mat, and starts inside.	Mitch seen	Static	Distant
47 MEDIUM CLOSE SHOT Melanie watching.	Melanie seeing	Static	Close
48 LONG SHOT (POV) The house; no movement	House	Static	Distant
49 CLOSE-UP Melanie watching off-screen house.	Melanie seeing	Static	Close (close-up)
50 LONG SHOT (POV) Mitch comes out of house and runs right toward driveway, stops, shades his eyes, looking off right.	Mitch seen	Static	Distant
51 CLOSE-UP Melanie watching.	Melanie seeing	Static	Close (close-up)
52 LONG SHOT (POV) Mitch turns, starts toward house, stops and looks to foreground, shading his eyes (reframing).	Mitch seen	Static	Distant

43

44

45

46

47

48

49

50

51

52

THE SHOTS *(cont.)*

53 CLOSE-UP Melanie reacts, ducking down.	Melanie seeing	Static	Close (close-up)
54 LONG SHOT (POV) Mitch lowers hand and runs to house, going inside.	Mitch seen	Static	Distant
55 MEDIUM CLOSE SHOT Melanie sits up fast and tries to start motor. (Sound of motor not catching.)	Melanie seeing	Static	Close
56 LONG SHOT (POV) Mitch comes out of house with binoculars and moves toward foreground as seagulls appear in foreground at top of screen.	Mitch seen	Static	Distant
57 CLOSE-UP Mitch moving binoculars up to his eyes as he looks off foreground right.	Mitch seeing	Static	Close (close-up)
58 MEDIUM SHOT (POV) Through circles of binoculars—mask shot—Melanie seen in boat trying to start motor.	Melanie seen	Static	Distant
59 CLOSE SHOT Mitch lowers binoculars, smiles, exits right fast. (Sound of motor catching off-screen/sound of seagull cries off-screen.)	Mitch seeing	Static	Close
60 MEDIUM CLOSE SHOT Melanie smiles as she pilots the boat left.	Melanie seeing	Static	Close
61 LONG SHOT (POV) Mitch moving quickly to his car.	Mitch seen	Static	Distant
62 MEDIUM CLOSE SHOT Melanie pilots boat left.	Melanie seeing	Static	Close

53

54

55

56

57

58

59

60

61

62

THE SHOTS (cont.)

63 LONG SHOT (POV) Camera pans right with Mitch driving car away from house right.	Mitch seen	Movement	Distant
64 CLOSE SHOT Melanie in boat watching off-screen left in direction of Mitch.	Melanie seeing	Static	Close
65 LONG SHOT (POV) Mitch drives car right on road and toward background.	Mitch seen	Static	Distant
66 CLOSE SHOT Melanie reacting as she watches off-screen Mitch.	Melanie seeing	Static	Close
67 LONG SHOT (POV) Mitch drives car fast left to right background.	Mitch seen	Static	Distant
68 CLOSE SHOT Melanie watching off-screen Mitch.	Melanie seeing	Static	Close
69 LONG SHOT (POV) Mitch driving car left to right along road. At the end of the shot, slight lateral movement following the car.	Mitch seen	Static ($\frac{1}{2}$ movement)	Distant
70 CLOSE-UP Melanie watching off-screen right Mitch.	Melanie seeing	Static	Close (close-up)
71 LONG SHOT (POV) Mitch drives car out right, followed in lateral movement by a very slight pan.	Mitch seen	Static ($\frac{1}{2}$ movement)	Distant
72 CLOSE-UP Melanie smiling as she watches off-screen Mitch.	Melanie seeing	Static	Close (close-up)

63

64

65

66

67

68

69

70

71

72

THE SHOTS (*cont.*)

73 MOVING FULL SHOT Camera moves in on pier as off-screen Melanie approaches it.	Pier	Movement	Distant
74 CLOSE-UP Melanie smiling.	Melanie seeing	Static	Close (close-up)
75 MOVING LONG SHOT Camera moves in on pier as Mitch appears from background and camera pans right with his run to edge of pier, where he stands waiting.	Mitch seen	Movement	Distant
76 CLOSE-UP Melanie smiles, then her slightly tilted face sets.	Melanie seeing	Static	Close
77 FULL SHOT Sky with seagull in flight from foreground left off-screen background right.	Seagull	Static	Distant Close
78 CLOSE SHOT On Melanie, gull flies from right foreground, strikes her head, and leaves to background right.	Melanie, gull	Static	Close
79 FULL SHOT Gull flies from right foreground toward left background.	Seagull	Static	Distant
80 LONG SHOT Mitch, strolling on the pier, stares closely at Melanie, off-screen.	Mitch seeing	Static	Distant
81 CLOSE SHOT Melanie, who had raised her hand to her head, removes it and looks at glove.	Melanie seen-seeing	Static	Close
82 CLOSE-UP (INSERT) Blood on index finger of Melanie's gloved hand.	Melanie (her finger)	Static	Close (close-up)

73

74

75

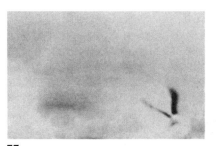

76

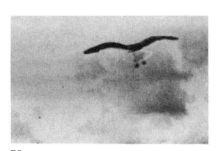

77

78

79

80

81

82

THE SHOTS *(cont.)*

83 **FULL PAN SHOT** Camera pans toward bottom left on Mitch, who leaps into a fishing boat background.	Mitch seen	Movement	Distant
84 **HIGH-ANGLE LONG TO MEDIUM SHOT** Mitch in right foreground in fishing boat approaches Melanie's boat and grabs it, pulling it into foreground. Melanie holds her head and leans toward the prow; he goes to her and helps her up.	Mitch Melanie	Movement	Distant Close

Mitch: Are you all right?

Melanie: Yes, I think so. What do you
think made it do that?

Camera pans toward bottom right as
he helps her onto ladder; camera pans
following her as she climbs it.

Mitch: That's the damndest thing I
ever saw, I don't know, it seemed to
swoop down at you deliberately. Oh,
you're bleeding, too; let's take care of
that, OK? That's the girl. Come on.

She holds her head with an expression of
pain. Mitch enters in close shot supporting
her, camera pans right following them.
They pass a man, camera travels forward,
pans right and stops with them close to the
door of The Tides Office.

Fisherman: What happened, Mitch?

Mitch: Gull hit her.

Fisherman: A gull?

Office Door.

83

84a

84b

84c

84d

84e

84f

III. COMMENTARY

The sequence is built on the symmetrical movement of a journey out and back, marked by an asymmetry in the difference between the first and second periods of this movement. The journey out is performed by one character, Melanie Daniels, the journey back by two, Melanie Daniels and Mitch Brenner. In this duplication, this simple action manifests a hierarchization of symmetry and asymmetry, which makes the image and the plot, whose secret and law it is, refer to one another.

The Two Centers

1.

Melanie's aim sustains the construction of the sequence at the beginning. The central point of her itinerary is the room in the Brenners' house where she intends to deposit the lovebirds. Thus, shots 32–36 (A3), which show her in the house, constitute the hinge of the sequence. They punctuate Melanie's journey out and back with a resting point; and the action at each end echoes that at the other, reinforcing their median positions. Moreover, they stand out all the more clearly against the rest of the scene in that they happen to be its only interior shots. Finally, their central value is recognizable in several features marked by differences in a formal operation of condensation and displacement at the three levels of the look, of framing, and of movement.

a) the look

Series A3 is surrounded by two series of shots that are deployed symmetrically on the one hand and, on the other, according to a strict binary alternation governed by a simple principle: Melanie seeing/what Melanie sees. This constitutes an unbroken harmony between shots 15–31 in the journey out (Al: the boat piloted by Melanie approaching the dock at the Brenners' house; A2 Melanie's progress to the house) and shots 37–56 of the return journey (A4, Melanie's movement toward and onto the dock; A5, her departure in the boat and her expectation): they echo and oppose one another symmetrically about a center.

But shots 32–36 explicitly break with this principle of alternation. Shot 32 (Melanie's movement in the hallway of the house and her entry into the dining room) and shot 36 (Melanie's route toward the door) rhyme with each other at each end of the series; but each one follows or precedes a shot of Melanie (31 and 37) that shows her outside the house at the moment she enters and leaves.

This is, of course, a perfectly normal technique: two shots from either side of a door ensure the continuity of the character's movement. It is only remarkable here, and all the more subtly so, in that the eye cannot be too forcibly struck by it because it upsets the rigor of a symmetrical alternation and, as we shall see, the relationship between the kind of framing that supports it.

Shot 33, on the other hand (the insert of Melanie's hands and the two envelopes beside the lovebirds' cage), is not part of Melanie's vision, it simply underlines a detail of her action. Only shot 35 (the Brenners' barn seen through the window) restores the principle of alternation—one vision of Melanie's between two shots of

Melanie seeing—and imposes the constructive continuity of the look in a group in which it is broken by a flagrant discontinuity.

But this is not strictly true: for if shot 34 does show Melanie seeing, shot 36 does not. This divergence is not very important: it happens at moments in series in which the alternation of shots does have the explicit function of expressing the subjectivity of vision. But on the one hand, shot 36 produces at the other end of the series a rhyming break which inverts that of shot 32. On the other, it materializes the difference by which it is marked in the relation of the framing.

b) the framing

The four series A1, A2, A4, A5, symmetrically distributed around A3, duplicate the alternation character seeing/thing seen with an alternation in the kinds of framing that can be formulated by the opposition close/distant (the first term includes the range from close-up to medium shot, the second from medium shot to long shot: it should be kept in mind that the relation between these terms, often hard to delimit strictly in an art of movement and in the relationship character/landscape, is always more important than their absolute scale). This opposition is upset in series A3. In fact, the only two shots that mark the alternation seeing/seen (34–35) in this series are defined by an equal framing in full shot. This non-opposition is reinforced by a relative equivalence between this framing and that of the two boundary shots in the series (32 and 36, long shots): Melanie ceases to be the seer and becomes the seen, explicitly so, although not by a character but by the camera and the cameraman. The effect is particularly strong in shot 32: when Melanie opens the door, the camera is waiting for her and marks the distance with a look that breaks the normal continuity of the double shot of her entrance with a slight spatial and temporal deviation.

The alternation of the framing, we should note, also governs the transitions between the series A2–A3, A3–A4: from shot 31 to shot 32, and from shot 36 to shot 37, there is a transition from medium shot to long shot and vice versa. But the progressive change of frame in shot 32 (from long shot to medium shot) somewhat diminishes the effect of the opposition, on the one hand; on the other, and in particular, it is simultaneously countered by the determinant break in the alternation of the look: a relation that is immediately duplicated in shot 33.

The only shot within this series that demonstrates the opposition close/distant is, in fact, shot 33 (the first close-up in the scene). But it is remarkable that, inversely, this shot avoids the alternation of the look. We have seen that at this level it is not in alternation with shot 32 but quite the opposite; it duplicates and details it. Furthermore, considering it in conjunction with the shot that follows (34, in which Melanie goes to look at the Brenners' barn through the window), it emerges that the alternation formula, that is, seeing/seen–close/distant, is transformed into non-seeing/seeing–close/distant. (Non-seeing in fact includes seen, but without the mediation of the character. The term is the more exact in that Melanie is here not only seen by the camera without being seen by anyone in particular, but that she does not see, since only her hands are shown to us.) Thus at this level shot 33 introduces into series A3 a displacement of the relation marked in the four neighboring series, which is confirmed by the articulation of a symmetry peculiar to the series.

c) the movement

Series A3 is in fact governed by the alternating opposition static/movement. This opposition is distributed through the five shots in the following ways: movement/static/ movement/static/movement.[4] The first effect of this alternation is to condense in the central series the double alternation static/static and movement/ movement, which opposes the series Al and A2 on the one hand and the series A4 and A5 on the other.[5] It supplements the break introduced into the alternation seeing/seen on the one hand, and the half-corollary of the framing on the other, thus making it possible to maintain the continuity of the relation of alternating opposition by displacing it to another level.

This displacement immediately unites shots 33 and 35, which maintain the rhyming of the static shots in the series. These two shots now also fulfill a regulatory function by reestablishing the alternation of framing and of the look in a series in which the one and the other are subject to a break. The modifications that occur in the terms of the oppositions echo this imbalance: on the one hand the double inversion of the look and the framing between shots 33 and 34, and on the other, as we have also seen, the non-opposition at the level of framing between shots 34–35, which alternate at the level of the look; finally, between the two static shots, a non-concordance of the opposition in framings since the framing of the first (close) is opposed to its function at the level of the look (non-seeing), while the framing of the second, on the contrary (distant), agrees with its function in the order of the look (seen). Thus symmetry and asymmetry develop in a condensed series, in a dual movement of centering and decentering.

2.

For this center by itself does not sustain the architecture of the scene. Melanie Daniels's return journey is not identical with her outward journey. In fact, groups A2 and A4 are in close correspondence at the dual level of the image but are in opposition at the level of the plot.[6] Hence the asymmetry that marks the sequence: the three shots, 12–14, that describe Melanie's outward crossing before she arrives in view of the Brenners' house are counterbalanced in the return journey by the long alternating series that leads her to the foot of the pier (60–71, B3).

This asymmetry is easy to explain. Between shot 44 and shot 56, Mitch Brenner discovers Melanie Daniels's presence. The plot, hitherto organized by the vision of one character, redoubles onto itself to respond to the dual vision. The center is then displaced, and after the moment in which Mitch sees Melanie, becomes *also* the four shots 56–60 (B2) in which the two see that they have been seen. The sequence conforms to the equation: one character, one center only, two characters, two centers. It would be more accurate to say: one single mobile center, which slips beneath the scene and sustains the development of the script with an architectural slide. The second center stands out less starkly than the first against the two groups that surround it: the series 44–56 on the one hand, which is both the last term of set A (A5) and the first term of set B (B1), and the series 60–71 on the other (B3), the third term in set B. The reason is clear: its first function is to carry to its highest pitch the binary action seeing/seen, governed by the principle of alternation, that is, to effect its reversal into seeing/seeing. The four shots 57–60 effect this break in the continuity: the change in the framing translates the reversal, forcefully materialized by the double circle of the binoculars in which Mitch's look imprisons Melanie. Note the divergence in framing: close-up for Mitch (57), medium shot for Melanie (58), and the divergence in the actions. Mitch attentively observes Melanie, who has removed her eyes from his for a second and is trying to start the boat's motor. The return to Mitch in close shot installs a reciprocity in the order of the look: close shot and medium shot are the framings that essentially define Melanie in the alternating action of the look throughout the scene.

But a clearer transition introduces the series. Shot 56 (Mitch reemerges from the house and hurries to the shore with the binoculars while gulls pass over), which continues the alternating action of the series 44–56 (B1), breaks it at the same stroke when it repeats a shot of Mitch in shot 57. This transition can be assimilated in its position to the ones at the beginning and end of the series 32–36 (center A), which group successively Melanie's entry and exit (31–32 and 36–37). But in reality it is much closer in its abrupt change of framing to the relation between ensemble and detail established between shots 32 and 33: when Melanie's hands in close-up tear up the letter she intended for Mitch, just as the latter lifts the binoculars to his eyes and observes the young woman who has entered his house by surprise to give him, indirectly, the two lovebirds. Furthermore, this transition is an open one, not like that of center A, inscribed in a closed series which is folded back onto itself by the rhyme established at either end of the series. That is why it is impossible to assign an exact number of shots to this second center.

Shot 56, onto which the break is grafted, rhymes at all levels in the series B1. At the other extreme, the end of shot 59 provides a point of division: Mitch leaves the screen, and the combined sound of the boat and of the seagulls announces the return journey. But that would be to cut in two the double smile which, in shots 59 and 60, unites the hero and heroine for the first time in the ironic and ravishing complicity of an exchange. We might say: 56–60, both in order to include everything, and for the pleasure of a numerical analogy with the first center. But this is only an image. Here the break is more alive, but less marked, for it develops the first one: a continuous action turns on itself around the relationship between two shots and a simple inversion in the framing.

The symmetry is balanced around this second center between shots 44–56 (A5 transformed into B1) and shots 60–71,[7] which orchestrates the joint return journey of Mitch and Melanie, one in a car, the other in a boat (B3). The two series strictly respect the principle of the alternation of the look in a binary distribution of shots which, as in the first pair of rhymes around center A, are articulated with a strict alternation in the framing: close-up to medium shot for the one who sees, full shot for what is seen. This double alternation is all the more significant in series B3 insofar as the reversal of seeing/seen into seeing/seeing is achieved in B2 and insofar as it would seem just as easy to conceive Melanie seen from a distance in the boat by Mitch framed in his car in medium shot or close-up. This contradiction is only apparent. The reversal of vision is formulated in the four alternating shots of center B: 57/58 for Mitch seeing/Melanie seen, 59/60 for Mitch seeing/Melanie seeing. The new break that is marked to Melanie's advantage, far from dislocating the plot or obeying a concern for pure form justified in the partial rhyme of set B, in fact makes it possible to join the two centers and, by a slide in two directions, to produce a formal and semantic fold in the scene, hierarchizing the relations of symmetry and asymmetry in the development of the script.

However, we should note straightaway that the contradiction is also resolved in group B3 itself, as it had to be, but by displacement to another level. In fact, if shot 61 (which shows Mitch running toward his car) echoes Mitch's movements between the barn and the house, the house and the shore, in the static shots of series B1, then shot 63 (which shows the departure of the car and thus inaugurates the boat-car duet that provides the rhythm of series B2) underlines the movement within the shot by a pan: the camera movement in this static series re-echoes the movements that underlined Melanie's actions in set A;[8] it identifies Mitch and Melanie as the two alternating shots in center B, 59 and 60, to make them equal and complicit in the order of the look. This equalization has its logical effect on the boat-car duet: the return to static shots in the rest of the crossing makes it possible to pursue the rhyme with series B1, but the opposition marked by the camera movement in shot 63 acquires a new relief in an opposition static/movement within the shot: the boat, filmed from close up, seems to be static; the car, filmed from a distance, seems all the more mobile in that its route around the bay is much longer than that of the boat. Thus, the opposition is analogous to the opposition revealed in series B1 between the motionless boat with Melanie in it, and Mitch's movements between the barn, the house, and the shore of the bay.[9]

Thus, series B1 is the first term in a strict comparison that is organized from the second center. But it is also the last term in an equally strict comparison organized from the first center, in which, you will remember, it balanced the series 15–24 (A1) in a first architecture of the scene whose symmetry is later broken, despite the support it receives from the folding of the first and last series: the departure and the arrival.

Let us examine the terms of this first comparison more closely. In both cases Melanie in the boat observes Mitch's action on the shore, the first time in order to get close to the dock without being seen, the second time in order to enjoy her surprise at the risk of being seen, or indeed, in order to be seen. The strictest rhyme in this equivalence is the term inversion of the outward journey and the return journey in the moving series that surround the center: A2 and A4, in which Melanie alone appears between moving shots of the trees, the house, and the barn. Mitch's movements, on the contrary, vary from one series to the other: the common art of symmetry and plot demands that he enter the barn once and the house once. But if both hide him, these two entries do not have the same value: the first makes Melanie's trick possible, the second reveals it. Furthermore, the second entry is repeated in shots 46 and 54. Mitch's first entry into the house (series A5, shot 46) rhymes with his earlier entry into the barn (series A1, shot 22); but Mitch's two entries and exits, which alternate term by term with shots of Melanie observing them, rhyme together with the two alternating series of Melanie's entry and exit (A2, A4), distributed on either side of center A. The movement of the character in the shot echoes the camera's movement following the movement of the character. Series A5 thus condenses series A1, on the one hand, and series A2 and A4, on the other, by rhyming with each of them.

But it also condenses the central series A3. Shot 48, in which the house is framed alone after Mitch has gone into it and before he comes out (recurring elliptically in the repetition of the entry and exit in shots 54–56: Mitch enters the house/Melanie seeing/Mitch leaves the house), occupies the position of the five shots 32–36, in which Melanie is inside the house. Series A5 thus condenses series A1–A4 which precede it, but *at the level of the plot*, just as the central series, A3, condenses the symmetrical series surrounding it (and beyond them, set B) but *at the level of the image*. In this new cleavage between symmetry and asymmetry, the first center slides and, when Mitch has grasped his binoculars in response to Melanie's provocation, is superimposed on the second center, which it implies.

This slide, which allows the ever redefined closure of a symmetry to be marked by successive condensations in the asymmetry opened up by the progression of the plot, should also allow another ideal folding of the sequence, in which, by recurrence, center B would slide beneath center A. It implies that series B3, the second term of set B, acts in place of the first term of set B (B1), with which, as we have seen, it rhymes perfectly, and thus that it rhymes with the first term in set A, onto which it can be exactly folded. This fictive recurrence makes the moment of provocation and the moment of discovery, which the logical progression leads us to read one beneath the other, coincide. It lets another opposition crystallize, one that is distributed between the two sets (a); and above all, it allows us to introduce a microseries we have so far ignored, although it is not part either of the Departure series or of the Arrival series (b): shots 12–14, which evoke Melanie's outward passage before she arrives in sight of the Brenners' house.

(a) When, in A1, Melanie is on her way toward the dock in the boat, Mitch is moving with his mother and sister toward a pickup truck that the two women get into. The pertinence of this opposition between the two actions is only revealed in order to reappear multiplied tenfold in the significance endowed it by the long double return that begins the moment Mitch runs to his car to follow Melanie, who has set off again in her boat. This equivalence by displacement of the opposition makes it possible to balance the movements within the shot in the series A1, A5–B1, and B3. In fact, the series A1 and A5 are in opposition at this level: in the first, Melanie advances in the boat, and Mitch, his sister and mother do the same, doubly, on foot and in the pickup truck. In the second Mitch moves and Melanie remains motionless (to the observer) in the boat.[10] But this is precisely the relationship, as we have seen, that is marked again in series B3 by the contrast between the very rapid movement of Mitch in his car and that of Melanie in her boat, which seems immobile by contrast but still reproduces the movement of series A1.[11]

(b) As for the return journey, it is clear that everything in it must echo the outward one. This symmetry is only rigorous if shots 12–14 are implied in the folding of series B3 on series A1. At the level of the plot and of the journey, these shots are the true equivalents of series B3 (hence their designation as A0). But in the interval there is a transition from one vision to two and from one character to two. This explains the fact that the first three shots in the complete series 12–24 (A0 + A1) are not alternating, whereas on the contrary, alternation extends beyond the series 60–71 (B3) into shots of the last series, the Arrival. The differences in the framing underline this imbalance: in shots 12–14 Melanie appears in the distance in full shots, during her return, in medium shot, close shot, or close-up. The difference in the movements within the shot underlines it even more: on the return journey Melanie seems to be motionless, while on the outward journey she crosses the entire screen. But it is clear that this movement within the shot rhymes with Mitch's return journey, just as the kinds of framing used in the outward journey for Melanie are used for Mitch in the return journey.

This divergence, marked in the terms of a highly determinate symmetry, suggests — to pursue the folding process — that we should define exactly how it is achieved at the extremes in order to assess what is played out between the departure and the arrival.

The End and the Beginning

One first symmetry is obvious: the arrival echoes the departure. But it hides a logical difficulty: the rhyme in the final series attains an extreme condensation; it has to make possible the folding and at the same time tie up all the loose ends. The plot in the two series is articulated around two multiple rhymes: the rhyme between the men, and the rhyme between the birds.

a) the birds

When Melanie arrives at the pier in Bodega Bay in shot 3, carrying the cage containing the two lovebirds in her car, gulls can be heard crying; and this recurs in shot 5. When on her return she moves, smiling, toward the pier where Mitch is waiting for her (shot 76), a flock of gulls is scattered across the sky, calling loudly (shot 77). In the next shot, Melanie is struck on the head by one of the gulls.

In one case, Melanie is linked to the lovebirds she intends for Mitch (or his sister); but as a surprise, without their seeing or speaking to each other, in the second case, she is linked to the gulls at the moment before their meeting. In the first case, she is the subject, in the other, the object. The logical conjunction between the birds is also suggested in shot 3 in the conjunction between the image and the sound: the lovebirds (unseen, but implied and seen again in shot 5) speak in this shot via the murderous shrieks of the gulls.

b) the men

On the one hand there is the fisherman, on the other, Mitch.

The first feature that unites them is their position. The former helps Melanie get down into the boat; the latter helps her climb onto the pier.

The second feature is the dialogue. It is remarkable because it is unique. The first exchange, in shot 6, deals with the boat that Melanie has reserved to take the lovebirds to Mitch's house; the second, in shot 84, deals with the gull that has just hurt Melanie. This exchange between Mitch and Melanie is duplicated straightaway by a dialogue between Mitch and a fisherman. We ask ourselves, in the strict sense, what this second fisherman, who appears at the very end of the sequence as Mitch is accompanying the wounded Melanie, rhymes with. Besides demonstrating the peculiar pleasure the mind takes in combining and varying figures, his presence seems to have to be justified as follows: he brings to bear on Melanie, wounded by the gull, an interrogation that echoes the silent question of the first fisherman as to the cage she was carrying and thus confirms Melanie's relationship to men and to birds; but in being called on to rhyme with the first fisherman by homology of behavior and function in this way, he displaces and clarifies the equivalence that unites Mitch and the first fisherman by focusing it onto the essential fact, the relationship with Melanie, especially as it is expressed in the third feature that gives the rhyme its real weight: the look.[12]

In fact, the fisherman watches Melanie depart just as Mitch watches her arrive. The equivalence in the plot takes its logical rigor from the equivalence in the image. The fisherman's look in shot 11 is subjective: back on the ladder and framed in a medium shot, he looks off-screen; high-angle shot 12 leaves no doubt that it is his viewpoint. The scale of the framing (long shot) makes it clear that this look is an insistent one, that it lingers on Melanie for a long time. In addition, it follows an interrogation of Melanie by the man, conveyed first by very explicit looks within the shot itself (shot 7), then by his shaking his head (shot 9). Melanie, on the contrary, pays no particular attention to the fisherman. Thus, the binary series defined by the alternation of the look, broken as soon as it starts by the repetition of Melanie in shots 13 and 14 (crossing the bay), but immediately restored to Melanie's profit as she observes the inmates of the Brenners' house (beginning with shot 15), opens to her disadvantage, so to speak, and puts her in the position of an object already, even though she has the initiative.

This reversal is extremely important. For Mitch's look, which only intervenes much later in the binary series, is thus marked from the beginning of the scene. It is inscribed in it by the substitutional mediation of the fisherman, in a dominant position, all the more so in that Melanie takes no notice of it, any more than she does of the premonitory cries of the seagulls. The alternation of the shots that defines the exchange and recognition of looks from one end of the scene to the other by a succession of breaks makes it possible to link together retrospectively these cries and this look, here distributed at the two ends of the series, united in the order of succession of the shots in the final series in which Mitch's look and the gulls' aggression together echo Melanie's triumphant look; Melanie is thus, and twice, doubly subject and object.

The end and the beginning of the sequence fold back on one another as the centers slide beneath one another. This double movement has its logic: center A is the moment of the gift, center B expresses the reversal of the look and their meeting. The presentation of the gift is sheltered from the look in the secrecy of the house; it consists of domestic birds. The meeting of the looks introduces the wild birds: gulls fly in shot 56 as Mitch hurries out of the house armed with his binoculars; they cry off-screen in shot 59 when he lowers the binoculars, smiles, and leaves the screen to run to the car. The beginning of the scene, which implies the gift and the meeting, introduces all the elements in half-constraint; the end, which links together the gift and the meetings, organizes the elements in a logical redistribution that echoes at every level their formal and semantic development during the sequence.

The delimitation of the series of shots, which, strictly speaking, constitutes Melanie's arrival at the Bodega Bay pier, requires that we make a semi-arbitrary cut in the very long alternating series that begins with the linked return of Mitch and Melanie after the shots of center B. A break in shot 71 allows this: Mitch's car, at the end of its route, leaves the screen to the right. Shot 73 shows the pier. Hence the series can be limited at shot 72 while respecting the play of alternation that ordered it to that point.

The first eight shots are divided into two micro-series of four strictly alternating shots each. The first (72–75) combines two shots of Melanie seeing (72, 74, both in close-up), with two shots of the object of her vision: the empty pier, then the pier with Mitch appearing on it (73, 75, both in distant shots). A third opposition, static/movement, complements the double relation seeing/seen, close/distant. This combination was outlined once at the beginning of the series 60–71 (B3), in the two shots 62–63. As we have seen, it persisted later in the series, relieved by the opposition static/movement in the shot. Hence, it is quite natural that the series 71–84, which follows the series 60–71, should develop an effect linked in both cases to Mitch's movement to beat Melanie to the pier. But we must look further for a more significant equivalence. It can be found in the series A1 and A2: the first, the crossing in the boat, conforms to an alternation static/static, while the second, the walk to the house, conforms to an alternation movement/movement. The four shots 72–75 condense these two series. The relation is further reinforced by a rhyme that has hitherto been absent: shot 73 frames the Bodega Bay pier as shot 24 frames the dock at the Brenners' house.[13]

Shot 24 (the last in series A1), significantly enough, has no equivalent in the inversion of series A1 in series A5: shot 44 (the first in series A5), which echoes it by position, shows Mitch's movement between the barn and the house. It propounds an equivalence between the entries of Mitch and Melanie into the house and thus participates in condensation at the level of the script of the three series A1, A2, A4, and of center A3, which, as we have seen, occurs in the series A5–B1. We can see what follows from the displacement to shot 73 of a rhyme that, by its position, is also operative in shot 44: it links Melanie's arrival at the dock on the one hand with Mitch's entry into the house and on the other with Melanie's arrival at the Bodega Bay pier, and thus their joint arrival at and on the Bodega Bay pier; but also, and above all, it links together these arrivals and entries.

This conjunction is verified by the relation static/movement/seeing/seen in shots 72–73, which condenses the relations seeing/seen-static/ static and seeing/seen-movement in series A1 and A2, in which static shot 24 makes a precise transition to moving shot 25, and on the other hand condenses the relation seeing/seen-static in the shot/movement in the shot in series A5. Furthermore, this conjunction is confirmed by the very succession of shots in which the first and second condensations act one after the other, the condensation of series A5 with respect to the series A1–A4 and the condensation of the final series with respect to all the others: shot 46, which continues the alternating rhyme with shot 44 of series A5, describes Mitch's entry into the house, just as shot 75, which continues the alternating rhyme with shot 73 in the final series, shows precisely Mitch's arrival on the pier.

We still have to explain why shot 73 is in movement while shot 24 is static, whereas their homology is implied by the analysis. Two complementary reasons can be adduced. In this sequence, camera movements underline the action, that is, the camera espouses the movements of the characters when they have the initiative: this is true of the many camera movements on Melanie at the Departure and in series A2, A3, and A4 in set A. If, however, in set B the initiative reverts to Mitch, this is little marked at the level of camera movement, for the reasons of symmetry and asymmetry we have discussed; rather, it is marked by a movement within the shot that then relieves the static/movement dialectic, which is only explicitly marked in series B3 by shot 63 with a camera movement underlining Mitch's departure. Hence it is completely right that at the moment of meeting, just as Melanie is about to find herself suddenly in the position of an object, the camera movement should predict this in some way and once again emphasize Mitch's action. The attribution of the static shot to Melanie also enables us to link shots 72–74 with the shots in series A1 and A5, which precede the boat's arrival at the dock (hence symmetry with the boat's arrival at the pier), on the one hand and, on the other, the meeting of the looks that interlock in the second center (something that is repeated tenfold here in the tenfold violence of the actual meeting). Inversely, the attribution of movement to what is seen by Melanie enables us to link shots 73 and 75 with the camera movements that illustrate her progress to the house and thus to assimilate her arrival at the dock more resolutely to her entry into the house, as if the former, acquiring movement in shot 73, rushed her by recurrence to beat Mitch to the threshold of the house. For Melanie's return journey is also an outward journey: when she arrives at the pier she is still carrying in her hands the birds she has just offered to Mitch Brenner.

The next four shots (76–79) are all static ones. They alternate two shots of Melanie (76 and 78) with two of gulls (77 and 79). But a double variation complicates this simple alternation of static shots. The first relates to a change in the object of vision: Mitch, who has just appeared on the pier (75), then the gull that crosses the sky (77).[14] Shot 76 juxtaposes them: the disappearance of the smile that has been on Melanie's face since shot 72 marks the change. The second variation relates to the conjunction seeing/seen (or seeing/seeing) in the same framing: in shot 77 the gull strikes Melanie on the head. This confirms a correspondence between Mitch and the gull or, to be exact, between Mitch's look and the gull. The alternation static/static reinforces the metaphorical effect. In fact, just as the alternation static/movement provides a condensed image of set A, the alternation static/static offers a condensed image of set B, distributed about its centers where the gulls' cries are already linked to Mitch's look (shot 59). As the centers slide beneath one another, the two successions of shots are superimposed: as Mitch hurries onto the pier, the gull descends on Melanie; the bird of the gift appears in its baleful double.

To be rigorous, we must clear up a point of detail here. I have said that these four shots, all static, condense all the series of set B. But one of the latter, B3, includes in shot 63 a camera movement whose importance I have emphasized, which thus opposes it to the static shots 76–79.[15] But in shot 78, the gull enters the screen to strike Melanie before leaving it in the right background. Two actions seem to be grouped together here: that of shot 57, in which Mitch looks at Melanie through the binoculars, and that of shot 63, in which Mitch's car is followed in a pan to the right (it leaves the screen in a static shot, shot 71). The essential point is clear: we are dealing in each case with a shot that marks Mitch on the one hand, Melanie on the other, in the play of a binary rhyme; hence, two actions that concern Mitch are condensed onto Melanie.

Movement within the shot is thus substituted for movement of the shot. But that is not enough. The two micro-series 72–75 and 76–79 have to be conceived as a unit and as superimposable on one another in order for shot 63 to find a continuation and a perfect rhyme in the movement that defines Mitch's appearance on the pier in shot 75: a movement that thus reintroduces as a unit the centers A and B, in which Melanie and Mitch have the initiative in turn, and in them the two sets A and B, distinct and intermingled. There is something remarkable about the fact that Mitch and Melanie, through the structure of the set and of the detail, are obliged to act in one another's places.

The shots that follow develop this condensation, which tends toward the final resolution. When in shot 80 and 81 the camera returns to Mitch and Melanie alternately, it is as if the narrative wished to return to the order of binary rhyme. But to do so strictly it would have had to invert the two shots 80 and 81 after shot 79 (the gull moving away). The order chosen witnesses to the fact that this scenic fragment could only strictly return to binary alternation by making shot 80 (Mitch on the pier looking at Melanie) follow the first moment of shot 76, before Melanie's second look: that is, by effacing the whole episode of the gull in which the divergences become significant. That is why shot 80 follows shot 79.

This successive conjunction of Mitch and the gull in which his look is duplicated with symbolic violence, introduces a break in the rhyme that serves to highlight the two earlier breaks in centers A and B. The first concerns Melanie, and is doubly repeated at her entry and at her exit from the house (31–32 and 36–37); the second concerns Mitch, in shots 56–57, when he discovers Melanie with the help of the binoculars. The analogy is particularly strong in the case of the second center. The break is indeed repeated with Mitch: Melanie, on the other hand, is in both cases imprisoned in Mitch's look without being able to respond as she does before and after by the challenge of her smile: in shot 58, in the circles of the binoculars as she tries to get the boat going, the second time in shot 81, because she is in a state of shock caused by the gull's aggression. But we should underline the fact that the dominance of the look, normally marked by the equivalence seeing/seen-close/distant shot, is here expressed by an inverse relationship: Mitch framed in a full shot, Melanie in a close shot. This inversion can be explained first from the succession of images: Melanie seen by Mitch is at the same moment looking, not at Mitch, but at her glove, red with blood from her wound. In the second place, the inversion marks the fact that the symbolic punishment that strikes her in Mitch's look in the metaphorical form of the killer birds has, from the beginning, spoken in her own look, in the first metaphor that her indiscretion proposed to Mitch with the symbolic gift of the lovebirds. If Mitch's look reverses and precipitates the sequence, Melanie's look guides it and organizes it until the moment of the meeting.

Moreover, the conjunction of Melanie and the gull arises in the formal succession as soon as the alternation is read backwards. Before establishing Melanie in shot 81 and Mitch in shot 80, it should have established Melanie in shot 79 instead of the seagull. The effect is clear: in this order it is Mitch who would be wounded hypothetically by the gull in shot 78.

If the break in the alternation in shots 79–80 also refers, as we have seen, to centers A and B, the break in the alternation in shots 80–81 marks a formal homology with center B; inversely, the new break in shots 81–82 marks a formal homology with the duplication of the break that occurs at center A. In both cases the break is effected by a transition to the close-up (insert) of Melanie's hands. In the first case, Melanie has just entered the house; the very close shot details her actions: she takes two envelopes from her purse, puts the one "To Cathy" on the front of the cage, and tears up the second one "To Mitchell Brenner," putting the pieces back into her purse. The transition from one shot to the next makes clear the *nature of the gift* and the double denegation that is expressed in the fate of the two envelopes. In the second case, the wounded Melanie lowers the hand she has lifted to her head and looks at it; the highly magnified detail shows the index finger spotted with blood. The transition from one shot to the next makes clear the *effect* of the gift. A double opposition marks the two pairs of shots: the first (32–33) is constructed out of an alternation movement/static and denotes a complete break with the alternation of visions: Melanie is released at the level of vision, as far as she is concerned, from the dominance that was expressed in the preceding movement.[16]

The second pair of shots (81–82) is constructed out of an alternation static/static and displaces the alternation of the look: Melanie replaces Mitch as the object of her own look at the same instant she becomes an object for Mitch's look. The relinquishment of dominance is expressed at the level of vision itself; it has a correspondence at the level of movement. Mitch has the initiative: the camera movement underlines his approach toward Melanie in shot 83 as it emphasized his departure in the car in shot 63. But this time Mitch is not explicitly seen: no shot of Melanie's look intervenes. Her look has been wounded, for it is only metaphorically, and for the sake of the rest of the plot, that the gull does not strike her eyes.

Shot 84, the last one, effects the meeting. For the first time since the beginning of the scene it groups Mitch and Melanie in the same shot. It completes Mitch's movement as he appears at the edge of the pier in shot 75 and, after the gull's aggression, reconfirms a complete break with the principle of alternation that marked its dominance. In a long movement that espouses the joint displacement of Melanie and Mitch supporting her, it ties together the many shots that broke up Melanie's descent at the side of the fisherman.

Shot 33

To bring the analysis to an end, we must here turn back and bring into play a deviation from the rhyme that has not yet been explained. It will be remembered that the rejection that gave shot 24 a double rhyme, one in series A5 at shot 44, the other in the Arrival series at shot 73, enabled us to link, on the one hand, the entries of Mitch and Melanie into the house, on the other, their joint arrival at and on the Bodega Bay pier; but it also and above all enabled us to link together the arrivals and entries themselves. However, the condensation that we have seen deployed at the double level seeing/seen and static/movement throughout set A is also operative at another less obvious or, equally, more latent level.

Series Al and A2 in fact manifest an opposition at the level of what is seen: Mitch in shots 15–20 (the first six shots of series A), and the house and barn, that is, non-Mitch (the last four shots of series Al and series A2, i.e., 21–31). Series A5, which follows series A4 in which the non-Mitch of series A2 is symmetrically duplicated, reproduces the difference between the first six and the last four shots of Al in quite another way. Mitch is seen in all the shots of the series that alternate with shots of Melanie seeing, except for shot 48, which shows the house alone, after Mitch has gone inside and before he comes out. This absence returns elliptically in the repetition of the entry and exit in shots 54–56 (Mitch goes inside the house/Melanie seeing/Mitch comes out of the house). But this opposition is condensed precisely in the four-shot micro-series 72–75. Shots 73 and 75 in fact include the opposition non-Mitch/Mitch; this correspondence further reinforces the relation previously established between set A and shots 72–75.

But there is more. Our analysis of set A has shown that it conforms to a double movement of condensation: of the four series Al, A2, A4, and A5 toward center A at the level of the image, of the three series Al, A2, and A4, and of center A toward series A5 at the level of the plot. This new condensation is produced at the level of what is seen, seen by Melanie according to the binary structure of the rule of alternation. The opposition Mitch/non-Mitch that is revealed as such in series Al and A2 (15–20/25–31) and duplicated as non-Mitch (37–43)/Mitch (44–46)/non-Mitch (48)/Mitch (49–56) in series A4 and A5, has no complete equivalent in series A3. Indeed, only shot 35 echoes it in the form non-Mitch, here the barn with Mitch in it, just as Melanie is in the house at that moment. Mitch is unseen, and the shot that should show him in the compressed alternation that would logically correspond within this short and condensed series to the relaxed alternation of series Al and A2, on the one hand, and of A3 and A4, on the other, is shot 33.

It is this same shot that breaks within the series the alternation of the look already fractured by the break that occurs at both ends of the series in repetitions of a shot of Melanie (31–32, 36–37), and that, on the other hand, makes possible the semi-alternation of the framing (up to shot 35, where it is interrupted), and particularly the alternation of movement which, as we have seen, the binary principle is both deployed in and displaced onto in series A3.[17] The result is that the lack of a shot marked Mitch-seen is underlined all the more vigorously in that the functions of the opposition and of the rhyme are here reaffirmed from shot to shot and perform formally in a roundabout way precisely where they are canceled in their first and primordial effect.

But shot 33, which shows Melanie—Melanie's hands—is linked, as we have seen, to shot 57, in which Mitch discovers Melanie with the assistance of the binoculars: first by position, since they effect a break in each of the two centers; then by nature, since they both express this by a transition from the ensemble to the detail, from full shot to close-up. This series of substitutional implications, which thus reduces the seen to the seeing and Melanie to Mitch in a chain of close-ups, enforces a leap capable of translating both the homology of the centers and their distances, which motivate the double slide: shot 33, which shows Melanie where it ought to show Mitch, shows metaphorically what Mitch sees when, in shot 57, he discovers Melanie fictionally—what he would see if he was in the house when Melanie entered it. This transference is confirmed precisely in the texture of the plot: the reciprocity of the condensation that links together the two series A3 and A5 and the conjunction produced by inversion between the barn and the house—each of which is seen in turn by Melanie in shots 35 and 48—make this missing shot a shot in which Mitch would already be on the path leading to his recognition of Melanie.

But it makes no sense to invoke the lack of this shot, we should remember, unless it signifies the transferential operation taking place between Mitch and Melanie in the break in the alternation of the look in series A3, where the development of the plot is structured in the deviation of the image. It is therefore legitimate to note that the alternation of the look that is thus broken could have been maintained, but with a lesser equilibrium of rhyme, in another relation of visibility that is disallowed by the respective dispositions of shots 32–33: Melanie seeing herself. But Melanie does not see herself, she cannot see herself here, indeed that is the whole stake of the scene, any more than she is really seen by Mitch or sees him here.

This double lack, as the reader will have guessed, is echoed in inversion in the final resolution of shots 80–83. We have seen how the two centers A and B are condensed in it. Shot 82 (the insert of the bloody finger) mediates the united look of Mitch and Melanie: she sees herself; and if she does not see Mitch, preoccupied as she is with her wound, she knows that she is seen, as she did in shot 58, for she is seen directly and not by metaphor. The two shots 33 and 57 are united in the symbolic violence of this last close-up, in which a common look marks the effect of the gift, the fact that it is impossible for Mitch and Melanie to see each other as seen without opening up a dual and murderous relationship.

The Chain

But this is not an even relationship. It is formulated at a privileged level where the asymmetry of the action and of the broad architecture of the scene is duplicated in the privileged constraint of form. The scene is traversed by a chain: it links together the close-ups and draws out the positions of the hero and heroine in the structural order of vision. It can be written as follows:

33 *Melanie's hands, lovebirds, letters to Cathy and Mitch*
49 Melanie, boat
51 Melanie, boat
53 Melanie, boat
57 *Mitch*
70 Melanie, boat
72 Melanie, boat
74 Melanie, boat
76 Melanie, boat (double look)
82 *Melanie's wounded finger*

The three shots underlined have two features in common that distinguish them: they detail the preceding shot (that is why they are, as we have seen, the three determinant breaking points in the sequence); and they are isolated and autonomous. They are divided, finally, according to the opposition seeing/seen, in the order non-seeing (seen)/seeing/seen: at both ends of the chain, the two /seen/ shots, which echo one another, at the center the /seeing/ shot, which acts as a pivot. The eight others are distributed into two internal series. They all concern Melanie seeing, and they rhyme in twos as the alternating play of the look demands.

Nine shots concern Melanie, only one Mitch. The only two *non-seeing* (seen) and *seen* shots concern Melanie. The object of the scene is to show Melanie subjecting by her look and subjected to a look. It could be given a reversible title: *the vision of Melanie Daniels.*

The close-up marks the most privileged moments in the order of the look. It intervenes in Melanie seeing as soon as the plot moves toward dual vision. The first, shot 49, is inserted between the shot of the house that Mitch has just gone into (48) and the shot in which he comes out (50). The first series follows Mitch's discovery of the lovebirds and his investigation on the shore. The second is a prelude to the meeting; it closes with the double look that groups Mitch and the gull, a ravishing smile and terror, in the same shot, shot 76.[18]

The chain of close-ups thus outlines the logical deployment of desire across the scene; Mitch and Melanie are both its mutual subject and object, but it is formulated first of all on Melanie from one end of the chain to the other, in a synchronic condensation of the image that mirrors the plot. The chain confirms the fact that shot 33 is both the center of the scene and its beginning and that it is echoed in shot 57, which is at the center of the chain, before reappearing at the other end in its inverted form. We still have to explain why the binary series marks Melanie with possession at the level of the look and dispossession in the breaks; why shot 82 is seen by Mitch and Melanie and shot 83 apparently by nobody; and lastly why shot 57 has the median position in that set since it is both seeing and marks a break.

The Author

One last character remains to be introduced. An author of films who makes his characters' visions intervene in the succession of the pictorial plot delegates his own powers to them, all the more so because this operation of duplication characteristic of every plot is in this case effected at the level of the form itself, which is where the *metteur en scène* reveals what is essential in his art. When, in a single scene, Hitchcock constructs several series of shots according to the binary alternation Melanie seeing/what Melanie sees, he effaces himself behind her look, so to speak; he relinquishes his own vision in favor of his character. But this game, a serious one, should never make anyone forget that it is fictional; it is the less capable of doing so in that the breaks in the character's vision constitute so many explicit returns to that of the *metteur en scène*, and in that if one can say here: this shot is seen by Melanie, one is only the more insistent on adding something that, however naive and weakly operational it may seem, is less likely to be said of another *metteur en scène*: but this shot is seen by Hitchcock.

This game, which successively identifies the author with one or a number of his characters and then differentiates him from them, in this case determines the articulation of the sequence and illuminates many of its turning points. Hitchcock is here, apparently, at Melanie's side. She has the initiative in the action; and her look, on which is based the binary alternation, organizes the breakdown of the real. But this look, as we may remember, acquires a limit right at the beginning, by the transference of it that Hitchcock effects in favor of the fisherman—for the length of an introductory shot that is immediately canceled—since Hitchcock, in a first break that also constitutes a first variation of his purely possessive and playful look at Melanie, repeats and varies shot 12 (Melanie seen by the fisherman) with two shots that see her moving in the distance, thereby marking the order of the plot and, at the same time, the camera's special pleasure in assuring itself of its object. The camera does the same thing deliberately in shot 33 duplicating the break which makes the transition from series A2 to series A3 in shots 31–32.

As we have seen, this rupture is determining. The privilege of the look that is established in favor of Melanie in the binary series from shot 14 on is overthrown in shot 33, all the more violently so in that this shot is the first close-up in the scene and subjects Melanie's body to a fragmentation clearly expressed in the term "insert," which describes the relations between the ensemble and the detail. The importance of the fact that this shot is seen by Hitchcock without any mediator is also clear. The result is that direct access is obtained to Melanie as an object. But this reversal is illuminated in the first place by the inversion it defines: Melanie is seen by Hitchcock when the structure of alternation would dictate that she should see Mitch. Remember also that everything combines to inscribe this shot as a metaphor for Mitch's vision in shot 57. This duality enables us to specify the relationship between the author and his characters on the basis precisely of the form he assigns logically to their relationships.

If indeed Hitchcock does espouse Melanie's look in order to get to Mitch in a common discovery in which the latter has the position of an object, the reversal effected from one center to the other clearly means that Mitch is the mediator, Hitchcock's main double in the inquiry he is conducting into the desire that speaks in Melanie's look. In this the fisherman is both their doubles: he enables us to identify the author and the character directly in the change of gear peculiar to the form of the plot. Shot 57, furthermore, condenses this movement. Here Hitchcock simultaneously subjects Mitch to his own look and Melanie to Mitch's look (we should note the power of analogy provided by the instrument of vision: the binoculars, which are also the camera). This is the sense of the break by which Hitchcock duplicates an implicit look at Mitch with an explicit one and reverses the dialectic of looks by giving Mitch dominance in the look: he does so by a shot similar to those that attribute it to Melanie (close-ups of the face), a shot that on the other hand opens a binary series completely similar to the one in which Mitch, before the reversal, is in the position of an object beneath Melanie's look. Remember that if the advantage is with Melanie in the series opened in this way, the movement compensates Mitch for this; that, on the other hand, it is explained by the requirements of symmetry, which in itself allows the folding of the scene and the identity and overlap of the characters that signifies the author's double identification; and finally, that it announces a new reversal capable of formulating the relations of implication between the characters and the *metteur en scène* by the conjunction of all the models of the mise-en-scène. The last break can be divided into three periods. The first (79–80) enables Hitchcock to unite Mitch and the gull but also, reading the alternation backwards, as we have seen, to unite Melanie and the gull to the point of fictionally substituting Mitch wounded by the gull for Melanie wounded in shot 78. The third groups Mitch and Melanie in the last shot, in the grasp of the camera of the *metteur en scène*, who both follows and leads their movement. The second period (80–83) avows a more secret structure. Here Hitchcock's look does not, apparently, reveal its explicit power: Mitch observes Melanie, who observes herself. But this look is of itself implied by the displacement of the alternation in which is inscribed the cleavage of looks: the condensation achieved conceals it, while the conjunction of looks, which it espouses and guides by turns in the development of the scene, stamps it with its mark.

Thus, Hitchcock is simultaneously Mitch and Melanie in the double look that ties them together. This does not mean that he is so in an equal or similar way; on the contrary, the relation he has with each of them is revealed in the double movement of the image and the plot by which the relations of his two characters are structured. Here it is impossible to say any more, except that they bring into play a mutual desire whose transgressive violence is directed at Melanie, who makes the gift and receiver its threatening sign, in the opposed forms of good and bad birds. This duality reproduces, but does not overlap, that of the hero and heroine, who are linked together by a rhyme as constant as it is diverse that allows them to be united but also opposed in a cunning orchestration whose subtle harmonies have been suggested by our analysis, to the point where we must find in its most secret heart, in the ultimate contradiction between symmetrical constraint and asymmetrical openness, the place, combining insistence and discretion, of the author.

To tell this double relationship accurately it would be necessary to go beyond the scene and establish it in the Hitchcockian dialectic of desire and law, which is revealed in the reversible shape of guilt and false guilt, linked together by the mutual constraint of the inquiry. *The Birds* provides this inquiry with a new scenario by displacing the detective story scheme onto the level of the symbol in order to mark more clearly the reality of the phantasm it contains.

Let me simply recall, to express this most vividly, how Hitchcock chose to introduce his film: on a busy San Francisco street the camera reveals a motionless girl on the sidewalk at an intersection. As she crosses the street, the camera follows her. She walks along on the other side, then stops and looks up. The next shot reveals her vision: a flock of birds wheeling above the city. A third shot shows her surprise; then, as she turns and goes into a pet shop, she passes a man clearly leaving it, with two white poodles on a leash. The girl is Melanie Daniels, the man Alfred Hitchcock. A few moments later, Mitch Brenner, too, arrives at the pet shop to purchase some lovebirds.

By this detour, which constitutes one of the most inspired of his traditional appearances, Hitchcock suggests a number of things. First of all, the mind's special delight in playing on the joint effects of repetition and variation as well as in formulating its most powerful ideas in the humorous mode. He also implies that, like Mitch and Melanie, he is inscribed in the dual dialectic of desire whose social image he gives and disguises by leading this pair of paradigmatic domestic animals. Finally, he suggests to us that, just like the fisherman, he might be a first double on the route that leads Melanie to Mitch; but he might equally well be the opposite; for even if he does disappear, it is he who directs the film in which Mitch is a double on the route that guides Hitchcock to Melanie.

If Mitch is one of the two principal characters of the plot, Melanie has one privilege over him: she is the heroine. It is her look in the very first shot that raises a flock of wild birds into the sky, just as it is her gift of a pair of lovebirds to a man that unleashes on Bodega Bay the irrational anger of primitive forces.

There is no doubt that Hitchcock identifies with Mitch, who interrogates Melanie's look and allows himself to be bewitched by it; but there is even less doubt that Hitchcock identifies with Melanie, whose eyes bear the phantasm whose effects Hitchcock narrates and analyzes in that purely narcissistic art that mise-en-scène is for him.

1969
TRANSLATED BY BEN BREWSTER

3. The Obvious and the Code
■ (on *The Big Sleep*)

Let us take as an example twelve shots from *The Big Sleep*. They are inscribed between two major "scenes." The first, in Eddy Mars's garage—where Vivian enters the action on Marlowe's side for the first time—culminates in the death of Canino; the second, in Geiger's house, is the end of the film—Eddy Mars's death brings the open series of enigma and peripeteia to a close and sets the seal on the emergence of a couple. In between the two there are twelve shots showing Vivian and Marlowe in the car on the way from the garage to the house.

As a specific unit of code, they correspond exactly to what Christian Metz, in his *grande syntagmatique*, calls a "scene," that is, an autonomous segment, characterized by a chronological coincidence between "the unique consecutiveness of the signifier (deployment on the screen) and the unique consecutiveness of the signified (= the time of the fiction)."[1] On the other hand, as a specifically textual unit, they also constitute what I have chosen to call, in work toward a description of the classical narrative film, a *segment*,[2] that is, a moment in the filmic chain that is delimited both by an elusive but powerful sense of dramatic or fictional unity and by the more rigorous notion of identity of setting and characters of the narrative. (When, as is most often the case, the two pertinences do not overlap completely, i.e., when a significant variation in location or character appears within one and the same segment, the segment divides into sub-segments.) In this case the dramatic unity is obvious—a pause between two strong times marked by the deaths of Canino and Eddy Mars, respectively, and a resumption of verbal relations between Vivian and Marlowe. Identity of characters and location is absolute—throughout the segment we have a car and the two main characters in intimate conversation. Finally, the segmental nature of the shots is reinforced by an element which, for all that it is not inherent in its definition, is often consubstantial with it in the classic narrative; the twelve shots open and close on lap dissolves—a punctuation that here functions as a (redundant) sign of demarcation.[3]

1

2

3

4

5

6

7

8

9

10

	Framing	S/M	Angle	Characters	Speech	Time	Elements of Narration
1	MS→ MCS	M	↗	VM	–	+	
2	CS	S	↗	VM	+VM	+	
3	CU	S	↗	M	+M	–	
4	CU	S	↑	V	+VM	–	
5	CU	S	↗	M	+M	–	
6	CU	S	↑	V	+MV	–	V: "I guess I am in love with you."
7	CS	S	↗	VM	+VM	++	Marlowe's movement as he takes a corner
8	CU	S	↑	V	+M	–	
9	CU	S	↗	M	+M	–	
10	CS	S	↗	VM	+VM	+	M: "I guess I am in love with you."
11	CU	S	↑	V	–	–	
12	CS	S	↗	VM	–	+	Vivian puts her hand on Marlowe's arm.
	a	b	c	d	e	f	

The interest of this segment lies in its relative poverty. Even an attentive viewer will not retain anything with certainty except the impression of a certain amount of vague unity. Questioned, he will very likely hazard the view that the segment consists of a long take supported by dialogue, or at best, of two or three shots. But Hawks needed twelve shots to secure the economy of this segment. Undoubtedly, that economy was designed so as not to be perceived, which is in fact one of the determining features of the American cinema. But it exists, and from it the classical mode of narration draws a part of its power. It is true, as Metz has observed, that "(that mode) is geared toward the sequence, and it is the sequence (and not the shot) that is its preoccupation, its constant problem."[4] But the organic material of this preoccupation is the prior set of formal, hierarchically ordered relations between the shots. What I want to show here is how the simplest narrative fact imaginable—two characters talking in a car—can come to set into play a series of elementary but subtle operations that ensure its integration into the development of a narration. It is on this level that the—relative—poverty of this segment is exemplary.

According to Rivette's famous formula, "obviousness is the mark of Howard Hawks's genius."[5] No doubt—provided we recognize the extent to which that obviousness only comes to the fore insofar as it is coded.

The text of the segment is constituted by the concerted action of six codes, listed from (a) to (f) in the accompanying recapitulatory table. The first three concern variations in scale between the shots, whether they are static or moving, and camera angle (symbolized by the arrow). These are three specific codes that manifest the potentialities of one of the five materials of expression proper to all sound film, that is, the image track.[6] The three others are non-specific codes; the presence or absence of this or that character or characters from the units considered (and note the lack of extension of this code here—there is no shot without a character), whether they express themselves in dialogue or not, and finally whether these units are of greater or lesser duration, does not depend on cinema. In the case of the last code, a relative imprecision will be noted—the times of each shot are brought into clear opposition, and this is just one of the multiple abstractions to which the codes subject the text. As for those elements consigned to the seventh column, they do, of course, fall within a code; but its extension differs radically from that of the remaining six. It differs in two senses: as a code of narrative actions it is of itself broader than the rest, pluri-codic from the outset through the different levels on which its elements are located; in addition, it only takes on its specific value as code in the light of the body of the text (e.g., the film), for which it determines one of the principal semantic axes. It is a reflection of this extension that it figures here in only a restricted number of elements capable of entering into combination with the action of the other six codes in the circumscribed space of twelve shots.

The most direct oppositions of the segment emerge between shots 1 and 2. Shot 1 is the only moving shot; it tracks in to frame the front right window of the car, and (from medium shot to medium-close shot) delimits two frames that are to have no equivalent in the remainder of the segment. I should stress (something which does not seem to have constituted a distinct code but might have done so) that it is the only shot taken outside the car. A fourth—correlative—opposition is marked in the transition between presence and absence of dialogue. But from shot 1 to 2 the narration is at pains to soften any excessive difference, ensuring continuity on three levels: through the relative identity of duration of the shots; the combined presence of the two main characters in both shots; and above all by maintaining the initial camera angle (from left to right), which is the simplest way of ensuring a sense that one is watching one and the same shot (see stills 1–12).

Shot 3 starts from an unevenly graduated transition (it is static like shot 2, and preserves the same camera angle as shots 1 and 2) to introduce another series of differences. The two characters/one character (Marlowe) change has its three correlates: passage from medium-close shot to close-up, from long take to short take, and the centering of the dialogue on one character.

Shot 4 refines this beginning of a system. We pass naturally from one character to the other, from Marlowe to Vivian, as if shot 2 had been divided to show us in turn the hero and the heroine, giving each of them the same reduction in framing and duration. But this comes only at the cost of a double difference: Vivian does not speak alone in shot 4 as Marlowe did in shot 3. Instead, they both talk. And above all, the angle changes completely to show Vivian full face, enclosed by the space of the car interior—the reverse of Marlowe, beside whose face the night landscape continues to flow, discernible through the left front window of the car.

Thereafter the segment organizes itself on this twofold opposition, alternating between two characters and one character, and between each of the two characters. But while the static nature of the shot, the distribution of the scale of framing, and the camera angle remain invariable, the other pertinences undergo notable changes.

a. First, the distribution of the characters. The shots that show the characters alone follow a very precisely graded pattern that complicates the initial 2/1-1 alternation. This pattern may be broken down as follows: four alternating shots (3–6), then two (8–9), then one (11). Inevitably, within the gradual contraction that marks the curve of the segment and ensures its internal acceleration (what might be called its "suspense"), a privileged status is assigned to Vivian, who figures in shot 11. Note that this privilege is secured by a delicate transition that inverts the initial data of the alternation—the M/V/M/V order that succeeds shot 2 becomes V/M after shot 7, as if to pave the way for the absence of Marlowe in the last occurrence.

b. But the privilege conceded within one code (presence in the image) is overthrown in another (presence in the dialogue belonging to each shot). We have already noted that while Marlowe alone speaks in shot 3, where he is in the image, Marlowe and Vivian both talk in shot 4, which shows Vivian alone, an opposition that is continued in shots 5 and 6. The shots that follow accentuate this imbalance in accordance with a progression which is at the same time inverse, similar to and different from that of the image-presence progression. For Marlowe alone speaks in shots 8 and 9, which show the two characters alternately; and while he does not speak in shot 11, where Vivian marks her privilege in the image, she—far from speaking—is quite silent.[7]

This silence, which opposes this shot of Vivian to the whole anterior series of shots showing one character, is followed by another silence. Shot 12, which shows both Vivian and Marlowe again, is silent, thereby giving the other end of the segment a symmetry with shot 1, whose singularity in relation to those that follow has been noted. A folding effect that clearly demonstrates the way in which the narration, even down to its details, proceeds through a differential integration of its constituent elements.

c. Third, time. While the two characters–long take/one character–short take equivalence is respected throughout the segment, the first term of the opposition undergoes profound internal variation. Shot 7 is in fact much longer than corresponding shots 1, 2, 10, and 12, to the point where it is almost as long as the set of the remaining eleven shots. The strategic placement of this shot will be noted—it occurs in the middle of the segment, thus delimiting a beginning that makes it possible and an end that it motivates and which echoes the beginning through a multiple process, a process simultaneously of equivalence through symmetry, of resolution through repetition and variation, and of acceleration in balancing.

The arrangement shown by the work of the codes is the same one that shapes the meaning of the fiction. From the mass of narrative elements ebbing and flowing throughout the segment (conversations, turning on a deepening of the relations of the enigma, and the more or less continuous-discontinuous field of the characters' actions and reactions) I have isolated only two phrases and two gestures. "I guess I am in love with you." This phrase, which occurs twice, uttered first by Vivian and then by Marlowe, clearly shows the extent to which the reduplication effect—in this instance a simple mirror effect linked to the avowal of love—is constitutive of the narrative. But this is so at the cost of an inversion that underscores the fact that repetition is constitutive only inasmuch as it takes its starting point from the difference circumscribing it, within a movement of bi-motivation that is in fact the specific necessity of this type of narrative. It is in shot 6 in which she appears alone that Vivian makes the first avowal of love, whose effect carries over onto shot 7, thereby justifying, among other things, its exceptional length. Inversely, it is in shot 10, in which Vivian and Marlowe appear together, that he reiterates the avowal whose effect will focus on shot 11, which shows Vivian alone and silent.

The two gestures, on the contrary, are relatively heterogeneous. They are nevertheless of interest, the first, which shows Marlowe, gripping the steering wheel in a difficult curve, by specifying him as he is throughout the film, on the side of action; the second, Vivian's tender gesture, is an explicit and conclusive response to the mutual avowal of love, permits us to place her clearly on the side of a feeling that she recognizes and expresses only when she has committed herself to the action on Marlowe's side.

This double narrative inflection has its effect, moreover, on at least two of the codic implications of the narrative whose articulation appears that much more strongly motivated as a result: on the one hand the divergence between presence in the dialogue and presence in the image, which privilege Marlowe and Vivian, respectively; on the other, the difference in camera angle, concentrated on Vivian and abstracting her face on the surface of the screen. Easily recognizable here is a double sign of the mythologization of the woman. Hawks, we might note, is one of the Hollywood directors who has most profoundly re-orientated the Hollywood tradition of the woman-object. The well-known independence and initiative of his heroines brings to certain of his couples—and to none more than that of *The Big Sleep*—the slightly legendary character of a relationship of adult reciprocity. But this is only achieved through the codified marks which, in this instance, make it the woman whose magnified face simultaneously and wholly expresses and receives the avowal of love.

Nevertheless, it would be overly simple to move to a neat conclusion and find something like the "secret" of the text in this correspondence, to see it as the rationale of the text, discovered in its meaning, or even in a meaning. On the other hand, if there is nothing but meaning, and if it has a meaning in the sense that one might say it has a direction, this must, I think, be expressed in quite a different way. In these films, let us say in the classical American cinema, meaning is constituted by a correspondence in the balances achieved—as a law of the text in development—throughout its numerous codic and pluri-codic levels, in other words, its systems. Multiple in both nature and extension, these cannot be reduced to any truly unitary structure or semantic relationship.

But, to confine ourselves to what has been produced by this analytical description of twelve shots isolated from a film that can justifiably figure as one of the models of American high classicism, we note:

a. the number of shots, which is relatively high given the exigencies of the action. This allows for a discontinuity capable of ensuring a certain degree of variation of the filmic space within the given time.

b. This variation, which the narrative adopts as one of its basic options, is, on the other hand, limited by a profound tendency toward repetition. Repetition essentially takes the upper hand through a number of strictly similar shots: on the one hand shots 3, 5, and 9 of Marlowe, and on the other, shots 4 and 6 of Vivian. (The similarity in question is, of course, on the level of the codes that constrain the constitutive variation of dialogues, actors' comportment, etc.)

c. This tendency toward repetition, which, as we saw, also expresses itself clearly through numerous relationships of partial similarity between shots (and beyond that between codes) carries with it a natural after-effect. It underscores the codic differences that give effectiveness to the basic variation constituted by the successive plurality of the shots. These differences are powerful and discrete in their distribution and transitions, having as their primary object to ensure the natural continuity of the narrative—that is, to sustain its artifice but without ever making it too obvious. A balance that in its own specific mode echoes that inscribed in the playing of the actors and the style of the photography.[8]

d. This balance thus reveals a constant relationship from shot to shot between symmetry and dissymmetry, which is, moreover reinforced by a general arrangement in the segment as a whole. In this respect we might recall the unequal deployment of the shots alternating between Vivian and Marlowe around the central axis represented by shot 7, which is itself inscribed into the alternation on another level. It is not surprising, therefore, that it should be the regulated opposition between the closing off of symmetries and the opening up of dissymmetries that gives rise to the narrative, to the very fact that there is a narrative.

Nevertheless, it should be noted that there is a particular arrangement that seems to me not specific to, but profoundly characteristic of, the American cinema. The progressive relationship (in the literal sense) outlined above seems more or less to resolve itself within each unit of narration — in this case within a short segment of twelve shots that might be taken for a secondary transition — by means of a suspension and folding effect, as if to allow the segment to close back on itself more effectively and leave to the new fold the problem of unrolling its new elements. Take the final shot, for example. It is conclusive and synthetic undoubtedly, by virtue of Vivian's tender gesture, which closes off the dialogue marked by their double avowal. But it is so in another way as well: by the silence between the characters, which has its equivalent only in shot 1, it ensures a kind of overall symmetry; but it is tipped over into dissymmetry, so to speak, because it is opposed to the shot it recalls through the identity it sustains with shots 2, 7, and 10, the final silence being the distinguishing mark.

1973
TRANSLATED BY DIANA MATIAS

4. Symbolic Blockage
🔳 (on *North by Northwest*)

For Dominique

We are all precious-little-me at the theater, watching Oedipus and crying out, "Now there's my type of guy! There's my type of guy!"
—Gilles Deleuze and Félix Guattari

The death of the Father will deprive literature of many of its pleasures. If there is no more Father, what's the use of telling stories? Doesn't every narrative lead back to Oedipus? Isn't storytelling always a search for origins, an account of one's entanglements with the Law, an entry into the dialectic of tenderness and hate? Today Oedipus and the narrative are dismissed in one stroke: we no longer love; we no longer fear; we no longer tell stories. As fiction, Oedipus served at least one purpose: it helped write good novels, it helped tell stories well (written after seeing Murnau's City Girl*).*
—Roland Barthes

I. THE FILM

North by Northwest illustrates in precise terms the Hitchcockian dialectic of the ordeal that leads the hero—the heroes—from the enigma to its resolution, from error to recognition. That this dialectic, inaugurated by the mistake that defines the reality of the ordeal, turns out to involve the common destiny of a man and a woman, implies no more than that this is the driving force behind the oeuvre, its origin and its vanishing point. That Hitchcock here yields to the seduction, to the ironic glamour of the implausible in order to give a more radical turn of the screw to the logic of the everyday is in my view only an intensification of the abstraction in which the pleasure proper to the glittering play of meaning gives rise to a more deliberate acknowledgment of the ruling principle of the Hitchcockian fable—morality and perversion linked.

This abstraction, in *North by Northwest*, lies in the controlled and pointed distance Hitchcock maintains toward a genre whose system he uses and perverts the more clearly to define his own. Note that this genre—the spy movie, more precisely, the spy movie as chase—constitutes for Hitchcock himself a sort of tradition whose effects he already experimented with many times in his best English period and in his first American films: in *The Thirty-Nine Steps*, to which *North by Northwest* is in many ways a lavish rejoinder; *The Lady Vanishes*; *Foreign Correspondent*; and *Saboteur*. In all of these films, but much more radically here, distance and control depend largely on performance, above all on the acting of the hero, which produces the clearest and most solid of identifications between the spectator and the director.

Cary Grant's performance is the supreme example of this, his hesitation pushed to the point of ambiguity between the mechanical and the sentimental, the reserved and the provocative: it conveys the fundamental derealization of the intrigue that defines it; it emphasizes its motifs, thus creating at the very level of narration as rhythm, between shots and within shots, a sort of permanent irony that is as difficult to formalize as it is easy to identify and that makes the film the privileged site of a dissociation, of a provocative shuttling backwards and forwards between the gratuitousness of the game and the gravity of the stake.

It is the nature and constitution of this stake whose successive terms I would first like to establish: that is, I wish to show the transformation that takes place, for the hero, from the moment that the director plunges him into the crucial dialectic of appearance and identity, of innocence and guilt. This transformation unfolds, symphonically, in three grand movements in which the relations of knowledge and ignorance that define the generation of the film, its dynamic, are raveled and unraveled by the metamorphoses of the enigma, according to a distortion that the director cunningly maintains between the knowledge of his characters and the knowledge of the spectator.

First Movement

When Roger Thornhill, in the Plaza Hotel bar, gets up to send his mother a message just as the public address system and the bellboy call George Kaplan's name, Vandamm's men seize him and open up a series of effects that govern the development of the film. The mistake (which apparently marks for Vandamm a successful outcome to his search—initiated before the film began—for Kaplan) produces two perfectly correlated quests:

a. Thornhill's search for Kaplan, the only man who can rectify the misunderstanding, the mistaken identity; for Vandamm (hidden for the moment under the name of Townsend), who takes him for Kaplan, this search functions as a trap insofar as Thornhill is logically drawn by it to coincide for Vandamm with the role of Kaplan;

b. the police's search for Thornhill insofar as the mistaken identity inscribes him in the position of guilty before the law: first for drunk driving, when he escapes Vandamm's hit men for the first time after they have forced him to drink; then for murder when Thornhill, looking for the false Townsend, ends up meeting the real one, whom the impostor causes to be killed in his arms.

The murder takes the double mistake to its extreme: it marks the culmination of an initial enigma whose dissolution ends the first movement. A dialogue scene, wedged into the sequences of Thornhill's flight, reveals to the spectator that Kaplan is a fictitious character; he has been invented by the CIA to thwart the schemes of Vandamm, who thus emerges as the objective, ideological, absolute guilty one that everything has led us to expect. The "Professor's" reply, exacting silence from the secret service on the reality of the murder and the unreality of Kaplan—"If we . . . give any hint to Vandamm that he's pursuing a decoy instead of our real Number One, then Number One, working right under Vandamm's very nose, will immediately face suspicion, exposure, and assassination"—contains a clue that is immediately forgotten, is made to be forgotten. This clue ushers in a displacement of the enigma that alone will justify a revelation that could otherwise seem clumsy and that, far from alleviating the playful anxiety of suspense, intensifies it.

Second Movement

This movement is articulated around a new character, Eve Kendall, in a plunge that is all the more radical insofar as Thornhill owes his escape from the police to his meeting her on the New York–Chicago train. Her refusal to accept the name "Jack Phillips" adopted by Thornhill in their first encounter suggests from the outset that the truth of the first enigma, for Thornhill, will be played out around Eve, and that the very reason for this enigma (that is, for the film) is evident in this relation— sealed by Hitchcock with an interminable kiss that reiterates in its violence, both passionate and ironic, the famous kiss from *Notorious*.

The enigma that then takes shape around Eve and that inscribes her in her turn in the ambiguous play of identity and guilt is formulated in three moments, the discrepancies between which, for Thornhill and the spectator, guarantee the jubilation attached to suspense:

a. Eve Kendall, industrial designer, saves Thornhill from the hands of the police. The note she sends Vandamm after the seduction tells the spectator what Thornhill will not know until the outcome of the famous airplane scene:

b. Eve Kendall is Vandamm's accomplice—and mistress—and only saved Thornhill in order to have him killed. Thornhill ascertains this in two scenes, in which his investigation logically shifts from Kaplan to Eve, in the double name of truth and desire: in Eve's room at the Ambassador Hotel and in the auction gallery, where he finds her at Vandamm's side and learns the latter's true name.

c. Eve Kendall is a counter-espionage agent.

Here we should note the rigor and duplicity of the scenario. The revelation that enlightens Thornhill as to Eve's identity comes only at the end of a first disclosure, which makes Thornhill's knowledge coincide with the spectator's: after provoking the arrest that allows him to escape Vandamm's hit men, Thornhill learns from the Professor who has had him freed that Kaplan is only an empty image he has happened to fill, an image the Professor presses him to embody further in order to mitigate the dangers weighing upon his actual agent as a result of the mistake. Thornhill, recovering his innocence through this objectification of his identity, refuses and thereby, given the dissolution of the inaugural enigma, seems to bring the film to an end. The second revelation, which precisely reintroduces as an enigma an apparently already settled interrogation of Eve (although its resolution contradicts both a clue and the heroic positivity of the couple so dear to American cinema), is required in order to ensure, via Thornhill's change of tack, continuity in the literal sense, the continuation of the film in a third movement, which turns the ultimate recognition of the truth into the very space and time of an exaltation of suspense.

Third Movement

This movement unfolds from Eve's faked murder of Thornhill, which brings about the indispensable renewal of the action and clears Eve of all complicity with the CIA, between the meeting in the woods and the famous chase on Mount Rushmore.

In the first scene, Eve Kendall reveals who she is, what woman hides behind the adventuress: a woman disappointed by men's infidelity, by their unfitness for marriage and family life.

> *Thornhill*: Has life been like that?
> *Eve*: Mm hmmm.
> *Thornhill*: How come?
> *Eve*: Men like you.
> *Thornhill*: What's wrong with men like me?
> *Eve*: They don't believe in marriage.
> *Thornhill*: I've been married twice.
> *Eve*: See what I mean?

In the second scene, at the moment of supreme danger, Roger Thornhill lets Eve know that behind the seducer she thinks she sees in him hides a victim of women's fickleness.

> *Thornhill*: If we get out of this alive, let's go back to New York on a train together. All right?
> *Eve*: Is that a proposition?
> *Thornhill*: It's a proposal, sweetie.
> *Eve*: What happened to the first two marriages?
> *Thornhill*: My wives divorced me.
> *Eve*: Why?
> *Thornhill*: I think they said I led too dull a life.

Between the two, the action, over and above the investigation, becomes a trial of love, the suspense the uncertainty of its consummation. Deceived up to this point by appearances, even if he does force them to strip off their masks, Thornhill now dominates the action; he takes the initiative, defying both the Professor's prohibitions and Vandamm's threats to rescue and win Eve. Seizing the spies' secret, he fulfills the destiny of the national law that saves him in return (a policeman's shot will cut down Leonard, Vandamm's secretary, just as he is about to push Eve and Thornhill off the cliff). But the excellence that, in this art of subjectivity and personal odyssey so often leads the wrongly accused hero, rather than the police, to the goal of the investigation (marking him, the hero, once again, as in *The Thirty-Nine Steps* or *Saboteur*, with a sort of ideological perfection) is only meaningful insofar as it reconciles the Law with the Desire that puts it in play: here, with Thornhill's fantasy reflected in Eve's, not to mention Hitchcock's fantasy, which feeds on this relation.

The two penultimate shots are well known: the movement Thornhill makes to draw Eve toward him, on the vertiginous slope of Mount Rushmore, is completed in the couchette of a sleeping car in an echo of the first seduction. From one image to the other, these words make it licit: "Come on, Mrs. Thornhill." They show that the transgression of the adventure closes with the sanction of bourgeois marriage; but they also indicate that the limit where desire is fixed can only find recognition in this transgression as trial and site of truth: the loss of identity and the guilt that from the inaugural mistake define the adventure as the traversal of an enigma thus lead the hero from an ignorance to a knowledge, from a lack to a possession, from the misrecognition to the recognition of (socialized) desire.

Hence the last jarring shot, which Hitchcock did not fail to emphasize, in the denegating form of a secret: "There are no symbols in *North by Northwest*. Oh yes! One. The last shot. The train entering the tunnel after the love scene between Grant and Eva Marie Saint. It's a phallic symbol. But you mustn't tell anyone."[1]

II. THE OTHER FILM: THE SAME

If we delve further into the dynamic of the play of desire that controls the progressive resolution of the enigmas, we realize that it is by signifying the relationship that links him to his mother that the hero finds himself logically carried toward the possession of a wife: Eve, the woman. This substitution, at the end of an ordeal in which the hero completes his itinerary (which may justifiably be called "Oedipal") opens the way to the *jouissance* symbolized by the last shot.

And so let us return to the point at the beginning of the film where this Oedipal itinerary, coinciding with the hero's trajectory, crystallizes. In this narrative, indeed, it is the omnipotence of the hermeneutic code resulting from an unconditional rejection of verisimilitude that gives rise to the symbolic code as its internal and ineluctable dimension. This narrative coalescence, which Barthes showed so well in S/Z, here achieves a sort of perfection. Some of Hitchcock's other, explicitly psychoanalytic, films—for example, *Spellbound*, *Psycho*, *Marnie*—have interrogated this relation of enigma, act, and symbol through the plot, if only to try to reflect on a layering that Hitchcock's work has made its principle. But never, I believe, did he attain such a supreme point of fusion. This is due, I believe, to a dazzling art of the surface that seems to render ever more immaterial the depth it never ceases to make its stake. In *North by Northwest* the symbolic is never beneath the film or above it; it constitutes its matrix only through the movement that carries it from enigma to enigma and from action to action. The other film is truly the same film. Oedipus is truly the subject who both answers the Sphinx and bears the weight of its demands.

And so it is just as Roger Thornhill, in the Plaza Hotel bar, gets up to send a message to his mother that narrative improbability seizes him in the name of George Kaplan. This coincidence, of course, reverberates throughout the film as a formal index of his Oedipal predestination. The effect of mistakenness here is multiplied by the insistence of the message. Already, in the taxi that takes him to the Plaza, Thornhill has twice asked his secretary to contact his mother—only to remember the moment he gets out of the cab that he has forgotten to explain how she can do so. The content of the message (Thornhill confirms with his mother that they are to go to the theater that night) is also far from immaterial to the symbolic opening that the rest of the film circulates back toward this moment of error and illusion. For, remarkably, this theme of the theater will be constantly reaffirmed as the internal metaphor of the film, arising from this postponed show. "With such expert play-acting, you make this very room a theater": this is Vandamm's response to Thornhill when, in the library where the latter is brought after his kidnapping, he insists there's been a mistake and, in order to reestablish the identity denied him, reminds Vandamm that he has to go to the theater. The pretext that establishes the inaugural mistake is thus from the beginning in very close accord with the scenario it gives rise to the next day, when Thornhill, accompanied by the detectives, his mother, and his lawyer, comes back to this room in which the transformations, though small, suggest a change of setting, and cries out with disarming accuracy when faced with the deceptive welcome given him by the false Mrs. Townsend: "What a performance!" Vandamm echoes him at the other end of the film, saying to Leonard: "When you return to New York, do say goodbye to my sister for me, and thank her for her superb performance as Mrs. Townsend." But it is of course Thornhill, the object of the mistake, who finds himself assuming the metaphor, having introduced it into the fiction in spite of himself. When, toward the end of the second movement, he catches up with Eve, Leonard, and Vandamm at an auction in Chicago, the dialogue remarkably condenses the manifest theatricality of the film as the reflexive space and conducting rod of the fiction:

> *Vandamm:* Has anyone ever told you that you overplay your various roles rather severely, Mr. Kaplan? First you're the outraged Madison Avenue man who claims he has been mistaken for someone else. Then you play a fugitive from justice, supposedly trying to clear his name of a crime he knows he didn't commit. And now you play the peevish lover, stung by jealousy and betrayal. Seems to me you fellows could stand a little less training from the FBI and a little more from the Actors' Studio.
>
> *Thornhill:* Apparently the only performance that will satisfy you is when I play dead.
>
> *Vandamm:* Your very next role. You will be quite convincing, I assure you.

There is a follow-up to this exchange, first between Thornhill and Vandamm, in the Mount Rushmore cafeteria: "By the way, I want to compliment you on your colorful exit from the auction gallery. . . . And now, what little drama are we here for today?"; then between Eve and Thornhill when, in the forest, she congratulates the amateur for having played to perfection this "little drama" (the fake murder), anticipated by Vandamm with an irony that destines him to become its victim. The instrument of this drama, a revolver loaded with blanks, will reappear twice, to be recognized first by Leonard, then by Thornhill, for the prop that it is, a deceptive part of this theater of illusions.

theatricality (handwritten margin note)

The narrative is constantly fascinated, in a ludic and reflexive reduplication, by the evident theatricality of its machinations. It does so to the point that, plunging into its own fiction the moment Thornhill gets up in the Plaza Hotel bar, it seems altogether to come instead of and in the place of the theater performance Thornhill was supposed to go to with his mother. The first conversation in the library, which

insists on this temporal equivalence, inscribes a parallel equivalence in the image: on both occasions when Thornhill mentions the show, his movements and those of the camera conjoined frame him in medium long shot in front of the huge curtains Vandamm drew when he came in. In these moments, no other element impairs the substitutive character of a representation: Thornhill seems truly to stand at the front of the stage he alludes to, as if to announce that the fiction in which he finds he has been caught arises from the projective fantasy initiated by a theatrical performance. We learn nothing about the play itself, except for these words of Thornhill's: "It was a show I was looking forward to." Given the mythic collusion between psychoanalysis and the theater so insistently emphasized since Freud, we must suppose that this play is the ever-revived version of *Oedipus the King* that psychoanalysis attributes to Western consciousness. Thornhill, having fictitiously entered the theater beside his mother, can do nothing to undo the ties that bind him to her except to go on the stage himself and live out his fantasy. *North by Northwest* is the film that results, producing in its systematic perversion the fantasy of the American citizen reflected in that of the author and the methods of his mise-en-scène.

The dialogue between Thornhill and his secretary in the taxi taking them to the Plaza Hotel allows us to grasp the image of this mother straightaway. It is a mother who is close: Thornhill is to dine with her before taking her to the theater. He knows how she spends her time; everything seems to suggest a richly habitual intimacy between them. She is an abusive

mother: she sniffs her son's breath to see if he has been drinking. "Like a bloodhound," says Thornhill, displaying the irritation he feels at this dependent relationship whose despotism he nevertheless seems to accept. This relationship is eventually confirmed in various ways. When he arrives dead drunk at the police station after successfully escaping Vandamm's hit men, it is to his mother that Thornhill makes the one telephone call allowed by law. It is difficult to render the piteous tone, at once infantile and provocative, of this call: "Hello, mother. This is your son, Roger Thornhill." These opening words show the same structural solemnity as those with which Thornhill sums her up to the sergeant who comes to stop him: "That was mother." The next day, in court, the exchange between the judge and the lawyer ("Counsellor, how long have you known your client?" "Seven years,

Your Honor." "Do you know him to be a reasonable man?" "Absolutely.") is greeted by Clara Thornhill with mocking contempt, which an indignant exclamation from her son is unable to dissipate. This contempt is evident in the next two scenes in which she accompanies him: to the false Townsend's house, where the police conduct their investigation; and to the Plaza Hotel, where her son begins his. It is there, in the elevator where they have been joined by Vandamm's hit men, that she asks them in an ironic and protective tone: "You gentlemen aren't really trying to kill my son, are you?" Finally, the last shot showing her at the hotel entrance just as Thornhill flees puts a fermata on this relationship of dependence: "Roger! Will you be home for dinner?" This son actually lives with his mother. We shall never know if this was true during the two failed marriages that the narrative will later attribute to him. But we cannot but see here a reason for their failure. Thornhill is nothing but a big baby, and only Cary Grant could confer on him the equivocal status of a man of forty and an ill-grown adolescent.

This infantilization of the hero is underscored at the outset by the first movement's only reference to his sexuality. On the way to the Plaza Hotel, Thornhill's secretary mentions, among other messages he must answer, a woman's name: that of Gretchen Sabinson.

> *Thornhill* (grimaces): Send her a box of candy from Blum's. Ten dollars. You know the kind—each piece wrapped in gold paper? She'll like that. She'll think she's eating money. Just say to her, "Darling, I count the days, the hours, the minutes—"
>
> *Maggie* (interrupting): You sent that one last time.
>
> *Thornhill*: I did? Oh well. Put, "Something for your sweet tooth, baby and all your other sweet parts." (Maggie gives him a look and he winces) I know, I know.

This dialogue suggests a sort of sexual immaturity; the latter reduces the love relationship to the level of the advertising slogan, which Thornhill, an advertising man, represents socially. In this context, it confirms his infantile fixation on the mother. But Thornhill seems completely conscious of this reduction, just as he is irritated by the excessive dependence he is subjected to, without being able to avoid it.

The mistake that plunges him into the adventure begins to break this circle. By this very movement, it gives Thornhill, through Eve, access to a depth forbidden by repression in his relationship with his mother, a relationship which, however immature Thornhill may be, is one of adulthood. That is why, with the excessiveness proper to the conventions of a semi-comic tone, everything helps to inscribe the mother in this world of surfaces of which her son is the professional echo. This is also why she must remain absolutely incredulous as to the reality of what is happening to her son. No doubt she cannot but be inscribed there; not, at least, until the moment she yields her place to Eve in the unfolding of the adventure and the fulfillment of the fantasy. The phenomenon of narrative substitution between the two women is both literal and radical. The telephone call by which Thornhill, in the New York train station, tells his mother he is leaving for Chicago announces the mother's disappearance from the film as, in a sequence in which metonymy astonishingly coincides with metaphor, it clears the way for the appearance of Eve, whom Thornhill meets as soon as he boards the train. Only two cursory allusions will occur after this to designate the now empty place of the mother, until the final apostrophe that symbolizes the substitution: "Come on, Mrs. Thornhill": the man who utters these words while pulling the conquered woman into his bed is formally marking his substitution of wife for mother.

By a perversion characteristic of most narratives based on splitting and substitution, this last telephone conversation between mother and son allows us to inscribe the son, through the mediation of the mother, with a virtual narrative element that will be actualized in Eve toward the end of the film: "You want me to jump off a moving plane?" Thornhill replies to his mother in order to explain his preference for the train; he thereby foretells that other plane which Vandamm, having discovered Eve's treachery, wishes Eve to board only so that he can throw her out of it. This narrative micro-displacement, which is only a detail but possesses precisely the force of a detail, underscores the fact that the relationship of substitution between the mother and Eve is marked by the theatricality of death, which will define the relationship between Eve and Thornhill and which emerges in the narrative with the mistake and the first attempt to murder Thornhill. It is thus inscribed in a particularly demonstrative way within the movement that draws Thornhill away from his mother and carries him toward Eve. This movement is in fact mediated by a murder: that of Townsend at the United Nations, where Thornhill arrives in flight, we might say, both from Vandamm's hit men and from his mother, and whence he leaves to board the train on which he meets Eve.

Townsend's name first appears on a board at the entrance to the Glen Cove property where Vandamm's men take Thornhill after the kidnapping. The question he poses to the hit men, "Who's Townsend?" is, of course, left unanswered: while perfectly natural, this question has no object but its own insistence. A few moments later, in the library to which he has been led, Thornhill rapidly reads the address on a package and finds this same name, Lester Townsend; he naturally grants it to Vandamm when the latter enters the room to interrogate him. The next day, at the end of the hearing at which Thornhill tries to justify his drunk driving, the investigators visit Glen Cove with Thornhill, his mother, and his lawyer. They are shown in by the same servant who let the hit men in the day before, and they are received by "Mrs. Townsend," of whom Thornhill had caught a glimpse during his conversation with Vandamm. She responds so as to confirm Thornhill's guilt and, to his stupefaction, dispels any of the police's remaining suspicions when she adds that her husband is that very afternoon addressing the United Nations General Assembly. It is thus quite natural that, once he has tried in vain to find George Kaplan at the Plaza Hotel where instead he meets Vandamm's men again, Thornhill races to the United Nations to meet "Townsend," to

whom he has himself announced as Kaplan. Of course he does not recognize his abductor in the man who approaches him and answers his questions courteously before beginning to get annoyed. At the precise moment that Thornhill, in an attempt to explain himself, shows Townsend a photo of Vandamm found in Kaplan's

room and asks him, "Do you know this man?" Townsend suddenly chokes, lets out a strangled cry, and collapses in Thornhill's arms—a knife plunged to the hilt in his back. The spectator has seen what neither Thornhill nor Townsend nor the spectators at the scene could see: one of Vandamm's men, Valerian, standing a few yards away from the two, threw the knife and fled. When Thornhill gets back to his feet, having fallen to the ground under the weight of Townsend's body, he is holding the bloody knife around which his fingers have mechanically closed. Amid the tumult that ensues and the looks that converge on him, a flashbulb crackles, fixing the hallucinatory image of the "United Nations killer."

We should linger over this image that so admirably overlays the mendacious authority of the cinematic message with the illusion of theatrical representation. It serves the narrative's unbridled hermeneutic so well that we may be tempted to ignore the burden of fantasy and symbolization woven into it. In having the real Townsend killed by both Thornhill and the false Townsend, who thus duplicates them both, Hitchcock in fact achieves a veritable symbolic tour de force, effecting the Oedipal itinerary of his hero by logically inscribing him in the problematic of the murder of the father. But, it will be asked, if Townsend is the father (assuming we are right to accord him this place), why have him killed by Vandamm when it is Thornhill's symbolic destiny that is at stake? The fact that Thornhill appears to be the logical victim of Vandamm's hit man makes the question all the more pertinent. He is the one they have followed from the Plaza Hotel in order to reattempt the murder postponed the night before. But, beyond all verisimilitude, the symbolic must be transformed into the verisimilar; and it must be Townsend who is killed by Vandamm through his representative and, in Thornhill's place, fictitiously killed by the latter at the same stroke. The tour de force lies precisely in the fact that Vandamm, through a remarkable effect of differential complementarity, serves both to establish the problematic of parricide in its extension and to negotiate it narratively, since it is only through him that the real Townsend can come to fill the place of the father.

It will be understood that our analysis, while respecting the narrative and in order to respect it, cannot at this point help tending toward more synchrony. At this level, the text of the film becomes equivalent to that of the dream or the myth. In S/Z, Barthes emphasized the specifically differential character of the symbolic field, which counterposes to the hermeneutic and proairetic (narrative-action) codes the pressure of another logic, one of atemporality, substitution, reversibility. This differential pressure is incomparably clearer in S/Z. This is so first, because Balzac's text may tend to close the symbolic into itself less than does Hitchcock's film; but also, and much more fundamentally, because Barthes consistently refrains from structuring the symbolic field, however slightly, in order to underscore its essentially productive function of textual dispersion. The goal of this text is rather, starting from the opposite excess, to emphasize in it (not, at times, without regret) a certain ineluctable character of compulsion.

Three elements would of themselves inscribe Townsend in the place of the father. The first, age, is a strong element: in generational terms, Townsend is clearly a "father" for Thornhill. The second element, the identity of the first letter of their surnames, is weak, to the extent that nothing (e.g., in their forenames) reinforces this phonic equivalence. The third is a subdued element that only acquires significance within the structure as a whole: Townsend does not have, or no longer has, a wife ("What about Mrs. Townsend?" "My wife has been dead for many years"). Similarly, but with no allusion to mark it, Thornhill's mother has no husband. This absolute silence concerning Thornhill's father obviously reinforces the hero's maternal fixation and invites an articulation of the two series, which thus turn out to be metaphorically interlocked. This is a figurative process that is far from rare in narratives of high symbolic charge, one of the means at their disposal to negotiate, through the development of the action and the placement of the enigmas, the symbolization functions that constitute their most pressing interiority. Thus, I have found several examples in Alexandre Dumas's great novel series from *Joseph Balsamo* to *La Comtesse de Charny*, and even more in the vast four-voice text constituted by the juvenilia and the novels of Charlotte, Emily, Anne, and Branwell Brontë. Classical American cinema, which in so many respects inherits the great tradition of the nineteenth-century Western novel, provides numerous examples; especially so Hitchcock's work, where reduplications and splits are arrayed to a vertiginous degree.

But with these clues alone, our interpretation could only inscribe the function of the father in Thornhill's destiny by a kind of leap. Carried along by the Freudian and Lacanian problematic of the father's murder, it would recognize in this simulacrum of murder the possibility that the hero could both accomplish and not accomplish this murder: that is, he could assume the symbolization that allows desire to be joined to the law while avoiding the impasse of an open fight to the death with the father for possession of the mother. He could thus gain access to a substitute object at the price of accepting his own castration by forging a positive identification with the father that at the same time puts him in the position of the symbolic father or the dead father.[2] Thus Thornhill, having killed the father without killing him, can bid his mother farewell and meet Eve. But we must locate Vandamm's place in the structure so that, without modifying this still virtual problematic, we can adjust it, enrich it, diversify it, and above all inscribe it in the text of the film. It is in fact Vandamm and not this so eminently symbolic father that Thornhill must first fight to win Eve. It is Vandamm's mistake that plunges Thornhill headlong into an adventure in which he holds the strings, only to be all the more surely its lure. It is Vandamm, finally, who, apparently against all logic, kills, or has someone kill, the father whose house he occupies and whose name he usurps.

This substitution is, clearly, enough to bring Vandamm into the place of the father. In this relation, "Mrs. Townsend" occupies a structural position. She consti-

tutes, indeed, the mediating term between the real Townsend and the false one, thus allowing the formation of a parental image that echoes the metaphoric complementarity formed by Townsend and Mrs. Thornhill. This replicatory effect is reinforced by the scene that brings the two women face to face around Thornhill at Glen Cove: though not really resembling each other, they nonetheless seem doubles at this moment—thanks to the deceptive, peculiarly maternal solicitude that Mrs. Townsend shows toward Thornhill to fool the detectives, so close to the mother's condescending irony and so well understood by her, even if she is fully its victim. But this equivalence, which thus makes the two women and the two men circulate in a scrambled network of glittering parental images, is posited so that it may also be undone, displaced in a remarkable manner. Toward the end of the film, just before the final confrontation between Thornhill and Vandamm on the slopes of Mount Rushmore, Vandamm lets us know who Mrs. Townsend really is: not his wife, but his sister.

This revelation is no doubt partly due to classical narrative's fundamental concern that all shadows be dispelled and that no enigma be diegetically introduced without eventually being resolved. The rest of Vandamm's words to Leonard confirm this, tying the Glen Cove servant to Valerian in a relationship to that point left unspoken: ". . . and you might tell your knife-throwing chum that I've reassured his wife." But why do these explanations bear so exclusively on family relationships? And why do they come so late if not to act retroactively upon a narrative in which their excessive clarity invites us to displace them in order to shed an even brighter light upon it? The cinematic fiction that comes to take the place of the theatrical performance Clara Thornhill and her son were to attend thus retrospectively attributes to Vandamm's sister the role of his wife at the moment that he himself plays the role of Townsend. A new equivalence is born, this time between Vandamm and Thornhill: both men find themselves, in fact, in an incestuous position, the one

virtually with respect to his mother, the other metaphorically with respect to his sister. This equivalence is reinforced by the parallelism that makes the two women disappear in the first third of the film and makes Eve, as it were, appear in their place to become a central term in the confrontation between the two men. We have seen how this substitution was initiated for Thornhill by the murder of the father. In a sense so it was for Vandamm.

Of course, Eve will later be retrospectively inscribed in the sequence of the story[3] at a point well before Townsend's murder and the beginning of the film. (She will confide to Thornhill in the woods: "I met Phillip Vandamm at a party one night and saw only his charm. I guess I had nothing to do that weekend, so I decided to fall in love. [. . .] Eventually the Professor and his Washington colleagues approached me with a few sordid details about Phillip, and told me that my . . . relationship with him made me 'uniquely valuable' to them.") But Townsend's murder is still responsible for allowing Eve to appear in the narrative and bringing her to the side of Vandamm, Leonard, and their acolytes, in the place once occupied by the false Mrs. Townsend. It is always very difficult to make fictitious modifications to the unfolding of a narrative (even when it is clearly to restore to it what one is thereby trying to steal from it). Still, on reflection, it is possible to imagine Eve in the Glen Cove scenes already playing the part of Mrs. Townsend whose relay she will later assume so perfectly for Thornhill. But this would be to deny the symbolic and hermeneutic exigency that requires her to appear, in a position of substitutive condensation, as the enigmatic stake in a struggle between two men, one of whom has lived with his mother and the other with his sister.

Vandamm is thus the inverted image, the negative, of both the father whom he kills and the son whom he tries to kill. He thereby introduces the psychoanalytic image of the idealized father: in himself he represents both terms of the dual relationship that perpetuates the Oedipal conflict by establishing a murderous reciprocity between father and son.[4] The masterstroke of the narrative is to have articulated in opposition to one another two structures in a single narrative matrix, to the extent that they coincide in the gesture of murder. One can often see the richness of a narrative, specifically its symbolic charge, in the presence of what might be called the "knots" of its fiction. At these moments, the narrative seems literally to condense into itself by tying together two series in one and the same event and thus emphasizing their interdependence. Townsend's murder is the perfect example. But if these two series are both strictly necessary to the economy of the narrative, they are not equally necessary, or not necessary in the same way. They attest to an asymmetry that reflects within the signifying contraction the fundamental asymmetry of the narrative and emphasizes above all the constitutive illusion of this narrative condensation, since it is only from the point of coincidence of the two structures that we can really speak of their duality.

The image of the idealized father that is organized around Vandamm after the murder supports nothing less than a structural mirage. Indeed, one cannot invoke the idea of Vandamm as an Oedipal structure that could introduce into itself the differential problematic of the idealized father without having immediately to oppose that psychoanalytic logic to itself. Of course, it is always more or less in vain that we ask a text to furnish strict clinical equivalents; all the more so in a narrative where the fantasy, in an entirely ludic externality, is expressed most of all through a play of differential positions. But this externality cannot interfere with the logic of the positions that constitute the fantasy; rather, it reinforces it, since it implies a supplementary symbolization. But the move effected for Vandamm, by the murder, from the false Mrs. Townsend to Eve has, strictly speaking, no meaning. Eve is not in fact the mother that the murder of the father ought, however fantasmatically, to restore to the son. She is even less the sister, who disappears at this point and whose place she takes. Thus, for Vandamm, Townsend's murder, symbolically, has no meaning. That is precisely why it introduces an effect of structural mirage, which can only be undone by shifting the fiction from Vandamm's Oedipus to Thornhill's. For if, at the moment he kills Townsend, Vandamm brings on through his victim the problematic of the idealized father, thus appearing to be the murderous son, we must never forget that this is true only because he kills him in Thornhill's place, in two senses: he kills Townsend instead of Thornhill killing him (but also so that Thornhill will be the one who kills him—this is the second mistake, which determines the rest of the film), and he kills Townsend instead of killing Thornhill (something the logic of the actions allows us to expect but which the narrative clearly cannot have). The murderous son, Vandamm, symbolizes the fact that Townsend could have been killed by Thornhill for the sake of the possession of the mother. As murderous father, both before and after the murder but because of it throughout the film, he symbolizes the "retaliation"[5] the son becomes subject to for having killed or wished to kill the father (since, in theory, filicide is never anything but a cover for the desire for parricide). In this sense, he is nothing but a projective image circumscribed in the logic of Thornhill's Oedipus, which happens to bring into play the two complementary and opposed figures of the symbolic father and the idealized father.

The projective image that divides Vandamm from the standpoint of Thornhill is divided in its turn. It is never Vandamm who kills or attempts to kill; it is Leonard, on the one hand, and, on the other, above all the character that the narrative calls

the "knife-thrower" and the script "Valerian." "[Since] the villainous James Mason is competing with Cary Grant for the affection of Eva Marie Saint, I wanted him to be smooth and distinguished. The difficulty was how we could make him seem threatening at the same time. So what we did was to split this evil character into three people: James Mason, who is attractive and suave; his sinister-looking secretary; and the third spy, who is crude and brutal."[6] This tripartition of the villain entails a differentiation of the symbolic structure and, through an effect of regulated contagion, permits its extension to the narrative as a whole. Indeed it subdivides the dual image of Vandamm, murderous father and son, disjoining on the basis of an indissociability guaranteed by Thornhill's fantasy Vandamm as father, on the one hand, and on the other Leonard and Valerian as sons.

The two substitutions that inscribe Vandamm in the symbolic structure underscore this functional prevalence of the image of the father: the first by putting him in Townsend's place; the second by making Mrs. Townsend his sister and thus instituting, through the incestuous similarity thereby tying him to Thornhill, a generational discrepancy that the physical immaturity so specific to Cary Grant's acting does much more to support than does the real age of the actors. On the other hand, while Vandamm's and Thornhill's rivalry over Eve is strongly marked, justifying the tripartition of the villain and endowing the plot with an indispensable psychological determination, it ultimately seems fictitious, immaterial. There is never any sign of it, really, in Vandamm's body—as if Eve were more his daughter than his wife or his mistress, as if his conquest of her was only illusory, for Thornhill's benefit, as if he only defended her so that Thornhill might win her away. An image of the transgressive excess that the son may always commit against the father, Vandamm is an inverted mediator. Until the end of the film, he embodies the menacing possibility that Townsend remains for Thornhill in the position of the idealized father. But just as he does not really kill, he does not die, in keeping with the code that does not allow the death of a star and confirming, on the basis of the very disjunction of which he is the object, that the violence of Oedipus is structurally determined by the desire of the son.

Leonard and Valerian are thus found to be caught up in the logic of the fantasy, doubly specifying the dual image of Vandamm as son. Through the material violence with which the narrative invests them, they take on the symbolic violence of the Oedipal confrontation opened up around Thornhill: the merciless struggle that opposes them to the hero and condemns them both to death thus makes them, through a covering process whose terms must be perpetually unraveled and displaced, two inverted representations of Thornhill, two complementary virtualities of the negative Oedipus, whose image is defined by Vandamm. This double symbolic inscription conveyed by the movement of the narrative crystallizes toward its end, according to a process of concealment and avowal whose effects we have already seen. For Leonard, Oedipal desire is expressed by a latent homosexuality whose effects are clearly brought to bear on Vandamm by the representational perversion of the narrative. It erupts when Leonard unmasks Eve's false murder of Thornhill: first in words, leading Leonard to invoke his "woman's intuition" and Vandamm to accuse him openly of being jealous of Eve; then in deed, when, to explain his conduct, Leonard shoots Vandamm with blanks just as Eve shot Thornhill, in an inversion in which desire, it is clear, is inscribed in the aggression, in the threat of castration for which it serves as a metaphor.

As for Valerian—professional killer, agent of the parricide—he nominally acquires a wife at the very moment that Townsend's fictitious wife becomes Vandamm's sister. We have already seen this servant, whom we see again at Vandamm's house in Rapid City: in the two Glen Cove scenes that confront Mrs. Townsend and Clara Thornhill, whose age brings her even closer. Why should she reappear, so near the film's close and in an afterthought, as the wife of this young man, if not to figure the fruit of parricide and the object of incest: the mother, whose singular ugliness suggests a horrific doubling of Thornhill's mother? An image of castration that flows from the menacing woman to her metaphoric son, the castrator par excellence, whose knife is foreshadowed, in the last two shots of the second Glen Cove scene, by an enormous pair of shears  with which he decapitates a clump of flowers. To tangle the threads that allow the narrative to unreel the whole skein of the symbolic, it is with Eve's same gun that

"Mrs. Valerian" will in her turn shoot Thornhill—as if to foretell the fact that Thornhill, in a reversal of image that corresponds to the doublings for which he is the pretext, is going to push the parricide, the man who is his inverted Oedipal image, off a cliff.

Thornhill is thus the sole veritable hero of this Oedipal adventure, whose identificatory power he focuses. That is why the guilt brought into play by the film is exclusively focused on him through the hermeneutic development of the specifically Hitchcockian detective-story dialectic between the guilty and the falsely accused that attains its supreme point of parodic externality in *North by Northwest*. Vandamm (doubly divided through Leonard and Valerian) can thus be opposed all the more easily to Thornhill as the bad son to the good son, and to Townsend as the bad father to the good father—so much does the structural truth of the narrative here tend to coincide with moral truth, and the socio-political law to compel desire to internalize it as the basis of its symbolic function. But psychoanalysis, with its more or less driving ethic of Oedipal normalization, is far from remaining outside such a collusion. At bottom this is what Lacan puts so well when he reminds us that "the law and repressed desire are one and the same thing."[7] For if psychoanalysis, as it has always claimed since Freud, "recognizes in desire the truth of the subject,"[8] it has done so in order to accept immediately the inevitability of its prohibition and its regulation by the law, which amount to the same thing. The Oedipus complex, which opens up a path to desire through repression, is this law, which maintains desire under its law. That is why, when one is a boy, one cannot symbolically "leave" the Oedipus complex except through castration. That is why Thornhill, through a fantasmatic foreshortening of a compelling logic, comes to live its ordeal, once the simulacrum of a murder carried out against the father frees him from the mother and carries him toward the object substituted for her.

Of course, this ordeal begins with the inaugural mistake that separates the hero from the mother and consigns him, not to the theater where he was supposed to meet her, but instead to a first confrontation with death. Not that death in and of itself automatically connotes castration, of which it is, on the contrary, an internal dimension. But in this substitution of scenarios, the hero is in effect torn from the mother by the "castrating" father, whom the scenario's glimmerings have allowed us to recognize in the false Townsend. The scene in which the two hit men try in vain to send the dead-drunk Thornhill's car over a cliff takes place (in a perfectly motivated way) in the evening, the very moment of the postponed theatrical performance. And to signify the imminence of death, Hitchcock employs Thornhill's point of view as his car stops miraculously at the edge of the precipice, the same vertical tilt shot that will twice reappear: apparently quite, arbitrarily, after Townsend's murder, as Thornhill leaves the United Nations building; and at the end, with a natural insistence, on the slopes of Mount Rushmore. The fact that Vandamm, in order to continue to play his castrating role after the determinant point constituted by Townsend's murder, turns out to be the mediator of the woman who will replace the mother for Thornhill, can be seen as the distorting effect that allows relatively contradictory and rigorously complementary significations and functions to be condensed into a single story.

The relation between the Oedipus complex and castration that, for Thornhill, coalesces around Eve from the beginning of the second movement of the film, can be broken down into four successive stages, which closely espouse the hermeneutic variations in which Eve is the stake, for spectator and hero alike:

1. The first takes place on the train, in the sleeper where Eve has welcomed Thornhill after the promise of seduction implied by their conversation in the dining car. Leaning against the partition, Eve and Thornhill kiss and talk in a series of tight shot-reverse shots that follow on from those of their earlier conversation.

Eve: How do I know you aren't a murderer?
Thornhill: You don't.
Eve: Maybe you're planning to murder me, right here, tonight.
Thornhill: Shall I?
Eve (whispers): Please do . . .

The long kiss that follows Eve's reply thus metaphorically seals the alliance between sex and death inscribed by Hitchcock with such extraordinary insistence in all his films. The preceding scene already introduced this relationship: two police-men come to interrogate Eve, who has hid-den Thornhill in the upper couchette of the sleeper, informing her that she has dined with a murderer. This much she knows, of course, and more, since she also knows that he is in-nocent of this murder. But the frightened sur-prise she must pretend enhances the kiss scene and the metaphor woven into it. It ludically underscores the mutually inclusive relation-ship of the sexual drive and the death drive, here directly tied to the image of the murder  that allows it to be established. The instinctual energy with which Townsend's mur-der is metaphorically invested is displaced to mark the sexual relation between Eve and Thornhill with a murderous violence; the glamour attached to the father's mur-der thus opens the path of seduction, first in the dining car, then in the sleeper.

There is a remarkable rift in this second scene: between the kiss and the sex-ual act that follows it (chastely presaged by the open bed), three shots depicting Thornhill's retreat into the sleeper's washroom introduce a rupture as brief as it is insistent. (1) Thornhill, in a medium close-up, looks at himself in the mirror, picks up a tiny shaving brush from among Eve's toiletries on the shelf, looks at it and puts it down. Then he picks up an equally tiny razor. (2) A big close-up shows part of his hand and the tiny razor turning in his fingers. (3) The framing repeats that of the first shot. Thornhill's gaze shifts from the razor to the mirror that reflects his empty gaze. He turns away suddenly when he hears Eve's voice outside thanking the stew-ard and calling him back to her. This scene is narratively motivated: Thornhill en-ters the washroom to hide from the steward; the steward enters the sleeper to make the bed, assuming thereby a mediating role in the progression of the enigma orga-nized around Eve; these various activities allow her to give him the note he will then take to Vandamm ("What do I do with him in the morning? Eve"). But this motivation is itself far from indifferent: it is precisely during Thornhill's confinement to the washroom that Eve gives the steward the note that abandons Thornhill to the mercies of the castrating father. The nature of these three shots, as well as the interruption they create in the progress of the sexual advances, make it all the more possible to inscribe in them the mark of castration. The tininess of the razor and the brush mark, first, the threat of a reduction of the penis. Moreover, this image is divid-

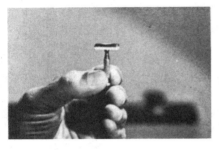

ed according to the two objects: the brush, whose bristles and handle evoke the penis fairly closely; and the razor, the instrument of a reduction that is materially similar to castration and symbolizes it. On the other hand, these objects that so strike Thornhill belong to Eve. They thus express castration in another way, in the form of a threat of incorporation: through the woman who replaces the mother, we see the threatening image of the phallic mother, the fantasy of which is inspired by Mrs. Thornhill the abusive mother, stand-in for the law in the father's absence.

Over and above this, the inscription of these two objects turns out itself to be further motivated by the development of the narration: the next day, in the men's room at the Chicago station, Thornhill uses Eve's brush and razor to shave. But the use to which he puts them takes diegetic implausibility one step further. It is indeed perfectly motivated that Thornhill, pursued by the police, should take refuge in the men's room to change out of the uniform a porter kindly let him steal; it is less so that he should waste time shaving, a time increased by the tininess of the razor. Two shots emphasize this departure from verisimilitude and reinscribe the castratory difference: next to Thornhill, a burly man shaves with a cut-throat razor and stares with a sort of contemptuous stupefaction at the thin streak of lather that Eve's razor is able to remove from Thornhill's cheek. But just then the two policemen who had questioned Eve on the train the night before and on the platform that very morning appear. They stop, glance at the two men and leave: the lather covering his face has

saved Thornhill. Eve's toiletries recover their diegetic motivation without their use becoming any more plausible. The admirable duplicity of the narrative lies in its always making the symbolic emerge in the distance, causing narrative verisimilitude and the lack of it to exist side by side without ever coinciding. A few moments later, when Thornhill finally rejoins Eve, she asks him, "What took you so long?" He answers, "Small razor. Big face." We want

to answer in his place, "Big face. Small penis," so much is it through Eve that the ordeal of castration is structured for Thornhill, the ordeal that from this point on will be sealed by the repetition of his confrontation with death.

2. Over the slowly dissolving image of Eve's beautiful face there appears the bus that is carrying Thornhill through an open plain to Kaplan. The mortal ordeal is doubly marked in this famous sequence. On the one hand by Eve, who gives Thornhill the deceptive message that is supposed to enable him to find Kaplan. A mortal reciprocity is thus established between them: the real but of course thwarted murder to which Eve condemns Thornhill corresponds to the metaphoric murder of which she was the object in the romantic relation. On the other hand, this mortal ordeal—via Vandamm, who orders it—brings into play the prohibiting father, thanks to the projective paradox that needs Vandamm to re-impose, for Thornhill, the law whose rupture was instituted by Townsend's murder. The victory Thornhill gains over death and the father by avoiding the killers' airplane thus allows him to attain the object of his desire, even if  he does not yet know—dupe that he is, as is the spectator, of the displacement effected around Eve—that this second encounter is a step in the long itinerary that leads him toward possession of the object.

The scene that reunites them again in the room at the Ambassador Hotel reconjugates in a remarkable way the narrative's verisimilitude and non-verisimilitude. It was, in fact, virtually inscribed in the film's development from the moment of the encounter between Thornhill and Vandamm, when the latter invested Kaplan with a retrospective reality and assigned his fate to Thornhill by making three successive hotels coincide with the three grand movements of the film:

> *Vandamm*: On June 16, you checked into the Sherwyn Hotel in Pittsburgh as Mr. George Kaplan of Berkeley, California. A week later you registered at the Benjamin Franklin Hotel in Philadelphia as Mr. George Kaplan of Pittsburgh. On August 11 you stayed at the Statler in Boston. On August 29 George Kaplan of Boston registered at the Whittier in Detroit. At present, you are registered in room seven ninety-six at the Plaza Hotel in New York as Mr. George Kaplan of Detroit. [. . .] In two days you are due at the Ambassador East in Chicago. [. . .] And then at the Sheraton-Johnson Hotel in Rapid City, South Dakota.

After the United Nations murder Thornhill is justified in going to Chicago to find Kaplan; and after the scene in the corn fields, he is justified in showing up at the Ambassador, where Eve ostensibly telephoned Kaplan that very morning. It is, on the other hand, much less justified, in the logic of the plot concocted with Vandamm, that Eve should turn out to be staying (with or without Vandamm and Leonard, the narrative does not specify) in the very hotel at which Kaplan has fictitiously checked in. But everything requires it. First, for the sake of the joint development of actions and enigmas, Thornhill must find Eve again, and through her Vandamm; second, and more precisely, Thornhill must find Eve in her room, to complete a rhyme with the earlier scene in which he found himself with his mother in Kaplan's room at the Plaza Hotel—thus insuring the symbolic progression of the narrative.

This rhyme is initially produced by the structure of the two segments. The first is divided into two parts that show, on the one hand, Thornhill's arrival with his mother in front of the hotel (one shot), then in the lobby (one shot); on the other, after a dissolve, Thornhill and his mother in the halls upstairs (three shots), then in Kaplan's room (many shots). The second segment is similarly arranged: Thornhill arrives in front of the Ambassador (three shots) and makes his inquiries in the lobby (ten shots); we see him again after a dissolve, in an upstairs corridor (one shot) before he enters Eve's room, where he remains until the end of the segment (many shots). There are many discrepancies between the two segments (as can be seen simply from our account of the respective numbers of shots); these discrepancies only put into relief the similarities that preside, in particular the partial homology of the two hotel room scenes, which accentuates the process of substitution between these two women narratively arranged as mirror images on either side of Thornhill. This homology is inscribed in the second half of the two scenes. Here are the elements of the first: a valet rings, enters, and naturally takes Thornhill for the Kaplan he has never seen; he explains that he is returning the suit Kaplan instructed him, by telephone, to pick up and have pressed the night before. As soon as the valet leaves, Thornhill takes one of the suits hanging in the closet, undresses, tries it on, and cries out—pushed to the limit by his mother's mocking attitude, which underscores the ridiculousness of the situation—"Well, obviously, they've mistaken me for a much shorter man!" In the second scene, at the end of a tense exchange in which Eve tries to get rid of Thornhill, she finally agrees to have dinner with him in her room, provided, she adds, that he have his suit sponged and pressed, as it has been sorely tested by the vicissitudes of the preceding sequence. Thornhill agrees and calls the valet, who says he will need twenty minutes to do it.

Eve: Better take your things off.
Thornhill (going up to her): Now, what could a man do with his clothes off for twenty minutes? (An afterthought, as he gazes at her reflection in the mirror.) Couldn't he have taken an hour?
Eve (turns, practically in his arms): You could always take a cold shower. (She starts to help him off with his jacket as he takes his things out of his pockets and places them on the dresser. Both of them are playing it just as though they were up to nothing but good, clean, healthy love-play.)
Thornhill: That's right. Mm—you know, when I was a little boy, I wouldn't even let my mother undress me.
Eve (peeling off his jacket): You're a big boy now. (She tosses the jacket on the bed, turns back to him, puts her hands on his belt buckle, starts to unfasten it. He takes her hands in his.)
Thornhill: Tell me, how does a girl like you get to be a girl like you?
Eve: Lucky, I guess.
Thornhill: Not lucky—naughty, wicked, up to no good. Ever kill anyone? (Instantly Eve's expression changes. He has gone too dangerously far; quickly he takes the curse off the remark.) Because I bet you could tease a man to

death without half trying. (He pats her cheek.) So stop trying, hmm? (He starts toward the bathroom, undoing the belt buckle himself as he goes. The door buzzer sounds. Eve goes to the door, opens it, lets the valet in.)

Eve (to the valet): Be with you in a minute. (She goes to the half-open bathroom door.) Trousers please. (Thornhill's hand comes out with the trousers. Eve takes them, picks up the jacket on the bed, gives the suit to the valet, and closes the door behind him.)

The double motif of the suit and the valet thus structures these two scenic fragments. In the first, the too-short suit suggests that the adventure into which Thornhill has been plunged by being mistaken for Kaplan has castration as its stake. He effectively undergoes a first "reduction," anticipating the metaphor of the razor and the brush. Through this ordeal, which reinitiates the threat of death in a remarkable counterpoint by using a telephone call to sig-nify the killers' return to the Plaza (just as Eve's "fatal" note to Vandamm is superim-posed, by substitutive similarity, onto the three shots in the washroom), Thornhill be-gins to escape the infantilization that governs his relationship with his mother and that for-bids him all true romantic realization. Thus,  the comparison with the mother seems to emerge of itself from the motif of the suit repeated in the second scene. "When I was a little boy . . .": these words refer both to a virtual childhood in which the son's repressed desire for the mother would be expressed by this prohibition, and to the first scene in which the mother, naturally, does not undress him. Eve can therefore respond, emphasizing how far he has come from this second childhood that he is only beginning to escape, "You're a big boy now." Of course, Thornhill here only allows himself to be half undressed, since this love scene is necessarily a decoy. For, in Eve, through the mortal threat she impos-es on him on behalf of the prohibitory father, we can glimpse the death-bearing woman who can only replace the mother by recathecting the castratory mother — the same castrating mother whose caresses, in a virtual family romance, are rejected by the child because of the anxiety awakened by his excessive desire for her.

This image reigns triumphant in the scene that follows, when Thornhill, whom Eve thinks she has duped but who has in fact duped her, finds her beside Vandamm and Leonard at a luxurious antiques auction. The presence of Vandamm, whom Thornhill sees here for the first time since he met him as Townsend, clearly gives its full extension to the image of Eve, dispelling any lingering doubts Thornhill may have had about her guilt; at the same time, it reactivates the whole scenario devel-oped since the inaugural mistake. When Thornhill reaches the group, his first words express quite well the sense of horrific fascination suggested by this global represen-tation: "The three of you together. Now there's a picture only Charles Addams could draw." At this moment the mortal threat attains its maximum fantasmatic intensity. When Vandamm, drawing out the theatrical metaphor, ironically runs through the inventory of parts played by Thornhill since they met, their brief exchange of retorts on his "playing dead" provokes Thornhill to say: "I wonder what subtle form of manslaughter is next on the program. Am I going to be dropped into a vat of molten steel and become part of some new skyscraper? Or are you going to ask this . . . female to kiss me again and poison me to death?" With a remarkable precision, these last words effect a reversal, twice underscored already, of the metaphorically murderous kiss that Eve asked Thornhill to give her on the train. In thus associat-

ing Vandamm and Eve by showing them together, the mortal threat articulates the two complementary but still distinct terms of the fantasy of castration to which Thornhill is prey: on the one hand, the castration with which the son is threatened by the father; on the other, the castration with which he is threatened by the mother, and from then on by any object that substitutes itself for her — in the form of a rape by incorporation, either di-

rectly or by a reversal of the sadism exercised against her thanks to an overlapping of sexual drive and death drive. Faced with this mortal threat, which the scenario begins to carry out the moment Leonard gets up to fulfill Vandamm's prophecy about Thornhill's next role, the latter's decision to give himself up to the police constitutes an outcome at once dramatic, hermeneutic, and symbolic. First dramatic: in provoking the intervention of the police by making a scene at the auction, Thornhill escapes Vandamm's hit men yet again. Next hermeneutic, since Thornhill's decision brings about the intervention of the Professor, who frees him from all objective guilt, clears up the mystery surrounding Kaplan's existence and introduces the third mutation in Eve's identity. Symbolic, finally, since, by dividing the image that joined Vandamm and Eve, this movement will take Thornhill to the point where he can assume his castration — that is, where he can positively and unmixedly substitute Eve for his mother and thus accede to paternal identification through the law the father symbolizes.

3. That is why, in the third stage of development, Eve really kills Thornhill, thanks to a sumptuous directorial detour whose theatrical power marks Thornhill's

accession to the symbolic order. This simulated murder, meant to restore Eve to Vandamm's confidence, is the last echo of Thornhill's murderous kiss. Its pretext is remarkable in that, by an inverted image, as it were a metaphoric rebound, it expresses Thornhill's desire for Eve in terms that take it beyond the seduction in which it has been fatally located until now. When Vandamm arrives with Eve at the Mount Rushmore caf-

eteria and asks Thornhill his price for the service he pretends to offer, Thornhill answers: "I want the girl [. . .] I want her to get what's coming to her. You turn her over to me and I'll see that there's enough pinned on her to keep her uncomfortable for the rest of her life." In this game of mirrors, it would be impossible to designate more clearly, through prison, the marriage that is symbolically sanctioned by the murder considered as an effect of demand. That is why the scene in the woods that immediately follows effects such a change in Eve, finally reduced to complete transparency in a true resolution of the fantasy. In it she loses cinematically her "vampiness" and symbolically everything that had identified her, as image of the castrating woman, with the forbidden mother inverted into the phallic mother. She becomes the disarmed *petite bourgeoise* who expects everything from the man who will be able to wrest her from the tangled fantasy whose object she has become in order to lock her up for the rest of her days in the silken prison of marriage.

This simulated murder clearly corresponds to the murder of Townsend, which established castration as the problematic of the narrative. In the first scene, Thornhill fictitiously killed the father: this murder allowed an object of desire to appear and substitute itself for the mother. In the second scene, Thornhill is fictitiously killed by the object of his desire. Between the two murders, the hero's acceptance of his own castration is played out through the dual relation that ties him to the object. We have seen the determinant role imparted to the woman in this process: in the execution of the hero that is its metaphor, she assumes a role parallel and complementary to that of the castrating father symbolized by Vandamm. This complementarity is again manifested when the process reaches its culminating point with the second murder. But this happens only at the price of a reversal as radical as this parodic murder, coextensive with the reversal introduced by Eve's new identity. It affects the figure of the father by substituting the Professor for Vandamm in the mise-en-scène in which Thornhill is a complicit victim. In this and this alone the murder can constitute for Thornhill an acceptance of his own castration and its

fictitious character institute its symbolization. Through an overlap of moral or political law and symbolic law, this murder is accomplished according to the law of the father: it thus inverts previous attempts and compensates for them. Retroactively, as it were, it even compensates for the guilt structurally inscribed in Thornhill, despite his innocence, by Townsend's murder. That is why the Professor, as he leads the way to the plane, absolves Thornhill of all implication in this death but asks him in exchange to help offset the effects it has progressively produced. The Professor thus occupies in his turn the place of the father assumed throughout the second movement by Vandamm, who is now consigned to symbolize fully that image of the idealized father he has never stopped projecting, caught up in the fatal dialectic of his double function: the son-father who kills (or seeks to kill) the father and the son and attacks the symbolic succession of the generations. The Professor stands for the necessity that the father, in order to be able to represent the symbolic father (to be a father dead according to the law, and not killed by the negation of the law), be also a living father: in the logic of

Thornhill's fantasy, he transforms Townsend the murdered father into the dead father. Narratively as well as symbolically, then, he is Townsend's stand-in, his complement and his transformation.

That, I think, is why the Professor's first appearance directly follows Townsend's murder. As we have seen, it is amply justified by the displacement it opens up in the relation between the spectator's knowledge and the hero's. But in those narratives founded on more or less strict coincidence between the hermeneutic and the symbolic, metonymic contiguity very often possesses more metaphoric value the more it is inscribed as a rupture in the "natural" sequence of actions. Townsend and the Professor are, furthermore, both official representatives of the American political machine and end up being opposed to Vandamm in strictly inverse ways: the first by being duped, up to his dying moment, by the man who usurps his name; the second, by duping Vandamm himself, with the projected image of an illusion that, through Townsend's murder, will entail Vandamm's downfall as the joint work of Eve and Thornhill. Thus is sealed, through Eve, the symbolic alliance between father and son. Of course, the term that founds this alliance immediately provokes its rupture. But it does so in a strictly delimited way, to perfect the Oedipal itinerary of the hero with a final term within the circle that gives him access to the paternal metaphor.

4. On the terrace of the Mount Rushmore cafeteria, a brief exchange between Thornhill and the Professor establishes the terms of the deal that they have made in the ellipses of the narration between their departure from Chicago and their arrival at Rapid City.

> *Professor:* I'm trying to remind you that it's your responsibility to help us restore her to Vandamm's good graces—right up to the point he leaves the country tonight.
> *Thornhill:* All right. All right. But after tonight . . .
> *Professor:* My blessings on you both.

After the simulated murder, the scene in the forest assures Thornhill of Eve's feelings for him; but the reticence she is obliged to show quickly betrays the fact that Thornhill is the victim of a certain non-reciprocity in the deal:

> *Eve:* He has told you, hasn't he?
> *Thornhill:* Told me what?
> *Professor:* Miss Kendall—you've got to get moving.
> *Thornhill:* Wait a minute . . . what didn't you tell me?
> *Eve* (to the Professor): Why didn't you?
> *Professor:* She's going off with Vandamm tonight on the plane.
> *Thornhill:* She's going off with Vandamm?
> *Professor:* That's why we've gone to such lengths to make her a fugitive from justice—so that Vandamm couldn't very well decline to take her along—
> *Thornhill:* But you said—
> *Professor:* I didn't tell you how valuable she can be to us over there.
> *Thornhill:* You lied to me! You said after tonight—!

Professor: I needed your help. . . .

Thornhill: Well you got it all right . . .

Eve: Don't be angry . . .

Thornhill: If you think I'm going to let you go through with this dirty business—!

Professor: She has to.

Thornhill: Nobody has to do anything! I don't like the games you play, Professor—!

Professor: War is hell, Mr. Thornhill—even when it's a cold one.

Thornhill: If you fellows can't lick the Vandamms of this world without asking girls like her to bed down with them and fly away with them and probably never come back, perhaps you ought to start learning how to lose a few cold wars.

Professor: I'm afraid we're already doing that.

Eve runs away and this dialogue ends with the Professor's chauffeur knocking Thornhill out. The latter wakes to find himself locked in the room where Kaplan is supposed to be hospitalized, critically wounded by Eve. A new conflict is thus opened up between father and son, around an object of desire that the son must conquer in defiance of the father's prohibition. In one sense, this conflict reintroduces the one that opposed Thornhill and Vandamm: like Vandamm, the Professor has used Eve as bait for Thornhill. But on the one hand the object of desire is not as such a source of conflict between father and son; and on the other the differences revealed between ideological and subjective options are not irreducible. The precise object of the end of this third movement will be to mediate between them, through a sort of implicit *Aufhebung* that will permit the son to emerge victoriously from the Oedipus complex by transgressing the law of the father, but only in the sense that it prescribes—to the point of embodying, its excellence. When, after duping the Professor with a false apology for his previous "childish" behavior, Thornhill escapes through the window to go to Vandamm's house, he truly becomes the "big boy" whose imminent appearance was foreshadowed by Eve's remark in the Ambassador Hotel room.

The very long segment that takes Thornhill from the approaches to Vandamm's house to the edge of Mount Rushmore's gaping precipice can be divided into two parts. The first is a period of observation. Thornhill learns that Leonard has exposed Eve's ruse and that Vandamm is preparing to avenge himself by throwing her from the plane they are about to board; next he learns that the microfilm Vandamm is carrying is hidden in the pre-Colombian statue he bought at the auction. The second part is one of action. Thornhill flees with Eve, who has managed to wrest the statue from Vandamm's hands; followed by Leonard and Valerian, they traverse the forest and reach the summit of the gigantic monument cut into the rock of Mount Rushmore. Valerian finds them first; after a brutal struggle, he is pushed over the cliff by Thornhill, who next tries to wrest Eve from Leonard, then to hold her up, suspended over the void by the hand that he extends to her, while Leonard brutally presses down his foot on Thornhill's naked hand, clinging to the rock and holding them both up. The miraculous gunshot that suddenly makes Leonard teeter confirms the sanction that the law of the father gives to the transgression of the son, just as Eve's and Thornhill's shared ordeal of thwarted death consecrates the mutual recognition of a desire inscribed in the promise of marriage. "Is that a proposition?" Thornhill asked Eve when she made advances to him in the dining car. "Is that a proposition?" Eve asks Thornhill on the slopes of Mount Rushmore, eliciting the desired response, "It's a proposal, sweetie."

As for the monument, a gigantic effigy of Washington, Lincoln, Roosevelt, and Jefferson, whose sudden appearance before the dazzled gaze of Eve and Thornhill is underscored by a shrill burst of music—how can we help seeing in it a fantastic,

 fantasmatic representation of the dead father? Subsuming the Professor and Townsend who are but its delegates, the very symbolization of the law, fixed in its eternity, the petrified images of the presidents seal the submission of desire to the law of Oedipus and of castration. History truly has as its signifier the dead father.[9] Presidential genealogy is its very image, uniting in a single chain the president still in office and those who precede him so that he may succeed them, symbolic, alive, but already dead, thanks to that sumptuous joke whose relations to historical consciousness Freud did not perhaps fully appreciate. The chamber theater of the familial scene broadens to the geographical dimensions of a State. The universality of the subjective law is reflected in the subjectivity that privatizes it and gives it its lustre. It is on the sovereign image of the four presidents that, on the terrace of the cafeteria, before the arrival of Eve and Vandamm, the third movement of the film begins, thereby placing itself under their sign. But this objective vision is then circumscribed into the circle of the telescope through which Thornhill observes them, thanks to the singular focalization to which the monument is subjected. Thanks to an effect that seems to move in the same backward tracking shot from outside to inside the telescope, the mise-en-scène expresses the relation of reflection between the externality of the law and its psychic internalization, which, psychoanalytically speaking, is the only foundation for its sovereignty as symbolic. The dialogue between Thornhill and the Professor that begins over this image develops this relation all the more clearly insofar as Thornhill stays close to the telescope throughout the scene, occasionally glancing through it and thereby virtually reconstituting the power of the first image.

> Thornhill: I don't like the way Teddy Roosevelt is looking at me . . .
> Professor: Perhaps he's trying to give you one last word of caution, Mr. Kaplan: "speak softly, and carry a big stick."
> Thornhill: I think he's trying to tell me not to go through with this hare-brained scheme . . .
> Professor: Perhaps he doesn't know to what extent you are the cause of our present troubles—
> Thornhill: I don't know if I care to accept that charge, Professor.
> Professor: If you had not made yourself so damnably attractive to Miss Kendall that she fell for you—

Thornhill: And vice versa.

Professor: —our friend Vandamm wouldn't be losing faith in her loyalty now. It was quite obvious to him last night that she had become emotionally involved, worst of all with a man he thinks is a government agent.

Thornhill: Are you trying to tell me [. . .] that I'm irresistible?

The subjective odyssey draws to it and incorporates History in the closure of its own system all the more insofar as it is welded to it by the figure that symbolizes them both. The Professor's first reply takes on the equivocation of this double meaning: "Speak softly, and carry a big stick." This is Roosevelt's famous injunction to the American people, in which the "big stick" policy opened the door to imperialism for American capitalism, further concentrating its symbolic power in the presidential image. The Professor's reference to it thus underscores the super-egoistic background with which Thornhill is invested as agent of the national cause. But how can we fail to see in this "big stick," which serves as metaphor for the scene of Eve's staged murder of Thornhill, the phallus that the father recognizes in the son once the latter, in order to have it, consents no longer to be it; that is, to renounce being it for the mother and, through the ordeal of symbolic castration, to surmount the fear of being stripped of it by the father (and/or of losing it in

the mother's body). Following Freud, we can even imagine that, confronted with the monument that so fascinates him, Thornhill's look suffers by rebound from Roosevelt's, which embarrasses him, the effect of petrification in which Freud recognized at once the castration anxiety awakened in the child "medused" by the sight of the mother's genitals, and the consolatory erection by which he reassures himself when faced with the fatality of the primal scene.[10]

In assuming the terms put into play in the inaugural scene of this third movement, and those that logically develop from them, the final chase thus vibrates

with an extraordinary symbolic resonance. It is while trampling on the heads of the single and multiple father represented by the four most illustrious presidents of the United States that Thornhill fully accedes to a positive identification with the father and definitively leaves the Oedipus complex: in one and the same blow he is inscribed in the cultural genealogy, fulfilling the law of the father (that is to say his politics) and acquiring a wife. In a shot whose absence he seems to regret, Hitchcock even thought of showing Thornhill forced to hide in Lincoln's nose and becoming the victim of a sneezing fit, thus symbolizing through corporeal synecdoche the identification between father and son.[11] And it is literally up the body of the father that, at the moment of supreme confrontation with death, Thornhill slowly pulls Eve's body to draw her, in a sumptuous effect of metaphoric succession, into the couchette of the sleeper where he can finally welcome her with the name heretofore reserved for his mother: "Come on, Mrs. Thornhill."

"To come": the word for *jouissance* in a language without a specific verb to denote it. On the petrified body of the dead father, something very like an inverted primal scene is played out: the father, in his double living image (the Professor, Vandamm), excluded from the picture but recalled within it by the finally triumphant image of the law, thanks to the saving gunshot that rescues the son from his negative image; the son, entering upon the scene to free himself from it, to kill the captivating image within him and outside him, to accept the symbolic inevitability of castration, and finally to *jouir*, but by the law, upon the scene that seems to shift, to pass without transition from the horrific and theatrical night of fantasy to the symbolic clarity of pacified narrative. "Come on, Mrs. Thornhill."

Lastly, we need to explain just what is raveled and unraveled in the name of Kaplan. The mistake engendered by the bellboy's call in the Plaza bar first opens up the possibility of the fiction. Later, at the end of the first movement, we learn that Kaplan is only an empty image, intended to act as a decoy distracting Vandamm and protecting the "Number One" who is at work under his nose; this is the image that Thornhill finds himself occupying. Later still, at the end of the second movement, Thornhill learns this truth about Kaplan from the Professor, and we learn along with him that the "Number One" whose immunity Kaplan is supposed to guarantee is a woman, and that this woman is Eve Kendall. Between the two scenes the little mystery surrounding Kaplan is thus dispelled. But the void he circumscribes is terribly full, full of an extraordinary fictional effectivity. Indeed, Kaplan is only a decoy that allows Thornhill and Eve to meet. But it is above all to allow them to do so while each is this non-existent character that neither of them is nonetheless. Thornhill can only come to fill the place of Kaplan because Eve occupies it too. He is only the false Kaplan to the extent that Eve is the true one. This illusory character is thus both the occasion for their meeting and the site of their coincidence. In light of all that precedes, one merely has to retrace in imagination the narrative operations played out between the meeting on the train and the simulated murder in the Mount Rushmore cafeteria to be seized by dizziness at the paradoxical chain of events that links the hero and heroine around this illusory representation. The projective image of Kaplan supports in the fiction the fundamental relation of narcissistic reduplication that governs the relationship between Eve and Thornhill. It is the vanishing point of their mutual recognition and, as such, of their identity. It is through the image of Kaplan that they both find themselves the improvised heroes of this ultimate adventure of love and death, which is a privileged fantasy of the Western imaginary and of American individualism. And it is through this fantasy that is founded, formulated, and virtually realized an even more fundamental fantasy, which is its inverse and its complement: the fantasy that makes them both aspire to the golden rule of marriage and to the serene eternity of hearth and home.

But the name Kaplan means even more. In that narcissistic structuration which in Lacanian terms corresponds to the register of the imaginary, Kaplan's name intervenes as the differentiating term that structures the imaginary according to the symbolic. It is, *par excellence,* the object = x defined as the phallus, always lacking and always in excess, which never ceases to be missing from its place, and which articulates out of this lack the structural series of the narrative: Thornhill and his mother on one side, Vandamm and Eve on the other.[12] But it does so in order to constitute at the same time their symbolic resolution. Remember the scenes in which Thornhill fully assumes Kaplan's name: after the one with his mother at the Plaza Hotel, where he still only half assumes it under the pressure of circumstance, there are on the one hand those of Townsend's murder at the United Nations, on the other that of the simulated murder in the Mount Rushmore cafeteria. These two scenes constitute for Thornhill the two central stages, complementary and inverted, of the process that leads him to accept his own castration and to form a positive identification with the paternal figure. Kaplan's name thus marks Thornhill's access to the paternal metaphor: it is itself that metaphor. One detail, in the airport conversation between Thornhill and the Professor at the end of the second movement, underscores this fact remarkably. When he asks for Thornhill's help, the Professor emphasizes the necessity of reassuring Vandamm about George Kaplan; Thornhill then stares at him and says, in level and considered tones conveying his conviction that the mystery of his adventure has finally been cleared up, "You're George Kaplan, aren't you?" The Professor responds, "Oh, no, Mr. Thornhill. There is no such person as George Kaplan." He adds, "Believe me, Mr. Thornhill, he doesn't exist. Which is why I'm going to have to ask you to go on being him for another twenty-four hours." The Professor, who sustains for Thornhill, in his complementarity with Townsend, the figure of the symbolic father, is also that father to the extent that he is the inventor, the father of that imaginary figure who commits Thornhill to his Oedipal itinerary. Certainly, the Professor is not George Kaplan. The question that for a moment assigns him to this place, the place that Thornhill must agree to occupy to finally accede to the law, underscores the fact that the Professor himself turns out to be in a metaphoric position in relation to this metaphor to which Thornhill's destiny is symbolically subordinated. But he gives it a specific origin and thus assigns it the destiny of an end. By drawing back to bring together the actions of Thornhill, Eve, and the Professor on the petrified body of the dead father, this signifier is at once what determines them and what allows them. That is why, despite the false air of naturalness given it by its "George," to which nothing corresponds unless it be Washington's forename, the name Kaplan is symbolic through and through. In it, the signifying effect of the phallus is determined as law through the proper name. Kaplan is nothing but the Name-of-the-Father.

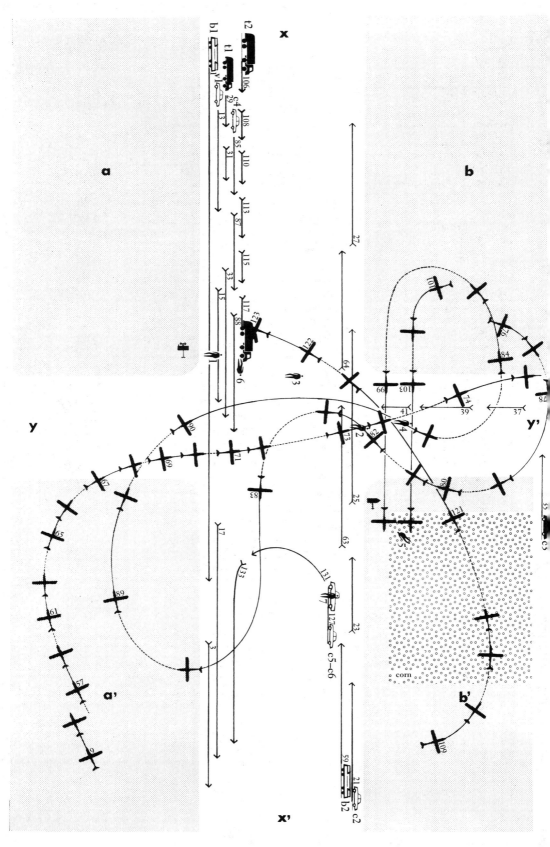

III. SEGMENT 14

After a first extremely long shot that inscribes the hero in a space spread out as if seen from an airplane—and everything suggests that the imminent fragmentation of this space is what is at stake in this scene—the segment is arranged according to a methodical alternation punctuated by interruptions. This binary movement opposes and unites subject and object from shot to shot, illustrating the same dialectic of the look that sustains Melanie Daniels's two-way boat-ride in *The Birds*. But this movement is manifestly more insistent here, playing on the vision that establishes and defines it to the advantage of its own abstraction. Interruption is being used here to mean whatever breaks the alternation, postpones it for the time of a single shot or sometimes a number of shots. Here it works through a duplication of the shot of the subject, the first effect of which is to conjoin the hero, within the frame, with the object of his vision, whose gradual insistence produces the economy of the segment.

We could just as well speak of the management of a suspense whose duplicitous preconditions have been furnished by the narrative. For at this point it is quite obvious that Thornhill has set out to meet a man who does not exist; after the revelation of the note to Vandamm, we know that, by setting up an appointment with Kaplan (whose terms were set by Leonard), Eve is sending him to face his death. Thus, in this open setting, whose unsettling force Hitchcock understood quite well,[13] we cannot but expect the imminence of an, as it were, already postponed death (in the classical code the hero cannot die in the middle of the film). This is one reason among others that seemed to justify preferring a *successive*, continuous-discontinuous reading, suited to marking the regulated progression by which Hitchcock was able to modulate the identification whose object is Thornhill.

1. The alternation established in 2b,[14] when Thornhill, standing, turns to watch the bus he has just got off disappear in shot 3, is followed without interruption until shot 32. Beginning with shot 4, a constant framing (Thornhill in tight medium long shot[15] to the right of the bus stop) produces a permanent back-and-forth between Thornhill and his vision, whose effects underpin the first accidents of the fiction and establish a matrix by segmenting the space.

The alternating micro-series that, by dividing the first series onto itself, opens this very long sequence of alternations, the longest in the segment, consists of shots 2b–4a: it shows the disappearance of the bus, at the other end of the highway on which it appeared in shot 1; but this time it is seen by Thornhill and thus defines a first subjective point of view from his position.

The second series (4b–12a) sets out, without the assistance of any other element, four successive point-of-view shots in two symmetrical pairs around the axis of the highway: on the one hand, the fields on both sides of the highway (5 and 7, in A and B); on the other, behind Thornhill and across from him, the two parts of the byroad that crosses the highway at right angles (9 and 11, in A' and B').

The third series (12b–18a), marked by the arrival of a car, has closed by shot 13 (in x) the succession of symmetrically paired point-of-view shots opened in shot 3 (in x'). After this point, until the end of this set of series and even through shot 57, when Thornhill crosses the highway, what he sees will be arranged according to one of these six framings: in this respect, they form a matrix.

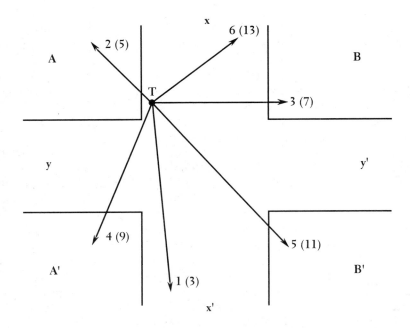

No doubt these three symmetries (or at least the two lateral ones of series 4b–12a) could seem more or less obligatory given the space, here essentially divided up by the intersection of the highway and the byroad, if we failed to note that they are defined in relation to the position of the subject of vision who is both on one of the two sides of the highway and on one of the two sides of the byroad. This explains their uneven angles in relation to the axes of the byroad and the highway that constitute their material reference. This divergence thus manifests the very inscription of the focalization of the look as a difference invested from the position of the subject of vision, that is, as a constitutive asymmetry of the narrative.

2. These symmetries climax in a final effect that both accentuates their closure and helps to open the narrative: the car that appears in x in shot 13 is the inverse of the bus that disappears in x' in shot 3. But this arrival also repeats the initial arrival, thus forming—given the difference which shot 1, denied to Thornhill's vision, imposes on the succeeding shots in this respect—the second link of a chain, a paradigm (let us call it the paradigm of means of locomotion) that will determine the architecture of the segment and that is immediately confirmed across series 20b–29 with the arrival of a second car.

3. Between these two series lies shot 19, constituting, together with the shots of Thornhill that bracket it, a short series in itself; it exactly repeats shot 7, one of Thornhill's four lateral visions; it thus divides the alternation of the look onto itself by a second alternation between "full" vision and "empty" vision, or between the highway-fields motif and the cars motif. This alternation immediately stops, inca-

pable of elaboration beyond this shot, whose strategic position is clear: after the disappearance of the first car in shot 17, it marks a sort of respiration whose systematic character (reiteration, opening of a rhyme between series) heightens the sense of expectation and suspense by a rhythmic contraction. For if neither Kaplan nor Vandamm's hit men are in the first car, they could turn up in the second, which appears on the inverse axis in x'.

4. The symmetry is clear, as is the repetition that brings out the differences. The first difference lies in the number of shots; they can be counted, in the two series 3 and 5, on the basis of the shots of objects of vision. The first of these series contains three such shots: a stationary shot of the car seen from afar (13), a shot in which its passing is emphasized by a pan that ends in a close framing (15), and a stationary shot in which it recedes (17). On either side of a central shot (25), whose movement makes it stand out amid the systematic uniformity of stationary shots, the second series has two shots (21–23 and 27–29) that divide the space onto itself and the time by a decomposition that Hitchcock has always seen as the very instance of suspense. A gesture of Thornhill's attests to this and institutes a second difference: just as the second car passes, he starts to take his hands out of his pockets, where he had put them in shot 10. What is particularly odd about this decomposition is that the shots are of practically equal length (from 3 1/2 to 4 seconds), that is, the four shots in the second series cover twice the time of those in the first. Thus, as if per contra, it entails an acceleration of the narrative: this is the third difference, which makes the disappearance of this second car at the very beginning of shot 29 coincide with the appearance of a truck by a nesting of the two series in which the logic of the progression is to find the motif of a first interruption in the alternation of the look.

5. The principle of this interruption is simple: like shots 15 and 25, shot 33—to maintain the alternation—ought to have followed the gradual entry of the truck into the field of vision; instead it conjoins Thornhill and the truck in the same field. It does this by means of two effects: a 180-degree inversion of the lens axis and a jump in the framing from MLS to VLS.

One difference asserts itself immediately: shots 15 and 25, in which Thornhill sees the cars, are both moving shots; shot 33 is stationary. This divergence isolates the interruption all the more; in particular, it marks the fact that the suspense, far from being a result of the dramatization that a univocal representation too often attaches to camera movement, here results quite precisely from an effect of difference: first from the effect of the moving shots of the two cars amid a set of stationary shots; then, when the truck passes, from the effect of the stationary shot in relation to the two previous camera movements.

On the other hand, apart from a difference in axis, shot 33, whose framing makes it materially possible to see the truck pass in front of Thornhill, reiterates shot 2, where Thornhill's look was first inscribed. But in the earlier case, the shot that follows (3, in which the bus disappears into x') opens the backwards and forwards alternation established in shot 4 with the reiteration of the same framing of Thornhill in MLS. Conversely, in the later case, the shot that follows (34), by returning to the same framing, brings about both the continuation of the interruption and the resumption of the alternation. We might be tempted to explain the modalities of this first interruption (the variation in framing and number of shots) for purely material reasons (the size of the truck, the dust thrown up onto Thornhill). But while the system obviously seizes upon material motivations without which it would have no raison d'être, it is in no way reducible to a technico-perceptual determinism. For example, the resumption of alternation could perfectly well have been brought about in 33b as it was established in 2b. But this would, first, have interrupted the serial regularity endowed, since shot 4, on the alternation of this framing with Thornhill in MLS. Second, shot 33 would have had to be a relatively long one, threatening a loss of the rhythmic unity to which Hitchcock seems to have been sensitive. Last and most important, it would have less sharply emphasized the difference opened by the metaphoric pressure of the truck, which is thereby inscribed in the very regularity of the closer shot that sustains the alternation. This aggression is thus produced from shot to shot, through an overlap that clearly establishes the interruption of alternation as a conjunction of subject and object and loss of the look. For the conjunction of Thornhill and the truck, which literally occurs in the middle of shot 33, and insists in 33b–34a via the cloud of dust that blinds Thornhill, postpones the vision reestablished in 34b.

6. A final divergence emphasizes the difference between the "truck" series and the two "car" series. Thornhill does not in fact see the truck disappear. In its place, we might say, but across from him, on the byroad, he sees another car appear. Starting with the disappearance of the bus, then, we can observe a continuous acceleration in the narrative progression of elements belonging to the paradigm of means of locomotion.

The framing of shot 35, which serves as prelude to the seventh series, is taken from one of the four lateral vision shots of micro-series 4b–12a (11). But a slight change in the axis of the look, now less oblique, accompanies a distinct difference of framing: the signpost has disappeared and the row of corn now occupies only the right third of the frame rather than filling four-fifths of it. And while Thornhill has not moved, the framing is a bit tighter, as if to accentuate the dramatization. The first divergence, the most distinct, will be reabsorbed: thanks to a short pan from left to right, the signpost will reappear in shot 41; and the reverse shot of the approaching car will simply repeat, with a slight tightening, the framing of shot 11. On the other hand, the systematization of the alternation back to Thornhill (36) is marked by a change of frame: slightly longer and much more oblique, it repeats the first of Thornhill's four lateral vision shots (5), except for the height of the camera, which now tightens the receding lines of the byroad around the character. Through a more or less variable recourse to two framings from series 4b–12a, alternately affecting the hero's vision and views of him where they had previously been assigned to his vision alone, the progressive differentiation of the new series is thus accentuated in relation to those more or less immediately preceding it. This differentiation is confirmed in shot 46 by a tightening of this same framing of Thornhill, which goes beyond the moderate framing of 4–34. This variation thus emphasizes the difference inscribed in the object of the vision, that is, in the dramatization of the narrative, when a man gets out of the car that leaves again and the man stands facing Thornhill—next to a signpost on the other side of the highway across from the bus stop.

7. Shot 49 constitutes the second interruption in the alternation of the look. According to an already stated principle, it conjoins the subject and object of vision, but in a way palpably different from the effects that organize it in shots 33–34. Here there is no overlap from shot to shot in the interruption to emphasize both the loss of the look and its recovery. Rather, there is an overt substitution in shot 49 which, instead of a progressive reduplication of shot 47 (the man seen by Thornhill), brings the two men to face each other on opposite sides of the highway. And this occurs without in the least affecting the first member of the alternating series, since shot 50 manifests a complete continuity with shot 48. This substitution radicalizes the "resumption of enunciation" by the subject producing the narrative, the author-enunciator, with respect to the character that serves as his relay. If any interruption of alternation in fact marks this resumption, it is, as it were, naturalized at the moment the truck passes or, later, when the airplane attacks; it is naturalized by the effects of dramatization that provoke it, to just the extent that it reinforces identification with the character. This is what justifies making the interruption in shot 33 act on the same axis as that of the previous shot, despite an enlargement of the framing (from MLS to VLS) demanded by the requirement of visibility. Shot 49 contravenes this continuity, replacing the oblique axis of the preceding and succeeding shots with a longitudinal axis that shows the highway disappearing into the distance in front of the camera. Axis and framing repeat, with very slight variations, those of shot 2, which inaugurated the alternation that it comes to interrupt; this is all the more true insofar as Thornhill, in shot 2, was watching the departure of the bus that had brought him, while the man across from him, although we do not know this yet, is looking out for the arrival of the second bus. The singularity of shot 49 lies in the fact that nothing happens in it; that, breaking the progression of the alternation, it does nothing but postpone expectation and dilate time in the interests of suspense. There is in fact a narrative gradation in the succession cars ⟶ truck (which sends up dust) ⟶ car ⟶ man (who might be Kaplan). It is postponed by this immobile insistence which, in shot 49, maintains the third term of the progression, as it were at a lower level than the second.

8. But the interruption, motivated by the movement of the truck in shot 33, heralds Thornhill's movement (52b–56), after a reinscription of the alternation (50–51). Before Thornhill advances, the framing in 52a exactly duplicates that of microseries 36–44 (Thornhill in long MLS/the car coming down the byroad, the man who gets out of it), thus accentuating the differentiation from micro-series 46–50, divided by the interruption of alternation (Thornhill in MS/the man standing by the signpost beside the highway). But this duplication is immediately compensated for by a radical differentiation in coding: micro-series 52b–56 follows a strict alternation of tracks backward and forward, until the encounter in 56b that conjoins Thornhill and the man on the other side of the highway.

9. This conjunction, however, entails no interruption of alternation, insofar as it is articulated with a simultaneous displacement and reinscription of the look. For while Thornhill looks at the man within the frame, the man looks out of it, thereby logically defining the new series 56b–63, in which the alternating terms of the previous series turn out, after their conjunction, to constitute the first term for a new alternation without altering the binary arrangement.

This series is further organized according to an alternation prior to the object of vision (on the one hand, the airplane that passes in the distance, in A, on the other, the bus approaching on the highway, in x'). In 56b–63 it thus sets up a nesting of oppositions that dialecticizes the chiastic repetition of the same framings. The first two shots, 57 and 59, are seen by the man alone, whose neutrality makes him master of the objective elements of the situation; shots 61 and 63 are seen by the man and Thornhill jointly. The airplane is just as far away in 61 as in 57, while the bus moves from far away in 59 to very close in 63, heralding the man's departure and thus preparing, as anticipated by his remark in shot 60 ("That plane's dustin' crops where there ain't no crops"), the relationship that will be established between Thornhill and the airplane.

10. Shots 64–65 carry forward series 56b–64 but by forming, through a new conjunction, a series that turns out both to open the fiction and to close a first loop in the development of the segment. The conjunction effected in shot 64 is a conjunction of conjunctions. It integrates one of the two terms implied in series 56b–63 by the alternation of the look: the bus, which enters the frame at the beginning of shot 64 and which, after the man has boarded it, we see driving away until the end of the shot; whereas the alternation, reestablished on the basis of Thornhill's look as he stands at the edge of the highway, is logically organized around the second term introduced in the previous series: the airplane, which since shot 57 has been identically insistent through three strictly similar shots (57, 61, 65), as if to mark clearly the difference whose object it will soon become in the series that, beginning with shot 66, will oppose it term by term with Thornhill.

This difference is triply conveyed in shot 66: by the disappearance of all internal conjunction between the subject and the object of his previous vision; by the change in the axis of the framing, oblique since shot 36 (in relation to the axis of the highway), now again transverse; finally, by the scale of the framing itself, which returns to tight MLS. These three qualities allow us to go back recursively to the first interruption of alternation in shot 34, and beyond it all the way to shot 4, in which the alternation of the look was established, in this framing.

A first loop is thus closed in the very movement that reopens it. Through the insistence of its linear progression, the narrative turns back upon itself in a kind of fold. That an inversion—and in this same inversion a divergence, a difference—is the mark of the fold, of its fundamental lopsidedness, and that this fold is only in effect at either end of this part of the segment (the end sliding beneath the beginning and reiterating its displaced effects), as if to save the body of the text for subsequent effects of symmetry and inversion, of repetition and difference, for a general folding, we might say—is because that is the very condition of the generation of narrative, of this narrative, this type of narratives.

Here is this fold, in play at three levels, repetitions riddled with differences on the basis of an initial symmetry that arranges the beginning and the end on either side of the highway, in AA' and BB', respectively.

First, the bus. The first one, in shot 1, appears in x, stops at the intersection of the highway and the byroad to let off Thornhill, and disappears in shot 3 in x', seen by Thornhill. The second, in shot 59, appears in x' seen by the man, then comes nearer in shot 63, seen by the man and Thornhill, stops at the intersection of the highway and the byroad to let the man board in shot 64, and drives off in x both seen and unseen by Thornhill: for, preoccupied as he is by the new object that has come into his vision, Thornhill only glances at the bus twice. This is enough to oppose shot 64 to shot 1, in which he could not do so, being essentially conjoined with the bus inside as he is here outside. But through an effect of inverted similarity, the man resolves this opposition by carrying Thornhill toward the difference of the narrative: in fact, he moves from conjunction outside to conjunction inside when he boards the bus in shot 64, the converse of what happened to Thornhill when he got off in shot 1.

Next come the three shots that establish or reestablish the alternation of the look between Thornhill and the object of his vision. At the beginning: from shot 2 (Thornhill in VLS and three-quarter view, along an oblique axis favoring side A) to shot 4 (tight MLS of Thornhill, transverse axis). Intermediate shot: in 3, the disappearance of the bus. At the end: from shot 64b (long MLS, Thornhill in long MLS, three-quarter back view, along an oblique axis, favoring side A, seen from further off) to shot 66 (tight MLS of Thornhill, transverse axis). Intermediate shot: in 65, the airplane in the distance, beyond the byroad.

Finally, shots 4 and 66 themselves. In the first, Thornhill turns from left to right within the frame, his look operating on the axis of the highway; in the second, he looks steadily across it transversely. An effect of difference that is duplicated by the one marked out by the framing: in 4, to the right of the bus stop, Thornhill stands out against the fields; in 66, to the left of the signpost, he stands out against the byroad. Beyond the indisputable mirror effect that makes the two shots fold onto each other on either side of the highway, this displacement of action and axis contributes to the narrative development, ushered in by the man's comment in the hermeneutic form so dear to fictions of appearance.

11. This displacement is immediately inscribed in shot 67, that is, on the "seen" side of the alternation. Note the admirable subtlety of the narrative here, its duplicity. The initial framing of the shot almost exactly repeats that of shots 57, 61, and 65, which, as we have just seen, ensured the differential development of an alternation between two objects of vision (airplane/bus) in series 56b–63 and 64b–65. Only a slight difference of axis, now less oblique, seems to translate at the level of the object the divergence marked by shot 66 at the level of the subject: shot 67 thus comes to ensure the univocal continuity of the narrative that shot 66 ensured via the retroactive plurivocality that attaches it to earlier points in the filmic chain. But this overly clear naturalness of the narrative and of the opposition between the two shots is counteracted by the very slight camera movement (a left-right pan) that heightens the difference in axis to center the road more or less in the axis of the camera.

Thus, a more discreet inverse interruption that effects a slight change of axis (oblique/transverse) sanctioned by a movement of the shot comes to correspond to shot 66's frank interruption (conjunction/non-conjunction; longitudinal axis/transverse axis; 3/4 back/front; very long MLS/tight MLS), which does, however, maintain the continuity of the stationary shot.

The very discreet interruption in shot 67 is interesting in that, like the one in shot 66, it marks its difference by the return of previous elements in the segment. The reader will remember the three pans, in shots 15, 25, and 41, that emphasize the passage of the first two cars and the arrival of the third, as the man starts to get out. They thereby accentuate the movement of the look over the object of vision from Thornhill's stationary position. In the minor mode, they thus correspond to what is subsequently marked, in a major mode motivated by Thornhill's crossing the highway, by the series of tracks forward and backward on the man in micro-series 52b–56a. In this chain, which is constituted by the totality of the camera movements since the beginning of the segment, shot 67 is quite similar—in its course as well as its direction (right-left), from the other side of the highway and along the transverse axis of the byroad—to the slight pan in shot 31 (technically, both of them might well be called reframings rather than camera movements in the proper sense). Together they can thus be opposed to the first two pans, which follow the trajectory of the cars along the longitudinal axis. This similarity is reinforced by the numerical coincidence in the sequence in which the two reframings are inscribed: three identical shots are devoted in each (35, 37, 39 and 57, 61, 65) to the car and the airplane, before shots 41 and 67, even if this sequence is unevenly rhymed, linear in the first case, broken in the second by the alternation between the bus and the airplane. This arrangement is opposed to that which earlier presides over the appearance of the two cars, introduced by one and two shots, respectively (13, 21, and 23).

The camera movement or reframing in each case emphasizes, by a very natural dramatization, the relation of growing proximity between subject and object. But this is once again at the price of remarkable divergences. The two pans on the longitudinal axis correspond, in fact, to the maximum proximity between subject and object: in shots 15 and 25, the car practically fills the whole frame. The first reframing apparently has the same role: it corresponds to the maximum proximity between Thornhill and the car, since the latter then turns around and leaves, just as the two previous cars disappeared along the opposite axis of the highway. But the third car remains much more distant in the space of the frame, on the other side of the highway. This first divergence corresponds to a second one: the man who will emerge from the car. It is thus this new object of vision that is emphasized by the reframing, as much as the approach of the car: through the increased dramatization that it introduces in respect to "Kaplan," it will later motivate Thornhill's displacement and the alternating micro-series of tracks backward and forward that will bring about this long-postponed proximity with the object, reinforced by the conjunction already discussed. (Thornhill: "Then your name isn't . . . Kaplan?" Man: "Can't say it is, 'cause it ain't.") In this respect the second reframing differs from both the first reframing and the two pans, the better to partake of all three. Like the two pans, it is inscribed in the progression that links an immobile Thornhill to the same approaching object. But it marks the beginning of this approach and not its end, the farthest (or almost) as opposed to the nearest. In this it paradoxically recalls the first re-framing (which here functions as a mediator), thanks to the substitutive continuity existing between the two objects successively linked to Thornhill. Just as shot 41 emphasizes the moment in which, when the car approaches and its door opens, the man who emerges will represent for Thornhill an interrogation that will be pursued until their conjunction, so shot 67 allows us to situate across from Thornhill, on the axis of the byroad, precisely the airplane that the previous shots only let us glimpse in the distance. As if to firmly mark what narrative difference owes to similarity inscribed as variation in the insistence of repetition, this approach must logically increase steadily until it marks the redoubled proximity of subject and object.

12. Let us summarize the similar operations in these two shots 66–67, beginning with and going beyond the fold that slips the end of this loop under its beginning, shots 63, 64, and 65 under shots 1, 2, and 3.

Shot 66, as we have seen, reiterates and inverts the first term regulating the alternation in sequence 4b–32, whose ultimate effect can be read in shot 34 when Thornhill, temporarily blinded by the passing truck, finally sees the car emerging behind the cornfield. Shot 67 is inscribed for its part in a chain that links by camera movement, on either side of the truck dealt with in a stationary shot, the first two cars and the third (and the man connected with it).

These two recurrent successions thus bring together in a very uneven combination the set of objects that may suggest what Thornhill and the spectator contradictorily expect. A contraction, a sort of narrative condensation is thus at work within the two shots: in its own peculiar way, it emphasizes the imminence of a relationship with the new object hitherto held out of the action (though prophetically indicated by the man's remark) and the new effect with which it will be invested. The airplane in fact turns out, by progressive integration, to follow on both from the previous meetings lacking all aggressive reality and from the meeting with the truck, the only one that brought with it both an interruption in alternation and in this interruption the loss of the look, thus manifesting both metaphorically and really the reality of the violence.

One last feature emphasizes this imminence of a fulfillment and an acceleration of the narrative. The airplane that arrives in y takes the last of the four directions defined by the intersection of the highway and the byroad. This is the last possibility for the appearance, in this setting and this progression by symmetric oppositions, of Vandamm's hit men concealed behind the null figure of Kaplan.

13. Through progression and recurrence, a second loop is thus opened with shots 66–67, a loop whose effects will simultaneously integrate, develop, and metamorphose the elements of the first.

Let us consider together the two series delimited by the first two airplane attacks, each one punctuated in the middle by an interruption of the alternation of the look. The first one can be broken down as follows:

a. successively: a four-shot micro-series (66–69) opposing Thornhill in tight MLS and the approaching airplane; then a three-shot micro-series (70–72), opposing Thornhill in MS and the attacking airplane. The divergence indicated by the absence of a fourth term reveals

b. the interruption of alternation heralded by the loss of the look in 72b, the moment Thornhill turns away and drops down in the space of the frame. Shot 73 is matched on his movement with a 180-degree inversion of the axis: it materializes the interruption translated in a by the conjunction of subject and object and by the absolute loss of the look; it reinstates in b a new possibility for alternation on the basis of the look that Thornhill, on the ground, directs at the airplane as it flies off;

c. a micro-series that opposes, from 74–78, the plane flying off and Thornhill standing up again, framed in long LS, according to an axis in the direction of x, but oblique to xx'.

Here it is no simple task to make a strict division between the two series, which in fact are articulated around the same object grasped in its continuity. However, the axis of the byroad and the movement of the airplane allow us to distinguish fairly clearly, at shot 78, the end of the first attack and the beginning of the second, which is immediately specified by a completely different framing of the subject of vision. It can be broken down as follows:

a. a micro-series of four shots, from 78–81, opposing the returning airplane to Thornhill in tilted-up long MLS, standing against the sky;

b. the interruption of alternation heralded in 81b by the loss of the look the moment Thornhill, followed by the panning camera from right to left and from top to bottom, throws himself to the ground. Shot 82 exactly repeats the doubly disruptive and establishing effect of shot 73;

c. a micro-series that, after shot 82, opposes Thornhill lying along an embankment and the airplane flying off, followed in 83 by a right-left pan. This micro-series is brought to a close almost immediately by a movement of the look in shot 84, which shifts to a new object: a car arriving in x.

We cannot help being struck by the absolutely regulated play of differences that are inscribed, between the two series, in a strictly reiterative architecture based on a mirror inversion of the two axes of the byroad (y and y').

1. In the second series, the tripartite structure arrival-meeting(= interruption)-departure is subjected to an overall contraction (insofar as the interruption of alternation here occurs at the hinge of two shots; these shots, while constituting an autonomous kernel, should clearly be assigned, one, to the arrivals, the other, to the departures). The first arrival includes seven shots distributed according to two different framings of the subject of vision (66, 68 in MLS, 70, 72 in MS), the second four shots defined by one and the same framing (79, 81 in long MLS). The first departure includes six shots divided into two framings of the subject of vision (by a divergence between 73b, in MLS, which marks the interruption of alternation and its resumption, and shots 75–77 in long LS), the second three shots defined by one and the same framing of the subject of vision (82, 84 in MLS). At the level of actions, this contraction explains why Thornhill stands up immediately after the first attack and apparently does not do so in the second.

The interruptions are absolutely similar in principle, acting on the shots that end the previous alternating micro-series and begin the next, and basing themselves from the end of the first shot to the beginning of the second on the loss of the look and a conjunction between subject and object. But while the first shot of the first interruption is stationary, that of the second is mobile, accompanying Thornhill's movement as he throws himself to the ground. This differential effect, inscribed in the subject of vision, is, on the other hand, reinscribed as soon as the interruption is over in the object of vision: shots 74, 76, and 78 are stationary, whereas the corresponding shot 83 is underpinned by a pan that follows the airplane's departure. Finally, let us emphasize that in the first interruption Thornhill is on the ground facing front, in the second in profile; and in the first the airplane simply disappears above Thornhill, while in the second it remains indirectly conjoined with him until the end of the shot by the bullets furrowing the low earth bank against which Thornhill has flattened himself.

A double effect of difference and inversion concerning the scale of the shots harmonizes in the diachrony with the contraction that takes place from one series to the next.

Let us resume. The first arrival and the first departure are arranged, always in relation to the subject of vision, according to the opposition near/far. Let us write this out more precisely. The parenthesis delimits the interruption properly speaking, at the intersection of the two shots, and the bars its borders, one a dotted line crossed by an arrow to mark the continuity of framing, the other full to mark its disjunction and the opposition it implies.

$$
\begin{array}{cccc}
 & a & b \quad a & b \\
\textbf{Tight MLS-MS} \longrightarrow & \text{MS} & \text{(MS-MLS)} & \text{MS} \quad \text{long LS}^{16} \\
66\text{--}69 \quad 70\text{--}71 & 72 & 72 \quad 73 & 73 \quad 74\text{--}78
\end{array}
$$

The second series, conversely, shows the continuity of a single framing halfway between near and far (MLS) (differentiated only, between the airplane's arrival and departure, by the opposition standing/prone). The system thus maintains a fairly clear-cut opposition between the arrival and the departure of the first series so that the second series can in turn mark its difference by a reversal of framing capable of emphasizing a gradation far $\longrightarrow$ near (long MLS $\longrightarrow$ MLS) in the succession of vision shots.

Finally, a last and perhaps the most subtle effect, insofar as it depends on a pertinence not heard from hitherto: the distribution in the frame of ground and sky. This feature has, of course, been continuously in play from the beginning of the segment. Once the movement backwards and forwards of the alternation has been established, it more or less regularly opposes shots of Thornhill and shots of the objects of his vision: the former having a strip of sky at the top of the frame, in a proportion that varies from one-fourth to one-third of the space; the latter distributing ground and sky in a proportion that varies from one-third to two-thirds in the space of the frame. It will be readily understood that this entirely relative opposition has no meaning until the moment it is radicalized and becomes marked as a divergence in the production of the narrative. That is precisely what happens here, from one series to the next, in shots 70–73 and 79–81. In the first set of shots, the opposition is established as follows:

a. in 70 and 72, thanks to a tilt down onto Thornhill in MS, the ground almost fills the frame; in 71 and 73, the sky fills the top two-thirds of the image. Later, from 74–78, the proportions again range from one-third to two-thirds, starting with the repetitive continuity of the airplane shots and undoing any opposition.

b. in 79 and 81a, thanks to a tilt up on Thornhill, the sky fills the whole image, with shot 80 of the airplane remaining just the same as shots 71, 73, etc. The brutal movement 81a ⟶ 81b puts an end to this opposition within the shot itself, by a kind of reversal sky ⟶ ground that marks a slight fluctuation between shots 82 (one-third sky) and 83 (two-thirds sky), before being resolved in an indifferentiation similar to that which followed shots 70–73.

We see that the effect of inversion involves the shots of Thornhill preceding the interruption of alternation in the two series, both articulated around a single shot (the airplane's approach), whose regularity makes it function as invariant and support of difference. In the development of the first attack, this divergence makes the second micro-series (70–72) stand out all the more, thus accentuating the systematic character of the contraction achieved, as it were, by scissiparity, from one series to the next. In fact it is the opposition between the scale of the framings that is thus reinforced: for if, between micro-series 66–70 and micro-series 70–72 this is only between tight MLS and MS, in micro-series 70–72 and 79–81 it is between MS and MLS, the two thus forming a micro-system on the basis of several pertinencies (identity of position, near/less near, tilt down/tilt up ⟶ [ground-sky], stationary/moving in the first shot of the interruption of alternation).

14. The object of the next series (84–88) is the arrival in x of a new (fourth) car. It can be broken down into two micro-series. The first alternates the subject and the object of vision (from 84 to 86, or more precisely from 84b, in which the look shifts from the airplane to the car, to 86a, in which the look is maintained until Thornhill stands up); the second emphasizes Thornhill's movement and his encounter with the object by an interruption of alternation (from 86 to 88, more precisely from 86b, in which Thornhill starts to get up, to 88a, in which the conjunction is confirmed before the car leaves the frame).

This brief series has a remarkable function. In fact, it turns out to compensate for certain asymmetrical effects of the two preceding series (the two airplane attacks). But, of course, this is only to open of itself a second asymmetry, according to a movement that announces in a strangely precise way the generation of the fiction as displacement or dislocation of the systems on which it is based: an unassuaged limp for which the narrative is both site and stake.

The reader will remember the divergence, corollary to the reduction in the number of shots, that the two series display at the level of actions: in the first series, Thornhill throws himself to the ground and gets up again, during the second he throws himself to the ground and stays there.

a. In the first, in 73b, Thornhill, on the ground, watches the airplane fly off in 74. These two shots are repeated in the second series, in 82b and 83 (the only difference being the axis of Thornhill's body, facing front and in profile).

b. In the first, Thornhill stands up in two shots, 75 and 77, alternating with two views of the airplane (76 and 78).

To find an equivalent we must introduce the third series. But this is at the price of a constitutive divergence that emphasizes this first difference instituted, through the appearance of a new object, by the series itself. Shot 82b is in fact repeated by shot 84, which alternates with the arrival of the car in shot 85. Thus, in opposition to the radical divergence established between shots 73 and 75 with the first attack, the shot that carries the interruption of alternation in the second attack is the one that allows it to be confirmed while making itself the first term of a new series. It is this duplication that is confirmed in shot 86 when Thornhill begins to stand up, a movement to be completed in shot 87, which interrupts both the alternation and the reiterative regularity of shots 82b, 84, and 86a.

Shot 87 thus allows the reinscription of a narrative element that was missing in the symmetry of the two previous series. But at the same time it constitutes the fourth term of a corresponding opposition in framing that seemed to have been resolved by a mediating operation between the first and second series. It is established as follows:

> *1st series*
> **near (MS-tight MLS)** / **far (LS)**
>
> *2nd series*
> **tight MLS**

As we have seen, the mediation is continued in the third series by shots 84 and 86. Shot 87 reintroduces, on the basis of the mediation itself, the opposition, by a framing that varies from LS to VLS. We can write this out as follows, taking the terms of the first opposition as reference:

> *1st series*
> **near (MS-tight MLS)** / **far (LS)**
> **near (MLS)** / **far to far + (LS to VLS)**
>
> *2nd series* *3rd series*
>
> *3rd series*

Here, at three levels, the textual work attains a dizzying subtlety:

a. The reiteration of the narrative element, not to speak of its differences—internal (position of the body) or external (inscription in a different action leading to Thornhill's running toward the car)—is staggered in relation to the sequence of shots and the opposition of framings. The first time, Thornhill stands up in the two shots following the one that shows him on the ground; the second time, this sequence is suspended by an intermediate shot: shot 84, in which he sees the car appear. On the other hand, in the first case, Thornhill on the ground in tight MLS (near) stands up in long VLS (far) in two shots (75, 77); in the second case, he is again on the ground in MLS (near), but it is in this same shot repeated that he begins to stand up (86) before completing the movement (which is thus caught in the opposition of the framings) in LS ⟶ ELS (far).

b. A single shot, 87, carries the essentials of this operation of symmetry-asymmetry. First, it sustains a third difference, announced by shot 86b in which Thornhill, standing up, loses control of the look: the interruption of alternation that conjoins the two shots in which he stands up, in opposition to the alternating arrangement of shots 75 and 77.

It is perfectly obvious that the interruption of alternation, Thornhill's movement that provokes it, and the corresponding conjunction (Thornhill and the car) are the primary elements of this difference governing the production of the narrative. But it is sustained by a finer difference opposing and joining shot 87 to shots 75 and 77. As we have seen, the latter frame Thornhill in long LS as he stands up, without any modification in the relationship between framing and subject. Conversely, in shot 87 Thornhill is initially framed in LS (far−); but his movement toward the highway initiates a variation in the relationship between framing and subject that ends in VLS (far+). This opposition "stationary in the shot/moving in the shot" is enriched by an opposition "stationary/moving" of the shot itself: two slight right-left pans emphasize Thornhill's move and the appearance of the car. And these camera movements lead to an exact coincidence between the final framing of shot 87 and the identical frames of shots 75 and 77, from which it differs a bit at first through its greater obliqueness and its lower ratio between the quantities of earth and sky. Such is the discreet perversion of this reiterative game. The moment Thornhill begins to turn toward the highway, shot 87 coincides with shots 75 and 77, for an ideal instant (the instant of an imperceptible frame, since the shot moves), in the arrangement of the character in the frame; but a manifest divergence remains in the strict delimitation of the framing. Inversely, at the final instant when the spatial delimitations of the framing finally come to coincide, the spatial arrangements of the character in the frame mark the supreme point of their difference.

c. The two series delimited by the airplane attacks displayed an overall symmetrical arrangement, according to a tripartite schema arrival-meeting-departure, based, from series to series, on a contraction in the number of the shots. The third series turns out to compensate, as much at the level of narrative actions as at that of framings, for the asymmetry hidden by the symmetrical arrangement of the two previous series. But this work of symmetrization itself turns out to open a new asymmetry between the two series, since the second term of the second series tends to expand into the opening of a third series or even into a third interruption of alternation in order to sustain the systematic set of operations performed between the first two.

These three series thus form a system. Of course, this system only closes by what it opens, as is shown by the third series: breaking the succession of airplane attacks, it reintroduces both the central axis of the highway and the bus-car-truck paradigm that organized the first part of the segment. We shall return to this, but not without having first recognized how the third series ends with a shot whose obvious transitive value is accentuated by the very fact that it happens to conclude this ordered set of series by duplicating the shot that introduced it.

15. Shot 88 shows Thornhill, in the axis of the highway, in x, in a slightly oblique shot from the BB' side. Thornhill is in three-quarter back view, initially blocking the car that approaches and rapidly disappears left; a slight reframing punctuates his movement as he turns around, into a three-quarter front view, to follow the car's departure. The reader will remember shot 64: same framing and same frame, same position of Thornhill, same conjunction in the frame between subject and object of vision. The difference in the actions and in their arrangement thus marks the difference of the same by causing a logical hierarchization of the two shots: the bus the

man boards drives off into the distance through the end of shot 64, followed by two intermittent glances from Thornhill; in 88, the car, followed by Thornhill's constant look, is off screen by the end of the shot; then because this conjunction is articulated onto a double opposition car/bus, x (real)/x' (virtual), which inscribes the two shots in both the paradigm of axes and that of means of locomotion.

Finally, even if shot 64 is inscribed in the regularity of the alternation whereas shot 88 constitutes the last term of its interruption, the two shots are otherwise conjoined in a four-term relationship, via repeated couples, thanks to the identity between shots 65 and 89, which expose the common object of vision: across from Thornhill, the byroad that crosses the highway and the airplane in the distance turning in the sky. Note further, in the duplication, the minimal divergence that governs it in both image and narrative: the first, much more oblique until the slight movement that will modify it in shot 67, so that it remains more or less equal until shot 89, the last, thus opening the reiterative sequence whose object it will be in several series (65, 67, 69, 71, 74, 76, 78, 80, 89) and only allowing a very distant view of the airplane which, in shot 89, is preparing to swoop down on Thornhill for the third time.

This duplication allows the reintroduction of the airplane, whose insistence, if not its all-determining threat, has been provisionally postponed by the appearance of the fourth car. The reader will note the radical contraction marking this return: six shots separate shots 64–65 from the interruption of alternation that emphasizes the conjunction of Thornhill and the airplane; shots 90–91, in which a new conjunction is produced, on the contrary directly follow shots 88–89. This divergence does no damage to narrative realism: during the car episode, from 84 to 88b, the airplane has the material time to complete its flying off and returning, as it does in several shots between the first and second attacks. But beyond the function of lending manifest panic to Thornhill's situation, beyond the peculiar benefits it confers on the systematization of the narrative (symmetry-asymmetry of the three series, return of the bus-car-truck paradigm), the episode of the fourth car possesses a precise strategic value in the formalization of the suspense tied to the threat of the airplane. Indeed, it makes it possible both to adopt and to undercut the classicism of the process of acceleration and contraction which ensures by means of parallel montage the administration of the suspense so dear to cinematic narration, and especially to Hitchcock, who only varies and perverts it to serve it all the better.

Thus, from the first to the second attack, the acceleration is produced by a contraction in the number of shots; from the second to the third, this contraction is all the more radically accentuated insofar as it is postponed by the intervention of a new element (the car). This is what is emphasized, from the first to the third attacks, by the return of a similar shot, foreboding the one and already almost materializing the other: this duplication introduces an almost excessive acceleration which compensates, by a brusque rapprochement of shots in which, as it were, a sudden contraction takes place in the narrative, for the detour constituted by the appearance of the car in the progressive sequence of attacks by the airplane. We have seen the extent to which this detour was essential to the logical hierarchization of the image and the narrative that it gave rise to. Here, again, the narrative achieves equilibrium in one plane only to lose it all the more in another.

18. A succession of series is organized form the starting point of the vision of the cornfield. The first, from 91b to 98a, leads Thornhill from the place where he fell to the ground to the interior of the cornfield where he takes refuge. In the dramatic and formal economy established with the airplane's first attack, this series occupies a place in relation to the third attack similar in function to that of the series delimited by the fourth car in relation to the second attack. It can be represented as follows:

1st attack $\longrightarrow$ 2nd attack $\longrightarrow$ 4th car $\longrightarrow$ 3rd attack cornfield

This correspondence is called into question by the first three shots of the series, 91b–93, which are modeled on shots 84b–86, despite the manifest divergence of the initial half-shots: 91b, in which Thornhill notices the cornfield, is in fact the brink of an interruption, in which Thornhill's fall ends the moment that the bullets fired from the airplane hit the ground; whereas Thornhill's look finds the car in 84b after following the turning movement of the airplane. Shots 85 and 92 are identical in all but their objects of vision, confirming or reestablishing the alternation of the look. Shot 92, which shows the cornfield appearing in the distance, extending across the frame, brings into play the only element of this rigorously bare setting (besides the roads and the signposts), introduced in shot 11 in one of Thornhill's four "empty" visions and used from shot 35 to shot 55 in the two series in which the third car and the man who gets out of it appear. As for shots 86 and 93, they pinpoint in quite similar fashion, with Thornhill in the same lateral position and the same framing, the moment in which he stands up again to head toward the new object, thanks to which he hopes to escape the threat of the airplane.

At this point, this term for term correspondence comes to an end. Of course, the shots that follow establish an interruption of alternation in the same way. But the mere statement of their respective numbers (87–88 and 94–98) emphasizes the fact that the new interruption of alternation is by far the longest since the beginning of the segment and thus marks the productive divergence opened up between the two series. The beginnings of shots 87 and 94 are still quite alike, in action (Thornhill, crouching, manages to stand up) and scale (long LS). Then they rapidly diverge: the first, we will remember, emphasizes Thornhill's run toward the car and their meeting with two brief pans and a change from LS to VLS; the second allows Thornhill to leave the fixed frame as soon as he has stood up. This divergence between the two shots still starts from an identity: in shot 94, Thornhill is conjoined with the airplane that turns in the air to try to come back toward him, as in shot 87 he is conjoined with the car approaching on the highway. But in the first case the car is the object he heads toward to escape the threat of the airplane; in the second the airplane is the object that he tries to flee, having noticed the cornfield to which he is running. The airplane that occupies the place of the car in the conjunction now occupies the place of the corn by position, as presaged by the regulated identity of the two series. For the first time since the beginning of the segment, a conjunction is thus inscribed within an interruption of alternation.

There are two things to be noted here. First, a submission to the reiterative regulation that from the beginning of the segment to its end links the interruption of alternation to a means of locomotion, or to the subject that is linked to it—that is, to an object in motion. Next and above all, the ineluctable progression that demands an enrichment of the structure through a combination of its previous elements. Shot 95, which follows this displacement of conjunction, remarkably accentuates this process. Thornhill, framed in MLS, followed in a left-to-right tracking shot as he runs, turns around a moment to check the position of the airplane. This shot thus reiterates, except in the direction of the movement, the track back in shot 90 that follows Thornhill as he runs from the airplane that pursues him in the third attack. The difference between the two shots, conveyed by the divergence in length (almost from three to one: 90 = 13 1/2 sec.; 95 = 4 1/2 sec.), lies in the fact that shot 90 produces a conjunction between Thornhill and the airplane that is displayed in shot 94 and postponed in shot 95. This duality and this double displacement of conjunction thus effects in series 91b–98 a true condensation between the two series 84b–88a and 88b–91a, those of the fourth car and the third airplane attack. It is a condensation all the more acute in that shot 94 also reintroduces the shot that is missing from the third attack and produces the contraction whose effects have already been marked: that is, the shot that shows the airplane leaving after the attack. But it is in a doubly displaced form: within the new series defined by the new object of vision, and in this series within the interruption of alternation. The airplane thus takes the place of the corn in shot 94, just as the corn took the place of the airplane in shot 92—through an effect of inversion whose multiple effects of displacement underpin the process of combination and progressive integration, condensation of previous elements. This process is confirmed with shot 96, which brings about the till now postponed conjunction of Thornhill and the corn: thanks to a framing that varies from long LS to VLS, which seems to make it follow immediately from shot 94, whose similarity with shot 87a has already been noted, it recalls 87b, in which Thornhill reached the end of his run to the car. This condensation of the two series is effected, we can see, by a true effect of dilation. The encounter with the new object of vision, the corn, is indeed postponed through three shots (94–96), which happen to reiterate, on the one hand, the shot that established the encounter with the previous object (87, the car), on the other hand, the shot that brought about the conjunction with the airplane (90). This dilation takes on the dramatization of the narrative via the systematic work of the image, foreboding with tenfold intensity a new airplane attack.

19. The latter is carried out, no doubt, in a palpably different way. But shot 94 contributes to one last effect that must first be emphasized. If, as we have just seen, it fulfills the displaced function of the shot of the airplane leaving after the attack, it also occupies the place of the shots prior to the attack, and specifically shot 89, which serves as prelude to the third attack. The airplane, in this curiously polyvalent shot, is at once leaving and returning, outside the series, emphasizing the overlap between the series. In this respect, shots 94–95 are in inverse relationship to shots 89–90: the airplane seen by Thornhill in 89 is followed in 90 by the track back that brings about the conjunction of Thornhill and the airplane: the conjunction in 94 of Thornhill and the airplane he does not see is followed in 90 by the lateral track that leads him toward the corn. This inversion, which further accentuates the complementary effects of displacement and condensation, in itself emphasizes

the loss of the look, which is immediately confirmed in shots 96–98, thanks to a new object of conjunction.

At the end of shot 96, Thornhill, seen from behind, enters the field and disappears into the corn. Shot 97 shows the corn from closer up; we see the wake produced by Thornhill's entrance, and the movement that shakes the corn betrays his progress. Shot 98 leads us into the very thick of the corn where Thornhill, followed by a slight reframing, throws himself to the ground, then, half lying down, tries to lift his head to see the airplane that he hears. It is at this moment, with the opening of a new series, that the loss of the look reaches its extreme, insofar as the alternation reestablished around the new airplane attacks operates beneath the level of the look, even if it seems to find a support in it.

It is not that Thornhill does not look, since, on the contrary, he is constantly raising his head; it is just that he does not see what he looks at, even if he hears it. It is easy to miss this, so much on the one hand do Thornhill's movements and the fixity of his look make us think the opposite, so much on the other does the alternation that emphasizes the two attacks up to shot 104 follow on from the regularity of the previous alternations. But the framing that from shot 99 to shot 103 introduces the second term of the alternation (the field of corn seen longitudinally in the axis of the highway in the direction $x'x$) can in no case be seen from within the corn. To ensure that this is not really missed, Hitchcock has in reserve a second differential sign to mark clearly the moment in which a true alternation of the look is reestablished: shot 105, in which Thornhill parts the cornstalks, is logically followed in countershot by a shot in which the stalks constitute a sort of mask (*repoussoir*) in the center of which he sees the highway. If the look is what establishes the alternation, the latter also goes beyond the former, through a derivation for which the look remains the pretext, thus emphasizing through similarity of construction the continuity of actions and their progressively differential acceleration.

20. The two successive series in the cornfield correspond without intervening interruption to two successive airplane attacks. The first is quite logically circumscribed in shot 99, to the extent that the previous shots allow the airplane the narrative time necessary to modify its course as a function of Thornhill's movement. This is the final effect of shot 94, whose polyvalence has already been emphasized. Within the series that carries Thornhill toward the cornfield (but without any effect of preconjunction, since the cornfield is not visible in it), it constitutes an equivalent to the shots of the airplane's approach in the three previous attacks; by the same token, as it were projected into this fourth attack by an overlap between series that at once dilates and accelerates the narrative, it justifies the fact that the attack thus seems to occupy only one shot. The airplane that we see from the front, in a line parallel to the axis of the highway, passes over the cornfield and leaves from the top of the frame. For the first time, thanks to the screen constituted by the cornfield, the airplane attack brings neither a true conjunction between subject or object nor an interruption of alternation. In a sense, we do have to speak of conjunction here, since the airplane flies over the cornfield in which Thornhill is hiding. But we do not see Thornhill in the shots where we see the airplane and, in addition, we see only a very limited part of the cornfield. And so the global conjunction is partially

undercut; but so it is at the level of each of the two partial terms, Thornhill and the airplane: the cornfield becomes more a setting for the action than an object of vision, as it already was when it served as a horizon line for the appearance of the third car. There is enough ambiguity in the situation, however, to mark through the serial gradation an effect of progression by inclusion of elements, even if this ambiguity on the other hand points up the lack of conjunction between subject and object and interruption of alternation in the first attack. This divergence further accentuates the differentiation of this fourth attack from the three previous ones; it also differentiates between the two successive attacks and allows the fifth attack to be articulated with the first three in a very subtle way. Indeed, the airplane's second traversal of the cornfield turns out to cause, after an alternation between Thornhill and the airplane from 101 to 104, an interruption of alternation in shots 104–105. Shot 103 explains this: when the airplane arrives over the field, it releases a huge cloud of material, probably an insecticide, which spreads through the corn. As in the interruptions of the first three attacks, the interruption of alternation in 104b and 105a is produced by a redoubled loss of the look that shows Thornhill struggling in a cloud of white smoke until he manages to separate the cornstalks enough to look at the highway at the end of shot 105. Of course, properly speaking, there is no conjunction of subject and object. In this respect, the fifth attack duplicates the fourth, in the same way that it exactly repeats its trajectory. But the conjunction created by the blast of insecticide half takes its place, less direct than real vision but more insistent, more structuring, since it underpins the interruption, than the bullets fired in the second and third attacks.

If we follow through the comparison of this fifth attack to the first three, we can see that:

a. as in the third attack, the return of alternation, ignoring the airplane, is immediately established around a substitute object—in that case the cornfield, in this case the truck;

b. as in the second attack, however, this object is a means of locomotion, advancing on the highway in x, shown in an equivalent framing except for a slight divergence in axis and distance and the mask constituted by the cornstalks.

In this we can see the usual process of differential progression through synthetic integration of previous elements within the same set. In its extreme singularity, the fifth attack condenses traits specific to the first three. Still, it is closest to the second, in position, if one bears in mind the fourth, which it duplicates. Thus it is a sort of recurrent loop that runs through the narrative when, after the two lengthwise attacks on the cornfield as after the two crosswise attacks along the byroad, Thornhill sees something appear on the highway, in the first case a car, in this case a truck toward which he runs to escape the threat of the airplane. The reiterative effect is reinforced by the functional similarity of the two shots which, after shots 85 and 106 (the car and the truck), each establish a new interruption of alternation. In shot 107, Thornhill, framed in MS, separates the cornstalks and leaves the frame to be seen again in 108 in VLS and move progressively away toward the truck appearing in the distance. In the same way, in shot 86, Thornhill was lying down in MLS and began to stand up, then completed his movement in shot 87 in long LS to run away from the camera toward the car. There are, of course, many differences between the four shots, especially 87 and 108, the former punctuated by a pan and going so far as almost to make the subject and the object of his vision meet on the highway, the latter stationary and maintaining a distance between the two that is sufficient to serve the difference that the narration, starting from each of these two points, chooses to maintain between a car whose effect remains limited and a truck whose arrival will determine the outcome of the segment.

But the effect of looping and nesting, of progressive recurrence, is no less striking for this difference. We can now complete the linear scheme of the successive series that emerge after the first airplane attacks:

1st attack ⟶ 2nd attack ⟶ 3rd attack ⟶ 4th attack ⟶ 5th attack
⟶ 4th car   ⟶ corn   ⟶ 2nd truck

The series in which Thornhill takes refuge in the cornfield after the third attack corresponds to the series opened by the appearance of the fourth car. On the other hand, it makes possible the last two airplane attacks, which in turn generate, with the arrival of the truck, a series reiterating that of the fourth car. The concatenated series of grouped attacks thus seem to slide into each other according to a process of generation by circularity. The effects of repetition and similarity borne by this process thus all the more vividly emphasize the differentiation produced in it by the operations of displacement, condensation, resumption, and progressive integration that are raveled and unraveled throughout the series: hence this effect of real illusion, through which the progression of the narrative incessantly defines itself by its regression.

21. When Thornhill enters the cornfield, he avoids the threat of the airplane; but at the same time he loses that mastery of the look which, between the interruptions, defines his relations with the object. Here, as we have seen, alternation acquires thereby a second dimension, inscribing its effects of binary regulation beyond the look that is its principal agent. Of course, the interruption caused by the clouds of insecticide, transforming the relative loss of the look into an absolute one, reestablishes it in order to open a new series with the arrival of the truck, in conformity with the generative rule in force since the beginning of the segment. But it is only to postpone it immediately thanks to the new interruption of alternation established at the conjunction of shots 107–108 (107: Thornhill looks into the distance and leaves frame left through the corn; 108: he runs toward the truck, which approaches in the distance on the highway). But shot 108, which sanctions the interruption, immediately becomes the first term of a new alternation, according to an arrangement that recalls that of the two attacks over the cornfield but entails an infinitely more radical loss of the look. This series, from shots 108–111, is established as follows: in 108, Thornhill, in stationary VLS, runs toward the truck, in an oblique rear view in relation to the highway along the $x'x$ axis, with the cornfield to the right as mask. In 109, the airplane, in stationary ELS, turns above the corn. In 110, Thornhill, in stationary long LS, enters frame left, still seen from behind, nearly in the axis of the highway, and raises his arms to stop the approaching truck. And in 111, the airplane continues to circle above the cornfield, followed by a very slight right-left pan.

The progression is clear. In the cornfield, Thornhill, conjoined with the previous object of his look, tried to see the airplane and alternated with it as it flew over the field in two successive attacks. The cornfield, object of vision become setting, provided, as it were, complementarily to Thornhill's unanswered look, a sort of link between the two terms of the alternation, as if to undo the nesting effect of the alternation initiated at the conjunction between the subject and the object of his vision. Hence there is a sort of illusion that might, with insufficient care, allow it to be considered an alternation founded on the look. Here, there is no longer anything of the sort, but rather a pure alternating montage of the most classical variety if it were not for the fact that beneath its apparent simplicity, it constitutes the result of a complex process that confers on it a fully differentiating value in the more and more urgent rise of the suspense, and drives it to divide immediately upon itself in order to carry to its highest point the dramatization inscribed up to this point through the alternation of the look.

22. The new series that opposes Thornhill and the truck is made up of nine shots. The first seven emphasize the alternation, the last three the interruption produced by the conjunction (the seventh shot is clearly part of both groups, hence the total greater than nine). The principle of this alternation is simple: on one side Thornhill, immobile in the middle of the highway and facing the camera, stretches forth his hands to ward off the approaching truck; on the other the truck steadily approaches him until they meet. Only two glances out of the frame, behind and to the left, still testify to the presence of the airplane during this alternating series in which the mise-en-scène, borne along by the relative rhythmic regularity and the accumulated subtlety of all the previous series, does not despise the tricks of temporal acceleration and scalar progression dear to traditional parallel montage. But, once again, it is a finesse that turns opposition within similarity into the principle of a contrasting complementarity that guarantees the harmonic and hierarchized development of the fiction.

To get a sense of the subtlety of this series, we must consider the elements of the short series that preceded it. The first term of the alternation (Thornhill and the truck) displays a double variation in scale and axis of framing: on Thornhill and the truck as they approach each other in shots 108–110, first along an oblique and changing axis showing Thornhill in VLS to ELS, then along a longitudinal axis showing Thornhill in long LS. The second term (the airplane flying over the cornfield in the distance) is, conversely, the object of two shots that are similar except for a very slight right-left pan in the second, in opposition to the stationary character of the shots of Thornhill. In the second series, the shots of the motionless Thornhill (112, 114, and 116) are identical, in stationary MLS. Conversely, the shots of the truck (113, 115, and 117) move progressively from ELS to CU in a fixed framing as the truck approaches until it occupies the whole surface of the screen in 117. Shot 118 of Thornhill, the last in the alternation, is a jump to MCU, intensified by a very fast track in to BCU or insert.

Thus a layered opposition is structured through the two series, at the three levels of shot scale, camera movement, and movement within the shot. The first opposition is internal to the first series. It clearly opposes to the variation between the two shots of Thornhill and the truck the identity of the two shots of the airplane (except for the variation of the very slight pan in the second), which circumscribe a distant object that moves transversely, crossing the frame from right to left. Thornhill and the truck move longitudinally toward each other in the stationary frame of shot 108, thus by definition inverting their respective distances from the camera, Thornhill moving away and the truck approaching; the shift to a closer scale on Thornhill in shot 110 (from ELS to long LS) displaces the oppositional relation between discontinuity and continuity, since Thornhill remains motionless in the frame while the truck continues to advance. But this same opposition (internal to the second shot of the first term of the alternation in series 108–111) continues from shot to shot in the series based on the alternation of the look between Thornhill and the truck. Of course, thanks to the reverse shot that inaugurates this alternation in shot 112, Thornhill shifts from long LS to MLS. But this change is discontinuous, like the previous change between the end of shot 108 and shot 110 from ELS to long LS, in opposition to the truck, which steadily grows larger in the shot. This imbalance, which considerably reinforces the physical violence of the suspense sustained by this alternation, is finally compensated for by shot 118 as if after the event: by its framing in MCU, which effects a jump on Thornhill (the third jump, if one takes both series into consideration), and then by the very short fast track that is modeled on the movement within the frame performed by the truck in shot 117. Thus, to the continuous progression of the truck's approach is counterposed the discontinuous gradation of the camera's relation to Thornhill, which leads them both through the two series from farthest to nearest until their inevitable conjunction.

But shot 118, whose necessity is clear in respect to the truck's final approach, gives, in one final inversion, as it were, one last turn of the screw to the progression by scissiparity from one series to the next. Let us recall shot 108, which distances Thornhill as it inaugurates the truck's progression at the beginning of their conjunction. It is essentially justified by its reiteration of shot 87, which ushered in the conjunction of Thornhill and the fourth car in the same way. It is thus inscribed in a hierarchization of framings, whose terms have already been laid out. On the other hand, the growth in the distance between Thornhill and the camera obviously favors the asymmetrical progression of the framings, from farthest to nearest, which are organized around Thornhill and the truck from this point on. But it is also in order to take on this inversion of distances, necessary to the setting up of the movement of paired progression, that the last shot of the alternation in the second series (118) corresponds to this first shot of the first series (108): by a rapid track in the shot that frames Thornhill most closely (for the only time in the whole segment) and reverses the long movement in the shot that takes him the farthest he has been from the camera since the beginning of the segment, except in shot 1.

23. As in the airplane attacks, the interruption of alternation is effected by a loss of the look at the end of the first interruption shot. It is particularly striking as it is not crystallized until the last few frames of the very short shot that is concerned to capture to the utmost degree the advance of the threat and of the fear in Thornhill's look: he literally disappears from the bottom of the frame, his clenched fist the only dent in the sudden white blur of the image. As in the first two airplane attacks, the conjunction is effected in the second shot; but unlike the conjunctions marked by the violent irruption of danger, that is, the successive airplane attacks, Thornhill's look is not reestablished at the end of the second interruption shot, thus emphasizing the temporal dilation of the shock that throws Thornhill between the truck's wheels, even though the shots themselves are very short. Not until the third shot

does Thornhill, lying on his back and framed in MS against a wheel that acts as a mask and insists on the conjunction, turn slightly to see the airplane emerging over the cornfield and coming straight toward the truck.

The alternation that begins here, in the length of a shot, has a synthetic value that alone would be enough to mark the gradual perfection of the suspense on the segment's surface. Shot 121, indeed, continues the alternation of shots 108–111 between Thornhill and the truck on the one hand, and of the airplane flying over the cornfield on the other. From the outset this alternation was established beyond the look, much more distinctly than in the two airplane attacks over the cornfield. It is very much the same alternation that is reestablished here, having been temporarily split onto itself by the alternating series between Thornhill and the truck. But this time it will be based upon the look, given the conjunction effected between Thornhill and the truck. The long detour that, beginning when Thornhill entered the cornfield, has hidden the airplane from his look (except for a look offscreen in shot 112, at the beginning of the alternating series with the truck) thus ends in this shot 121 where he sees it coming toward him for the sixth time. The second term of this alternation also turns out to bring a conjunction into play, all the more ineluctably to anticipate the one to follow. It is with his head and shoulders barred on the right of the screen by the truck's wheel that Thornhill sees the airplane. Shot 121 — a banal reverse shot transformed into the central element of a system — takes advantage of the wheel, which emphasizes the conjunction, and of the look, which can logically include it in its field by bringing it to the left of the frame to serve as a mask, thus effecting a formal conjunction between the airplane and the truck.

Shot 122, which puts an end to this barely established alternation, is thus a conjunction of conjunctions. In this sense it marks the acme of the segment, at the level of action as well as at the level of the combination of elements. At the moment when the airplane goes out of control and reaches the truck, with which it will collide in the succession of shots 122 and 123, Thornhill has truly met Kaplan.

Music has hitherto been absent from this segment, which the extreme scarcity of dialogue and the nearly constant subordination of sound to image allow us without exaggeration to reduce almost entirely to the image track; here the music returns with a generic stridency and a suddenness that confers on the final accident an extraordinary symbolic violence, as it does later on the sepulchral immensity of the "Monument" looming before Eve's and Thornhill's eyes.

These shots of interruption and conjunction do not allow us to see Thornhill. The first, which has to show the final trajectory of the airplane, is an ELS; the second, which shows the collision and then the explosion followed by a huge whirlwind of flames, is a closer shot that maintains nonetheless a relatively long framing. Not until shot 124 do we see Thornhill, still lying between the wheels of the truck, get up and begin to retreat toward the camera, in long LS. This divergence, which — unlike all the previous interruptions — seems to leave Thornhill out of the first two interruption shots, is easily explained by the peculiar necessities of this conjunction: only an ELS could show the collision between the airplane and the truck, underneath which we still see Thornhill, even if he is not really visible.

But another and much more significant divergence governs this interruption and emphasizes its culminating and convergent character. After these shots, no re-

sumption of alternation is established around Thornhill's look. The transition between shots 124 and 125 demonstrates this clearly: Thornhill still has his back
turned toward the inferno at the end of shot 124 when the two truckdrivers leave the
frame and run away on the dirt byroad in shot 125 in a framing that almost exactly
reiterates the one that showed the approach of the third car at the end of shot 41 and
that we might for a moment have thought was seen by Thornhill.

24. Beyond this, there is apparently almost nothing to say about the end of the
segment. Shot 126 again provides the motif for the ghost of a system with shots 123
and 124. All three are shot at the same angle, obliquely from Bx' towards $x'A$. The
first is a VLS of the truck and the airplane in flames; Thornhill is beneath the truck,
but we do not see him. The second, in long LS, shows Thornhill standing up and
beginning to move away. The third exactly repeats the framing of the first: inversely,
in it as in the second, we see Thornhill continuing his retreat, this time framed in
MLS. On the other hand, shot 126 is jointly opposed to the other two by the brief
backward tracking movement that follows Thornhill's movement and reveals the
white signpost marking the bus stop at the left of the frame.

Stationary shot 127 shows in reverse shot along the x' axis a car and a pickup
truck stopping at the side of the highway. Here again the mise-en-scène is careful to
disavow all possibility of interpreting this shot as a subjective vision: Thornhill in
fact enters the frame at the beginning of the shot and rushes toward the three men
and one woman who get out of the vehicles. Like the shots of the airplane in the two
successive attacks over the cornfield, shot 127 thus postpones the inscription of the
look though everything still indicates its presence: Thornhill sees the arrival of the
cars, since he heads toward them, just as he plausibly guessed the airplane's movements amid the cornstalks. But these visions are postponed: the first in favor of an
alternation outside the control of the look, in the second in favor of an avoidance of
alternation demonstrated by the immediate conjunction of Thornhill and the cars.

Shot 128, also stationary, returns to the airplane and the truck in flames in an
extremely long shot (longer than 123, tighter than 122), this time almost on the axis
of the highway. The mask constituted by the arm and part of the body of one of the
three men (a farmer) once again ensures the desubjectification of the shot. Next,
shot 129 shows Thornhill laterally in LS as he gradually backs through the group
while they move forward to stare at the accident. Shot 130 is a match on action,
repeating the framing of shot 128, in which the four characters in rear view gradually move up. Thus, from the interruption shots on, the mise-en-scène steadily avoids
any return to alternation, whether based on the look or on a parallelism of actions.
There is, however, a sort of derivative alternation established in 125–130 between
two fields, between which the characters' exits and entrances ensure a steady continuity of conjunctions: on the one hand the variable shots of the truck, conjoined
with Thornhill in 124, with the farmer's fragmented body in 128 and with the people
moving up in 130; on the other, diversified reverse shots that form a succession of
actions taking place on the dirt byroad in y' and the highway in x', on the other side
from the burning truck.

True alternation of the look is, however, reestablished one last time. But unlike
the one whose interlocking underlies the segment as a whole, this alternation is not

established around Thornhill. The look was shared once before, displaced onto the man who got out of the fourth car when the airplane first appeared in the far distance. But this happened in spite of the privilege accorded the man in shots 57 and 59, as it were for Thornhill's benefit, in the constant play of alternation in which he was center and subject. Here, in contrast, the farmer fully becomes its center. When the sound of a motor is heard at the end of shot 130, the farmer turns around to see in 131 his pickup truck making a U-turn on the highway. Shot 132 immediately reiterates shot 130, thus confirming that shot 131, inserted between two shots of the subject looking, is indeed the object of his vision and that the alternation of the look is thus reborn in this derivative alternation that constitutes a very remote echo of it. The farmer turns and then rushes off to be conjoined in shot 133—which reiterates shot 131—with his departing truck, which he chases along the deserted highway, on which Thornhill flees the same way he arrived, until he is nothing more than a point on the horizon, like the bus that brought him.

We may wonder about the reason for this last alternation and this last interruption-conjunction. No doubt we must invoke the dramatization inherent in the look, in localized point of view, which is capable of generating its effects even through the mediation of a character who is absolutely secondary to the genesis of identification. On the other hand, it seems quite natural that, in a segment structured throughout by a shuttling back and forth between alternation and its interruption, this dialectic should be reaffirmed one last time at the end of the segment, having been postponed for several shots in favor of a more differentiated editing pattern. But we might expect this final effect, in keeping with all the others, to take shape around Thornhill's view. He would see the pickup truck in an alternating pattern two to four shots long, then be conjoined with it as he was before with the other vehicles, only this time he would get in and disappear as we hear the off-screen cries of the farmer or even see him appear as we do here—in the same field of vision that produces the conjunction of Thornhill and the vehicle through an interruption of alternation.

There are three apparent reasons for the solution adopted by Hitchcock. First, we have seen how the last true alternating series, which ended with the conjunction of the truck and the airplane, constituted a sort of acme that condensed the progressive violence of earlier operations. Any resumption of alternation around Thornhill after this point would have fallen fatally short of this acme and thus have risked weakening the gradation of suspense, whereas resort to another character ensures its relay by differentiation. Second, the importance thus accorded to the farmer allows the development of a closer rhyme with the only other character who has appeared thus far in the segment. Finally, this last solution has the advantage of introducing into the continuity of a single dramatic movement the differential element that the man's run introduces into the symmetrical folding of the segment as a whole, since the pickup truck disappears on the horizon of shot 133 just as the bus appeared on the horizon in shot 1.

25. This folding is remarkable. It is all the more so in that it is double, or rather triple. For the segment only folds at its two extremities in this way thanks to the earlier folding that already joined its beginning and its center—what we can now call its center. Thus is organized, in an eminently strategic way, one last network of systematic relationships, between the beginning, middle, and end of the segment,

on the basis of the scintillating rhyme effect that joins shots 1 and 133. Between the center and the beginning, a loop formed, producing, through a set of repetitions riddled with differences, as it were, a recommencement of the narrative. It is by reinsisting on certain of these repetitions and differences that we can bring out an architecture, a singular sub-system in which, in an effect emphasized on many occasions, the center will play, among other things, a mediating role between the beginning and the end of the segment.

The first bus, we will recall, appears in x in shot 1, stops at the intersection of the highway and the byroad to let Thornhill get off, and disappears in shot 3 in x', seen by Thornhill. The second bus appears in x' in shot 59, seen by the man, then draws nearer in shot 63, seen jointly by the man and Thornhill; it stops in the same way to let the man get on and drives off in x, conjoined with Thornhill and apparently unseen by him, thanks to the diversion of his look produced by the airplane (which appears in the distance in shots 56–63, in which Thornhill's and the man's paired looks alternate between the successive visions of the airplane and the bus).

This identity of object, this inverted symmetry of axes and actions, this conjunction in common, can be seen both to reduce and to accentuate the fundamental divergence opened up in the image and the narrative by the duality of characters. Indeed, it is between the man and Thornhill that there crystallizes, in the same way as at the levels of the actions and the axes, an effect of inverted symmetry at the level of the conjunctions: from inside to outside for the first, from outside to inside for the second. The conjunction between Thornhill and the second bus is thus, as it were, supererogatory to this self-enclosed pairing. It opens a second effect, one of repetition, which is immediately undermined by a double difference. First, of course, in the conjunction itself: moving from inside to outside in the first case, restricted to outside in the second. Next, logically, in an echo at the level of the look: Thornhill, fully preoccupied by the airplane, nevertheless twice glances quickly over his shoulder to the right at the bus as it drives off. This double divergence thus corresponds to the asymmetry introduced by the simple duality of the two men, limited and compensated for by the inverted symmetry whose closure we have already felt.

This asymmetry is further reinforced by the general arrangement of these two subsets: in the first, there is no shot of the object before the conjunction; in the second, there is none after it. But this is at the price of a divergence inscribed in the alternation itself: on the one hand, the bus disappears in one shot (3); on the other, it appears in two shots (59 and 63), but above all in an alternation with the airplane. The duality of the objects of the look thus corresponds to the duality of the subjects; when Thornhill looks at the airplane in shot 64, it justifies his conjunction with the departing bus and the fleeting look he gives it. The closure of a multiple rhyme is thus established in the very movement that ensures the narrative opening of the segment.

But this man who leaves in a bus arrived in a car. The effects of inverted symmetry organized in a mirroring between the beginning and the center of the segment thus turn out to have a sort of systematic polyvalence. On the one hand, they prohibit overly clear and complete effects of symmetry between the arrivals and departures, the means of locomotion and the characters; on the other, they both compensate for and refine the constitutive asymmetry opened up by the duality of the characters; finally, they emphasize all the more vividly the divergence between the car and the bus, which bring about, respectively, the man's arrival and his departure. Thus they allow us to infer the existence of a fourth term capable of balancing the system through a chiastic symmetry: that is, a car that Thornhill will get into in his turn.

This car exists; it is, of course, the pickup truck of shot 133. Unlike the buses, the cars are opposed to each other from the outset: by a difference of axis, which attributes to the first the direction y', and to the second the direction x'. On the contrary, a remarkable effect of inverted symmetry brings them together in a kind of nesting of actions. The first car, which arrives, does not really depart; it makes a U-turn in shots 45 and 47, but we cannot see it drive off on the byroad (the pan in shot 41, which emphasizes its approach and its moment of arrival, alters the amount of the byroad visible in the image: the car thus leaves the frame as soon as it has completed its U-turn). The second car, which departs, does not really arrive. It has, practically speaking, stopped at the side of the highway when we first see it in shot 127. And in shots 131 and 133, it will make a U-turn to depart into the distance on the highway in x', just as the first car arrived along the byroad in y'. Nothing, furthermore, could be less alike than these two movements of arrival and departure, which are organized around a U-turn in the axis: the first, divided into four short shots seen by Thornhill (35, 37, 39, and 41), the second in one long shot (133), which brings about the conjunction between the farmer and Thornhill, object of his vision. But they nonetheless allow an effect of inverted symmetry, which is articulated with the one bearing on the two buses to produce a global effect of chiastic symmetry between the man and Thornhill, their arrivals and departures, and the means of locomotion that are linked to them.

But there is still a divergence inscribed in this symmetry. Properly speaking, we do not see Thornhill get into the car as we saw the man get out. His movement occurs during the elliptical time corresponding to the overlap between shots 129 and 130, in which Thornhill retreats until he disappears among the people who move forward to stare at the airplane and the truck in flames. When the farmer turns around at the end of shot 130, it is to see his car break into the U-turn that rhymes with the one made by the earlier car. This divergence conveys, first, logically, the narrative contraction carried out after the final accident, particularly through a relativization of the alternation of the look. The effect of surprise in shot 131, which precisely reestablishes the alternation one last time around the farmer, is the greater for it. Furthermore, for the first time in this segment in which Thornhill's look so constantly scans the horizon, this contraction puts him in conjunction with the new car in shot 127 without a prior look. But this conjunction only marks the first of the two stages proper to any movement of getting on or off, inside and outside a vehicle. Shot 131 thus corresponds to the second stage of the conjunction: Thornhill is joined with the car outwardly in shot 127, inwardly in shot 131, as, inversely, in one sense or the other, but always one after the other, Thornhill is with the bus in shot 1, the man with the car and the bus in shots 43 and 64, the two drivers with the truck in shot 125, the farmer and the other people with the two successive cars in shot 127.

This divergence, finally, seems to correspond to the imbalance introduced by the arrival of the farmer in the chiastic symmetry to which that arrival is an indispensable mediation. Through the nesting effect that yokes the man's arrival to Thornhill's departure, the farmer's arrival comes to repeat the man's and, helped further by the similarity of vehicles if not of axes, to organize the two characters in relation to Thornhill, on the basis of and within the structure of chiastic symmetry. This relationship of the two characters adjacent to the hero is thus manifested through him by a double effect of inversion at the level of the look, referring the last alternation of the look back to two previous alternations: first to the man's arrival, which Thornhill sees in the same way the farmer sees his departure; then, more subtly, to shots 56–63: in the first case, the man's look serves to relay Thornhill's, on the basis of a conjunction that reestablishes the alternation and expresses his mastery of the situation in relation to Thornhill, since he first sees the approaching bus and the plane whose contradictory behavior he notes; in the second, the farmer's look serves to relay Thornhill's by reestablishing the alternation in which Thornhill will this time be the object, but insofar as he is master of the situation in relation to the farmer who is its victim. Nevertheless, the farmer's intervention at the same time preserves the integrity of the structural effect of chiastic symmetry between the man and Thornhill. That is why, through a double complementary effect that testifies to its profound systematic perversity, the narrative associates the arrival of the farmer and the pickup truck with that of a second car, and thus includes the farmer in a group of characters whose movement is then organized in relation to a movement immediately preceding it in the diegesis: in shot 127, the four characters get out of the two cars just as the two drivers get out of the truck in shot 124; and in shots 129–130 they approach the scene of the accident just as the drivers move away from it in shot 125. Thus, the farmer is inscribed both in a simple and immediate rhyme and in the microsystem hierarchized by the chiastic symmetry in which he intervenes as both constitutive and divergent element. The final shot becomes the echo of this double determination: the condensation achieved in it indicates that once the narrative has begun, and with it the asymmetry that carries it, it can only be stopped by constantly readjusting that asymmetry.

As we have seen, the trajectory of the pickup truck in shot 133 is in complete opposition to that of the car in shots 35–41, though it is still its complement in the play of inverted symmetry. The reason for this is simple: the final shot must rhyme with shot 1 to produce the effect of symmetry that brings into coincidence, as if in a mirror, Thornhill's departure and arrival and through them the segment as a whole. But by the same token, if one thinks about it, shot 133 also inverts shot 64, whose effects in relation to shot 1 have already been outlined in great detail. It does so in a very different way, if only to mark the median and mediating function that makes it more or less the organic center and the pivot of the fiction. Indeed, in the second period of this very long shot, could we not say that the immobile Thornhill is conjoined on the outside with the bus driving off in x', to which the man is then conjoined on the inside; just as, inversely, the farmer is conjoined on the outside with his pickup truck, which he chases as it disappears in x', and conjoined with Thornhill on the inside? This is a way, moreover, of accentuating the rhyming effect between the man and the farmer, the one arriving in the place of the other, in order to emphasize the fact that the narrative, this fragment of a narrative, is reaching its end. So it is this inverted similarity that is inscribed as difference in the mirror effect adjusting one to the other shots 1 and 133, and that thus condenses in the final shot of the segment its median and initial shots. It would be impossible to imagine a more perfect image of classical fiction than this progression through differentiation of the same, which makes the final shot a reflection of the first, marked with an element of complementarity and a paradigmatic divergence.

26. And so we have reached the end of this ten-minute segment, cut into 133 shots, divided into 22 series, punctuated by 13 interruptions of alternation. The various successive conjunctions of Thornhill with the object that he flees, the airplane, and with the objects that, on the contrary, he approaches with increasing terror, lead to this acme logically summed up in their meeting. I will not try to tie everything neatly together by going back over the reiterative progression of the series, the differential regulation of the alternations, the similarity and diversity of the interruptions. First, because it is impossible. Textual analysis is irreducible in that it cannot be summarized without yielding only the bare bones of a structure that, although not null, can never be the multiple whole which is constructed in it, around it, through it, upon it, beyond it. In different kinds of language, which one is sometimes tempted to see as contradictory but which are only partly so, Lévi-Strauss and Barthes have said this again and again. Analysis of itself generates a second text that it would be vain to wish to reduce in its turn. In the two tables and the collection of frame stills the reader will find a schematic image of the succession whose reiterative and differential progression the step-by-step traversal that has guided this reading will have rendered palpable.

But I would still like to remind the reader briefly of its characteristics. The first is the multiplicity of the codic levels and of their constitutive elements. This multiplicity seems all the more significant insofar as one is dealing with particularly homogeneous and relatively impoverished filmic material. But this poverty is obviously deceptive. Is it not the very condition of the system's richness and the reason for its brilliance? The second characteristic concerns the nature of the progression. It is double, profoundly linear and non-linear at once: on the one hand, it ties the system's elements together step by step, in a more or less immediate contiguity, between one series, alternation, or interruption and the next; on the other, it ties them together at a distance, at a more or less great distance, in a play of echoes that simultaneously produces a contraction and a perpetual dilation of the system. Hence, thanks to the systematization by contiguity, there sometimes emerge third characteristic, partial ensembles, micro-systems, sub-systems that testify profoundly to the global systematicity of the segment: always closed and always open, advancing by a progressive and regulated integration of their previous elements, an accentuation of effects of substitution, condensation and displacement, as evidenced, for example, by the three series 11, 12, and 13, formed by the first two airplane attacks and the arrival of the fourth car. Finally, the last characteristic, the most fundamental and the most difficult to isolate, so closely is it bound up with the global and micro-elementary experience of the filmic text for which this analysis would like to be the site: the imbalance, the constitutive asymmetry that, across the flood of repetitions, symmetries, rhymes, equivalences, and similarities, guarantees the development of the narrative. This productive imbalance is at once constant and pluralized—plural, Barthes would say,—and the one in proportion to the other. That is to say, it governs both the relations between the levels, codes, and sub-codes, specific or non-specific, and the relations within each level. The continuous operations that produce the putting into play of the multiple narrative elements are performed in such a way that any compensation for this imbalance in one plane immediately reestablishes it in another, with a fatality that perfectly expresses what Lévi-Strauss calls the ineluctable asymmetry of structure. This fundamental imbalance is the point of absolute coincidence between structure and structuration, the too perfect dream of the one and the always slightly utopian reality of the other.

The more or less recursive step-by-step progression that has guided this analysis has attempted to bring to light the multiplicity of the successive operations that effect the generation of the segment. It is to experience once again its exemplary expansion that we shall rearticulate the terms of a network whose systematic breadth has hitherto been slightly underemphasized. I mean, of course, the chain I have baptized the paradigm of means of locomotion. Its terms have the advantage of covering the field of the syntagm where it takes shape from one end to the other, thus constituting a true framework for the segment, one that, except for a few divergences, coincides with the framework constituted by the regulated system of alternations and interruptions. This is, as it were, to complete the analysis by recommencing it, through a sort of imaginary adjacency of all the previous operations. And because of the privilege thus conceded to one system, however prevalent it may be, among a plurality of systems, it is also to undo the illusion of analytic exhaustiveness: we think we have analyzed everything and we have not, since this or that was missing from the analysis; but also because a system is not really the same if it is grasped in the displacement, the fractioning of its ungraspable exhaustiveness, or if it is grasped for itself, in an ideal closure, as real as it is illusory. Which is to recognize that analysis may need a number of strategies to do justice to that strangely relative truth at stake between the text that serves as its pretext and the text that it becomes.

27. Three levels specifically determine the hierarchization of the elements in this chain: the nature, number, and order of the vehicles; their movements according to the two axes and four directions established by the intersection of the highway and the byroad; and the characters that get in and out of them. This third level, determinant despite the scarcity of instances, immediately brings into play via the characters, essentially via Thornhill, their looks, his look, and from there unreels the whole skein that takes us from the look to its loss, from alternation to its interruption, to the conjunction of subject and object, of characters and means of locomotion. This to emphasize, if that were necessary, the castrating blow of the chisel inflicted by the exhaustion of a code or system on the text in which it is inscribed. But this surplus-value operation is also the one that we perform when we read, or analyze, a text, and that the text itself carries out, as it were against itself, precisely because it is multiple.

The first bus appears in the distance in x in shot 1 and disappears in x' after stopping to let Thornhill off.

The first car repeats this movement of appearance and disappearance in shots 13 and 17, from x to x'. Between the car and the bus a double divergence is inscribed: a divergence in character (or in stopping, as the two constantly coincide, except in the case of the airplane) and in vehicle.

In shots 21, 23, 25, 27, and 29, the second car follows a path exactly opposite to that of the first car. The differentiation from the bus is reinforced by this symmetry to the extent that this second car and the one immediately preceding it constitute a closed subset.

The first truck, which follows it from shot 28, accentuates the opening of the system. It arrives in x, like the bus and the first car, which, however, it does not resemble; but unlike the three vehicles that precede, it does not disappear on the opposite axis and thus leaves an empty term in x' in the balancing of the systems whose constraining force has already been suggested by the subset of the two cars. In response to this balancing, we might be tempted to consider the appearance of the truck in x and the disappearance of the bus in x' as mirror images of one another. But that would just be to isolate all the more vividly shot 1, which endows direction x with a supernumerary term, not to mention the difference that continues to be inscribed, through the bus, at the level of character.

The appearance of the third car in shot 35 marks a radical opening up of the system. It adds the axis yy' of the dirt byroad to the axis xx' of the highway that it crosses. This major divergence is reinforced by a minor one: after stopping, the car makes a U-turn in shot 47 to take the same road it came on in y'. Even if we do not really see it leave, this beginning of a movement is enough to distinguish it both from the bus and the first two cars, which we see traveling along the whole length of axis xx', and from the truck that continues its course virtually in x'. On the other hand, in one respect it reiterates the first bus, in relation to which it is on the other hand in a maximally differential position (in kind of object, in axis, in length of path). Just as Thornhill got out of the bus to station himself at the side of the highway in AA', the man gets out of the car and stops at the side of the highway in BB'.

Like the arrival of the second car in the wake of the first, the arrival of the second bus in shots 59, 63, and 64 allows a relative closure of the system whose differential expansion was emphasized by the third car. Indeed, it strictly inverts the first bus. While the latter arrived in x and left in x', the former arrives in x' and leaves in x. On the other hand, the man who got out of the third car gets onto this bus, as Thornhill got out of the first bus. This effect of inverted symmetry thus constitutes the two buses as a subset, by means of an element that contributes to the radical differentiation of the subset "cars," until this point symmetrically closed upon itself through the first two cars.

It is on the transverse axis yy' introduced by the third car that the airplane will be deployed. As we can see on the schematic table, its paths are, of course, less systematizable than those of the other vehicles and are defined by the rectilinear layout of the highway and the byroad. But we can still assign them directions with relative precision. This is what is emphasized in the first attack in shots 66 and 67 by Thornhill's look and position and the slight pan that inscribes the airplane's arrival on the axis of the dirt byroad in y. In fact, the airplane's paths depend virtually as much on the definition within the frame of the byroad's axes as on their actual trajectories. This first attack coincides with the last of the four directions defined by the intersection of the highway and the byroad. From the first moment, then, the airplane produces the maximum extension of the system at the level of axes and compensates for an asymmetry introduced into the subset "cars" by the divergent arrival of the third car; but it does so while accentuating this asymmetry through the displaced overlapping effect thus marked among the elements of the paradigm.

Let us see how the elements are organized through the two successive airplane attacks in series 11 and 12. Thornhill sees the airplane that headed toward him from y disappear in y'. Then he sees it come back the other way in y', still along the axis of the byroad. But in contrast the airplane does not depart in y, as we would expect from the inverse symmetry of the two attacks that reiterate along this new axis the opposed paths of the two successive cars along the xx' axis. In shot 83, the airplane in fact leaves obliquely over the fields, in a direction that can be approximately defined as $yA'x'$. This divergence, which thus prevents us from really collapsing together the two successive airplane attacks, on the other hand reinforces the divergence previously constituted by the arrival of the third car in terms of the axes, since the first departure of the airplane corresponds to a single arrival of the airplane in y, the second arrival of the airplane to the arrival of the third car, all in y'.

The arrival of a fourth car is interposed between the second and third airplane attacks. This has three structural effects. First, it reestablishes at the level of number the symmetry of the subset "cars." Second, like the first two cars and in opposition to the third, it arrives on the highway. But, like the third, we see only its arrival; a similarity that is immediately undermined by a difference: it continues its path virtually along the axis of the highway, whereas the third makes a U-turn and leaves virtually the same way it came. Finally, this fourth car increases the privilege accorded the direction it takes from the beginning of the segment: like the truck, it arrives in x without disappearing in x'.

The third airplane attack takes place from y, according to the same process of narrative acceleration. It is not until shot 94, after Thornhill has seen the cornfield in place of the airplane, that we see it flying above him in the distance as he flees along the byroad. His position is certainly less easy to define than it is in shot 83 at the end of the second attack, where he leaves obliquely in respect to the highway in the direction $yA'x'$. But it seems fair to assume that he is moving in the direction $y'Bx$, which inverts, along an imaginary median axis, the direction of shot 83, whose displaced function is fulfilled by shot 94. Balance is thus reestablished between the directions in the subset "airplane," but at the price of an imbalance between the arrivals and departures along the central axes, since to two departures in y' correspond one departure and one arrival in y. Not to mention, of course, the divergence that continues to be inscribed at the level of the directions themselves by the arrival of the third car in y'.

The two airplane attacks that then occur one after another over the cornfield are distinctive in that they are enacted outside the frame specifically delimited by the intersection of the highway and the byroad. The presence of a line of telephone poles stretching away into the distance at the left of the immovable frame of shots 99, 101, and 103 confirms that they take place parallel to the highway, along the edge of the cornfield that borders it. These two attacks situate the airplane along the longitudinal axis reserved until now for the multiple category "bus-car-truck"; they thus fulfill a contrastive function of the same type as the third car opening, for automotive vehicles the yy' axis subsequently strictly reserved for the evolutions of the airplane. But the price, of course, is a double asymmetry: the two attacks do not really take place on the axis of the highway; furthermore, their similar paths are reduced by the constancy of a single framing (tied to Thornhill's postponed look): the airplane starts from a point in *xB*, arrives in *x'B'* above the corn and leaves at the top of the frame. Thus we cannot make a strict division between arrival and departure, since the airplane's passage is not divided in relation to Thornhill's look or even to his position. However, the direction of the attacks from *x* to *x'* in itself defines the preference accorded to arrival by the mise-en-scène, further increasing the imbalance that causes the majority of the operations and particularly the arrivals of the vehicles to be concentrated around direction *x*.

Like the second bus, the second truck to appear opens and closes a subset within the paradigm. But the two buses are organized according to an effect of inverted symmetry. Here there is nothing of the sort, but rather a no less systematic effect of repetition. Arriving in *x*, the second truck repeats the arrival of the first. And its departure, of course, does not take place—no more or even less than the first truck's departure, postponed by the arrival of the third car—since it stops as it knocks Thornhill down and explodes on the impact of the airplane. But a divergence is inscribed between the two trucks: two men get out, as Thornhill got off the first bus and the man got out of the third car.

The airplane's final arrival is not as strictly transverse as are the first three, on both sides of the highway over the byroad. This is explained by the variation of Thornhill's position and the previous movements of the airplane over the cornfield. But it can still be assimilated to them without too much systemic artificiality, if only because of the almost exact return to the framing used in series 35–47 for the arrival of the third car. Closing the circle of means of locomotion on the *yy'* axis with the accident, this return accentuates the constitutive asymmetry that, sliding into the heart of the repetition, binds together this series of operations. It can be schematically summarized as follows:

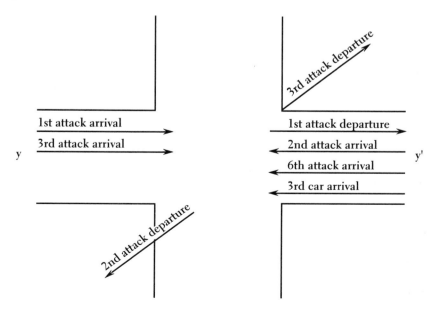

Here we see that:

a. airplane attacks 1, 2, 3, and 6 are symmetrically organized in pairs in y and y' in terms of arrivals, but

b. the departures progressively undercut the rigorous symmetry of the first attack, either by marking a distortion of the paths with respect to the axis (departures 2 and 3) or by being postponed by the exigencies of the action (sixth attack); and

c. the car implicated in the subset "airplane" doubly accentuates this imbalance, increasing on the one hand the number of arrivals, on the other the advantage accorded direction y'.

Let us examine on the other hand how the elements are organized along the xx' axis with the appearance of the last elements of the paradigm: the two cars arriving in x' just when the airplane and the truck collide, allowing Thornhill, who steals the first one and leaves in x', to close the segment thus by absconding from the mise-en-scène of which he has been the victim. We can schematize the series of operations performed along the xx' axis in the same way.

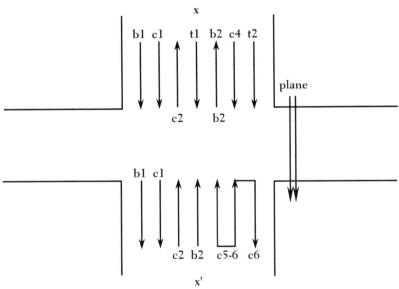

The last cars clearly make it possible to redress the marked asymmetry that has favored direction x from the outset. We might even believe for a moment that a perfect overall equivalence has been achieved: at the price of an inverse divergence between the number of arrivals and the number of departures, it would redress the manifest divergences between the automotive vehicles (excluding the two buses), the cars thus compensating for the missing truck in x'. But this equivalence is not altogether without artifice; it suggests an illusion of symmetry only the more surely to bring out the many asymmetries that haunt it:

a. The first lies in the unequal number of arrivals and departures: 9 versus 5, according to a movement recalling that of the yy' axis. After the first bus and the first two cars, the arrivals, as on the yy' axis after the first two airplane attacks, are more numerous than the departures, in a process of acceleration that logically governs the progression of the segment and contributes to the effect of suspense. (Logically speaking, we can also find this progression at the level of the characters, in the imbalance between the motions of getting in and getting out. For two characters who get into vehicles, Thornhill and the man, the latter onto the second bus, the former into the pickup truck, four get out: Thornhill from the first bus and the man from the third car, in a chiastic symmetry; but also the drivers who get out of the second truck as the farmer and the other people do from the two final cars.)

b. This equivalence does not take into account the two successive airplane attacks over the cornfield. Hardly reducible to such strict terms, they nonetheless increase the privilege accorded both direction x and the arrivals. As we have seen, in this respect they play a comparable and inverse part to that of the third car, which similarly accentuates the imbalance inscribed in the airplane attacks along the yy' axis.

c. Finally, the two last cars arrive one behind the other in shot 131. A single axis thus delimits two arrivals that are really only one. This divergence, which introduces a kind of irresolution into the relation between symmetry and asymmetry, is sharply accentuated by the fact that the clustered arrival of the two cars is not like that of the previous vehicles. To varying but hardly opposing degrees, they all appear or disappear in the distance, defined on the horizon by each of the four directions. Here the two cars are already quite near and ready to stop by the time we see them one behind the other at the side of the highway.

The segment thus involves two buses, two trucks, six cars, and one airplane. The singularity of the airplane is striking. In the numerical symmetry that governs the three other means of locomotion, there is a very slight divergence: the car in which Thornhill leaves is a pickup truck; it introduces a kind of classificatory ambiguity between cars and trucks, in kind and number. Finally, the succession of the elements of the paradigm reveals a remarkable arrangement. It can be broken down as follows, leaving aside the airplane attacks:

$$
\begin{array}{l}
\text{bus} \\
\qquad \left. \begin{array}{l} \text{car} \\ \text{car} \end{array} \right\} \ \text{(successive)} \\
\qquad\qquad\qquad \text{truck} \\
\text{bus} \dots\dots\dots\dots \overset{\text{car}}{\underset{\text{car}}{}} \dots\dots\dots\dots \text{airplane} \\
\qquad\qquad\qquad \text{truck} \\
\qquad \left. \begin{array}{l} \text{car} \\ \text{car} \end{array} \right\} \ \text{(grouped)}
\end{array}
$$

This schema emphasizes, first, that the paradigm is organized according to a relatively strict rhyme, around a division into two parts, the second duplicating the first and demonstrating two divergences: on the one hand an inversion of order since the first two cars in the first part of the segment precede the truck and in the second follow it; on the other, the first two cars arrive consecutively, while the last arrive together. In this rhyme, the airplane has no place. But we can note that it comes into play at the very moment that, with the arrival of the bus, the second flap of the segment opens, at the level of the paradigm. This correlation is sharply emphasized in shots 60–63 by an arrangement which, starting from the alternation of the look and going beyond it, alternates vision of the airplane and vision of the bus until the disappearance of the bus and the first airplane attack.

The segment is thus divided upon itself from the moment of the appearance of the airplane, a unique term in the paradigm of means of locomotion, and by the rhyme then established as a reprise of all the other elements of the paradigm. This division established on the basis of the paradigm of means of locomotion exactly confirms the division that allowed us to locate a center in the segment by the articulation of three sets of elements systematically distributed between the beginning, middle, and end of the segment. On the other hand, the segment is further divided upon itself starting from this point as soon as it becomes necessary to define the vehicles in their occurrences and numbers: during the second part, the six airplane attacks are inscribed in the succession of the other elements of the paradigm. The specific treatment given from its appearance to the only element in the paradigm external to the rhyme thus opposes it, by a kind of alternation and rhyme, to the elements that on the other hand themselves organize the second part on an almost exact model of the first. This movement of division underpins the progression of the segment, its suspense; it allows the repetition of the rhyme on the basis of the difference that undermines it, and makes out of the difference between the two series of events within the paradigm, in the second part, the difference that orders the two parts in the very movement of their repetition.

Now I have to confess that the airplane arrives in shot 9, making on the horizon at the left of frame the same short fragment of a trajectory that it performs in shot 57, when it appears to the man's look. This is the fate of analysis: the print I was able to work on was too dirty or too mutilated for me to see it. By a sort of fate, this positioning can only refine the system as any new element would. First, it introduces a variation in the neutrality of Thornhill's four "empty visions" within series 4b–12a. It also provides a rhyme, in which a radical effect of variation is all the more logically inscribed, for shot 57, in which Thornhill does not see the airplane that the man points out to him. Next, it drops a clue, made to be forgotten but introducing a sort of narrative trouble once it acquires its value as clue. Finally, in doing this, it produces a rhyme between the two parts of the segment, since the airplane appears in the first as it does in the second, but to the advantage of an extreme asymmetry, which thus contrasts all the more with the even distribution of the other vehicles, whose alternation with the airplane then ensures a rigorous progression of the segment.

1a   1b

2a   2b

3a   3b

4a   4b

5a   5b

6a   6b

7a   7b

8a   8b

9a   9b

10a   10b

11a   11b

12a   12b

13a   13b

14a   14b

15a   15b

16a

16b

17a

17b

18a

18b

19a

19b

20a

20b

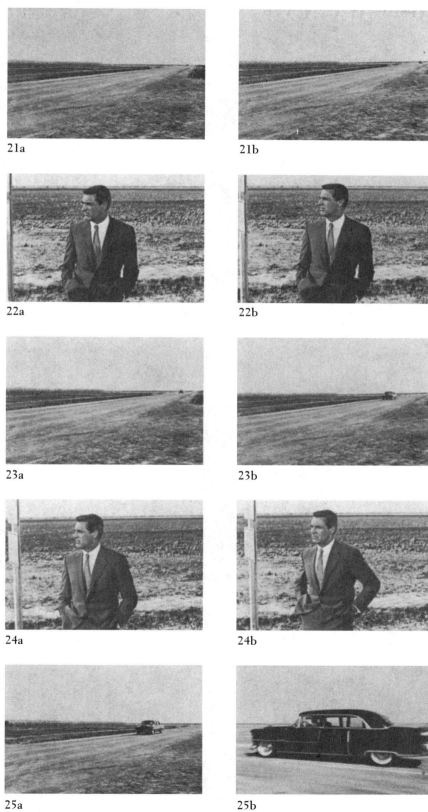

21a

21b

22a

22b

23a

23b

24a

24b

25a

25b

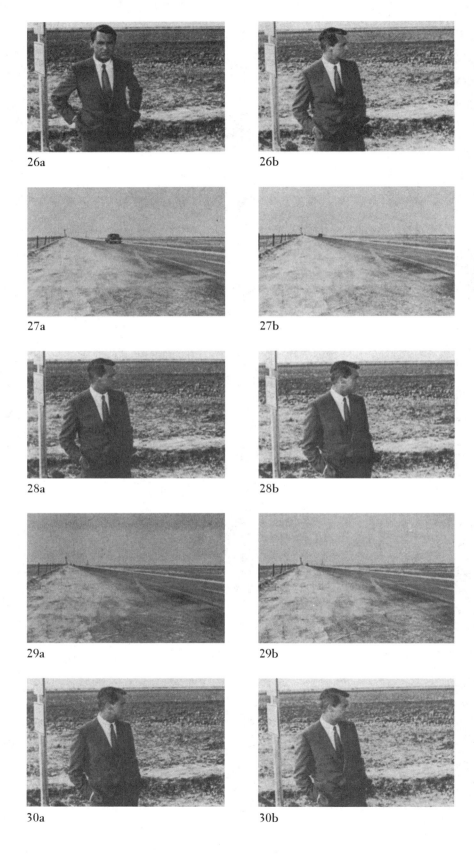

26a

26b

27a

27b

28a

28b

29a

29b

30a

30b

31a   31b

32a   32b

33a   33b

34a   34b

35a   35b

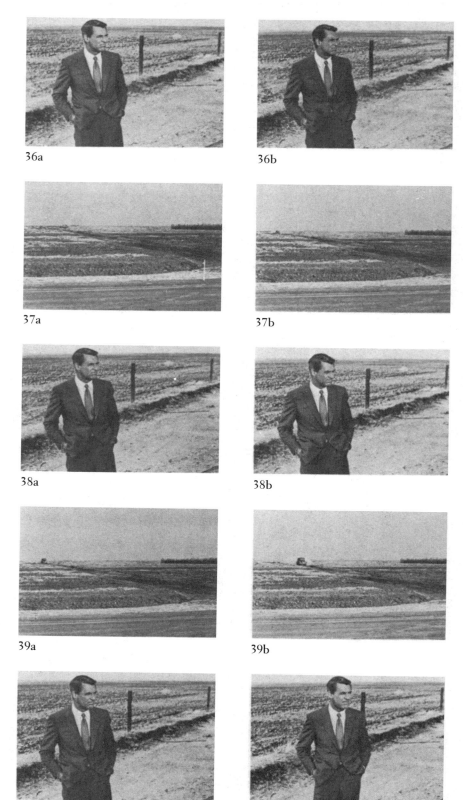

36a

36b

37a

37b

38a

38b

39a

39b

40a

40b

41a

41b

42a

42b

43a

43b

44a

44b

45a

45b

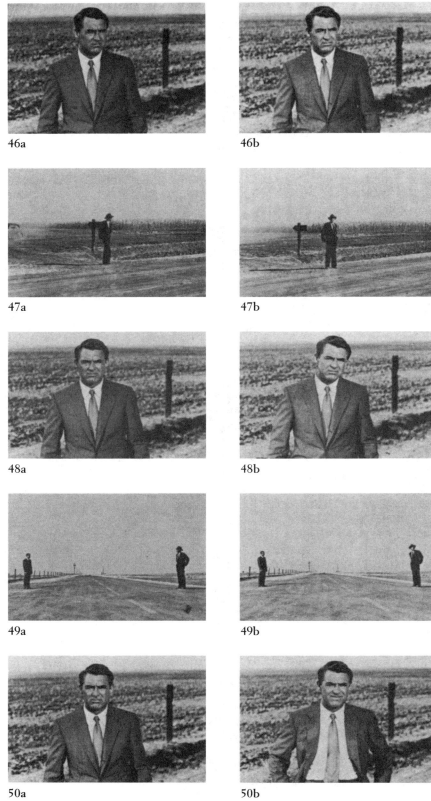

46a

46b

47a

47b

48a

48b

49a

49b

50a

50b

51a

51b

52a

52b

53a

53b

54a

54b

55a

55b

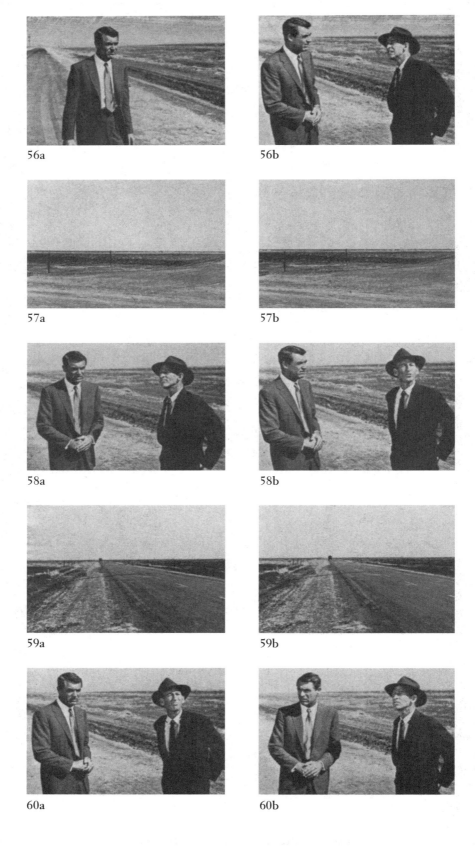

56a

56b

57a

57b

58a

58b

59a

59b

60a

60b

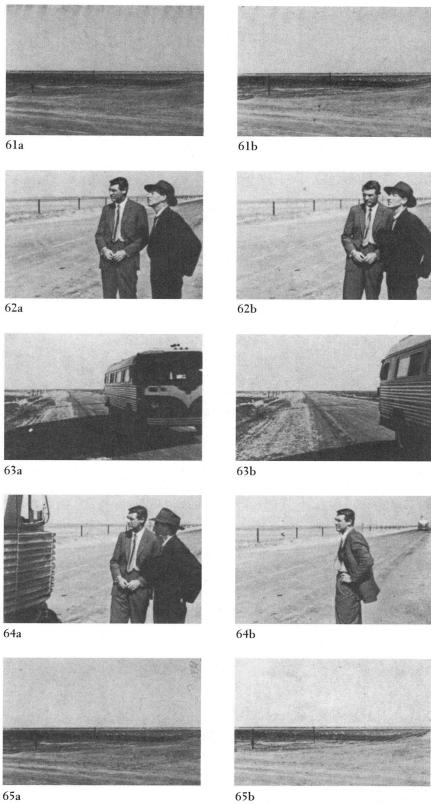

61a

61b

62a

62b

63a

63b

64a

64b

65a

65b

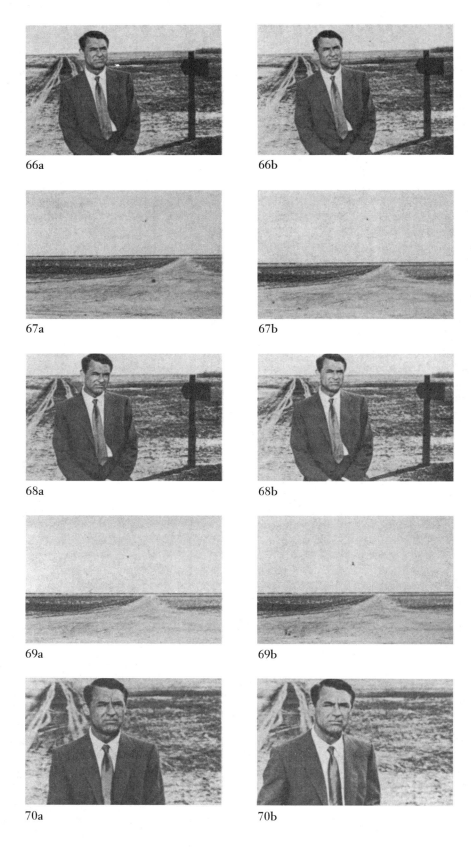

66a

66b

67a

67b

68a

68b

69a

69b

70a

70b

71a

71b

72a

72b

73a

73b

74a

74b

75a

75b

76a   76b

77a   77b

78a   78b

79a   79b

80a   80b

81a

81b

82a

82b

83a

83b

84a

84b

85a

85b

86a

86b

87a

87b

88a

88b

89a

89b

90a

90b

91a

91b

92a

92b

93a

93b

94a

94b

95a

95b

96a

96b

97a

97b

98a

98b

99a

99b

100a

100b

101a   101b

102a   102b

103a   103b

104a   104b

105a   105b

106a 106b

107a 107b

108a 108b

109a 109b

110a 110b

111a

111b

112a

112b

113a

113b

114a

114b

115a

115b

116a

116b

117a

117b

118a

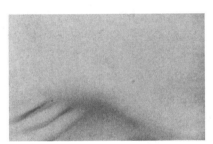

118b

119a

119b

120a

120b

121a

121b

122a

122b

123a

123b

124a

124b

125a

125b

126a

126b

127a

127b

128a

128b

129a

129b

130a

130b

131a

131b

132a

132b

133a

133b

SERIES

1. The first bus	1 – 4a
2. The highway, the fields	4b – 12a
3. The first car	12a – 18a
4. The highway, the fields	18b – 20a
5. The second car	20b – 29
6. The first truck	29 – 34a
7. The third car	34b – 41
8. The man	42 – 56
9. The man, the airplane, and the second bus	56 – 64a
10. The second bus and the airplane	64b – 65
11. The first airplane attack	66 – 78
12. The second airplane attack	79 – 84a
13. The fourth car	84b – 88
14. The third airplane attack	88b – 91a
15. The cornfield (and the airplane)	91b – 98
16. The fourth airplane attack	98b – 99
17. The fifth airplane attack	100 – 105a
18. The second truck	105b – 108
19. The truck and the plane	108 – 111
20. The second truck	112 – 120
21. The truck and the plane	120 – 126
22. The farmer and the other people, the fifth and sixth cars	127 – 133

PARADIGM OF MEANS OF LOCOMOTION
IN SEGMENT 14

bus 1   Thornhill gets out

                (the airplane)

    car 1

    car 2

        truck 1

    car 3   The man gets out

bus 2   The man gets in

            the airplane → attack 1

                 attack 2

    car 4

                 attack 3

                 attack 4

                 attack 5

        truck 2   The drivers get out

                 attack 6

    car 5   The occupants get out

    car 6   Thornhill gets in

INTERRUPTIONS OF ALTERNATION	/1/ /2/	ALTERNATIONS — SEEING/SEEN	UNSEEING/UNSEEN SEEING/UNSEEN
		2b T/the bus	
		4a	
		4b T/the highway, the fields	
		12a	
		12b T/a car	
		18a	
		18b T/the highway, the fields	
		20a	
		20b T/a second car	
		29a	
		28 T/a truck	
		32	
T-TRUCK	33		
T-TRUCK (with dust)	34a		
		34b T/a third car, then a man (43)	
		48	
T-MAN	49 (50)		
		50 T/the man	
		56a	
			56b T-MAN
		56b T-MAN/the airplane, the bus, the airplane, the bus 63	
			64a T-MAN-BUS
		64b T-BUS FAR/the airplane	
		65	
		66 T/the airplane	
		72a	
			72b T bottom of frame
T-AIRPLANE	73a		
		73b T/the airplane	
		81a	
			81b T bottom of frame
T-AIRPLANE	82a		
		82b T/the airplane	
		84a	
		84b T/a fourth car	
		86a	
			86b T gets up

INTERRUPTIONS OF ALTERNATION		ALTERNATIONS SEEING/SEEN		UNSEEING/UNSEEN SEEING/UNSEEN
T-CAR	87 88a			
		88b T/the airplane	89	
T-AIRPLANE	90			
T-AIRPLANE (with bullets)	91			
		91b T/the cornfield	93a	
				93b T gets up
T-AIRPLANE	94 95			
T-THE CORN	96–98a			
				98b T in thecorn(seeing) /the airplane over the corn(unseen) 104a
T-THE AIRPLANE (with powder)	104b 105a			
		105b T/a second truck	107a	
				107b T gets up and exits from the frame
T-TRUCK	108			
				108 T-TRUCK/the airplane
		112 T/the truck	118a	
				118b T falls until he leaves bottom of frame
T-TRUCK	119 120a			
		120b T-TRUCK/TRUCK- AIRPLANE	121	
T-TRUCK-AIRPLANE	122 123 124			
				(124 THE TRUCK-THE AIRPLANE/countershot 130)
		130b FARMER-TRUCK- AIRPLANE/T-CARS	132a	
				132b The farmer exits from the frame
FARMER-CAR (T)	133			

SEGMENTS		ACTIONS	MEANS OF LOCOMOTION	
1		Rush hour in Manhattan: Madison Avenue. Two women have difficulty getting into a taxi. A man (Hitchcock) raps on the doors of a bus, which have closed in front of him.	taxi bus	transit (−) transit (−)
2	a	T. and his secretary: they leave an office building and get into a taxi that takes them to the Plaza Hotel. T. gets out.	elevator (inside) taxi (inside)	arrival transit
	b	The lobby and the bar of the Plaza. The name Kaplan and the mistake: T. is kidnapped by Vandamm's hit men.		
	c	Through the city: T. between the two hit men in the car.	car (inside)	departure
3	a	The Townsend estate: T. between the two hit men.	car (inside)	arrival
	b	The Townsend house: from the lawn to the library.		
	c	In the library: T., Vandamm, and Leonard; the mistake continues. Leonard and the two hit men make T. drunk.		
4		On the road (night). T. escapes from the hit men. Chase between the two cars, which ends with an accident engineered by T. and the arrival of a police car.	cars (outside-inside) police car	transit (+) transit (−)
5		At the police station, T. telephones his mother. Sergeant Klinger, the doctor.		
6		In the courtroom, T., his mother, and his lawyer. Judges and policemen. Further inquiries are granted.		
7	a	The Townsend estate. T., his mother, his lawyer, and policemen arrive in front of the house.	car (outside)	arrival
	b	The Townsend house. From the lawn to the library.		
	c	In the library. "Mrs. Townsend" fools the police and T.		
	d	From the library to the lawn. They leave.	car (outside)	departure
8	a	T. and his mother arrive at the Plaza Hotel.	taxi (outside)	arrival
	b	In the lobby. T.'s mother asks for the key to Kaplan's room.		
	c	In the corridors and in Kaplan's room. T. makes inquiries about Kaplan. Arrival of Vandamm's hit men.		
	d	In the elevator and in the lobby. T. escapes from the hit men.	elevator (inside)	transit
	e	T. and then the hit men take taxis.	T. taxi (inside) hit men taxi (outside)	departure

SEGMENTS		ACTIONS	MEANS OF LOCOMOTION	
9	a	The two taxis arrive one after the other at the United Nations building.	T. taxi (inside) hit men taxi (outside)	arrival
	b	The United Nations building (inside). T. meets Townsend and interrogates him. Townsend is murdered by Valerian.	Taxi (outside)	departure
	c	T. escapes.		
10	a	Offices of the CIA. The entranceway.		
	b	Offices of the CIA (inside). The Professor and his colleagues discuss the story of T., accused of the murder of Townsend, and reveal that Kaplan is an imaginary character whom they have invented.		
11	a	The concourse of the New York rail station. T. telephones his mother. He is recognized by a ticket clerk and breaks through the ticket barrier.	airplane (evoked)	
	b	The station platform. T. boards the Chicago train and meets Eve, who misleads the police and rescues him.	train (inside)	departure
12	a	T. and Eve in the restaurant car. First seduction. She alerts him to the arrival of the police.	train (outside to inside)	transit (+)
	b	Eve's sleeper. T. is hidden while the police interrogate Eve.	train (inside)	
	c	The train.	train (outside)	
	d	Eve's sleeper (night). The seduction: the kiss.	train (outside to inside)	
	e	Eve's sleeper. T. hides in the washroom while the steward makes the bed. He looks at Eve's razor and shaving brush.	train (inside)	
	f	Eve's sleeper. The kiss (continued).	train (inside)	
	g	The steward takes Vandamm a note from Eve, which reveals their complicity.	train (inside)	
13	a	The Chicago station. Eve and T., disguised as a redcap, walk along the platform. The police look for T. among the redcaps.	train (inside)	(arrival)
13	b	T. shaves in the toilet with Eve's razor.		
	c	The station concourse. Eve telephones Leonard, who then returns to Vandamm.		
	d	The station concourse. Eve transmits "Kaplan's" instructions to T.		

Segments		Actions	Means of Locomotion	
14	a	The prairie. T. arrives for his meeting with Kaplan. He is attacked by an airplane, manges to avoid it, and leaves again in a pickup truck after bringing about a collision between the airplane and a truck.	bus (outside)	arrival
			car (outside)	transit (—)
			car (outside)	transit (—)
			truck (outside)	transit (—)
			bus (outside)	transit (—)
			plane (outside)	transit
			car (outside)	transit (—)
			truck (outside)	transit (—)
			car (outside)	transit (—)
			pickup (outside)	departure
15	a	The police find the stolen pickup truck. T. in front of the Ambassador Hotel in Chicago.	pickup (outside)	(arrival)
	b	The lobby. T. asks the clerk for information about Kaplan. He spots Eve and follows her.	elevator (outside)	transit
	c	The hotel corridors. Eve's room: she plays a trick on him and escapes without learning that he has seen through all her tricks.		
16	a	T. arrives in front of the auction gallery.	taxi (outside)	arrival
	b	In the gallery. He finds Eve, Vandamm, and Leonard. The Professor is among those attending the auction. T. makes a scene so the police are called, which allows him to escape from Valerian.		
	c	T. leaves between two policemen.	police car (inside)	departure
17	a	The police car arrives at the airport.	police car (outside)	arrival
	b	The Professor takes T. and leads him to a waiting airplane. He reveals all the ins and outs of the story to him and asks his assistance in exculpating Eve in Vandamm's eyes.	airplane	(departure)
18	a	The Mount Rushmore cafeteria. On the terrace, T. and the Professor. T. looks at the Monument's four presidents carved into the cliff.		
	b	The cafeteria (inside). T., Vandamm, Eve, and Leonard. Faced with T.'s proposition to hand her over, Eve shoots him and escapes by car while the Professor takes care of T.	car (outside)	departure
	c	The cafeteria. The parking lot. The Professor has T. loaded into an ambulance.	ambulance (outside)	departure

Segments		Actions	Means of Locomotion	
19		Woods. The Professor helps T. out of the ambulance. Eve is beside her car. They explain themselves. T. discovers that the Professor has tricked him and wishes to retain Eve, who runs away. T. is knocked out by the Professor's driver.	ambulance (outside) Eve's car (outside) Eve's car (outside)	(arrival) (arrival) departure
20	a	Hospital room. T. and the Professor, who believes T.'s feigned repentance.		
	b	T. escapes from the hospital by climbing out of the window and through a woman's room.		
21	a	T. arrives in the neighborhood of Vandamm's house.	taxi (outside)	arrival
	b	Valerian arrives, is seen by T.	car (outside)	transit (—)
	c	T., outside the window, hears the conversation inside the house. Eve, Vandamm, and Leonard speak of their forthcoming departure. Then Leonard reveals Eve's plot to Vandamm; he decides to kill her on the plane. T. learns that microfilms are concealed in the pre-Columbian statuette.		
	d	T. climbs into Eve's bedroom and manages to warn her.		
	e	Vandamm, Eve, Leonard, and Valerian make their way to the airstrip. T. is delayed by the housekeeper. When they arrive at the airplane, T. speeds up in a car, Eve grabs the statuette and runs to him pursued by Leonard and Valerian. She jumps into the car, which they have to abandon almost immediately.	plane car (outside)	
	f	Woods. Eve and T. run, pursued by Leonard and Valerian.		
	g	Eve and T. arrive on top of Mt. Rushmore. Valerian is pushed over the edge by T.; Leonard is shot down by a policeman just as he is about to push T. off together with Eve, whom T. is holding. T. pulls Eve slowly up the rock face.		
22	a	A sleeper. T. helps Eve climb into the upper bunk.	train (inside)	transit (+)
	b	The train enters a tunnel.	train (outside)	

IV. MULTIPLE PARADIGM

The fact that the airplane thus emerges as the only irreducible element within a paradigm in which all the other elements refer to each other according to a strictly hierarchized network of correspondences, the fact that it alone carries the threat of death attached to Thornhill, further radicalizes the effect of symbolization ushered in by the inscription of the segment in the second movement of the film. Let us recall the segments that came before and after it: on the one hand the scene on the train, where the threat of castration takes shape for Thornhill in Eve's seduction; on the other hand the two scenes in the Ambassador Hotel and at the auction, where threats of death, seduction, and castration culminate in the image of Eve and Vandamm together.

The airplane as symbol of castration: before and after *North by Northwest*, this image resonates in Hitchcock's work. It first appears in a displaced form that is a nice example of the intertextual unconscious. In 1935, Hitchcock very freely adapts John Buchan's novel *The Thirty-Nine Steps*. He cuts out some fundamental aspects of the plot, which will be reinjected into *Foreign Correspondent* some five years later. Among many other things, he does not use one situation sketched in Buchan's narrative. The hero, alone on a deserted heath, is spied on by an airplane; without actually attacking him, it comes dangerously close the second time it appears: "It [. . .] began to circle round the knot of hill in narrowing circles, just as a hawk wheels before it pounces."[17] One thinks, of course, of the scene in *North by Northwest*, displaced and systematized from one film to the other. In Buchan's narrative, this abortive attack immediately precedes the moment when Hannay, in an isolated farmhouse, finds himself face to face with the head of a German spy ring. In Hitchcock's film, soon after this same scene of chase and wandering from which the airplane is absent, the hero takes refuge at a Scottish notable's house and explains that he is looking for a gang of spies whose leader is identifiable by the little finger missing from his left hand. When the man asks, "Are you sure it isn't the right?" we are shown the striking image of his raised hand, with the missing finger standing out against the bright light of a windowpane. Through this detective-story clue, Hannay finds himself facing the symbolic image of his own castration, conveyed throughout the film by the relationship formed around him by the woman and death, until the inevitable positivity of the ending. Two superimposable and complementary representations are thus displaced from one film onto another, articulated from the starting point of a novel lacking any real symbolic charge. To close this retrospective excursus with the beginnings of a system, we could even bring in *Foreign Correspondent*, which borrows part of its theme from Buchan's novel. Here again we find an airplane; when it plunges into the sea, the death of the father provides an ending to both the politico-detective-story scenario that makes him a Nazi spy, and the symbolic scenario: from this point on, the hero need no longer share the place of this too-much-loved father next to the heroine.

After *North by Northwest*, the airplane is transformed into a bird. The first time is in *Psycho*, through the stuffed birds artfully arranged in Norman's den. They are a metaphor for the mother's embalmed corpse, and they seem to take flight from the moment Norman's psychotic body becomes its living envelope: draped in a long dress and wearing a wig, his arms wide-stretched as he brandishes the huge theatrical knife that returns onto the body of the other the symbolic wound that tears him apart, Norman resembles a giant bird. It is on this basis that the bird assumes the function of generalized metaphor in *The Birds*: it takes on the whole collected weight of suspense and enigma, and beyond it the whole symbolic charge of the narrative it defines, in which it only materializes the savage elementarity of desire in proportion to the regulated fatality that implicates it in the symbolic straits of Oedipus and of castration.

But in *North by Northwest*, the threat of death and the accompanying threat of castration are not restricted to the airplane, even if it is their most perfect embodiment. The hit men first try to kill Thornhill with a car, at night, by pushing it off a seaside cliff with him almost dead drunk inside. Furthermore, the airplane is not univocally linked to the threat of death. It does, to be sure, repeat this threat twice, thus providing at the level of the textual system as a whole the rhyme missing for the airplane in the restricted textual system of segment 14. It is repeated in a minor key when Thornhill, on the telephone with his mother in the New York train station, must justify his preference for trains over airplanes ("You want me to jump off a moving plane?"). It is repeated, now in the major key, near the end of the third movement when, through a parallelism whose weight as symbolic substitution has already been emphasized, Eve must escape the threat enunciated by Vandamm, who plans to push her out of the plane in which they are to fly off. But an opposition is quite naturally inscribed in this subset of the airplane, turning its negativity into positivity: it is on an airfield that the Professor reveals the machinations around Kaplan, and it is in the landing lights of an airplane that Thornhill decides to board it in order to ward off the threat of death directed at Eve. This set of relations, which demonstrate yet again how symmetry and asymmetry are hierarchized at every level of the textual system, can be set out as follows:

1. *Airplane* (not seen, mentioned on the phone) Thornhill might fictitiously have to jump out of it if he took it.

2. *Airplane* that tries to assassinate Thornhill.

———
———

3. *Airplane* that Thornhill takes to go to rescue Eve. It arrives at the airfield.

4. *Airplane* Eve will really be thrown from if she takes it. It arrives at the airfield.

The rescuing airplane and the murderous car thus undo any semantic or symbolic univocality of representation. They emphasize the necessity of conceiving the paradigm of means of locomotion in richer and more differentiated terms, from the moment we bring into consideration the film as a whole in which it has a no less noteworthy extension.

If one thinks about it, the means of locomotion in segment 14, except for the airplane, are almost all marked by a coefficient of uncertainty that makes each in turn or sometimes all together really or virtually serve the threat of death or the saving mediation. After the arrival of the bus and before the arrival of the airplane, from Thornhill's point of view, they may each herald the arrival of Kaplan, and from the spectator's, the threat of death held over Thornhill by the telephone conversation between Eve and Leonard. After the arrival of the airplane, they all represent for both Thornhill and the spectator the possibility of escape from the threat specified by the airplane. But a remarkable amalgamation affects the truck: nearly killing Thornhill, who falls between its wheels, it ultimately saves him from the increasingly inescapable aggression of the airplane. Furthermore, the initial bus and the final car are themselves ambiguous: the first because it should allow Thornhill to pay off the mortgage of the inaugural mistake but in reality leads him toward a confrontation with death; the second because it allows him to escape the scene of this confrontation, but only to carry him immediately toward the risk of its reiteration.

Such is the function imparted to most of the means of locomotion in the overall paradigm: a transitive function, which materializes and punctuates the stages of Thornhill's itinerary. *North by Northwest* is an itinerary, a route. "Let's take *North by Northwest*, which isn't based on a novel. When I start on the idea of a film like that, I see the whole film, not merely a particular place or scene, but its direction from beginning to end."[18] This is why *North by Northwest* constitutes the apogee of the chase film, what Hitchcock calls "a story that covers lots of territory."[19] If we leave out segments 5 and 6 at the police station and the courtroom (which mark the movement of the journey just begun with a half pause), segment 10 in the CIA office (the only one in which the fiction abandons Thornhill's route for a moment in order to advance its meaning), and segment 20 (which takes advantage of the contraction of a double ellipsis in respect to the movements it implies), all the other segments of the film are organized via the mediation of one or more means of locomotion. "Aside from that [the direction from beginning to end], I may not have the vaguest idea of what the picture will be about."[20] This denegation in turn summons the truth that confirms it: "I'd thought about it for a long time [. . .]. The whole film is epitomized in the title—there is no such thing as north-by-northwest on the compass. The area in which we get near to the free abstract in movie-making is the free use of fantasy, which is what I deal in."[21] The two arrows pointing in different directions that prolong the initial

"N" and the final "T" of the title in the credit sequence attest to the fact that, through this wordplay, the hero's itinerary is subject to the manifest irrationality of a symbolic direction, "its direction from beginning to end," which resolves its enigmas by a traversal of the Oedipus complex and castration.[22]

The various means of locomotion that so incessantly punctuate this itinerary thus jointly determine its material and symbolic possibility. When they are not themselves its terms, they are the mediators of this confrontation with death, which is inscribed as the dramatic and externalized form of the threat of castration in the fantasmatic race that leads Thornhill toward the conquest of the object. Nothing illustrates this better than the scene Hitchcock planned but then left out of the scenario because he could not integrate it into the action, a scene that he liked for its very "gratuitousness." In keeping with the enigma it subtends in terms of reality, it emphasizes the symbolic charge with which the means of locomotion is invested throughout the film, a metaphoric body subject to the power of death because it carries that power in itself: "I wanted to have a long dialogue scene between Cary Grant and one of the factory workers as they walk along the assembly line. They might, for instance, be talking about one of the foremen. Behind them a car is being assembled, piece by piece. Finally, the car they've seen being put together from a simple nut and bolt is complete, with gas and oil, and all ready to drive off the line. The two men look at it and say, 'Isn't it wonderful!' Then they open the door to the car and out drops a corpse! [. . .] Where had the body come from? Not from the car, obviously, since they've seen it start at zero! The corpse falls out of nowhere, you see! And the body might be that of the foreman the two fellows had been discussing."[23]

To pinpoint more precisely the symbolizing effect of the paradigm, we can start with the last shot. Without invoking the discourse of the *auteur*, we can still accept his commentary as a supplement to the text, whose denegatory character cannot fail

to evoke the interpretation glittering in it. He says, we may recall, "There are no symbols in *North by Northwest*. Oh yes! One. The last shot. The train entering the tunnel after the love scene between Grant and Eva Marie Saint. It's a phallic symbol. But you mustn't tell anyone."[24] Here "love scene" means the penultimate shot in which Thornhill draws Eve into the upper couchette of the sleeper, continuing the movement with which he snatched her from death on the slopes of Mount Rushmore. In the logical sequence of actions, the train naturally takes on this symbolic value in order to translate what the film hides from us, and at the same time to add what is at once a final term and an indispensable rhyme to the paradigm that runs through the film like a chain. In doing this, it invites us, by an effect of generalized recursiveness, to see in the chain itself as a whole the insistence of phallic symbolization that the entire film manifests as the fundamental determination of the subject who is its hero. Which is not to say, of course, that any given vehicle is magically endowed with this phallic representation. It is the chain itself as a signifying whole that, both beyond and in its purely material justifications or the internal necessities of its own systematicity, comes to take on the physical and fantasmatic itinerary of the hero and lead him progressively to this final erection in which desire triumphs in the possession of the object because in it it is at last fused with the law. This affirmation in no way contradicts the fact that certain elements of the paradigm and the paradigm as a whole serve throughout the film as metaphors for the threat of castration. I even see in this a

confirmation of phallic symbolization. This about-turn effect, which condenses the phallus and the agent of threat into the same series of figures, allows us to specify more precisely the nature of the fantasy of castration and the symbolization functions woven through the paradigm.

The threat of castration is first specified for Thornhill around Vandamm, through the substitutive projection of the image of the idealized father, which opens up a path for Thornhill to a positive identification with the symbolic father, via the fictitious murder of which he is the agent and the repeated at-
tempts at murder of which he is the object. But the threat of castration is no less specified on the woman's side: first through the mother, who occupies the place of the absent father and keeps her son in a state of infantilization that prohibits any truly reciprocal relationship; next and most importantly, because Eve, replacing the mother, reactivates the fantasies of incorporation and loss of the penis projected onto the mother all the more in that she appears as an object of rivalry in the struggle joined with the father and comes herself to send Thornhill to face death, by a seduction effect that turns her into a castrating woman. The first train, where the seduction takes place, is thus not really equivalent to the final train that forms its necessary rhyme in the overall economy of the paradigm. We can metaphorically assign a phallic role to this first train because it is one of the essential elements in the chain punctuating Thornhill's Oedipal progression; but to the extent of the threat of castration at stake in it for Thornhill through the woman, it should also, and more fundamentally, be seen as the metaphor for her sex, in which the hero cannot assure himself of his own except by running the risk of losing it. This film, which tells the story of the possession of a woman, assigns a third metaphorical dimension to the paradigm of means of locomotion: it designates both the phallus and the threat it is subject to through the woman's sex. Which again is not to say that each of the means of locomotion assumes this function of symbolization any more than it is required to assume specifically one or the other of the two previous representations, or all three together. But the singular force of this paradigm of means of locomotion lies in the condensation (longitudinal, distributed at anchorage points throughout the film) that it performs among these three determinations linked to the problematic of castration, and in the phenomenon of symbolic diffusion with which it marks from end to end all the elements of the chain that constitutes it, without ever really constraining any of them.

In this third symbolic assignment, Thornhill's whole body becomes the phallus undergoing the ordeal of castration. This explains a motif that connotes in a very special way a penetration into the inside of a means of locomotion. At the very beginning of the film, when Thornhill emerges from the elevator with his secretary and starts through the crowd, continuing to dictate his correspondence, she begs him to call a taxi. Thornhill runs up to a taxi that a man is about to get into, blithely pretends that his secretary has fallen ill, and sweeps into the car with her while thanking the bewildered man. This behavior first of all defines the hero's character, the adroit self-confidence and ruthlessness proper to his career in advertising. In this sense, his conversation with Maggie in the taxi is an insistent presentation of the artificiality of this character, of this cog in the industrial and technocratic machine

whose most alienating surface effects he so perfectly embodies. But while this feverish haste is in perfect keeping with the hero's socio-professional situation, it is also the beginning of his journey. In relation to what it brings about, it has an overdetermining value: a material haste that changes of itself into a symbolic haste, to mark clearly the trap that the hero will fall into because it is his destiny. It is in this first taxi that we see the infantilization still inflicted on Thornhill by his mother and his resultant sexual immaturity. As if this immaturity, conveyed by the fantasmatic gluttony of his note to Gretchen Sabinson, were expressed in the physical haste from which will arise, through a regulated sequence of ordeals, the possibility of an accession to the symbolic order.

This is precisely what is marked by the repetition of the process when Thornhill takes the initiative in the investigation and returns to the Plaza. Through an effect attributable to the systematic regulation of the narrative, Thornhill is this time in the elevator again with his mother, accompanied by Vandamm's two hit men. As soon as the elevator stops, he rushes into the hotel lobby, runs down the front steps, and plunges into the taxi that a couple is about to enter. This motivated haste brings about the physical separation of Thornhill from his mother, just as in the earlier scene it was supposed to ensure their meeting, since Thornhill there gave Maggie the message confirming their date for the theater that very night. At this moment, Thornhill is beginning his mad race toward Eve's body. After Townsend's murder, which is its indispensable symbolic intermediary, this haste can be seen in a new insistence on excessive penetration into means of locomotion: first into the New York–Chicago train, which Thornhill boards by breaking through the ticket barrier; second into the car that he steals after the airplane explodes, to end up, borne by the accidents of necessity, in Eve's bedroom at the Ambassador Hotel; and third and last into Valerian's car, which he jumps into in order to snatch Eve from death. It will subside with the last vehicle, which ends this reiterative sequence of accelerations. Significantly, we do not see the moment of entry (this is the only time a scene takes place inside a vehicle); it suffers no threat of either death or castration. That is why this railway sleeping car, in which Thornhill for the first time penetrates the woman's sex with a kind of symbolic obviousness, can so clearly change into a phallus—suggesting by this metaphor that one cannot have it unless one renounces being it.

This final image is all the more logically emphasized by Hitchcock insofar as it refers, by a recursive effect that begins with the first taxi Thornhill enters, to an image that precedes his first appearance. As usual, Hitchcock appears, signing the film as a body in the body of the text. But he does so strikingly, this time placing himself at the origin of the chain through an effect of radical inversion: a bus brusquely shuts its doors in his face just as he is about to board it. How could one establish a more precise relationship between this bus and the first taxi Thornhill enters by a kind of break-in, and that final calming which sets the seal on its symbolic resolution? As he will again do at the beginning of *The Birds*, where he is seen walking with a pair of poodles on a leash, Hitchcock thus emphasizes the identificatory relationship that links him to his character. A delegating identification, which provides a remarkable measure of the extent to which fiction and oeuvre partake of fantasy, and of the oeuvre as fantasy ("It's a fantasy"),[25] since in it Thornhill accomplishes what Hitchcock cannot, except by a symbolic transmission made possible by the film as imaginary discourse.

Distributed along the chain, this micro-system opposing the bus Hitchcock cannot enter to the two taxis Thornhill enters excessively displays reiterative effects in each case. The first, two shots before Hitchcock appears, shows two women trying in vain to enter a taxi; the second, just as Thornhill is usurping a taxi for the second time, shows the two hit men rushing after him down the stairs and grabbing the next taxi from the same increasingly dumbfounded couple. Thus inscribed in the paradigm, these opposing events indisputably reinforce, through the power proper to repetition mechanisms, the effect of symbolization with which the other elements in the chain are invested. They do not participate in it strictly speaking; it is impossible to implicate these two anonymous women or even so directly Vandamm's two hit men in the symbolic play that governs the distribution of representations according to Thornhill's desire (even if the hit men, representing Vandamm, are here the agents of death and through it of the threat of castration to which Thornhill is subject). But both pairs are linked to it by system, by the peculiar power of an organization which, without ever being detached from the overall system, in particular from its major narrative and symbolic determinations, is still never strictly dependent on it.

Thus the paradigm of means of locomotion is constantly and multiply diffused over the whole textual surface. Leaving aside the unmarked vehicles assembled womb-like in the opening segment and then scattered here and there at the whim of the action, the paradigm includes thirty-seven different vehicles, divided into six categories: two trains, two trucks, three buses, four airplanes (of which one, and this is the sole case, is only mentioned), twenty-three cars, which are themselves subdivided into three categories: eleven private cars, eight taxis, four police cars (two marked as such, one plain, one ambulance). Given this classification of vehicles into subsets, three pertinencies, or three levels, define their systematic inscription in the narrative syntagm. The first emphasizes the relationship (or non-relationship) among the vehicles and the characters; the second the opposition between actions taking place outside or inside the vehicle (when it becomes a setting); the third the distribution of each vehicle in the division into segments, whose validity it often confirms: the vehicle is in a position of arrival and/or departure (in which case it is almost always at the edge of a segment) or in a position of transit (in which case it may cover the whole space of the segment or only pass through it, briefly or at length).

This paradigm, which is coextensive with the film as a whole, is specified as a restricted paradigm in segment 14. There it possesses its own systematicity: its levels of organization clearly duplicate those of the paradigm as a whole; but at the cost of a generalized displacement consisting essentially in the fact that the tripartition arrival/departure/transit is modulated according to a simple opposition arrival/departure subdivided by the axial quadripartition of the highway and the byroad. This intra-segmental micro-system is thus added to the inter-segmental micro-systems that subject a certain number of elements of the overall paradigm to the systematic pressure of this or that particular determination, respectively. It thereby emphasizes the fact that the paradigm of means of locomotion reveals, within its own (vertical) system, the same polysystematic organization that segment 14 does at the level of its own (horizontal) system. But the restricted paradigm of segment 14 is not really equivalent to these micro-systems of the paradigm as a whole (let us call them sub-systems to distinguish them), some of which traverse it and thus mark the inter-systemic overlap of which any system (micro-system or sub-system) is the stake. The generalized displacement to which it is subject, its disproportionate number of vehicles (eleven of thirty-seven, in one segment out of twenty-two), the actantial subdivision concentrated on the airplane, all display not so much the effect of disconnection characteristic of every partial system but rather a true mirror effect between the restricted paradigm and the overall paradigm in which it is inscribed. This mirror effect lies in the fact that the restricted paradigm is in turn divided, within the limits of its own system, into more or less similar subsets, more or less different from those that determine the polysystematicity of the overall paradigm. In thus dividing upon itself, it is constantly inscribed deep in the body of the segment, just as the overall paradigm is constantly inscribed in the body of the film.

On the one hand, through the overall paradigm, it is the entire film as a narrative, hermeneutic, symbolic system that emerges, in the displaced progression that carries it from its beginning to its end via segment 14, which is one of its knots. It is because it takes on the whole weight of the narrative through the duplicitous image of Eve that the restricted paradigm can, at either margin, be so closely modeled on the paradigm as a whole, reflect its operations while displacing them, be referred to it by the imbalance of a rhyme — the airplane — which would be sufficient to attest to the narrative openness of a chain for which the restricted paradigm is offered as a metaphor. But in this movement, the narrative that thus crystallizes on itself, via the divided image of the paradigm that symbolizes it, is sharply illuminated in return. For, on the other hand, it is by inscribing itself in the most micro-elementary operations of the filmic text that each element of the restricted paradigm comes, via the segment, to enter the fiction, to bear it and to be caught up in it. It is one of the players in this infinitely systematic materiality of the image that produces the narrative and hierarchizes the segment from its first shot to its last. The light thus projected by the paradigm of means of locomotion through its double, superimposed inscription is that of a systematic homology, of a textual correspondence between segment and film.

In the same way that the film takes Thornhill from the inaugural elevator from which he emerges with his secretary to the final sleeper where he is united with Eve, the segment takes him from the first bus he gets off to the last car in which he disappears, pursued by the farmer. From this beginning to this end, the segment, in traversing its center, shifts in relation to itself as it incessantly hierarchizes its constitutive elements: characters, framings, vehicles, looks, fixity, movement, actions, direction, conjunction. The film does exactly the same thing through its actions, its characters, its figures, its three grand movements, its vehicles, its motifs, its segments. Just as the framing of Thornhill in series 11, 12, and 13 of the segment (the first two airplane attacks and the arrival of the fourth car) alternates between near and far and distributes this opposition unevenly among the three series, the three bedrooms corresponding to the three cities and the three hotels mapped out by Vandamm reveal in their uneven distribution through the three movements of the film an uneven division that expresses, by a divergence from similarity, the regulated difference of the narrative. (If Thornhill, borne along by his investigation and his desire, is first discovered in Kaplan's bedroom with his mother at the Plaza in New York, then with Eve in her bedroom at the Ambassador in Chicago, he does not appear in a bedroom at the Sheraton in Rapid City but rather in the hospital room, where he takes on the role of Kaplan after the simulated murder in the Mount Rushmore cafeteria. This divergence, which temporarily keeps the bedroom from being the setting for the desire inscribed by Eve and the mother in the previous scenes, immediately enables it to be reinscribed by a differential arrangement: first, when in order to leave the room in which he has been locked by the Professor, Thornhill leaves by the window and enters another bedroom where a young woman, frightened at first, tries to interrupt his flight with a heartfelt "Stop!"; second, when in order to warn Eve of the danger she is in, he goes right into her bedroom in Vandamm's house.) And just as the uneven distribution of the near/far opposition in series 11, 12, and 13 is differentially articulated with the continual gradation from farthest to nearest governing the second truck's approach in series 20, so the uneven distribution of bedrooms in the film's three movements naturally brings with it in its wake the displaced repetition of its own motif constituted by the two sleepers, where, in the second and third movement, the seduction and conquest of Eve are played out.

On the one hand a micro-system, since it is circumscribed by its (segmental) limits, tends toward the smallest units of the filmic system, takes on its entire material specificity; on the other a macro-system, since its limit is the film and, in the film, the narrative as a whole. Between the two there is a profound concordance of balancing effects: at both levels it subjects the narrative to a convergent hierarchization of symmetry and asymmetry, of repetition and difference. Everything suggests it at every moment; but strictly speaking it is not based on anything, unless it be the circular experience of textual systematicity. The paradigm of means of locomotion fixes this circularity in its very motion: by gathering in the effect of concordance between film and segment, it is both its point of reflection and its field of expansion. Through a kind of calculated artifice intrinsic to the strategy of this film as to that of the analysis that duplicates it, the two sides of the paradigm thus seem only to emerge from their respective textual bodies in order to make them fall back toward each other, projecting the exact image of that elusive object: the textual system of the film.

It emerges from it, rich in its twenty-two segments, its more than a thousand shots, from end to end and indistinctly micro-, macro-, poly-system, improbable but incessant, irrepressible, incompressible systematic body, ever one and ever fragmentary. Its image is all the more real for being more virtual. Here that image is all the more rigorous and more intense for being born of the articulation of a segmental micro-system and of that textual level so hard to define and yet so suggestive that we call the narrative system of a film. It thus designates the profound tendency of the classical film, specifically the American film, to constitute itself into scenes, into segments, whose closure guarantees systematic autonomy: to the point of perversion, to the point of turning a partial system into an almost limitless nesting of relations. But this closure is deceptive; it has no reality but to found the narrative that traverses it, feeds on it, reproduces itself in its image in order to seem in turn to close into its own system. That is why the narrative, what is usually called the narrative of a film, is always torn between pure narrative surface and the depth of the overall system. Between the two the various systems, segmental, inter- and intra-segmental, that endlessly restore the fragmented image of this depth.

It follows that in the most systematic text there is a system only because there are several systems, a plurality, an infinity of systems. For if each system generates systems inferior to it in extension, these systems—micro-systems, sub-systems, and so on to infinity, down to the most elementary relationships—never stop marking the displacement of the system in relation to itself, its subdivision onto itself, bearing witness to the fundamental irreducibility of any textual structure. In this sense we could say that there are only degrees of system and try to oppose to the system what Barthes calls the systematic. But this is because each is the condition of the other; because the text, this text, that of the classical film, is the conflictual and harmonic space of their coincidence. The relativization of the system is the condition of its absoluteness. In its effect of generalized rhyme, the system, or the systematic, subjects to itself the filmic text from end to end. Starting from the multiple systems put in play, as if beneath them, the systematic perversion of the rhyme eventually designates a kind of degree zero of the system, which is the indirect sign of its omnipotence. Hence that dizzying impression that there is no element whatsoever that does not herald a second element implying it, duplicating it, redistributing it in the glittering play of the fiction. Hence that sense of déjà-vu, of endless recognition, programmed expectation, surprise set up and deflated, that cyclic impression of an eternal return of similarity that presides over the novelistic progression of the most accomplished works of great American classicism. And so it is on the basis of the omnipotence of this effect of generalized rhyme, of the multiplicity of the systems that it supports and that sustain it, that, through a film like *North by Northwest*, we get the idea that there is a system, the mirage that makes us believe in the pressure of a unitary system imposing from top to bottom and end to end an organic hierarchization of the filmic text.

A justified mirage: it is based on the superior rhyme of the classical textual system, the one that takes control of it, carries it from its beginning to its end, assigns it an end. This rhyme has to assume the premises that it posits, the problems that it initiates, the enigma that it formulates, the lack that it reveals and that justifies it. It must repeat in order to resolve. The first words (or almost the first) of *North by*

Northwest, just as Thornhill emerges from the elevator with Maggie, emphasize a fight between the elevator operator and his wife: an interruption of dialogue and communication (Thornhill: "Say hello to the missus." Operator: "We're not talking." (2)), through which the film opens to send the hero toward the conquest of the object that allows it to be reestablished: the good object, the one that at the end of the ordeal, because the ordeal has made it good, is consecrated by the good marriage, the algebraic product and ineluctable end of the film. Between mother and wife is established the major rhyme of the narrative, without failing to rhyme with the indexical motif of the elevator operator: between Thornhill and his mother, in the same way, there is an interruption of communication: the lack of a telephone, which makes vain Thornhill's instructions to Maggie about their theater date, justifies the telegram, thrusts Kaplan into the circuit, the Name of the Father which Thornhill grasps and in which he is grasped by an ineluctable movement, the film, until Eve, at the end of the race, comes to occupy the place of the mother.

The superior rhyme of the film is that of the narrative, because in it is the rhyme of its story. The story, the signified of the narrative, is born to exceed it, projecting beyond the text an imaginary effect constituting its symbolic reference. After the film: it is the supposed eternity of marriage, of desire reconciled with the law. Before the film: the narrative constantly retreats before itself until it reaches a point that allows it to institute itself throughout as a rhyme, a response, of which its internal rhyme is the ever repeated echo and its ulterior rhyme the resolution. This retreat, made possible by the story, may go as far as myth or fantasy. "When I was a little boy. . . ." It ascends, through the two previous marriages, to the supremely insidious image of the mother. Castration anxiety, image of the phallic mother, of the phallus that she lacks, fascinated projection of the primal scene, of which the entire film constitutes the reversion, the reactivation, through the hero's entrance upon the scene of the fantasy. The theatrical metaphor takes on this simultaneously reversible and progressive relationship of before and after; it refers it to the fundamental relationship between the psychic apparatus structured according to the symbolic and the cinematic "apparatus" *(dispositif)*. Through the twin powers of repetition and identification, it joins the author-enunciator, the hero and the spectator in a single desire to see and to know—the scopic drive, endlessly reinscribing in the specularity of the cinematic spectacle the image, always one further step back, always out of reach, of the primal scene.[26]

The film is subject, subjects itself to the narrative as the subject to Oedipus. Thus it tells the story that the filmic corpus never stops rehearsing: the passage from one equilibrium to another, from a first term to a second, which repeats it and resolves it. The second train repeats the first, and in doing so resolves it: by a radical movement of elliptical contraction, of clausula, which inscribes in the filmic signifier the convergent effect of symbolization linked to the sanction of marriage and to the *jouissance* it promises, symbolized in its turn by the displacement of the last shot. This effect, a more differentiated example of which is provided by the similarly paired scenes in the hotel rooms at the Plaza and the Ambassador, is here carried by the major signifying units of the filmic system. But it is constantly inscribed and propagated down to the system's smallest signifying units, through the movement of repetition/resolution in which they are perpetually at issue. The effect is much more indirect, since this micro-elementary movement, involving all the codes specific to the materials of cinematic expression except the segmentation codes of the larger narrative units, always seems more or less to escape the narrative while never ceasing to construct it. And it does so to the point that, consigned by its very nature to be specified essentially in a step-by-step progression within relatively restricted sets, it gives the illusion of incessantly closing back upon itself, as if stricken with a sort of symbolic atopia by its material specificity and the extreme fragmentation of its semantic contents. But the indirect character of the effect of symbolization is precisely what gives it its force. This character is all the more suggestive because it is continual, irrepressible, it never ceases to produce and to reproduce, and to produce because it reproduces, the major rhyme of the narrative, of the story become narrative. Like the narrative, it resolves because it repeats, and repeats because it resolves, constantly going in its sense from its lack of sense. It is the narrative, in its compartmentalized mass, inscribing symbolic structuring at every one of its points through an endless movement back and forth and an endless recuperation.

There is in every great classical film, and this could be its most exact definition and the precondition of this double unitary movement of symbolization, one or more systems that more specifically produce the circularity of symbolic structuring by a double projective effect of concentration and dilation of the textual system in relation to itself. The paradigm of means of locomotion is one of these systems. The exemplary systematicity of *North by Northwest* can thus be expressed by the fact that in it the projective chain is duplicated by a nested rhyme between the narrative and the segment that displays the highest degree of micro-systematic organization in the textual system as a whole. The chain of the look is grafted onto it, in all its structuring, enunciative, identificatory, narcissistic insistence, so as to make the form of the image doubly fantasized on the basis of the fantasy of the narrative. By its effect of projected abstraction and systematic contagion, the paradigm of means of locomotion inscribes the symbolic in every micro-systematic relationship of segment 14 and, from there on, in every relationship of the textual system deployed virtually as an immense signifying chain with multiple points of entry. The back-and-forth movement that carries the general rhyme from degree zero to the absolute limit of the system is the pulse of the symbolic, commanded from its beginning to its end by the signifier of desire subject to the law that governs it. It makes us hear, as if in a continuous vibration, the destiny of Oedipus and of castration even in the minimal textual operation, the smallest divergence from similarity. Oedipus: the difference of the narrative, its very repetition, assigning its (psychological) destiny to repetition. By an effect that only appears paradoxical, the force that produces the narrative also enables it to be brought to a halt. This force endlessly opens it and closes it, in one and the same movement; reproduces, in order to define it and define itself, this continual movement, which hierarchizes, as it were to infinity, the productivity of the filmic text. This effect can be called SYMBOLIC BLOCKAGE.

When, in the United Nations lobby, Valerian slowly takes his knife out of his pocket to murder Townsend, we see a statue, the bust of a nude woman, on a stand at the left of the frame. Later, when Thornhill finds Eve in her room at the Ambassador, two tiny oriental statuettes on the dresser frame Eve as she tries to undress Thornhill ("When I was a little boy . . ."). A few moments later, in the auction gallery, Vandamm gives Leonard instructions to bid for a pre-Colombian statuette representing a Tarascan warrior. Looking at Eve while the bids rise and the sale is completed, Thornhill says to Vandamm, "I'll bet you paid plenty for this little piece of—sculpture [. . .] She's worth every dollar, take it from me. She really puts her heart into her work. In fact her whole body." Still later, when Thornhill succeeds in entering Eve's bedroom in Vandamm's house, he lets her know what he has just overheard from Leonard and Vandamm: the statuette from the auction is filled with microfilm. Finally, when Leonard plunges from the slopes of Mount Rushmore just as he is about to push Eve and Thornhill off the rock face, he drops the statuette that he has taken from Eve just as she had grabbed it from Vandamm in her flight. It breaks, and among the shards we see in a big close-up the microfilm unreeling among the rocks.

Eve has two bodies. The first, threatening, is inscribed by the metaphoric insistence of the chain in the murder of the father in which she is at issue. It is the body of the forbidden mother, whose primordial image is reactivated by the conversation in the hotel bedroom, whose threatening aspect is actualized in the fatal image of the kiss by the conversation in the auction gallery. But repetition brings, through the reiterated motif of the elements of the chain, the image of its resolution. This threatening body breaks when the statuette slips from Leonard's hands, put to death by the law of the State refracted in the representation of the symbolic father. It breaks in place of Eve, who is reborn from the abyss in which she was to have been smashed to pieces, a glorious body devoted to the reconciliation of desire and the law. In breaking, the statuette releases the actual stake of the spy movie, since the microfilm justifies the actions of the CIA and the spies. But, metaphorically born from Eve's body, it is the symbolic stake of the film that is presented and unreels, in a movement that imitates that of the real film and refers its unreeling to the body of the woman whose possession justifies the hero's itinerary. A miniaturized body of the mother, the statuette breaks to allow the fantasy of the oeuvre to be born on the gigantic body of the father.

Hitchcock reappears in the text, enunciating that if the woman is forbidden to the author, the enunciator (who cannot enter the initial bus), she is only permitted to the hero (hastened into the final train by an ellipsis) via the sublimated fantasy for which the film is the stake as imaginary object, for the director who makes it and the spectator who sees it. In doing this it delivers an image for the desire of the analyst: that of analysis itself. In this paradigm of statues thus deployed from  micro- to macro-statuary, analysis experiences once again the hypnotic reduplication by which the film is constantly granting itself the spectacle of its own systematicity, in the unbridled form of a symbolic contagion that eventually affects all its representations from end to end. In these rolls of film that fall from the paradigm, as its remainder, analysis must recognize that the relation of reciprocal inclusion of system and symbol has no sense but to perform the endless back-and-forth between the film and the micro-film. Through its mise-en-abîme, the generalized rhyme of the classical film presumes, in its final textual effect, the fascinated desire of the analyst.

1975
Translated by Mary Quaintance

5. To Segment / To Analyze
(on *Gigi*)

1. 1/47

The film opens. Paris, the Bois de Boulogne, the Avenue des Acacias. The choryphaeus (commentator) of the musical comedy (Honoré) introduces himself and, in a voice that is part-song, part speech, states the theme: "Little Girls." It is a theme immediately focused by the appearance of its instigator: "This is a story about a little girl . . . in particular . . . Her name is Gigi." Gigi passes by and slips away, opening up the theme to the narrative that borrows her name.

The film ends. The theme is taken up again: same set-up, same place, same shot. But now, behind the commentator a couple comes into view, moving in a different, mythical, time, a time apparently outside the narrative since it constitutes the solution of the narrative's enigma: Gigi, accompanied by her husband, Gaston.

Classical cinema (especially classical American cinema) depends heavily on such "rhyming" effects. They carry narrative difference through the ordered network of resemblances; by unfolding symmetries (with varying degrees of refinement) they bring out the dissymmetry without which there would be no narrative. The classical film from beginning to end is constantly repeating itself because it is resolving itself. This is why its beginning often reflects its end in a final emphasis; in this, the film acknowledges that it is a result, inscribing the systematic condition of the course it follows by signing with a final flourish the operation that constructs it throughout.

In this instance the repetition-resolution effect has a specific, but very common, character, and this is its whole strength. It operates on a broad scale and very precisely, *from segment to segment*, that is, from one major narrative unit to another, from one major syntagmatic unit to another.

But what actually is a segment for the purposes of analysis? This comes down to asking first: With what kind of truth and applicability does the *grande syntagmatique* endow the definition of the segment and the reality of analysis?

2. ON THE *GRANDE SYNTAGMATIQUE*

Much has been written about the *grande syntagmatique*: for it, against it, based on it. The work for it has perhaps been excessively subservient. That against it has recently lacked intellectual generosity and imagination. I shall not recapitulate, but at the same time I shall assume familiarity. However, I shall need to retrace the line that carries it in the thinking of Christian Metz, in order to set my own procedure in context.

The constitution of the *grande syntagmatique* combines two complementary lines of thought, determined by the logic of discovery. We are speaking here of 1966, just two years after the impetus provided by "Cinéma: langue ou langage?"[1] (translated as "Cinema: Language or Language System?"). On the one hand it is necessary to demonstrate by means of *a* code, that is, *this* code, that *some* code is involved, in other words, that codicity is no less effective in cinema than in other fields and that it is possible to try to master it and activate it there. This is something no classification, taxonomy, "montage table," etc., had been able to demonstrate, either because they were too formal, or because they were not formal enough. In this sense, the *grande syntagmatique* is a theoretical operator: it actualizes the concrete possibility of a semiology of the cinema because it brings its virtualness onto a material level. Moreover, this specific code seems, from both the logical and historical viewpoints, to be preeminently suited to illuminating the cultural makeup of film as the basis of a fiction, using a closed series of commutable syntagmatic types.

The interacting pressure of these two lines of thought explains how Metz was able to yield, though only in part, to the immediately punctured illusion of having "found" *the* code of cinema. Very soon, indeed almost at once, the *grande syntagmatique* ceases to be *the* code, to become quite simply a (specific) code among others (an assertion *Language and Cinema* makes over again and again to the point of codical vertigo). But the shadow of ambiguity is valuable. For while the *grande syntagmatique* may be one code among other codes that juxtapose and cross it, it envelops them and is superior to them in the proper sense of the word, that is, manifestly, as the consequence and condition of the fiction.

On the other hand, from its origins, or almost so, the *grande syntagmatique* was the object of a patient and rigorous self-criticism on Metz's part. It is therefore constantly deepened by contradictions turned on itself, in step with a logic of still improbable effects, which in a sense undermines the direct positivity of the code but augments its potential pressure. From the first *Essais*, Metz confronted three basic objections. First, the gap between the autonomous shot and the seven other syntagmatic types. The shot sequence (as the name indicates), through a kind of spatio-temporal expansion, proves to contain the possibilities of seven other types; it thus imposes the need for a genuine bipartition of the initial chart.[2] Then in the seven other types, there is the discrepancy between the "hard" and "soft" types (which emerges in concrete form in the syntagmatic analysis of *Adieu Philippine*): for example, between the bracket syntagma and the non-diegetic insert on the one hand, said to be "clear configurations, 'recognized' with certainty and no possibility of error"; and on the other hand, the ordinary sequence and the scene, said to "have fairly fluid contours so that it is sometimes difficult to draw them out of the mass and isolate them from the general filmic flux."[3] (I would add to these a vacillation, first between the scene and the sequence, then between successions of scenes and/or sequences and weak instances of the episodic sequence, which sometimes raises questions.) Finally, the third and in my view most important point: "The set of problems posed by the fact of alternation," which the two complementary forms (one achronological, the other chronological) of parallel and alternate syntagma are powerless to resolve.

The solution would seem to assume that a rigorous semiological theory be established in order to account for two facts that are both pronounced in films, though neither of them has yet been satisfactorily explained: (1) the phenomenon of what one might call the *transformation of the insert*: an autonomous segment with a single insert can easily be "transformed" into an autonomous segment comprising multiple inserts, and thus into an alternate type; (2) the distinction between *true alternation* (which establishes a narrative "doubling" in the film) and *pseudo-alternation* (which may be reduced to a mere visual alternation within a unitary space or else derives simply from the fact that the *filmed subject* itself assumes a vaguely "alternating" aspect within a certain relationship).[4]

Finally, a third line of thought deriving logically from the other two: through the methodological investigation carried out by *Language and Cinema*, the code becomes genuinely a code, in other words, radically detached from the filmic text for which it is simply an abstract exponent, actualized there in the concrete form of the autonomous segment.[5] In an article written soon after, this concern prompted Metz to establish the triple criterion of demarcation for the autonomous segment in the "diegetic film" (actually put into operation by Metz with his syntagmatic analysis of *Adieu Philippine*): "The analyst of the classical film is justified in considering as a single autonomous segment any passage in the film that is not interrupted by a major change in the course of the plot, by punctuation, or by the abandonment of one syntagmatic type for another."[6] The autonomous segment is thus consciously set off to the side of the text, in the direction of its obligatory intercodicity and of textual analysis.

All this has meant that today, Metz thinks (as I know from talking to him at length) that a new version of the *grande syntagmatique* is possible. (If so, why not do it, you may ask. Quite simply because science exists only as borne up by a desire and desires are displaced—as Freud discovered. Only the imaginary realm of science believes that one always insists on finishing—in a limited period—what one has begun.) The new version of the *grande syntagmatique* would need to break down the positivist illusions frequently linked to the beginnings of any formalization. It would thus more surely guard against the new positivism, which the evolution of linguistics might tend to project onto film theory, by seeking simply to replace the structural model by the generative and transformational model. In safeguarding itself against both, the new version could combine the advances they have made. It would be wary of the plurality of levels that prohibits a strictly Chomskian model from ever rejoining its object, film, in the singularity of its textual system. Cinema will never be a language, nor film a grammar. It is not by chance that Nicolas Ruwet's poetic and musicological analyses owe as much if not more to the structural model as to the generative and transformational model. On the other hand, the new version of the *grande syntagmatique* would need to reinforce the level of abstraction in order to stamp out definitively any flattening structural effect, or any descriptive application between code and text, thus correcting earlier inadequacies. Current syntagmatic types, after an internal editing of their list, their number, etc., would take on a new status there: they would become so many matrices for logical spatio-temporal organization, arising from a deep structure. Each of the segments reflected in the text would be conceived as a (final) surface unity, a singular combination of several types of matrix. Thus a movement of partial or limited generation is at work, springing from the two different depth levels (but only two, for strategic reasons linked to the present state of research in the domains concerned). Then the surface level, that is, the level of textual actualization, would alone merit the name autonomous segment, presenting analysis with the constantly renewed singularity of a precise decomposition of the filmic chain.

This very special situation of the *grande syntagmatique* as a problematic, incomplete code, on the one hand prime and primary, on the other, a code among others, seems to have had two opposing results in the field of film analysis. Numerous works have developed in the direct line of the *grande syntagmatique*, either applying it literally, or occasionally seeking to perfect it by trying to diversify, enrich, and lend flexibility to one or the other of its types (but still necessarily remaining within the bounds of Metz's self-critique, which implies its transformation). These works thus reasserted the determining stability of this code, its capacity for historical and stylistic induction and its specific, practical (descriptive) and analytical instrumentality in the textual study of the large narrative units.[7]

On the other hand a number of textual analyses developed within the movement to establish a semiology of cinema and with a more or less explicit reference to Metz's thinking found themselves not ignoring but skirting the test of the *grande syntagmatique*. For some this was doubtless because they only placed themselves on the level of the segment (or fragment) in order to concentrate on the work of its smaller units.[8] Or because they started from a segment or a number of segments (or fragments) in order to evaluate their function in the productivity of the textual whole.[9] But this detour extends even to analyses bearing on a film as a whole and thus more or less consciously situated within the perspective defined by Metz as that of the global textual system. I have in mind, consciously bringing together works of very varied nature and intention, *Foetus astral*, by Jean Monod and Jean-Paul Dumont;[10] the collective work of *Cahiers du cinéma* on *Young Mr. Lincoln*;[11] the book by Claude Bailblé, Michel Marie, and Marie-Claire Ropars on *Muriel*;[12] Stephen Heath's long study of *Touch of Evil*;[13] and my own analysis of *North by Northwest*.[14] The detour is all the more notable in the last two examples in that the analyses (in other ways very different) depend on a segmentation: a primitive or semi-primitive segmentation that justified Stephen Heath's note following his narrative breakdown of the film: "The segmentation here operates at the level of the narrative signified according to simple criteria of unity of action, unity of characters, unity of place; it has no analytic status other than that of allowing reference to the film as narrative." I would have had to add that note to the segmentation tables in my own study were it not obvious that, like Stephen Heath's, they constantly brushed up against the *grande syntagmatique*, without seeking to constrain it and, above all, without risking being constrained by it.[15]

This is the risk I would like to take here because of what it seems to me it can teach us. Starting from the *grande syntagmatique* and going well beyond it, I will concentrate on the systematic modeling of the narrative units of the classical American film. Perhaps as a genre film, which is profoundly coded, *Gigi* shows this modeling better than others. But I remain convinced that, within the irreducible arrangement of each of its textual instances, such a modeling process governs the majority of the films of American high "classicism."

This beginning of an analysis of *Gigi* does not aim to fill any gap between the present state of the *grande syntagmatique* and a second, as yet virtual state. Analysis could no doubt situate that gap and consider it in terms of its own logic. But no more. Here, therefore, the *grande syntagmatique* is fully applied (that is, with all its "lacks") as the operator of the analysis: given, first, the descriptive logicalization it effects on its own level; then, the syntagmatic reference it opens up in the analysis by its capacity to instigate a generalized syntagmatic segmentation. As we shall see, segmentation is a mise-en-abîme, a "plumbing of depths," a process that has no end theoretically—which does not mean that it no meaning, in fact, that is its whole meaning. Through the differential play it sets up between various levels, segmentation allows us to experience the increased plurality of textual effects.

But this approach to *Gigi* is only a beginning, and within such limited bounds it is by definition far more the setting in place of an analytical framework, a setting in perspective, than analysis itself. I have limited myself to a major extent (but on the level of the smaller units, minimally) to the recording of the differential rhyming and repetition effects that structure the development of the narrative. Their fundamental determining role in the constitution of the classical film at the level of the fragment, the segment, or the film as a whole has been shown by my earlier analyses. To me it seemed striking to make them stand out within the crossing of levels at work here. I could obviously not do much more than categorize and list these rhyming effects; what I could not do was produce them in the logic of their textual progression, the material work of their traversal: analysis is not reducible to its framework.[16] But one cannot endlessly recommence the work of analysis without the risk of losing oneself in it, for in a sense it is truly without end. (This is what I hope to show here, by keeping myself somewhat on the outside.) There is also the risk of beleaguering a point already well made (for classical film, I think especially of Thierry Kuntzel and Stephen Heath). This is why the layout of the analytical framework can itself take the place of analysis and thereby discover virtual space as a model (whence Barthes's remarkable "call," which is his "first analysis" of *L'Ile Mystérieuse.* Intellectual imagination, mine and yours, has to give back to the elements I have broken down the space that constitutes and is constituted by them, in other words, their textual volume.

3. SEGMENTAL

The syntagmatic breakdown of *Gigi* which reveals 47 autonomous segments in the image track of the film (1 to 47 in the summary table) calls for a number of observations:

a. The extreme redundancy between the three demarcatory criteria demonstrates a high degree of classicalness.[17]

b. In this sound and musical film, the image is sovereign on the level of segmental demarcation. The instrumental or vocal numbers are lower or equal to the segmental limits, with one exception: Gigi's song ("I don't understand the Parisians") straddles segments 9 and 10, thus creating a kind of autonomous sound segment. Were this a frequent occurrence rather than an exception, we would see a partial doubling of the segmentation, along a second axis. The voice and dialogue are strictly subject to the phenomenality of the image, to its temporal outline. As far as the music is concerned, while its fades occasionally do not coincide with the fades of the segmental demarcation, overall and in connection with the song, it simply reinforces the stability of the autonomous segments of the image. The *grande syntagmatique* of the image track in the classical film, because of the power specific to the diegesis, is clearly something like *the* code — the one that permits the rest.

c. This strict application of the *grande syntagmatique* ran up against two difficulties:

on the fringes of the scene/sequence vacillation (not generally very strong here) two hesitations in the breakdown: between segments 10 and 11, and within the very long segment 30. A (relatively) slight impression of continuity led me to mark a segment in the first instance. In the second I hesitated over a sequence/scene/sequence tripartition (found as a/b/c in the sub-segmentation).

the impossibility, in a film that significantly includes no alternating syntagmas, of giving an account of the alternations (where does the true begin or the pseudo end?) that more or less structure numerous segments: 1, 8, 13, 15, 17, 21 (an episodic sequence which is at the same time an alternate syntagma but lacks simultaneity between the two temporal series, like the alternate syntagma of *Adieu Philippine*, which Metz used as a basis for raising the question of alternation); 24, 25, 26 (in which the segmental level loses a true scene between Honoré and Mamita); 30, 35 (a bastardized episodic sequence whose first two episodes are a kind of abbreviated version of an alternate syntagma); and 47.[18]

d. The autonomous shot, despite its frequency (nine segments), results in few complications — here again the classical model is in full play.

This breakdown demonstrates two conditions essential to the development of the textual logic:

a. first, the high number of repetitions and rhymes which, within the mirror effect of segments 1–47, operate *from segment to segment* — though not through their syntagmatic forms, of course. At this level, the syntagmatic type is simply one pertinence among others, although profoundly different: as a specific exponent of the textual surface it affects, it is the form in which pertinences of varying stability (places, characters, actions, musical or sung motifs) are inscribed in the cinematic signifier, their disposition within each segment being that which conveys the narration from segment to segment.[19] In this sense, what I am here calling segmental (i.e., the textual surface delimited by different forms of autonomous segments) corresponds to the level Metz calls "suprasegmental" in terms of codic units.

One has only to refer to the summary table to recognize the operations taking place, that is, the repetitions, scored by differences, between segments:

1 and 47
4 and 37
6, 16, and 20
7 and 31
8, 28, and 29
14 and 40
15 and 41–42
19, 27, and 32
23 and 46
24, 25, and 26
36 and 39

b. from segment 36, certain of these operations touch a large number of the final segments of the film (37, 39, 40, 41–42, 46, and 47). Such concentration is worth noting: it shows how, through its segmental breaks, the film resolves itself by repetition, through a kind of generalized condensation of the narrative which, on the formal level, conveys it to its ending.

But these chains of repetition-resolution effects are inscribed within the bounds of autonomous segments only to break them down in multiple ways. For if the classical film tends, as Metz saw clearly, toward the sequence (the autonomous segment)[20] far more than toward the shot, it does so at the cost of an equally profound tendency to inscribe the segment within a system of narrative commutation with units that are both superior and, above all, inferior to the segment, with a bearing well beyond the divisions of the filmic chain.[21] These two major movements simultaneously attract and repel, contradict and complement each other. This is what makes it both necessary and difficult to distinguish them: their (decomposable) merging, which turns the film into the space of a generalized segmentality, is the condition that transforms the filmic surface into a textual volume.

4. SUPRA-SEGMENTAL/SUB-SEGMENTAL

On the one hand, the classical film thus tends toward units that can be superior to the segment (supra-segment or macro-segment), even though they very often coincide with it. Both ordinary and specialized language refers to these as "sequences"; they often correspond to "units of scenario."[22] They are generally determined by a kind of global unity of time, place, and action. In Gigi this is the case with segments 24, 25, and 26, all situated at Trouville in the course of the same day and involving the same characters (thus constituting a kind of episodic supra-sequence). It is also the case, in a very different way, with segments 12 and 13, the one denoting, by means of an extremely rapid autonomous shot, the front of the Palais de Glace (neither Gaston nor Gigi are visible, but we know that they are walking toward the building and that they are going to go in); the other is the scene that unfolds inside the rink. But unity of place is not an imperative if narrative movements prove too dissimilar in spite of the transitions that bind them; it thus seems more correct not to combine segment 27 (XVI), where Alicia persuades Mamita to accelerate Gigi's education, and segments 28 and 29 (XVII), which are devoted to the educational sessions. The supra-segment is a kind of unified minor dramatic mould, and this is what justifies its also being able to cover several different locations in succession, hence segments 3, 4, 5, and 6 (III), which preside over the meeting of Gaston and Honoré; or segments 30 and 31 (XXVI), which present in one block Gaston's contradictory reactions to Gigi's transformation.

The determination of the supra-segments is obviously less rigorous than that of the autonomous segments because it is not determined by any cinematic specificity but derives solely from the pressure of the textual system. It is therefore to a profound degree subject to the singularity of each film; and it depends on analysis that gives it an intermediary function between the segments and the large film sections (A, B, C, D, and E here) that distribute the dramaturgy of the narrative.[23] Its interest, like that of any breakdown, is primarily descriptive and involves circumscribing the rhyming effects that unite or superimpose themselves on those of the autonomous segments. Through a kind of internal tautology, segments grouped into a supra-segment rhyme among themselves all the more strongly within this new unit. This is an operation that in one sense adds little, but it is nevertheless striking since it concentrates the rhyming effect in the narrative succession. This is so in the case of segments 24, 25, and 26 at Trouville, mentioned earlier, which group three "sequences" supported by the same characters; likewise segments 28 and 29, which bring together into one "education" syntagma the two episodic sequences in Alicia's apartment. But the most eloquent are clearly those large-scale rhymes that are established across the film from supra-segment to supra-segment: the one clear example relates to the two "Maxim's" sets, which unite segments 14 and 15 and segments 40, 41, and 42 in VIII and XV, respectively. There are other effects at work between sets, but their nature is more partial and is determined by the complementary test of sub-segmentation.

For in this film, as in the classical film generally, it is clearly on the level of the units lower than the segment that the multiple echo play, which structures and constrains the progressive resolution of the textual system throughout, is systematized in a much broader way. At this lower level, let us consider what I shall call *elementary* sub-segmentation, that is, the sub-segmentation that defines two or more successive times within the continuity of the same segment, each circumscribing a small scene. I mean, obviously, in the dramatic, not the syntagmatic sense.

It should be noted that Metz invoked a third criterion to determine the demarcation between two autonomous segments, that is, "a major change in the course of the plot." The criterion is clearly imprecise. What is a major change? Yet this is to pose the question badly. For demarcation, in terms of the "plot itself,"[24] is nearly always obvious: the absence of the two other criteria almost automatically entails the transparence of the third. This stems from the fact that the classical film defines its segmental units by a series of breaks in the signified of temporal denotation: only a major change in the course of the plot can manifest the break when it is not done by punctuation or variation in treatment. The imprecise criterion is therefore the sure one. Through a kind of tautological proof, a narrative change that entails no segmental mark can only be a "minor" change; but in return, the minor change will often be far less minor than others that are nevertheless sanctioned by segmental demarcation, precisely because the change introduced into the course of the plot by the other two criteria would not exist without them (except in cases of redundancy, of course, and these are always numerous). Consider for example the mutation introduced into the narrative by the appearance of a character (major or minor, as the case may be) and inversely, the slightness of the change denoted by the demarcation through punctuation between the autonomous shot of the facade of the Palais de Glace and the scene inside that follows. In other words, segmental breakdown determined by the multiple inscription of the signified of temporal denotation in the filmic signifier only half coincides (occasionally more, occasionally less) with the unfolding of the plot and the succession of narrative actions. Hence, there is a series of dissociations that open the way to an operation of sub-segmentation.

The episodic sequence (and the same would be true of the bracket syntagma) has a particular privilege in this context, arising out of the precise demarcation of each episode. This demarcation is effected again (but at a lower level, as a "sub-segmentation") by the diegesis itself, in most cases by internal punctuation (for the sake of consistency, let us call it a sub-punctuation). On the one hand, episodes are thus almost always linked together (as are the segments in certain supra-segments) by a succession of rhyming effects, as in the case of the various episodes of segments 14, 21, 28, and 29.[25] On the other, a certain episode may establish rhyming effects over a distance with some segment or sub-segment. This is how the overall rhyme linking segments 14 and 20 takes its precise shape: the fourth episode of segment 14 (14d), in which Liane and Gaston enter Maxim's, is repeated by segment 40, where Gigi and Gaston enter in their turn.

Inversely, the criteria of sub-segmentation in the other segments are determined outside any specific inscription in the cinematic signifier. Their indisputable indeterminate character should not be taken as a cause for hesitation. True scenes are constituted nevertheless. They rest on disjunctions provoked by characters' entries and exits, particularly emphatic in this genre film and strongly marked by the dynamic of theatrical representation. The locations, actions, and instrumental and vocal motifs clearly all give powerful support to the stage scene effects organized between characters. But they do not have the same degree of pertinence: the instrumental or vocal motifs, because their limits are almost always inferior or equal to the segment only partly coincide with that of the sub-segment; the actions, because they are not truly divisible into segments in the same way and tend to be diluted in the overall mass of narrative signifieds; the locations, because the temporal form that distributes them is already the precise object of the *grande syntagmatique*.

Scenes thus appear, opening up multiple networks of rhymes. Beginning with segment 1, the fifteen shots that succeed each other before Gigi appears show Honoré in the position of commentator (1a), as he will be again in the first episode of segment 14 (14a); then again in sub-segment 34b, after the disappearance of Gaston. In the same way in segment 22, the disappearance of Gigi in shot 154 opens a brief scene between Mamita and Gaston (22b), which responds to the one that preceded it in segment 7 and the one that succeeds it by the same means in sub-segment 30b, before being renewed in segment 31.[26]

On the other hand, the sub-segmental divisions allow the establishment of new commutations on the basis of intermediary sets between the sub-segment and the segment, the segment and the supra-segment. Thus, the first "education" set that overlaid segment 8 and sub-segment 9a finds its full echo in supra-segment XVII (28 and 29). In the same way the very long sub-segment 30c, sub-segment 43b, and the short segments 44 and 45 mark, with a very sharp repetition effect, Gaston's two departures and returns, which prelude his decision first to keep Gigi, then to marry her. In this way an overall rhyme is established between sub-segment 30c and seg-ment 31, on the one hand, and segments 43, 44, 45, and 46, on the other; this is, in other words, supra-segment XXVI. This last rhyme serves to increase in a major way the condensation that brings together in the final section (E) a series of earlier ele-ments from the four other sections. Space does not allow for a demonstration of the subtle way in which condensation, in this last example, only touches supra-segment XXVI from the starting point of the earlier effect, which condenses (pre-condenses) supra-segments XIV and XXVI in supra-segment XVIII. But to make the text's pro-ductive return on itself fully readable, it would be necessary to go much further into the decomposition of its elements, that is, it would be necessary to sub-segment the sub-segmentation.

5. (MICRO)SEGMENTAL/TEXTUAL

For sub-segmentation goes much further than this. Up till now I have chan-neled it into scene effects, corresponding to one or more shots, in the first case, always either to very long shots (like 34b) or to the more specifically determined units in the episodic sequence.[27] I have, moreover, simply brought out successive dissociations in terms of a linearity that sometimes corresponds exactly to the truth of the text, but more often only in part, mimicking its truth with a representative approximation that is neither altogether false nor altogether true.[28] This is the rea-son for my qualification of that first sub-segmentation as *elementary*.

Complex sub-segmentation goes much beyond this. It might be called *micro-segmentation*—indicating a movement, which is the progressive work of textual and analytical pressure. For here there is no longer anything that corresponds to the precise distinction between segmentation and sub-segmentation. Before segmental demarcation there are only degrees of narrative expansion. This is why complex segmentation does not have anything to do with the limits of the shot, even though the play that is set up with the demarcatory boundary of the shot in turn constitutes a textual pertinence and a stylistic index.

Here I can give only two very summary examples of this movement:[29]

a. *Segment 33*. Shot 302 shows Gigi in her room (this décor appears here for the first time); she is alone, stretched out on the bed, stroking her cat; she gets up to open the door to Gaston within the continuity of the same shot. This beginning of a scene is soon matched by a true scene, the long autonomous shot of segment 38, in which Gigi is singing in her room, holding her cat in her arms. The simplicity of this arrangement shows clearly the way in which the film proceeds through the varied duplication of its successive elements. A fragment of the shot (relatively brief, even though this is a long shot), turns out to be textually commutable with a segment that it anticipates: a shot that is prolonged into a scene that closes on itself. Thus, it completes the condensation effect operating between the fifth section of the film and the four others: from segment 37 to segment 47 there is not one that does not repeat a moment, a segment, or a sub-segment from the four others, scored by the variation that carries the film to its end.

The three quite unequal sub-segments that follow (b/c/d) are inscribed along three axes which, because the sub-segmentation is not developed, only emerge incompletely: the first, which covers almost the whole of the segment (302–307), is inscribed in the series of scenes between Gigi and Gaston; the second, determined by Mamita's appearance in shot 308, is inscribed in the series of multiple scenes or scene fragments between Gigi, Mamita, and Gaston (in particular, it ushers in the dramatic and equally very short scene 43a); the third, after Gigi has rushed to her room, is inscribed by means of a second internal split in shot 308, in the series of scenes, peaceful and dramatic by turns, that bring together Mamita and Gaston.

b. *Segment 47*. Here again, internal splitting of the shot brings out three minuscule sub-segments in the last two shots of the film: (a) in shot 348, Honoré is singing, leaning on a tree in close medium shot; (b) in shot 349, Gigi and Gaston advance at a slant across the lawn and go toward a cab they climb into, followed by the camera, which then loses them to rejoin (c) within the continuity of the same shot, Honoré in the same fixed frame of the preceding shot.

This final example gives a clear indication of how the progressive decomposition of the dramatic instances of the filmic chain, opened up by the decomposition of the *grande syntagmatique*, leads of itself and more or less inevitably toward internal analysis of the segments on the one hand and on the other, toward a comparative analysis of the segments that echo each other. It can be seen that the final segment, which displays a clearcut classicism, is constructed on an a/b/a alternation, which reproduces that of the initial segment of which it is the resolution: in both places, it is clearly between Honoré and "the rest" that a narrative alternation is established. But at the start it is done in twenty-one shots, which would need to be broken down, at the level of elementary segmentation, into two sub-segments, one devoted to Honoré alone, the other to Honoré and Gigi. In breaking them down, it would be seen that neither the first nor the last shot shows Honoré and that the last shows Gigi alone because the narrative is beginning and she is its title and subject. In the final segment the same movement is accomplished in two shots, both of which show Honoré, and in between these two, Gigi, but with her husband Gaston.

At this micro-systematic level, analysis encounters the increased dispersion and constraint of the specific codes (codes of camera movement, looks, scale of shots, etc.), deployed within and throughout the macro-systematic code of the *grande syntagmatique*. Analysis meets anew with the voluminous pressure of the textual system, the full organic play of its differential repetitions. From segment to segment, and from supra-segment to sub-segment, and again from segment to sub-segment, and from sub-segment to sub-segment (from the elementary to the complex), segmental analysis, thus multiplied tenfold, opens onto a permutational, oriented infinity—that of the classical textual system. It crosses paradigms, which allows it (like the means of locomotion in *North by Northwest*) to mirror and to experience the constant comings and goings and the sense of urgency, which is both perfectly traceable and completely irreducible, and from it to constitute the projected space—the "truth" of the reading reflected in that of the filmic text. For example, the segmental analysis thus increased, operating from segment to segment as from supra-segment to sub-segment, would end by constructing, on the basis of the multiple scenes "at Gigi's," the immense paradigm of entries and exits (there are others, but this is the most obvious) sustaining the micro-systematic structuration of the narrative units of the film (the large, medium, and the less large, which, as Metz clearly saw, are still remarkably large precisely because they are the smallest).[30]

6. TO SEGMENT/TO ALTERNATE

To avoid the double excess of both theorization and analysis I have here eschewed the treatment of the question of alternation—whose fundamental importance I have already nevertheless suggested—either in itself or in the totality of textual space.[31] I would simply like to emphasize how, not only at the level of the segment (and beyond that, the supra-segments and sub-segments of a certain diegetic extension, that is to say, at the level of the large narrative units) the entire film is submitted to a sort of generalized alternation between couples and sexes, which leads the film from its premises to its resolution, according to the transformation that regulates it: the substitution of Gigi for Liane d'Exelmans at Gaston's side.

Observe how the first part of the film is organized precisely in this way. The first segment stages, with the announcement of the commentator, a symbolic meeting (stripped of narrative implications) between Gigi and Honoré. Their separation produces, from that point, a series of crossovers that organizes the series of relations between characters, according to three determinations that proceed by alternating one with the other: women, men, men and women: in segment two, Gigi and Mamita; in supra-segment III (segments 3-4-5-6), Honoré and Gaston; in segment 7, the crossing of the sexes, Gaston and Mamita; from this point we return, in supra-segment V (segments 8–9), to the women, Gigi and Alicia, to stage then a second crossing, the one that determines the fiction, between Gigi and Gaston (segments 11, 12); this is prolonged in the segment that follows (13) by the doubled effect linked to the introduction of Liane, through which all the terms of the drama—or the comedy—come together.

Thus we have the presentation of the characters in the best theatrical tradition. But it is according to this regulated oscillation, which will continue to the very end, by diverse configurations of different scope: between the men on one side (the series of scenes between Gaston and Honoré and the very rare ones that show them alone); the women on the other side (the series of scenes between Gigi and Mamita; Gigi and Alicia; and, at the end, Gigi, Alicia, and Mamita; to which can be added Gigi alone, but rarely); and finally, and very diversely, between the men and the women but without exhausting, far from it, all the combinatory possibilities (Honoré never meets Alicia and meets Mamita only once; Gaston briefly meets Alicia), to the advantage of an intensive work of repetition, a repetition that tends, it cannot be said often enough, toward the resolution that is properly speaking the result of this play of alternation, in a final conjunction: that of the couple programmed by this code.

7. SEGMENTAL/FAMILIAL-CONJUGAL

To conclude, let me note a final, fundamental effect, proper to many American classical films, whereby the textual volume multiplies and closes off doubly the field of its own expansion. The systematic accumulation of symmetries and dissymmetries throughout the filmic chain, decomposed by the work of a generalized segmentation, constantly mimics and reproduces (because the one produces the other) the schema of family relations that founds the narrative space.

Gigi on the one hand, Gaston on the other, are two children brought up, in accordance with their sex, by a substitute mother (Mamita) and a substitute father (Honoré). A triple dissymmetry is inscribed in this symmetry, which pledges Gigi and Gaston to each other from the outset.

a. One man, Honoré, corresponds to two women, Mamita and Alicia, in the role of adoptive substitute parent.

b. A genealogical gap makes Gaston Honoré's nephew and Gigi the grandchild of Mamita and grand-niece of Alicia.

c. A clear difference in age between Gigi and Gaston reproduces this genealogical gap, making one already a man, the other still a child.

The mutual feeling between Gigi and Gaston is crystallized in the supra-segment (XV) at Trouville. These three segments (this analysis has had no opportunity to go into this point) are partly constructed on a narrative alternation that juxtaposes Gigi and Gaston on the one hand, and on the other, Honoré and Mamita, who meet in the film for the first and last time. They seem to be bound by an old love and go so far as to evoke the marriage that might have united them. This retrospective marriage clearly simply serves to reflect the as yet potential marriage of Gigi and Gaston. But it suggests much more than that. At this precise moment, the bar of dissymmetry jumps from one generation to another, with the help of a single reply. When Mamita tells Honoré with an insistence of no use to the plot but necessary to the symbolic level: "Gigi is my granddaughter," Honoré's gallantry, which is structural in the proper sense, prompts him to reply: "Granddaughter, no. Daughter." What clearer way of indicating that the children they have not had are obviously those they have both adopted, whom the film is to unite in marriage. Thus the film manages to rebuild a nuclear family of four, which allows the first generation to see itself mirrored in the second (all the more easily because the film keeps silent on the missing terms of this unfolding structure, terms that could have blocked the final condensation: both Gigi's maternal grandfather and her father). In this way, an incest fiction, so favored by the classic-romantic imagination, is established. The dissymmetry obviously reappears, like Alicia, who is absent from this four-term structure. But the dissymmetry of the structures serves what it hides and allows to be resolved: thanks to a discrepancy in age, Gigi is to recover in Gaston the substitute for a father even more strangely absent than the mother who is heard singing as a voice-off; and Gaston recovers in Mamita the obvious substitute for a mother of whom not a word is spoken.

This, then, is the story the film tells us, within a narrative that makes of the segmental the textual condition for a happy slide from the familial into the conjugal, and so assigns itself as an object the resolution of Oedipus. Thus Oedipus, the code generator or macro-code of the narrative, traverses the whole network of specific and non-specific codes that ensure the production of the text at multiple levels of the narrative. Through an effect that is all the more powerful because it is so hard to grasp, it sustains these operations, which are apparently heterogeneous to it, but only insofar as it derives from them its power, or better, its possibility. This is the effect of textual production that I tried to understand in terms that were both different and rigorously complementary in an analysis of Alfred Hitchcock's *North by Northwest*, as an effect I called "symbolic blockage."

1976
TRANSLATED BY DIANA MATIAS

SECT.	SUPRA-S.	S.	PLACE	SUBS.	CHARACTERS	SHOTS	SYNTAGMA	MUSIC	ACTION
A	0	0	Titles over engravings			x		Champagne Gigi	
	I	1	The Bois	a	Honoré	1–15	sequence	"Bois" theme	Honoré introduces the Bois de Boulogne and himself: the bachelor stockholder and a lover of women.
				b	Honoré Gigi	16–21		"Little Girls" theme/then sung by Honoré	He praises little girls and introduces Gigi, playing with some friends. She passes behind him and goes off through the Bois.
	II	2	At Gigi's (ext./int.)		Gigi Mamita	22–24	sequence	Mother's singing voice off	Gigi arrives at her Grandmother Mamita's and is reminded that it is the day of her visit to Aunt Alicia.
	III	3	Paris At Gaston's (ext.)		/Honoré/	25	autonomous shot	"Little Girls" variation	A cab crosses a square and stops in front of a luxurious building.
		4	At Gaston's (int.)		Gaston tradesman valet	26	autonomous shot		His uncle's visit is announced to Gaston Lachaille. He finishes dealing with a few matters and goes out.
		5	At Gaston's (ext.)		Honoré Gaston	27–28	sequence		The meeting between the uncle and nephew, who go off in a cab across Paris.
		6	Paris		Honoré Gaston	29–40	scene	"It's a Bore" theme, then sung by Honoré/Gaston	Honoré praises the charms of life (Paris, wine, women, high society). Gaston responds that everything bores him and stops the cab.
	IV	7	At Gigi's (ext./int.)		Gaston Mamita	41–48	scene		Gaston arrives at Mamita's. They talk about Gigi. Gaston is astonished by the "lessons" Alicia is giving her.

SECT.=Section SUPRA-S.=Supra-Segment S.=Segment SUB-S.=Sub-Segment

SECT.	SUPRA-S.	S.	PLACE	SUB-S.	CHARACTERS	SHOTS	SYNTAGMA	MUSIC	ACTION
	V	8	At Alicia's (ext./int.)		Alicia Gigi	49–64	sequence		Gigi arrives at Alicia's, running. The lesson is now on how to eat ortolans. Conversation on marriage.
		9	At Alicia's (int.)	a	Alicia Gigi	65–67	scene		Lesson (continuation): jewels, cigars. Conversation on love and art. Alicia leaves.
				b	Gigi	68–71		"The...."	Gigi inveighs against the Parisians and love and goes off.
	VI	10	Le Jardin des Tuileries		Gigi	72–75	sequence	...Parisians" sung by Gigi	Gigi continues singing as she crosses the Tuileries and ends up sitting on a bench.
		11	Le Jardin des Tuileries		Gigi Gaston	76–82	scene		Gaston arrives in a cab, recognizes Gigi ("Gaston, do you make love all the time?"), and teases her as he takes her along to the Palais de Glace, where he is meeting Liane d'Exelmans.
	VII	12	The skating rink (ext.)		/Gigi Gaston/	83	autonomous shot	waltz	The façade of the Palais de Glace.
		13	The skating rink (int.)		Gigi Gaston Liane skating teacher	84–90	sequence	waltz	They enter and sit down. On the ice are Liane and her skating teacher. Gigi finds her common and vulgar and leaves suddenly. Liane joins Gaston and reminds him that they are to meet Honoré at Maxim's. They leave.
	VIII	14	At Maxim's (entrance)	a	Honoré (+x)	91	episodic sequence	Maxim's theme	Honoré introduces Maxim's and praises it.
				b	Baron de la Cour Girl	91–92		Maxim's theme	The Baron de la Cour enters with a "belle."
B				c	Honoré Girl	92–93		chorus in speech/song	Honoré enters with a "belle."
				d	Gaston Liane	93–94		"	Gaston enters with Liane.

SECT.=Section SUPRA-S.=Supra-Segment S.=Segment SUB-S.=Sub-Segment

SECT.	SUPRA-S.	S.	PLACE	SUB-S.	CHARACTERS	SHOTS	SYNTAGMA	MUSIC	ACTION
		15	At Maxim's (room)		Gaston Liane Honoré	95–105	sequence	"She is so gay tonight," sung by Gaston	At the table, Liane is in high spirits, Gaston gloomy. "She is not thinking of me." Honoré asks Liane to dance. Liane grows more and more exuberant, Gaston increasingly bad-tempered.
	IX	16	At Honoré's (int.)		Gaston Honoré Manuel	106–121	scene	"It's a bore" sung by Honoré/Gaston, then Manuel	Gaston arrives at his uncle's to announce that Liane is being unfaithful with the skating master. Honoré takes him to Honfleur where the couple are hiding, to settle the affair in a gentlemanly way.
	X	17	At Honfleur (ext./int.)		Honoré Gaston Liane Skating teacher	122–134	sequence		Honoré and Gaston arrive at an inn and surprise the couple. Gaston offers the man a thousand francs to disappear and says goodbye to Liane who faints.
		18	Newspaper		(Gaston Liane)	135	autonomous shot		A front page with a photo of Liane. "Sugar Prince breaks with Liane d'Exelmans."
	XI	19	At Alicia's		Alicia Mamita	136	autonomous shot		Alicia and Mamita comment on Liane's "suicide."
	XII	20	At Honoré's		Gaston Honoré Manuel	137	autonomous shot		Gaston arrives at Honoré's and is congratulated by Honoré on his first suicide; he dissuades him from shutting himself away and advises him rather to live it up.
C	XIII	21	/At Gigi's (int.)/	A a	/Gigi/ (Gaston)	138	episodic sequence	"It's a bore"	Gigi's hands hold an illustrated program: "Gaston Lachaille opens Pré Catelan for a gigantic party."

SECT.=Section   SUPRA-S.=Supra-Segment   S.=Segment   SUB-S.=Sub-Segment

SECT.	SUPRA-S.	S.	PLACE	SUB-S.		CHARACTERS	SHOTS	SYNTAGMA	MUSIC	ACTION
			Pré Catelan	B	b	Gaston Girl Honoré	139–141			Honoré enjoys himself at a table with several girls while Gaston yawns.
			/At Gigi's (int.)/	A	a	/Gigi/ (Gaston)	142			Gigi's hands hold an illustrated program: "Who will be Gaston Lachaille's Queen at the battle of flowers?"
			The Bois	C	c	Gaston Girl	143–144			In a flower-covered float, Gaston, looking bored beside a girl.
			/At Gigi's (int.)/	A	a	/Gigi/ (Gaston)	145			Gigi's hands hold an illustrated program: "Two thousand guests invited to Gaston Lachaille's masked ball."
			At Gaston's (int.)	D	d	Gaston Honoré	146–148			Honoré looks for Gaston in the costumed crowd and finds him slumped in a corner on a couch.
			/At Gigi's (int.)/	A	a	/Gigi/ (Gaston)	149			Gigi's hands hold an illustrated program: "Gaston Lachaille invites the opera company home."
	XIV	22	At Gigi's (int.)		a	Gigi Mamita Gaston	149–154	scene	"Little Girls" whistled by Gigi	The bell rings. Gigi gets up and opens the door to Gaston. Mamita is preparing a cassoulet in the kitchen. Gaston decides to put off his party and sends Gigi with an apology.
					b	Mamita Gaston	155–156	scene	Mother's voice off	Mamita and Gaston talk about Honoré.
		23	At Gigi's (int.)			Gigi Gaston Mamita	157–175	scene	"Champagne" sung by Gigi, Gaston, Mamita	Gaston and Gigi play cards. Gigi makes him promise that if she wins he will take her with him to Trouville. She cheats and wins. Gaston is furious but gives in, agrees to take them. They sing and dance with Mamita as they empty a bottle of champagne.

SECT.=Section SUPRA-S.=Supra-Segment S.=Segment SUB-S.=Sub-Segment

SECT.	SUPRA-S.	S.	PLACE	SUB-S.	CHARACTERS	SHOTS	SYNTAGMA	MUSIC	ACTION
	XV	24	At Trouville The beach The sea		Gigi Gaston Girl Man Honoré Mamita	176–183	sequence	"Champagne"	While Gaston and Gigi frolic in the water, Honoré is about to pass a note to a girl when he catches sight of Mamita on the beach, greeting him. He puts away the note and a man goes into the girl's cabin.
		25	At Trouville Tennis		Gigi Gaston Girl Man Honoré Mamita	184–194	sequence	"Champagne"	Honoré arrives on the tennis court. The girl, dressed to kill, is solemnly playing with her admirer on one side. On the other, Gaston is playing with Gigi, who is running about like a mad thing under the amused eye of Mamita.
		26	At Trouville The terrace The beach		Gigi Gaston Girl Honoré Mamita	195–223	sequence	"I remember it well" sung by Honoré/ Mamita	Gigi and Gaston on the beach with a pair of donkeys. Mamita watches from the terrace, laughing. Honoré is about to follow the girl as she comes into the hotel when he catches sight of Mamita and goes to sit beside her. They evoke past love at length. Night falls. Gigi and Gaston return, dragging the donkeys.
D	XVI	27	At Alicia's (int.)		Mamita Alicia	224–235	scene		Alicia warns an amazed Mamita about Gaston's likely passion for Gigi and persuades her to speed up Gigi's education before the return of Gaston, who has left for Monte Carlo.
	XVII	28	At Alicia's (int.)	a	Alicia Gigi	236	episodic sequence	"Little Girls"	Lesson in manners: how to serve coffee, which Gigi spills.
				b	"	237			Lesson in manners: how to walk, how to sit down. Not very successful.
				c	"	238			Lesson in manners: tasting wine, on which Gigi gets tipsy.

SECT.=Section   SUPRA-S.=Supra-Segment   S.=Segment   SUB-S.=Sub-Segment

SECT.	SUPRA.S.	S.	PLACE	SUB.S.	CHARACTERS	SHOTS	SYNTAGMA	MUSIC	ACTION
				d	" "	239			Lesson in manners: choosing a cigar, which Gigi snaps in two.
		29	At Alicia's (int.)	a	Alicia Mamita Gigi model designer	240–246	episodic sequence	"Little Girls"	Presentation of a dress, which Mamita and Gigi like, but Alicia does not.
				b	Alicia Mamita Gigi, etc.	247–250			A second dress, which Mamita and Gigi like, but Alicia does not.
				c	Alicia Mamita Gigi,etc.	251–254			A third dress, which Mamita and Gigi don't like and Alicia chooses.
				d	Alicia Mamita Gigi, etc.	255–256			Gigi tries on the dress and is aghast.
XVIII		30	At Gigi's (int.)	A / a	Gigi Mamita Gaston	257–268	sequence	"Little Girls"	Gaston arrives at Gigi's. She rushes straight into her room and returns in a white dress. Gaston, who doesn't accept the metamorphosis, loses his temper and leaves, then returns to invite Gigi to tea at the "Reservoirs." Mamita is against it and Gigi goes back to her room.
				b	Mamita Gaston	269–275			Mamita explains to Gaston that she cannot let Gigi go out with him alone. Gaston loses his temper, insults Mamita and leaves.

SECT.=Section SUPRA.S.=Supra-Segment S.=Segment SUB-S.=Sub-Segment

SECT.	SUPRA-S.	S.	PLACE	SUB-S.	CHARACTERS	SHOTS	SYNTAGMA	MUSIC	ACTION
			From Gigi's back to Gigi's (ext.)	B c	Gaston	276–289		"She is a babe," by Gaston / "Gigi" sung by Gaston	He walks across Paris as far as the Tuileries, where he met Gigi earlier, and returns. When he left, Gigi was only a harmless child; on his return, she is a girl with whom he is in love.
		31	At Gigi's (ext.)		Gaston Mamita	290–291	scene		He rings and asks Mamita to receive him.
	XIX	32	At Alicia's (int.)		Alicia Mamita	292–301	scene		Mamita reports to Alicia Gaston's proposal on keeping Gigi: a private apartment, a car, etc.
	XX	33	At Gigi's (bedroom)	A a	Gigi	302	sequence	"I remember it well"	Gigi comes out of her room to open the door to Gaston.
			At Gigi's (living room)	B b	Gaston Gigi	302–308		Gigi	Gigi refuses Gaston's proposals, bursts into tears when she learns that he loves her.
				c	Gaston Gigi Mamita	308			Mamita rushes in, Gigi runs to her room.
				d	Mamita Gaston	308			Gaston says goodbye to Mamita and leaves.
	XXI	34	At the restaurant	a	Honoré Gaston	309–311	scene		Gaston arrives at a restaurant where Honoré is having lunch and explains his disappointment to him. Honoré consoles him and invites him to join him that evening with "Michele" at Maxim's.
				b	Honoré	312		"Poor boy" sung by Honoré	Honoré congratulates himself on having reached an age where conflicts like this don't matter.

SECT.=Section   SUPRA-S.=Supra-Segment   S.=Segment   SUB-S.=Sub-Segment

SECT.	SUPRA-S.	S.	PLACE	SUB-S.		CHARACTERS	SHOTS	SYNTAGMA	MUSIC	ACTION
	XXII	35	On the telephone At Alicia's	A	a	Mamita	313	episodic sequence		Mamita on telephone in tears.
				B	b	Alicia	314			Alicia puts down the telephone and has a cab called.
			In Paris	C	c	(Alicia)	315		"Little Girls" variation	A cab crosses a square in Paris.
		36	At Gigi's			Alicia Mamita Gigi Gaston	316–325	scene	Mother's voice off	Alicia arrives at Gigi's and reproaches Mamita for her clumsiness. Gaston rings; he has received Gigi's letter. She comes out from her room for a moment to tell him that she would rather be unhappy with him than without him and returns to her room. Gaston goes out. The two sisters look at each other.
E	XXIII	37	At Gaston's			Gaston jeweler	326	autonomous shot	"Champagne"	Gaston chooses jewelry for Gigi.
	XXIV	38	At Gigi's (bedroom)			Gigi	327	autonomous shot	"Say a prayer for me tonight" sung by Gigi	Gigi mentally prepares herself for the evening she is to experience.
		39	At Gigi's (int./ext.)			Gigi Alicia Mamita Gaston	328–329	scene		Gigi emerges from her room in an evening dress. She kisses Alicia and Mamita, opens the door to Gaston's ring, and they go out.
	XXV	40	At Maxim's (entrance)			Gigi Gaston	330–331	sequence	Maxim's theme	Gaston and Gigi enter Maxim's and move to a table.
		41	At Maxim's (inside)			Gigi Gaston Honoré	332–335	sequence	"She is so gay tonight"	At the table, Gigi applies Alicia's lessons to perfection: the coffee, the cigar, and the jewelry. They get up to dance, as they pass greeting a surprised Honoré, who recognizes Gigi.

SECT.=Section   SUPRA-S.=Supra-Segment   S.=Segment   SUB-S.=Sub-Segment

SECT.	SUPRA-S.	S.	PLACE	SUB-S.	CHARACTERS	SHOTS	SYNTAGMA	MUSIC	ACTION
		42	At Maxim's (entrance hall)		Gigi Gaston Honoré	336–337	sequence		Gaston offers Gigi his gift. Gigi exclaims like a real woman of the world over the beauty of the diamonds, which she offers to the room to admire. Gaston is angered and leaves, dragging her to the exit.
	XXVI	43	From Gigi's (ext.)	A a · · · · · B b	Gigi Gaston Mamita · · · · · Gaston	338 · · · · · 339–340	sequence		He drags Gigi by the hand up the steps. Gigi throws herself tearfully into Mamita's arms. Gaston goes back down the steps and walks across Paris.
		44	Le Jardin des Tuileries		Gaston	341	autonomous shot	"She is a babe" · · · · · "Gigi"	He passes in front of the Tuileries fountain, stops, and turns back.
		45	Toward Gigi's (ext.)		Gaston	342–344	sequence		He retraces his steps and goes slowly up Gigi's stairway.
		46	At Gigi's (int.)		Gaston Gigi Mamita	345–347	scene		Mamita and Gigi are sitting up. Mamita goes to open the door to Gaston and begs him to avoid a scandal. Gaston asks Mamita for Gigi's hand. She rushes into his arms tenderly.
	XXVII	47	The Bois		Honoré Gigi Gaston	348–349	sequence	"Little Girls" sung by Honoré	Honoré sings. Gigi and Gaston appear and leave in a cab. Honoré goes on singing.
	Repeat		Ending on painting				a shot		

SECT.=Section   SUPRA-S.=Supra-Segment   S.=Segment   SUB-S.=Sub-Segment

6. To Enunciate
▦ (on *Marnie*)

1.

The credits have barely begun and already a body has been snatched. Twice one name has staked its claim on another: the film's title by its director, and a woman's name by a man. Such a gesture is a familiar way of signing a text with one's own distinctive flourish. Here, it is also a possessive move that separates the heroine's name from those of the two actors ("Tippi" Hedren and Sean Connery), featured in the second and third titles following "Universal Presents" and already linked as a couple. Let's try, in theory nothing stops us, to imagine the contrary: "Chantal Akermans's *Bobby*."

Perhaps this explains the power of these subdued titles, which is so different from the compressed violence of the credit sequences that Saul Bass designed for earlier Hitchcock films such as *Vertigo*, *North by Northwest*, *Psycho*, and *The Birds*. More than anything else they suggest the film's roots in melodrama or soap opera ("If we want to reduce *Marnie* to its lowest common denominator, it is the story of the prince and the beggar girl" [304]).[1] But their impact most likely results from the unique way they are presented: instead of simply following one another, the titles dissolve like the turning pages of a book, with the shadow of the second title projected onto the first, eventually covering it. Thus they pile up on top of the film's title forming a block, until the last credit, "Directed by Alfred Hitchcock," which reiterates, from the point of view of the mise-en-scène, the effect of a virtual possession that the film will attempt to make real.

2.

No frame enlargement can ever reproduce the variable speed at which this body is offered and then taken away from us. The effect results from the difference between two movements, that of the character, and that of the camera. At the very beginning of the shot, the camera clings possessively to this body that it offers to us as an enigma ("The only way to do that is to travel the close-up" [266]). But almost immediately the respective speeds of camera and character are no longer evenly matched. From this point on, the camera follows this body only while pulling away from it, revealing its own presence through this separation and substituting for the partial body one that is total and thus all the more imaginary. This soon leads to the camera beginning to

0a

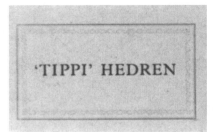

0b

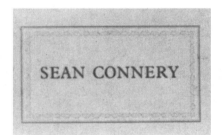

0c

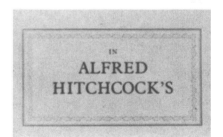

0d

0e

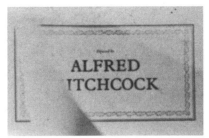

0f

1a

1b

1c

1d

immobilize itself, progressively and imperceptibly, sanctioning this separation without detracting from the almost excessive regularity of the walk and the time it takes to end such a lengthy shot—which it does, in complete stillness, during which time the body-object eludes us as it moves away, literally passing into the distance.

Several things can be noted here. First, there are the signs of the hermeneutic at work: a yellow handbag, a deserted platform, a woman with her back to us: is this really "Marnie," the woman-title Hitchcock appropriates for himself and offers us? Second, the work of enunciation in the body of the text. More than anything else it is the variation in distance between camera and object that serves to inscribe cinema in the realm of the scopic drive through an exaggerated manifestation of its effects.[2] This is the law of the "succession of shots" described by Malraux in *Esquisse d'une psychologie du cinéma*.[3] This law must be understood in terms of three complementary codic systems:

1. from shot to shot, as Malraux explained (the variation in distance is determined by the cut);

2. camera movement (which immediately renders ambiguous the concept of the shot: each frame becomes a new shot, with only the distance from the object varied);

3. movement of the actor within the shot, stationary or moving (with the ensuing multiplication of effects).

Exploiting the conflict produced by the articulation of these last two codes, Hitchcock (i.e., the director, the man with the movie camera, the kino-eye: the author-enunciator) underscores in a single shot that this variation in distance, this tension that erupts as an infinity of shots within the shot, constitutes his position of enunciation by moderating the trajectory of his scopic relation to the object.

Almost unnoticeably, this quasi-somatic effect operates simultaneously on both levels of spectatorial identification—with the camera and with the object (the perpetual dialectic between being and having, identification and object-choice). In the classical film, this effect is a function of a continuous suturing—and this is precisely its nature. Here, a segment is electrified by the abrupt cessation of the music, which comes to a full stop as the first shot begins, following the evocative magnificence of the credits. The impression is intensified by the eerie exclusion of all noise, except for the sound of Marnie's heels on the platform. Here, the final immobility of camera and character, momentarily in sync, switches into this *fascinum*, "where the power of the look exercises itself directly"[4] as a lack inscribed in the circuit of the drive ("the look as little object o"). This fascination has meaning only insofar as it is immediately sutured, setting off the dialectic of identificatory desire and the oscillation between these two points: the moment of seeing and the final immobilization, the *fascinum*.[5]

3.

Strutt: *Robbed! Cleaned out! Nine thousand nine hundred and sixty-seven dollars! Precisely as I told you over the telephone. That girl did it. Marion Holland, that's the girl, Marion Holland.*
Cop: *Can you describe her, Mr. Strutt?*
Strutt: *Certainly I can describe her. Five feet five, hundred and ten pounds, size eight dress, blue eyes, black . . . wavy . . . hair, even features, good teeth . . .*

Cop: *Ahem* . . .

Strutt: *Why, what's so damned funny? There's been a grand larceny committed on these premises.*

Cop: *Uh, yes sir. You were saying: uh, black hair, wavy, even features, good teeth. She was in your employ four months.*

Other Cop: *What were her references, sir?*

Strutt: *Well, as a matter of fact . . . yes . . . she had references, sure . . .*

Secretary: *Mr. Strutt, don't you remember, she didn't have any references at all.*

2

3

7

9

Strutt: *Well, she worked the copying and the adding machine. No confidential duties.*

Mr. Rutland, I didn't know you were in town. Just had a robbery, almost ten thousand dollars.

Mark Rutland: *So I gather . . . by a pretty girl with no references.*

Strutt: *You remember her—I pointed her out to you last time you were here. You said something about how I was "improving the looks of the place."*

Mark: *Oh . . . that one, the brunette with the legs . . .*

Strutt: *Excuse me, gentlemen, Mr. Rutland is a client.*

Mark: *I don't think we have got time to discuss business today, Mr. Strutt, what with this crime wave on your hands.*

Strutt: *Oh! no, no . . . always time for Rutland business, you know that . . . How are things in Philadelphia? The little witch! I'll have her put away for twenty years. I knew she was too good to be true. Always so eager to work overtime, never made a mistake, always pulling her skirt down over her knees as though they were a national treasure. She seemed so nice, so efficient, so . . .*

Mark: *. . . resourceful?*

A classical segment in 24 shots. The first 20 shots are organized as an alternation between Strutt (2, 4, etc.) and the various motifs that make up the reverse shots, thus creating several implied subjective shots—the safe (3); the secretary, the two police detectives (5); the two police detectives (7, 11, 13, 15); the secretary (9, 17, 19), up to Mark Rutland's entrance, when he moves into a shot of the secretary (21). But in shot 22, a tracking shot following Strutt framed in medium close-up (slightly wider than preceding shots), combines the two alternating terms in a final stage of the shot (22, 24a, during which there occurs a slight change in camera angle determined by the eyeline axes). This resolution becomes in turn a pole in a new alternation with the police detectives (23)—an alternation immediately broken when the camera, with a slow forward movement, frames the pensive face of Mark Rutland (24a, 24b), isolating a focal point centered on a single element of the first alternating term.

21a

22a

24a

24b

The text, the dialogue, speaks about itself, raising the enigma of its beginning only to reformulate it around the theft in yet unforeseeable terms. The theft figures here as the flip side of sex: the woman's reply to the aggression by the image, of which she is the object. Everything conspires in the production of this image. It is spun through Strutt's greedy, lascivious description (here again we need the texture of the voice, excited and vulgar, of this bourgeois businessman) and reinvigorated by Mark's half-complicitous irony right through to the end of the segment. It becomes clear that sexual reticence is the surest means of guaranteeing fascination with sex, as soon as it is presented in an image, because a woman corresponds only to the codes that reveal this sexuality. We also see that a "true" woman's only "reference" is her conformity to this image that constitutes her (hence the need for the other secretary as a counter-example, just as in the beginning of *Psycho*). In "improving the looks of the place," she is the very essence of décor. But this is also because, in English, one says, when describing a woman's appearance, "her looks"—as though her "looks" were nothing but that image constituted through the looks given her by men.

So too, and even more importantly, this imaginary image of Marnie comes to fill the real but empty image of the first shot. It is a full-frontal description of her that Strutt gives, thus completing in a kind of deferred reverse-shot the image that the camera gives us only from the back. (For the spectator, naturally, the expectation is intensified in this first instance of possession-dispossession.)

4.

24b   25a

Once the dialogue has ended and the camera has completed the slow forward tracking shot that isolates Mark's face, he turns toward the spectator with a thoughtful look that is obviously supposed to indicate that, during the time when the shot becomes stationary, he is daydreaming about this woman whose virtual image he has helped to create. The real image that follows (25a) repeats exactly the beginning of shot 1 and seems to materialize his pensive gaze, taking the place of the traditional subjective shot: in fact, this effect—associated with the succession of shots and the absence of any demarcatory punctuation—sutures, in a way, the transition from segment to segment. Mark thus sees what he cannot see but what he is in the position of being able to imagine by means of the camera that sees in his place. This repetition-effect, which makes Mark see/imagine what Hitchcock–the camera sees in shot 1, situates Mark on the trajectory of enunciation permitted by the camera-look. Mark's singular desire for Marnie is aroused by this relationship between himself and the image. He becomes the relay for that which Hitchcock can only possess through the camera, which forbids it to him precisely so that he may represent it. The fetishistic operation, thus redoubled, is extended from the director to the character who takes his place, which brings about a return to the narrative's initial condition of possibility: the essentially fetishistic position of the cinematographic signifier. ([In answer to Truffaut's question] ". . . I'd like to know which aspect of this book made you decide to do this film," Hitchcock answered: "The fetish idea. A man who wants to go to bed with a thief, just like other men have a yen for a Chinese or a colored woman. Unfortunately, this concept doesn't come across on the screen. It's not as effective as *Vertigo*, where Jimmy Stewart's feeling for Kim Novak was clearly a fetishistic love. To put it bluntly, we'd have had to have Sean Connery catching the girl robbing the safe and show that he felt like jumping at her and raping her on the spot" [277].)

Strutt is also inscribed in the trajectory of virtual possession of the object that Mark will help to assure. Mark does so by mediating between mise-en-scène and the spectator through the play of a double identification with the character and the camera. The shot of Mark that ends segment 2 is almost identical to the shot of Strutt that opens it and recurs throughout the segment, where Strutt, to evoke the woman who robbed him, seems to go back in turn to this first shot—as if he were the third term of an imaginary viewpoint in the structure seeing/seen/seeing, whose first term is conflated with the camera in order to be subsequently displaced onto Mark's look.

5.

Shot 25 (the opening of segment 3) repeats shot 1 (segment 1) in order to so-lidify what the work of enunciation is determining within this shot: its development in the narrative as narrative. According to the principle of repetition and regulated difference, now fairly well understood, which is the basis of narrative progression and expansion in the classical cinema (especially in the American cinema), shot 25 uses the same camera inflection (but never quite the same) to call attention to Marnie's forward movement down the hallway.[6] Here, notable differences are produced by the obvious discrepancy between action and décor (décor is different but the action is repeated) by which any difference that occurs in the narrative is marked by the seal of repetition. We have

1. movement. This time Marnie walks faster than the camera following her, which allows us to see immediately the difference in décor. The moving camera stops before framing her in a medium shot (as in segment 1, on the platform), while she continues toward the background, this time without stopping.

2. music. After expanding during the credits, it is interrupted abruptly with shot 1, in order to reappear, at the end of the dialogue, in shot 25, which seems to take up again where the credits left off ("Directed by Alfred Hitchcock"), by arising from Mark Rutland's daydream.

And there is more. On the left of the frame a door opens from what must be a hotel room. Hitchcock emerges, his back turned three-quarters toward the viewer, perfectly positioned to allow him to observe Marnie walking down the hall and away from him. He then turns toward the spectator staring at the camera that he himself is and whose inscription he duplicates. The spectator in turn (re)duplicates this inscription through his identification with both Hitchcock and the camera. Then Hitchcock turns again, or rather, he is about to turn toward Marnie, but the shot is abruptly cut off before he completes his movement. This is a way of conveying "the intelligence of a machine." He is telling us that his eye, virtually he himself, could, while Marnie walks away, her yellow handbag under her arm, that he could, if he were that camera lens he becomes by means of the film work, reframe her just as he has done at the beginning of shot 25, and as he did in shot 1. He formulates, in the full meaning of the term, his position of enunciation by inscribing himself in the chain of the look at the exact point that permits him to determine, however fleetingly, the structuring principle of the film.

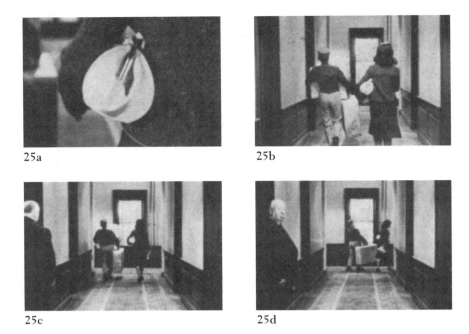

25a

25b

25c

25d

In thus observing Marnie, who is both object of desire and enigma (becoming the one because she is the other), Hitchcock becomes a kind of double of Mark and of Strutt, who have just contributed to the creation of his image but who, at the same time, are caught in it. This is possible because they too are nothing but doubles, irregularly distributed along a trajectory at whose origin is Hitchcock, the first among all his doubles, a matrix that generates them as well as his own representation as duplicate image of himself, embodying the pure power of the image, the desire of the camera, whose chosen object is here the woman.

6.

This explains his need to appear, almost arbitrarily, in all of his films since *The Lodger*. But it also explains why these appearances occur, more and more frequently, at that point in the chain of events where what could be called the film-wish is condensed. It is an authorial signature, of course, but an exaggerated one that punctuates the logical unfolding of the fantasy originating in the conditions of enunciation. This operation is similar to that of the Freudian pun. There, the whole biography of the subject is precipitated toward the point of crystallization constituted by the pun from which this biography can be read—the work of analysis—through the chains of displacement and metaphor.

Shadow of a Doubt: In the train going to Santa Rosa (in a later film, *The Birds*, the birds will attack Santa Rosa as well as Bodega Bay), Charlie, the uncle, is invisible. His voice is heard—a brief dialogue with the conductor—behind a black screen. But a few steps from him (one would like to be able to say, in his place) sits Hitchcock, a traveler who joins him on the path to the center of his fantasy (murder-possession of the mother, predicted during the credits by the waltz of the "Merry Widow"). He is playing cards, dealing the cards of the film. That is why he holds a full hand of spades (emphasized by a close-up, almost an insert). He holds all the cards, including those of the strongest house, the cards of death; taken in by his own game, he masters it only to lose himself in it.

Strangers on a Train: Here again a scene on the train, where the exchange of murders takes place; it is a train that makes the round-trip between Washington and Mulgate (the scene of the murder). Hitchcock gets on the train carrying a double bass that, by synecdoche, inscribes him in the fantasy—Miriam (object of the murder) works in a music store. The camera pursues her image as far as her reflection in her own glasses fallen to the ground, thus accentuating the nature of the impossible image (the fantasy of the real as impossible, according to Lacan) that gives the camera the power to film, since it wishes to become part of this same fantasy.

A spectacular twist to the enunciation: later it will be the glasses of *Patricia Hitchcock* that reawakens Bruno's murderous fantasy during the Morton's party, pushing him to repeat the act on the elderly society woman (double of the widows in *Shadow of a Doubt,* just as Barbara-Patricia is the double of Miriam here). Let us go on.

I Confess: Again master at the game, Hitchcock passes across the screen in a now famous image, silhouetted against the sky at the top of the steps (count them, about thirty-nine!).

Rope (which I have not been able to see for more than ten years—an inevitable hazard of film study): He passes again, either during the credits or after, I do not remember, but before the camera moves toward the window of the apartment building and fixes, as soon as the window is penetrated, on the scene of the murder.

Rear Window: Here Hitchcock delineates more precisely the mirror effect of seeing and seen, the reversibility of exhibitionism and voyeurism in the scopic drive. He does so by including himself among the tenants of the fragmented apartment house/screen that Jeff structures, divides, and redivides through his camera lens.

Then comes the "royal road"—the four films whose credits, designed by Saul Bass, crystallize the enunciative work:

Vertigo: Substitution and mimesis of the trajectory by means of segmentation. *Segment 1.* A roof-top chase: a policeman falls to his death; Scottie, police detective, discovers his acrophobia. *Segment 2.* Scottie and Midge (at Midge's): they talk about their former relationship and his acrophobia; then Midge tells him that, according to the experts, the only thing that will cure him is a second scare; Scottie reports an unexpected urgent telephone call from an old college friend, Gavin Elster. *Segment 3.* Elster's office on the Embarcadero in San Francisco; Elster asks Scottie, now retired from police work, to follow his wife, who is haunted to the point of madness by an image. Between segments 2 and 3, there is a sub-segment that introduces 3: a long shot of the Embarcadero, during which Hitchcock walks across the screen, in the time and space, the ellipsis, that leads Scottie from one situation, from one décor, from one segment, to another.

Shadow of a Doubt

I Confess

Rear Window

Vertigo

North by Northwest

Psycho

The Birds

Identification works here in ways both subtle and crude. It evokes, on the one hand, the fascinated-fascinating eye in the credits from which the title and names erupt; and on the other hand, the film that exploits this metaphor by linking the destiny of the subject to a passion for the image (twice over: Scottie is fascinated by Madeleine because she is herself fascinated by an image; we see here the infinite regression of the fantasy particular to the scopic drive, which itself constitutes the scene). It is a passion that precipitates, almost in a chemical sense, the peculiar affinity between the woman and the death wish that continues to exist for the man (and the woman who repeats this same construct).

North by Northwest: The bus that closes its doors on Hitchcock places him on the side of the lack, the absence (that the film as object [in turn] returns as its possession: the plenitude of the lure in the chain called "paradigm of the means of locomotion," which I have described as a principle of the film as a system and of desire as the logic of that system, and which works by means of an effect of "symbolic blockage" that ensures the film's textual expansion).[7] Here again, there is a train, or rather two, on which the dual game of murder-seduction is played out between Eve and Thornhill. This only goes to show the extent to which the chains, from one film to another, are interlinked in this more closed paradigm comprised of their (explicit) moments of enunciation.

We can also see in this doubled train the second train in *Shadow of a Doubt* on which Uncle Charlie tries to kill his niece, Charlie: in both films there is a similar logic of filmic repetition/resolution working through the internal opposition between the resolved desire of neurosis, which returns to the law, and the impossible desire—gaping, excluded, mortal—of psychosis.

Psycho: Hitchcock places himself on Marion Crane's path from the hotel (where she and Sam have just made love) to her office (where she yields to the temptation to steal, as if to get even for the sexual aggression, of which she was metaphorically the object, inflicted on her by the oil man in the Stetson). Hitchcock is on that path (also wearing a cowboy hat) so that, for a brief moment, they can figure together in the same image, thus enunciating the object of desire. But he does this in a singular way, by accumulating the metaphoric effects of displacement: the last images of the segment, after Marion leaves Sam in the room where she (almost grudgingly) has been the object of his desire, and the first image of the second segment allow Hitchcock, through the artifice of the lap-dissolve, to substitute himself for Sam before Marion appears, so that he can subsequently be included, through the mediation of money and the theft, in this desire that the camera will later take to its most extreme in the shower scene, through Norman's desire-delirium.

The Birds: Another crossing of paths. Shot 1 (following the credits, the names shredded to pieces by animated birds). A street in San Francisco: a bus passes in front of us, revealing Melanie Daniels walking down the street followed by the camera. Suddenly she stops and looks up. Shot 2. A flock of birds swoops through the city sky. Shot 3. Melanie is surprised; resuming her walk, she enters a shop at the precise moment when Hitchcock comes out of it with two white poodles on a leash. He leaves the store so that Melanie can enter it. It is Mrs. MacGruder's pet store, which, moments later, Mitch Brenner will in his turn also enter to buy a pair of "lovebirds,"

1   2

neither too demonstrative nor unfriendly, lovebirds that he wants to give to his younger sister as a birthday present. Thus does Hitchcock inscribe himself in the chain of the fantasy, of the imaginary body-symbol that engenders the film—a body torn between neurosis and psychosis, between desire and the law. Body-look of the woman, body-look of the man who captures hers and is fascinated by it, who will have to recognize himself in it, finally in order to dominate it. The pair of poodles that, like the lovebirds, symbolizes the diegetic couple, shows clearly enough where the film-catharsis, the mise-en-scène as ritual, orderly perverse transgression, will lead them.

Marnie: A new level of intensity is reached in the system of signature. Before, Hitchcock positioned himself diegetically and symbolically so as to figure in the logic of fantasy. But in *Marnie,* he assumes a specific position in the cinematographic apparatus, whereby he asserts himself as enunciator by representing himself in the scene and on such an axis that he comes to embody both the look and the camera.

7.

25d   26a

26b   26c

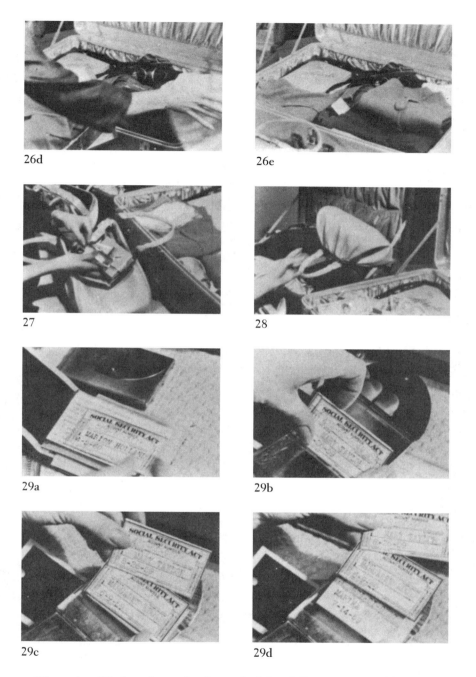

26d

26e

27

28

29a

29b

29c

29d

Thus what Hitchcock sees [at the end of shot 26] or imagines (like Mark and Strutt, but from even closer up because he is in a neighboring room of the hotel), is what we see: this same woman, still seen from the back but wearing a bathrobe, as the voyeuristic look moves in for a tighter view. The camera creeps up on the body, takes pleasure in fragmenting it to concentrate on what this sadistic fragmentation adds to the enigma: a division of the object, of its identity in four time-space fragments of the same shot [what is virtually only one shot has been deconstructed into four] that shows her hesitating between Marion Holland and Margaret Edgar as she flips through the social security cards, passing over Martha Heilbronn and Mary Taylor. This woman has no references because her identity varies. All she can offer is the surface of an image, and therein lies her seductiveness. She responds to this aggression against herself, which reduces her to an image, with the theft that serves only to increase her fascination, her "looks" (Mark's, Hitchcock's, the spectator's).

Marion-Mary-Martha-Margaret-Marnie and even Peggy, the nickname for Margaret under which a man thinks he recognized her at the racetrack, even the nickname Minnie Mouse that she borrows to tease Mark, even the Maryland license plate of the taxi she takes to her mother's in Baltimore: at that point, another signifying chain forms through too many films not to be deliberate: Miriam (*Strangers on a Train*), Madeleine (*Vertigo*), Melanie (*The Birds*), Margot (*Dial M for Murder*), and Marion (*Psycho*).

M, or the letter of the woman-object, inscribing, insisting upon, the relationship between sex and death. In *Dial M for Murder*, the significance of the phone call that is a signal to Margot's murderer is underlined by the close-up of a finger dialing the M digit—hence the film's title, which resonates like a pun (echo of Dial O for Operator). This minor but deeply personal film ("I immediately said I'd take it because that was coasting, playing it safe")[8] could provide the means to articulate the two chains: that of the signature system and that of the woman as emblem of the death wish. We must keep in mind that in *Dial M for Murder* we see Hitchcock in a college picture between the two men who intend to murder the woman—her husband and the killer. (So, too, in *Suspicion* does Joan Fontaine distractedly assemble letters into the word MURDER when she imagines that she is the object of a death wish on the part of her husband, the image of which she (re)constitutes fantas(ma)tically, to the point of fainting at the edge of a precipice.)

Hitchcock's motivation for this game of signifiers, made up of women's first names beginning with an M, originates, I believe, in a cultural fantasy arising from the ferment of his Catholic upbringing: M as in Mary, the Holy Virgin. In the tradition of the Western novel, especially beginning with the nineteenthth century, this double image of woman relayed through the American cinema, as whore and virgin, branded by the imminence of death; fatal curse of her sex in the Oedipal triangle that progressively superimposes itself on the double Christian constellation of the Holy Trinity and the Holy Family.[9] Thus, in the nineteenth century, for numerous historical reasons, love and death became interchangeable, organized as they are around narcissistic doubling and the fantasy of bisexuality. Freud demonstrated the importance of these two fantasies in his complete outline of the Oedipus complex: the two fantasies ensure that the man is constituted as a desiring subject by the transformation of love into death; and it will be the body of the woman that will have to bear the unendurable image of his own castration.

8.

Following the segmentation of the name, the segmentation of the body completes Marnie's change of identity. Through a clever organization of suspense, her face, hidden until now, is at last unveiled as it finishes its metamorphosis, now fully transformed into the image of archetypal (Hollywood) femininity.

The ending of shot 31 is ambiguous. After the very slight tilt of the camera when Marnie throws back her head, her eyes shut, delighted with herself, her face turns in our direction to give itself fully to the image. Marnie looks at herself, in what is supposed to be her mirror, contemplating the triumphant image of a split identity that responds with theft and metamorphosis to the sexual aggression that her being constructed as an image seems to spark. But she is not looking at the camera. The sustained look is intentionally too high, avoiding the camera axis that would link Marnie and the spectator or collapse the mirror into the screen. (In fact, they do coincide for a brief moment but in a way that is effectively virtual with respect to the unfolding [*défilement*] of the film: only when one slows down the film on an editing table to look at the scene where Marnie, in one continuous movement, raises her head and stares at herself in the mirror, can one see, and feel the full force of, the single frame that lines up her gaze, her image, the camera, and the spectator.)

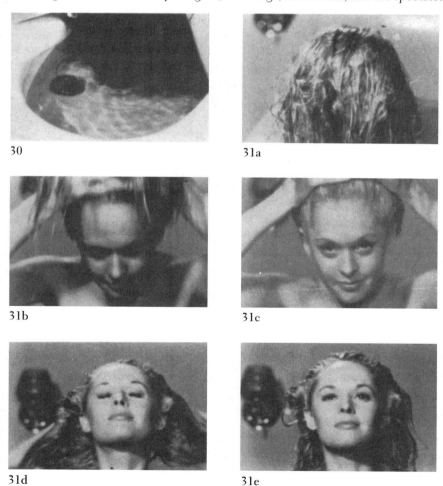

30

31a

31b

31c

31d

31e

Thus, we see her seeing herself, without her seeing us seeing her. In this way, the divergence dramatically increases the voyeurism as such, what might be called the passion for the image aroused by its missing part. This fixed, contemplative gaze suggests that Marnie imagines herself in terms of her own image in the mirror, just as Mark is stimulated by Strutt's description and his own memories (hence the segment that follows, and which, in a way, she anticipates, in the same way Mark anticipates, at the end of shot 24, that she will walk down the hallway of the hotel). And this is, in one sense, the condition that enables her to see herself and take pleasure in doing so.

In her absorption in the desire for her own image, a desire shaped by the threat of the masculine look that she counters with her symptoms, Marnie offers to the male spectator (to the camera held by Hitchcock, Mark, Strutt) the deferred pleasure of desire for an object; for any woman spectator, who, for all practical purposes is alienated by this structure, she stimulates a desire for identification.

9.

Once the enunciation is thus organized around this high point (31d), the film can truly begin, or begin again. In a subtle touch, the film recommences with a shot of Marnie's back. Resumed as well is the film's perpetual game of difference and identity: the narrative. This time (32b), shot from a wider angle, the lower part of Marnie's body is framed instead of the truncated torso with which the film began. Marnie is carrying two suitcases instead of one, and a light brown purse instead of a large yellow purse. The action takes place in a train station and no longer on the platform. Instead of seeing her body enigmatically move away, the camera stays with it, following it in two distinct movements, finally to reveal her when she turns around

32a

32b

32c

32d

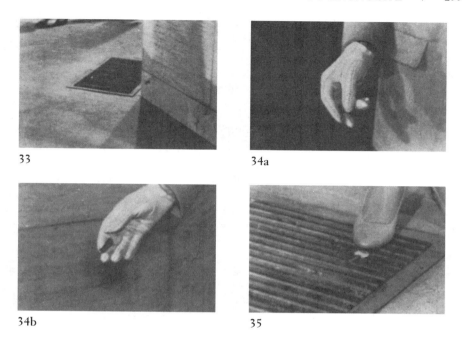

33

34a

34b

35

facing the camera in medium close-up (32d). In this particular instance, shots 1 and 31d
are condensed. This time there is also a displacement that pulls her look into the action
and sees her seeing, no longer with this strange structural glance (31d) that locks in the
enunciative apparatus but with one of those glances, at once partial and constant, that in
Hitchcock carve out the real that they constitute, giving the action its meaning.

Strictly speaking, shot 33 is thus the first subjective shot of the narrative (not-
withstanding the previous subjectivity implied by the reverse shots of Strutt in the
second segment). While Marnie is looking, Hitchcock borrows her look, identifying
himself with her since he makes her and the spectator identify themselves with the
camera, following the rule of delegated point of view. Two things can be noted: first
of all, the simple act of delegating the look, which in Hitchcock's films is done
insistently and frequently, makes possible the doubling of the look, in which the
enunciation is inscribed across the multiplicity of textual systems from a center at
once constant and shifting; second, and even more to the point, Hitchcock's fundamental need for the intermediary look of the woman creates, in a mirror structure,
the metaphoric possibility of the look as truth (look of the man/look of the camera).
This is also a necessary condition that effects a return toward her and her repossess-
ion as object. But here it is in the guise of a pleasure taken in a return to Marnie's
body, cutting it up, parceling it: *fetishizing* it (all "motivated," of course, by the
action: the key dropped, then pushed down into the grill by her foot, and so on).

10.

In all classical films there are periods of dead time. These are undoubtedly
necessary to the action, but we experience them as slumps. ("We often run into the

problem of the logic of time. You feel you must show a certain amount of preparation; yet that preparation can become dull. We're so anxious not to drag it out that we can't fill it with entertaining details that would make it more interesting" [230].) Thus, the inevitable problem of classical film insofar as it is hostage to two contradictory tendencies (make the film long enough, but never really too long).

There is, however, another reason, economic in the Freudian sense of the term, that explains these slumps. Extreme tension, it seems to me, must be avoided; the film cannot afford to let too many significant events or meanings pile up. In the characteristic order of the classical film (a motivated succession of representations), this tension may well threaten to subvert the continuity of perception, specifically the systematic relation of the film's parts to each other. It is almost as if dull or partly dull moments are necessary to recuperate or reorder what has just been seen, to unbind, even unconsciously, the condensations and displacements that have taken place; in short, these slumps make it possible for the spectator to undertake a first working through of the "film-work" (Thierry Kuntzel). That these periods of dead time are generally less noticeable during a first screening, when all the work is still to be done, also points up that fact that these films, in shrewd anticipation of their economic market, were never conceived for successive viewings.

Furthermore—but this is only saying the same thing differently—the classical film cannot run the constant risk of creating a density so apparent that it undermines the verisimilitude that structures the film from beginning to end. The film must maintain a certain slack in its fictional structure to avoid the risk of abstraction, of looking ridiculous, or worst of all, of having the plot seem improbable. Hitchcock is fully aware of this problem, having pushed to the extreme the classical narrative's capacity for figurative abstraction. (Talking about *Strangers on a Train*, he said: "The great problem with this type of picture, you see, is that your main characters sometimes tend to become mere figures" [146].) This explains the almost "useless" segment in which we see Marnie, arriving by car along a tree-lined street, enter into a hotel where she seems to be a regular and ask to be driven immediately to "Garrod's" before going up to her room to change clothes. (This is also the first segment to be defined classically by a lap-dissolve, which makes it stand out since, before this, in the beginning of the film, straight cuts were used, accentuating the effect of its being one solid block— although it is true that between the shots of the Social Security cards and of Marnie's hair in the sink (30) there is a first lap-dissolve, but so brief that I could only see it on the editing table because I had stopped accidentally at that point.)

36

40

11.

Man: *How do, Miss Edgar. Good to have you back.*
Marnie: *Hello, Mr. Garrod. Ah, there's my darling.*
Man: *That big old spoiled baby of yours. Knew something was up; he tried to bite me twice already this morning.*
Marnie: Oh, Forio, if you want to bite somebody, bite *me*. (He helps her get on the horse.) Thanks.

41

42a

Here, too, the dialogue speaks explicitly about itself. It structures Marnie's displaced love for Forio (logical complement of the theft), which, typically, takes the place of a man or a child. This is the woman's response to the phallus that she lacks, and that she disavows in the man at the price of her own frigidity. This is what happens when the woman is made to believe that man, instead of merely having the phallus, is the phallus. The film bases the genealogy of this fantasy on an actual infantile trauma, whose logic will be progressively constituted by the narrative until the culminating point in its reconstruction, a reconstruction that is also its unfolding and its resolution: a return to both reality and normality, represented by the couple, genital love, social mores, and property.

But what is really at stake here is the way in which this structure, which crystallizes around the desire for the woman, puts to work the processes of enunciation and vision: how the symbolic is deployed from the point that organizes it, from the imaginary object it is given. Here, too, Marnie is seen by a man whose implication in the structure is determined by the fact that he is inscribed in the chain (from Hitchcock, the enunciator, to Mark, his fictional delegate) that controls the relationship between the camera and its object. Garrod occupies a position similar to that of the fisherman who, in *The Birds*, takes Melanie to the boat and watches her leave, puzzled by the eccentric desire of this woman carrying her two lovebirds in a cage.[10] The fisherman functions as a relay (like Mitch Brenner's neighbor earlier in the film) between Hitchcock and Mitch, who reappears during the fragment in the position of the look and desire. Garrod, too, is a relay between Hitchcock and Mark Rutland.

But the look (shot 43, what Garrod sees in a classical point of view shot) rivets itself on Marnie (44). One could say that, in this reverse shot, his imagination becomes the logical continuation of his vision. This statement is undoubtedly exces-

42b

42c

43

44

sive; nonetheless, this metonymic effect cannot be disregarded. The camera's return to Marnie has such a powerful effect precisely because this interposed vision once again precipitates in the film-text the question of the scopic drive in relation to its position of enunciation. It is in delegating a look that he in fact never relinquishes, that the director takes on the position of enunciator, from which he proceeds to constitute, shot by shot, that unreal real that we call film.

This return to Marnie is not coincidental. In the shot that follows 42b ("Oh, Forio, if you want to bite somebody, bite *me*") the camera exposes and examines Marnie's pleasure and obliquely makes a link, through shot 31 (her jubilation in front of the mirror), to all the shots in which she appears. This interrogation of Marnie's pleasure works on two separate levels. On one level, the representation of her pleasure is almost embarrassingly excessive: the horse in its animality and as an obvious phallic substitute. On the second level, it is a pleasure that has its meaning only insofar as it can be represented as an image. That this pleasure is exactly the unreal real characteristic of film is underscored by the obviously fake movement of Marnie on the horse that is almost entirely off-screen, as the equally hokey rear screen projection of a forest flows by. In this image of her own orgiastic excitement, Marnie seems to be getting off on herself as an image, and to be turning back around on itself the question posed by both the camera and the enunciator: What is a woman who can take such pleasure in herself? What is the nature of her pleasure? And finally: What is pleasure?

This question is raised in two practices, whose terms are so close that they are like two sides of the same coin that recur throughout the Western novel (especially in the nineteenth century), classical cinema (the American cinema in particular),

and psychoanalysis (Freudian and Lacanian). The first consists in positing an irre
ducible difference: "the dark continent of female sexuality" for Freud, the privilege
granted to woman with respect to pleasure for Lacan (at the price of not being able
to know her own pleasure [méconnaissance]); in Hollywood cinema, the extreme
condensation of sexuality in the woman's body-image. The second process systematically reduces this exaggerated difference to a single term: sexuality (itself), which
is phallic, determined by symbolic law, and so on. The woman represents this monolithic sexuality for the man, reflecting back to him only his own image.

This double, linked process reveals the prerogative and the purpose of a certain
kind of cinema of representation: to privilege the *imagistic* nature of what is at stake
here by stopping, as it were, its vertiginous movement by doubling it; then the
mechanism of the lure, cinema, becomes, through the work of enunciation in the
film, the condition of pleasure by creating a mirror construction endlessly refracted,
the irreducible gap of the scopic drive. Pleasure is the image that must be assimilated, retrieved; the impossible real, like murder, which is the sadistic reversal of
pleasure. For the man-subject who is behind the camera, this image of fear or pleasure ascribed to woman as other is the bedrock of his fantasy. This is also, for
Hitchcock, what it means to enunciate.

1977

TRANSLATED BY BERTRAND AUGST
AND HILARY RADNER IN 1977;

REVISED BY CONSTANCE PENLEY
IN 1990

7. Psychosis, Neurosis, Perversion
(on *Psycho*)

> *Barthes said to me the other day: basically, when you give someone*
> *something to read, you give it to your mother.*
>
> —Philippe Sollers

I

Psycho is undoubtedly the most obscure of Hitchcock's films. Obscure, first of all, in a literal sense, because in none of his other films does night seem so black and day so somber. There is, of course, *The Wrong Man*: exactly like *Psycho* (inscribed between the colorful symphonies of *North by Northwest* and *The Birds*), it left a trail of shadow, three years earlier, between *The Man Who Knew Too Much* and *Vertigo*. The two films do have in common a kind of nocturnal excellence that permeates the gestures, faces, and image tones: Hitchcock sought, in one case, to endow them with documentary value, and entrusted them, in the other case, to a television cameraman. However, this material obscurity—fuller and duller in the realism of *The Wrong Man*—seemed eventually to dissolve away, or at least be balanced out by the exemplary linearity of the screenplay and by the ultimate resolution of the error, restoring to Christopher Balestrero the certainty of his identity, and to his wife the hope of a fragile mental balance. In *Psycho*, on the contrary, to the extent that a surrender to the codifications of romanticism and horror is always possible, the role of shadow grows incessantly, according to the interplay of ordering and disruption that guides the film from its beginning to its end.

The principle of classical film is well known: the end must reply to the beginning; between one and the other something must be set in order; the last scene frequently recalls the first and constitutes its resolution. *Psycho*'s opaqueness is contradictory in this respect: the end, apparently, in no way replies to the beginning— the psychiatrist's commentary on the case of Norman Bates has little to do with the love scene between Marion and Sam in the Phoenix hotel. The specific obscurity of *Psycho* is thus, above all, a rhetorical obscurity. It denotes the fact that the film, in a sense, contravenes the classical model of narrative—as well as that more singular model which is both an eccentric and exemplary version of it: the Hitchcockian system. Obviously, it does so not in order to elude the system but rather—through a greater degree of abstraction—to determine its regime(s): the system here performs displacements with respect to itself, designating with extreme clarity the mechanisms that govern its operation.

II

The first sign of this is the radical displacement of the investigation. In the Hitchcockian fable, investigations conform to two major modalities, complementary and interchangeable, in which the relationships of identification are established by the position of knowledge that Hitchcock reserves for himself (and thus for the spectator as well), as opposed to the various subjects (supports) of the fiction. The inquiry represents, first of all, an ideal testing-ground for the hero (or the heroine as mirror-image, or the couple-as-subject), who, constrained by chance and necessity, learns to acknowledge a certain truth about his own desire after a dramaturgy of violence based on the search for the secret. To achieve this the riddle must be solved, and the mistaken identity in which it was cloaked revealed; these two questions may then be traced back to their common origin, resulting in a final equilibrium between desire and the law. This renders possible, through the inclusion-exclusion process of the terms of the destructive drive, the ultimate integration (whether successful or not) of the imaginary into the symbolic by means of a general dovetailing of the textual operations. Such is the exemplary itinerary of *North by Northwest*, but the same model is used in *The Thirty-Nine Steps, Saboteur, Foreign Correspondent, To Catch a Thief,* and, in a slightly different form, in *Strangers on a Train* and *Rear Window*. In *Notorious*, by displacement, it is the hero, the man of the couple, who is the secret agent invested with the knowledge and initiative usually paradoxically divided up between the police and the false culprit. In *Spellbound*, of the two characters that make up the couple, it is the woman who leads the investigation of which the other is the object. And in *Shadow of a Doubt* the investigation is led by both the woman and the policeman, who eventually make up the final couple. Thus, most of Hitchcock's films can be seen as multiple variations or distortions of this same basic model.

Conversely, the second modality consists of denying the hero (or heroine or couple-subject) access to the truth of the investigation: even though they may share its diegetic benefits, they are dispossessed of this knowledge by some external factor. Take, for example, *Dial M for Murder,* in which neither the husband nor the wife lead the investigation of which both are the object; or *Under Capricorn,* whose highly improbable plot follows the same model; or even *I Confess,* in which the presumed culprit is, paradoxically, the only one who knows the secret, but can say nothing. However, these narratives in which the hero is deprived of the truth-seeking initiative are, in general, all the more constrained by a uniform dynamic leading from the riddle to its solution (*The Wrong Man,* for example). In addition, they often depend, very naturally, alongside the main couple, on a third important character: in *Under Capricorn,* Charles Adare, the outsider and friend; in *Dial M for Murder,* Chief Inspector Hubbard, who unravels all the elaborately tangled threads of the plot.

Psycho, however, apparently conforms to this second model, while breaking the system apart at its very core. Neither of the two main characters is invested as subject during the progression of the investigation; its indices of truth are divided up among Arbogast, the sheriff, Sam, Lila, and the psychiatrist. The former two, a private detective and a policeman, share the partial and misleading truth that is so often allotted them in Hitchcock's films: Arbogast succeeds in tracing Marion but gives credit to the fiction of the mother; the sheriff denies this fiction without being able to account for its effects. Sam and Lila, for their part, seem to fulfill—amidst the scattered functions of the second model—a function proper to the first, that of the couple whose action solves the riddle and opens the way to truth. This is actually due to a displacement, since the solution brings about nothing that concerns them directly (thus Sam and Lila merely mimic the diegetic couple, marking out its absence). In addition—and as a result—their solution is only a half-truth; it immediately requires the mediation of a superior truth. This is provided by the third important character, here embodied in the psychiatrist, with the significant difference that in this case he intervenes, very deliberately, as deus ex machina, a stranger to the action, strictly exterior to what is at stake. This is why the final explanation has sometimes been considered a useless appendix, whereas it is the ultimate result of the work of displacement that has taken place throughout the film. Thus, from an original dispersion of truth and its diegetic effects, a veritable split occurs between the materiality and the awareness of experience: the division of the investigation merely reproduces the central division organizing the film and determining, at all levels, its regime.

III

Psycho contains two narratives, slipping one under the other, one into the other. This relationship must be conceptualized in order to penetrate to a structural perversion to which Hitchcock opened the way by deciding to "kill the star in the first third of the film."[1] There is, first of all, the story of Marion. The opening scene in the hotel room calls attention to the problematic: marriage. The ensuing theft produces its dramatic effect. This is a weakened version both of *Strangers on a Train* (as regards marriage, Marion and Sam occupying the place of Guy Haines and Ann Morton, with the third person being a first wife, not yet divorced in *Strangers*, already divorced in *Psycho*) and of *Marnie* (as regards the theft). The story could have various outcomes along its own axis: one of these, the meeting between Marion and Norman, has the ambiguous function of ending the story in order to transform it. The second story, that of Norman, might thus be said to begin when Marion arrives at the motel and to continue, slightly altered (because of the persistent pressure of the first story), to the end of the film. Such, indeed, was the case in the novel by Robert Bloch that was used as a pretext for the film: Hitchcock immediately broke up the overly simple structure of the book, and later justified this in a singularly underdetermined way.[2]

> In fact, the first part of the story was a red herring. That was deliberate, you see, to detract the viewer's attention in order to heighten the murder. We purposely made that beginning on the long side, with the bit about the theft and her escape, in order to get the audience absorbed with the question of whether she would or would not be caught. Even that business about the forty thousand dollars was milked to the very end so that the public might wonder what's going to happen to the money. . . .

> The more we go into the details of the girl's journey, the more the audience becomes absorbed in her flight. That's why so much is made of the motorcycle cop and the change of cars. When Anthony Perkins tells the girl of his life in the motel, and they exchange views, you still play upon the girl's problem. It seems as if she's decided to go back to Phoenix and give the money back, and it's possible that the public anticipates by thinking, "Ah, this young man is influencing her to change her mind." You turn the viewer in one direction and then in another; you keep him as far as possible from what's actually going to happen. (269)

This statement focuses on what constitutes, properly speaking, the center of the narrative, its moment of extreme fascination. However, it denies the fact that, from this very moment onwards, the constitution of the "first story" is supported by its inscription within the "second," both at the level of narrative identifications and at that of the logic of its occurrences. Denied, too, is the subtle movement by which the narrative both masks and accentuates the division constituting its paradoxical unity. The singular genius of the film consists of indissolubly mixing together the two narratives that it is composed of, by using the meeting of the two characters as the means of their substitution. Everything contributes to this.

1. The time allotted to the meeting, which by itself takes up, strictly speaking, one-fifth of the film (more, in fact: a third, counting the rather short sequence that leads Marion, caught in the storm, to the Bates Motel, and the much longer sequence between the murder and the disappearance of Marion's car in the marsh).

2. The violence that concludes the meeting, which is so incredible that it obfuscates its own secondary effect: namely, the determining fact of the passage, in a sense, from one character to the other.

3. A major rhetorical shift contributes to this displacement and facilitates the reversal. Whereas the segmentation of the rest of the film systematically employs, in a highly classical manner, the three criteria of segmental demarcation,[3] the scene of the meeting (in the extended sense) is devoid of all punctuation: there is not a single fade-out between the moment Marion abruptly leaves the garage where she has traded in her car and the moment her new car sinks into the marsh. This does not mean that thirty-five minutes of the film make up a single segment; the two other criteria of demarcation do intervene, although much less distinctly than in most classical films. It is as though the sudden absence of punctuation were responsible for creating the illusion of segmental continuity, isolating the time of the meeting within the construction of a whole in order to give it a greater fluidity and the logical evidence necessary to carry out the substitutive shift.

4. Finally, "naturalness" acts like the musicality of a fiction, integrating with misleading obviousness the elements of the first narrative that contribute to the construction of the second.

IV

The perfection of the ternary composition both conceals and reveals the binary division between the narratives and the characters. Three movements, reiterated to harmonize term-to-term in coupled oppositions, reinforce the unfolding of the fiction and its organic cohesion by establishing a very stable hierarchy of repetition and difference. All three involve an itinerary leading to the motel, and all three end in a murderous aggression punctuated by strident music. The first takes Marion Crane from her room in Phoenix to the motel room, where she is assassinated by "the mother"; the second takes Arbogast from Sam's store in Fairvale to the motel and then to Norman's house, where he in turn is assassinated by "the mother"; the third takes Sam and Lila from Sam's store to the motel and then to Norman's house, where Lila only escapes aggression by "the mother" thanks to the intervention of Sam, who recognizes Norman through the disguise.

It is immediately clear, limiting the discussion at first to murder, what movements 2 and 3, 1 and 2 have in common, respectively and by pairs: the aggression is a response, in the two latter cases, to an intrusion into the house, first by Arbogast, then by Sam and Lila (whereas Marion's assassination takes place at the motel); but—conversely—in the first two cases the murder is accomplished, whereas its failure in the third case lifts the veil of mystery and carries the film to its resolution. Thus, with the benefit of an equivalence by pairs (1 = 2, 2 = 3), the third movement recalls the first, thus accentuating the repetitive circulation.

Nevertheless, on closer examination it can be seen that an intrusion into the house is suggested during the first movement, though in unlike manner, when Norman invites Marion to share his meal, provoking the indignation of "the mother" and, eventually, the murder and everything that ensues. Thus, by a regulated difference, the circularity of the fiction is ensured—what might be called its narrative (dis)similarity. In the same way, just as movements 1 and 3 are organized around the repeated motif of the rooms rented first by Marion, then by Sam and Lila, the second movement includes Norman's very natural proposal of his room to Arbogast (and later, failing that, his less natural proposal that Arbogast come and help him change the beds).

Again, one could evoke the three scenes of shot-reverse shot, identically distributed throughout the three movements, in the small motel office (with Norman on one side of the counter, Marion, Arbogast, Sam and Lila on the other, reflected in the mirror). However, in the third case, there is a repetition: Sam is later seen alone with Norman in the office (while Lila is on her way up to the house). Thus, the third movement constantly doubles back on itself to emphasize, within the regulated difference, the progression and accomplishment of the narrative. It has been seen that movements 2 and 3 are defined by an identical trajectory: from Sam's store to the motel and then to the house. However, in the third movement this trajectory is split in two by the emergence of the mystery, which constitutes a turning point.[4] When Sam goes to the motel the first time to look for Arbogast, he sees "the mother." He undertakes the same visit with Lila in order to initiate her fully into the secret; thus they follow, together, the whole itinerary leading from their rented room to Marion's, and then, separately, from Norman's office to the mother's room, and from Norman's boyhood room to the cellar where his mother is concealed. The (dis)similarity ensures the circular identity of the narrative by guaranteeing its unpredictable advance toward a final result.

Within this regulated succession, this elaborate interplay of identities, separations, intimations, and revelations that correlatively ensure the superimposition and interchangeability of the two narratives, the second movement, much shorter than the first, has a specific transitive value: following Marion's disappearance, it emphasizes the role of Norman, progressively establishing him as the new hero of the narrative before making him the center of the mystery. The latter is accomplished by the third movement, for which Hitchcock cleverly reserves the sheriff's revelation concerning the mother's death—since, logically, if Sam and Lila were only preoccupied with Marion's fate and the stolen money, the spectator could only expect, and dread, the solution of the undoubtedly horrendous mystery hidden within Norman.

V

This circular orchestration, by the very progression of its three movements, has a secondary effect: it sets off all the more plainly the segments bordering it on either side (the opening and closing scenes), and, within these segments, rigorously heterogeneous and yet connected, the speech of the psychiatrist and the love scene in the Phoenix hotel.

The speech of the psychiatrist, in the course of which those parts of the mystery that still remain obscure are finally illuminated, is the logical consequence of the radical exclusion of the first narrative. The speech concerns Norman; it is a commentary and explanation of his case: it says nothing about Marion, who has become the pure object of a murderous desire, and even less about Sam, who can only listen, at Lila's side, to an analysis that excludes him from the diegesis of which he too, through Marion, had been the subject.

This raises a series of questions. Why is this film about psychotic dissociation organized with respect to an original plot that, while supporting it to the point of appearing indispensable, nevertheless remains, in a sense, totally foreign to it? In this highly classically orchestrated film, whose three movements recall the hermeneutic tripartition of *North by Northwest*, how is the internal principle of classical film satisfied—namely, that the end must always reply to the beginning? In what way does the last scene provide a solution, or even an echo, of the first? I think it is necessary, here, to conceive of Hitchcock as pursuing, through fiction, an indirect reflection on the inevitable relationship, in his art and in his society, between psychosis and neurosis, inscribed respectively in narrative terms as murder and theft. These are general instances, fictional rather than clinical, those of a civilization in which a certain subject, who is both a singular subject and the collective agent of enunciation, finds a way to structure his fantasy and determine his symbolic regime. What appears from the fact that the subject of neurosis is offered up in the logic of the narrative to the violence of the subject of psychosis, man or woman, mutually interchangeable throughout the course of the narrative, is the obscure numinous point of a fiction that carries to a vertiginous degree of duplication the fascinated reflection on the logic of desire.

This position is a familiar one within the twists and turns of Hitchcock's labyrinthian scenarios. It is already enunciated with incredible precision in *Shadow of a Doubt* by the doubling of uncle and niece, manifested in the Christian name they share as well as in the repeated motif of the bedrooms (the uncle's hotel room and the niece's family room: both characters are revealed, lying in bed, by a single movement of the camera, and, in a pure mirror effect, there appears in the first shot, from the left, the woman who runs the hotel, and in the second, from the right, the young girl's father; thus is prepared the substitution that will later place the uncle in the niece's room). On the one hand, there is Charlie's—the niece's—profound, inexpressible dissatisfaction, the neurotic lack that she hopes will magically disappear thanks to Uncle Charlie; on the other, there is the uncle's psychotic split, the return of his childhood trauma that is compulsively acted out in the murder of widows and that ultimately, due to the progression of the inquiry, turns upon the young girl as the logical object of its deadly desire. Thus, as in *Psycho*, woman, the subject of neurosis, becomes the object of the psychosis of which man is the subject. This is a fundamental aspect of the Hitchcockian constant according to which, given a certain order of desire, it is above all women that get killed.

This is not to say:

1. That women do not kill. But the murder they commit is always the reverse side of the "psychotic" aggression of which they are the object. It is thus that, in *Shadow of a Doubt*, the uncle, in his struggle, falls off the train from which he had tried to throw his niece; in *Blackmail* the young woman kills the painter who had tried to rape her; and in *Dial M for Murder*, the husband's murderous desire having replaced, as in so many of Hitchcock's and other films, the psychosis he conceals, the woman kills to defend herself from the assassin he has hired. This is why, in a rigorously complementary manner, women may—or must—seem in the position of symbolic murderers: thus, in *North by Northwest*, Eve's fictitious murder of Thornhill is woman's response to the murderous desire she awakens in man—if only metaphorically, as a sexual object.

2. That women cannot "manifest psychotic tendencies" (as can be seen in *The Wrong Man* or in *Under Capricorn*). But that they do so only to the extent that the hero has suffered a loss of identity, and never from the same demented object-desire as he. This is why women can tolerate madness in men only if they can save them from it (in *Spellbound*, even at the cost of awakening their murderous desire; or, in a totally different way, in *Rebecca*). This modality may also be that of men (*Marnie*), but it then involves only, so to speak, a semi-madness, and this at the price of a fetishistic position that reinforces love and is related, through scopophilia, to murderous desire, of which it is the mitigated, possessive form.

Vertigo constitutes, in all respects, a marvelously complex counterexample. The woman is the object of an illusory psychosis; she is an image of psychosis, turned toward death in a twofold manner, through the image-painting of Carlotta Valdes. She awakens a passion in the man: the desire to see, mesmerized by death; this is the moment when Scottie tears Madeleine away from what fascinates him. Later, after the false-real death of Madeleine, the man wanders on the borderline of madness (between neurosis and psychosis: narcissistic neurosis, mourning, and melancholia). Still later, when the false living woman reappears, the desire to kill reemerges: an image must be modeled so that the "real" can at last be transferred onto it, thus accomplishing—with the help of God if necessary (the appearance of the nun diegetically motivating the second fall)—the subject's desire, sublimated in the scopic drive that transfixes the male subject.

3. Finally, this is not to say that men cannot be the subject of neurosis. Such, indeed, is their most common lot. Neurosis is what occurs when an encounter with the extraordinary, by way of the inevitable ritual testing of murder-psychosis, determines for the hero the resolution of the symbolic. There is always a "madman" who kills for the hero, turning the subject of neurosis into a false culprit, and thus inciting him—through a displacement in which neurotic guilt is resolved in the reality of action—to rediscover a certain truth of his desire. Here again the itinerary of *North by Northwest* is exemplary.

So, in another manner, is that of *Strangers on a Train*, through the meeting of the characters and the fiction of the exchanged murders. The issue of marriage, or in this case remarriage (elsewhere it is the question of stabilizing or restabilizing the couple: *Suspicion*, *The Man Who Knew Too Much*) serves to sustain what can be called Guy's "neurosis": the basic neurosis of American cinema. By a diabolical twist, this issue—in the interests of its own resolution (the final marriage)—provides psychosis with its object. Because of the exchange of murders, Miriam, Guy's wife, comes to occupy the place of Bruno's father, whom Bruno has vainly appealed to Guy to murder. As a part of the fantasy of the murder of the father, necessary to the symbolic resolution of neurosis, Miriam thus embodies the complementary fantasy that indicates, for Hitchcock, the psychotic's access to the real: the murder of a woman (and through her, of the too-well-loved mother; such films as *Shadow of a Doubt*, *Strangers on a Train*, *Psycho*, and *Frenzy* are directly connected around this motif).

These, then, are the terms that *Psycho* sets into play, frontally, through a reversible effect of the articulation between the two psychic structures, grasped in a doubling relationship carried by sexual difference. The criterion used here to associate and dissociate neurosis and psychosis remains, overwhelmingly, the one used by Freud:[5] both are avatars of desire that bring about an unsettling of the subject's relationship to reality. But whereas in psychosis the Ego is at the service of the Id and eludes what it finds intolerable in reality, in neurosis the Ego is the stage of a conflict between the Id and the Superego, such that the loss of reality "affects precisely that piece of reality as a result of whose demands the instinctual repression ensued."[6] This is Marion's situation in *Psycho*: the theft that draws her into this loss is her response to the socio-sexual aggression on the part of the "millionaire" in Cassidy's office, of which she was, metaphorically, the object. But on a much deeper level, it is her response to Sam's aggression, of which she feels herself to be the object, in the sordid clandestineness of the hotel room, when the conflict between the intensity of her sexual demand and her wish to have it legally sanctioned by marriage (continually postponed due to Sam's financial position) comes to a head.[7] This explains the focus here, just as later on in *Marnie*, on money, that polyvalent signifier of desire (sexual or social), which also serves, even better than hysterical conversion and perhaps with greater conformity to unconscious logic, the logic of the fiction.[8] This is what Marion's theft attempts to resolve, magically, "by a sort of flight," as Freud says of neurosis—dodging the fragment of reality that psychosis, for its part, simply denies in order to reconstruct a better reality.

VI

The long segment during which Marion and Norman are face to face in the small reception room of the motel thus places face to face, fictitiously, two psychic structures: man and woman, the latter destined to become the prey of the former. The mirror arrangement that organizes their dialogue in a regulated alternation of shot-reverse shots ensures, between the two characters, the interchangeability necessary to their future substitution. It is here that Norman's family romance is presented, in the deceptive form in which it has been restructured by his desire, by the truth of his delirium,[9] thus echoing the more disparate elements of Sam's and Marion's family romances, scattered throughout their dialogue in the hotel room. Thus, the two mental forms are brought together by similarity and exclusion: Marion grows aware of her own derangement because of the much more absolute derangement she senses in Norman. Their differential assimilation is concentrated in a metaphor with endless ramifications. "Norman: You—you eat like a bird." The metaphor is no sooner spoken than it is denied. "Anyway, I hear the expression 'eats like a bird'—it—it's really a fals- fals- fals- falsity. Because birds really eat a tremendous lot." Marion has to be a bird in order to be constituted as a body potentially similar to that of Norman's mother, object of his desire, stuffed just like the birds who survey their exchange. But Marion cannot really be a bird, because the bird's "psychotic" appetite has been reserved for Norman, as the body transformed into the mother's body (even if, by a remarkable reversal, Norman eats nothing during the entire scene: "It's all for you. I'm not hungry.").

The reception room scene is meticulously organized to lead up to the murder scene. After an opening shot during which Norman appears amidst the stuffed birds disposed about the room, there are four shots showing Marion, standing, in alternation with the birds: the order of these shots (bird a—Marion—bird b—Marion) denotes her feeling that she is seen by the birds as much as she sees them and that this disturbs her. After a repetition of shot 1 (Norman standing), there is a shot showing Norman and Marion together, seated on either side of a tray of food prepared by Norman. Then a classical alternation is established, dividing the shot between the two characters to distribute their dialogue. At the same time, a formal opposition emphasizes the fact that Norman, in this second alternation, has come to occupy, with respect to Marion, the place of the birds. In the various ways in which Norman is framed, he is associated with the outstretched beaks and widespread wings of one or several of the stuffed birds. Conversely, Marion is defined successively in two framings: she is beneath an oval painting whose theme was clearly visible during the second bird shot of the preceding alternation. The painting distinctly shows a band of angels, or, more precisely, a group of three women in which the central figure seems to be rising up to heaven, wings outspread. Next to the painting, in the same shot, the menacing shadow of a crow is projected onto the wall, penetrating the picture like a knifeblade or a penis. It is this complex whole that rivets Marion's attention, then splits apart when she takes her seat beneath the painting and becomes—through a double, metaphorical-metonymical inflection—defined by it, just as Norman is later emblematically defined by the birds. Thus the differential assimilation is continued: Marion, angel-woman-bird; Norman, bird-fetish-murderer. And thus is prefigured, in the intertwined motifs of alternation, the aggression of which she is soon to be the object (announced, when she rises, half concealing the painting, by the black beak of the crow that reappears inside the frame).

A few shots later, the alternation between Norman and Marion recommences, this time through an apparatus that mimics the cinematographic apparatus itself. Norman is concealed, significantly, by a painting that prefigures the effect he is to produce: *Susanna and the Elders*, virtually at the moment of the rape. Beneath the painting is a large hole that reveals, in the wall itself, the tiny luminous hole to which Norman puts his eye, creating—just like the projector's beam—an image that is for us virtual and for him almost real: Marion undressing, once again in the proximity of two birds, the portraits hanging on the wall of her bedroom near the bathroom door. The alternation then continues, obsessively marking the insert of the bulging eyeball, and shifting from the relationship between shots to the relationship between segments (or subsegments).

The next double series of shots, postponing voyeurism, intensifies it to the extreme:

a. Norman, under the influence of what he has seen, goes back to shut himself up in the house in order to imagine what will happen next—or better yet, what will happen metaphorically for him, given the premises that catalyze his desire.

b. Marion, in her room, soon gets into the shower: the spectator, by this advance intrusion, is witness to the scene for which Norman's obsession has prepared the way.

The moment of the murder marks the invasion by the subject (hero and spectator together) of the constituted image of his fantasy. Here, alternation must be abandoned; it is ruptured by the brutal inscription on the image of the living body-knife-bird of Norman-the mother, the reiterated fragmentation of Marion's body, the insert of her mouth agape in a horrendous scream and that of the dead eye that answers—at the opposite extreme of this very long fragment—the bulging eye of Norman given over to the inordinate desire of the scopic drive.

VII

That only men are subjects of psychosis (or that women are psychotic only by default, or by reflection) here implies, above all, something else: that only men are subjects of perversion (here and elsewhere, given a certain regime of fiction, and a certain order of civilization). It should be recalled that the manner in which psychosis and perversion can both be defined—although not in the same way—is by their difference from neurosis, through their common allegiance to the wishes of the Id: the former, as has been seen, by its indulgence in a form of delirious reconstruction, through an infinitely more radical loss of reality than in neurosis, implying a lesser subservience to repressive mechanisms; the latter, in the sense of the famous formula: neurosis is "the negative of perversion." Though it must not be taken literally—as its reversal (perversion is the negative of neurosis) would tend to define perversion as nothing but the raw manifestation of infantile desire—Freud's formula does imply, however, that perversion provides a more direct access to the object of the drive, according to its own defense mechanisms (denial of reality, splitting of the Ego), which in some ways link it to those of psychosis.[10]

More specifically, it can be seen how this twofold difference is articulated here with respect to the inscription of the scopic drive and its destiny. To go back to the beginning of the film: there is the first, continuous shot during which the camera wanders down from a high angle over the rooftops of a city, progressively closing in on a window with half-raised blinds, then going beneath these blinds to reveal, in a bedroom, a couple that has just been making love. Thus, from the start, emphasis is placed on the voyeuristic position, which deliberately constitutes the position of enunciation.[11] It is highly remarkable that this opening shot, quite common in Hitchcock's films (see *Shadow of a Doubt*), is especially reminiscent of *Rope*, in which the first interminable shot focuses—having passed through a similar window/screen—on the cold fury of a murder.[12] In this interplay of forms based on an endless interchangeability between murder and the sexual act (see, e.g., the scene of the kiss in the train in *North by Northwest*),[13] it is clearly the "unseen" of the primal scene in the hotel room that, at the level of the enunciating instance itself (Hitchcock-the camera), is displaced from neurosis to psychosis, from the hotel room to the motel room.

Thus, Norman obviously comes to occupy, with respect to Marion, the place of Sam (whence the resemblance, for some striking, between Sam and Norman, particularly during the scene of their confrontation across the counter in the motel office).[14] However, the substitution occurs at the price of a displacement, imputable to the respective identifications between Hitchcock and the two male characters. In the first scene, the camera almost always remains at a distance from Sam: he is held, like Marion, and usually with her, within the frame, that is, within the neurotic field that the two of them circumscribe. An essentially diegetic identification is thus set up (for the male spectator, who is *primarily* addressed), at the level of the sexual possession of which Marion has been the object, when Sam renews his demand and hears it refused.[15]

Conversely, in the shots preceding the shower scene, the camera reduces to an extreme degree the unforeseeable effect of the distance separating it from what is being filmed: it virtually coincides with the insert of Norman's bulging eye, due to the metaphor of the apparatus thus constituted. This is the point of maximal identification between the character and the instance of the mise-en-scène; it can only be surpassed by its own excess, when the eye-camera becomes a bodyknife, entering the field of its object and attempting in vain to coincide with it.

However, in order to go from one man to another, and from one position to another, the camera must also embody the woman and adopt her look, conserving a strong identification—diegetic, of course, but more specifically specular, determined by the organization of the point of view—with the subject it has taken as its object. (The latter can be maintained in a position of fundamental subjection through a series of carefully planned relays—the policemen, the service station attendant—that reiterate the question of which she has been the object from the start.) In conformity with its basic path, that of perverse structuration, the transformation from neurosis to psychosis is brought about by woman, who is both its foundation and its indispensable form.

This explains the lengthiness of the first half of the first movement, organized around theft and escape. It also explains the systematic series of shot-reverse shots that mark Marion's itinerary up until the moment of blindness (a mixture of fatigue and hypnosis) that causes her to turn off the wet highway and head for the motel. It explains, finally, the resumption and redoubling of these shots as a preparation for the moment of reversal, during the confrontation between Marion and Norman. In this manner, the diegesis participates directly in the aggressive potential, carried to an extreme by the reciprocity of the looks in the alternation of shot-reverse shots. The effects of this cinematographic code par excellence evoke the structure of the cinematographic apparatus, and thereby of the primitive apparatus it imitates, namely, the mirror wherein the subject structures himself, through a mode of narcissistic identification of which aggressivity is an indelible component.[16] However, this reference only makes sense—here very specifically (as in all of Hitchcock's films, and classical cinema in general, particularly American)—within the global system in which it has been constructed, that is, in a system in which the aggressive element can never be separated from the inflection it receives from sexual difference, and the attribution of this difference to the signifier that governs it. In other words, it is directed from the man toward the woman, and that difference which appears due to woman is nothing but the mirror effect of the narcissistic doubling that makes possible the constitution of the male subject through the woman's body, ordered by a double play of differentiated identity, based on an effect of imaginary projection subjected to the constitutive pressure of a symbolic determination.[17]

Between man and woman, through woman's look as appropriated by the camera, this mirror—or doubling—effect (hence also one of denial and splitting) serves to structure the male subject as the subject of a scopic drive, that is to say, a subject who imaginarily attributes to woman the lack he himself has been assigned, in response to the anxiety created by the fantasized threat of this lack within his own body. This is the classical dialectic—as described by Freud and Lacan—of the phallus and castration; its implications with respect to perversion (the conjugated motifs of voyeurism and fetishism) have been astutely analyzed by Guy Rosolato.[18] Lacan refers this dialectic, particularly as regards the scopic drive, to the lack—unevenly divided between the two sexes—of the signifier that structures it; it is this signifier, castration, that determines "the gaze as *objet a*."[19] In a different perspective, the same dialectic has been relativized by Luce Irigaray, who denounces the fact that in men (that is, in Sam, Norman, Hitchcock, Freud, Lacan, the subject writing these lines in an attempt to fissure the system that holds him) "the scopic drive is predominant."[20]

This is why, theoretically, there are no women fetishists,[21] nor even, more broadly speaking, women perverts: either because, in psychological terms, "perverse" as applied to women connotes perversity rather than perversion, or because theory—elaborated or directed by men—has avoided acknowledging perversions in women, not having discovered perversion itself.

This explains the fact that Norman's psychosis, his inordinate object-desire that rushes headlong into murder, is entirely structured by a fetishistic aim carried to the point of madness. Psychoanalytically, it might be said, Norman is a collage (which

neither confirms nor denies his clinical possibilities, which are not in question—
simply because, for me, that is not the question). He seeks to construct a chain in
which the excessiveness of the psychotic-perverse desire of the male subject can be
structured—from the man to the camera, his true measure—during the scene where
he establishes his presence at a distance, fascinated, in vertiginous mastery. This
chain may be written phallus-bird-fetish-mother-eye-knife-camera. A terrifying play
on words (suggested, rather than made explicit, in the film) connects this chain to
the omnipotence of infantile desire turned toward death: *Mommy, mummy:*[22] the
mother's body, fetishized to death, so to speak, becomes the body that murders, in
keeping with the desire awakened in the eye of the subject possessed by it. Through
the incredible incorporation of a metaphor become reality, Norman's fascinated
look carries within it the phallus immemorially attributed to the mother. But he can
acknowledge it in himself only on condition that he ceaselessly encounter it in his
mirror image, namely in the body/look of woman (which engenders the mirage),
and as an absolute threat to which he must respond; otherwise, it is his own body
that will desert him. Such (to complete the psychiatrist's speech) might be the motivations behind the genealogy of the case: the reiterative passage from the former
murder (that of the mother) to the murder of Marion of which Norman-the mother
is the agent, emphasizing in both cases, given an original identificatory fantasy, the
literally impossible desire for possession and fusion that is at stake.

   This allows us to describe the distribution of the three terms (psychosis, neurosis, perversion) within the logic of the process of enunciation. These terms define
the primordial relationship between the two scenes that most closely circumscribe
this process (the hotel and the motel), through a "breathing space" during which
the subject is presented as such. The possessive form used in the credits—"Alfred
Hitchcock's *Psycho*"—is a mark of enunciation that may be said to have a double
meaning: this film belongs to me; this psychosis is mine, or would be mine if . . . if it
weren't, precisely, for this film, which both involves me in and frees me from psychosis, positioning me elsewhere. A special lettering effect (something like the bulging eye during the credits of *Vertigo*) contributes to the singularization of this
relatively common signifying arrangement: a vibrato twice causes the center of the
letters to shift back and forth, first for the title *Psycho*, and then for the name in the
final enunciation: "Directed by Alfred Hitchcock." In addition, the opening scene
immediately reiterates the interplay of black and white lines that had striated the
credits from top to bottom: the camera must pass under Venetian blinds to enter the
room at the end of its movement, and it is on the background of these horizontal
lines, in the second half of the scene, that Sam and Marion are seen in reverse shot,
separately or together. Thus, by displacement and metaphor, what is inscribed in
this space communicates an implied relationship between the title and the name.
   In the first scene, the camera's power is intrinsically expressed by the bird's-eye
view of the city and its rooftops, then emphasized by its concentration on the voyeuristic point of reference: the couple in the bedroom after love-making. The "after" is important, since, in a sense, the camera intervenes in place of what happens
between man and woman at the literally mythical level of the primal scene: it is
a continually withdrawing instance, collecting—at the purified level of vicarious-

ness—what is fundamentally perverse and psychotic, given the logic of this perspective, in man's desire for woman, even within the neurotic configuration that is its most common destiny. The camera becomes, it might be said, the eye-phallus, projected and reprojected from one sex to the other; but on the basis of a signifying privilege assigned to only one sex, it transforms the camera into pure eye, look, dissociated from the scene, in proportion to the lack of the phallus of which it circumscribes the representation so that—and because—it is represented in it.[23] It is this dialectic, in slightly different terms, that emerges during the second scene, through a temporal actualization: "that which may not be seen" seeks to show itself, to break into awareness (into reality), but displaced from the act. The camera must still, obviously, remain outside its object. Yet it is also doubly inscribed within it, as has been seen: firstly by the mediation of the apparatus set up around Norman, and secondly through the invasion, by the subject of the apparatus, of the tableau of his own vision. From its perverse situation, already enhanced by an identification with the subject of the diegesis, the camera thus fully assumes the psychotic function that was potentially circumscribed during the first scene. However, it can of course attain only a more extreme perversion, since it is filming its metaphorical invasion of its own field. It thus reaffirms all the more strongly, by its very division, the unforeseeable effects of distance, lack, and denial that make it up—everything that psychosis (Norman-the camera) is at that very moment attempting to exorcise by presenting as real, through a rape ending in murder, the imaginary and ungraspable relation of the primal scene.

Within this configuration, one thing seems to me to be essential, namely, that it is through woman's pleasure *(jouissance)* that the perverse projection and psychotic inscription are carried out (just as it is through her actions, her body, her look, that the film moves from one scene to the next). The emphasis on Marion's pleasure in the shower goes well beyond all diegetic motivation: close-up shots of her naked body alternate with shots of gushing water; she leans into the stream, opens her mouth, smiles, and closes her eyes in a rapture that is made all the more intense because it contrasts with the horror that is to come but also because the two are linked together. By a subtle reversal, the pleasure that Marion did not show in the opening love scene at last appears. However, the pleasure is for herself (even if it can only be so for the camera, because of the image-nature assigned to her by the camera); it takes the form of narcissistic intimacy, which poses, for men, the question of sexual pleasure itself, with woman's body instituted as its mythical site. The masculine subject can accept the image of woman's pleasure only on condition that, having constructed it, he may inscribe himself and recognize himself within it and thus reappropriate it even at the cost of its (or her) destruction.[24]

VIII

Briefly, to resume and strengthen what has been said by considering several points in a spiral-like movement, that is, together, as a text does whenever one tries to make it appear as what it is, that is to say, as what it becomes, virtually, always in analysis: a *volume.*

1. The first scene(s) is (are) programmed as a matrix whose elements are distributed throughout the whole text by effects of dispersal, rebound, and repetition. This is one of the laws of classical film (see, in particular, the analyses of Thierry Kuntzel).[25] In *Psycho*, this process is at first carried out at a very general level. The first scene, through the shift in the screenplay, primarily serves as a preparation for the succession of scenes between Marion and Norman: their tête-à-tête in the reception room, the series of shots setting up Norman as apparatus [*dispositif de Norman*], the murder in the shower. From this is derived, at the end, the scene with the psychiatrist, which resolves not only the enigma but the (psychic) mystery of the murder: this final scene only replies to the first one at the price of the initial displacement caused by the shift in the screenplay.

There is also, however, the way in which the first scene inaugurates the sequence of bedrooms: the motel rooms, Marion's room, Arbogast's room (suggested), Sam and Lila's room, and thence, at the end of the third movement, the intrusion into the bedrooms of the house, especially Norman's and the mother's, under Lila's discovering look.

More subtly, there is a thread that leads from the first shot to Norman as apparatus, to the next-to-last shot. Norman-the mother is seen in a medium shot against the naked wall of his cell, smiling, while on his face is gradually superimposed the skull that will make of him, irremediably, the mother. Her voice is heard: "I hope that they are watching. They will see; they will see, and they will say, 'Why she wouldn't even harm a fly.'" This circular play on words goes from the fly to the bird, to the body-fetish of Norman-the mother. But it goes further still: to the omnipotence of the scopic drive. Norman's words are addressed to all the guardians of the law (policemen, judges, psychiatrist), presumably gathered on the other side of the door and peering at him through the keyhole. However, through them, his words are addressed to the spectator, who is trapped in the mirror by Norman's eyes, staring right into the camera as though to conjure away the power it exerts. The spectator is thus confronted, from within the shot itself, with the "*unauthorised* scopophilia" that places cinematic voyeurism "in direct line from the primal scene."[26] Thus, all of the opening shots have been condensed into the body-look of Norman-the mother, revealing the reflective structure of the apparatus, before the final shot, with an ultimate effect of resolution, brings the film to its close (in a single sweep, using a very long dissolve to link the last and next-to-last shots through the superimposition of the skull). In this way, two screenplays intermingle: male (Sam, Norman, and—in both—Hitchcock) and female (Marion, the mother); and the end, after a monstrous detour, replies to the beginning. Marion's dead body reappears in the white car dragged from the marsh only because it has been, from the beginning, the object of the conjugated desire of a man and the camera.

2. The apparatus is therefore present in the film, though not—as in *Rear Window*—by a mirror effect. Here, a certain rhyming effect of two images strikes me; first, on the roadside at dawn, the close-up of the policeman coming upon Marion asleep in her car; and secondly, in the cellar, the close-up of the mother's skeleton. The latter is seen twice, once when Lila puts her hand on Mrs. Bates's shoulder and the draped skeleton slowly swings around toward her, and again at the end of the segment, after Norman's intrusion. There is a similarity between these two faces, sustained by a striking reversal: the eyes have disappeared. In the second case they

are nothing but hollow sockets, and in the first they are totally hidden by dark glasses. This is a way of signifying, by its very absence, the unbearably excessive nature of the look. The dark glasses especially (like Mitch's binoculars in *The Birds*) suggest a metaphor of the photographic lens: super-vision of the law, symbolized by its representative; excess of the symbolic itself, which triumphs at the end "in the prolixity of the psychiatrist."[27] Film, both as discourse and as an institution, is subject to an order that is marked by the monolithic power of its ruling signifier. However, this super-vision is also that of disorder, the breaking of the law, of which fetishistic psychosis is the most inordinate form. Moreover, the signifier is perpetually imaginary, subject to denial and splitting. The hollow eye-sockets of the mother are the verso of an apparatus whose recto is the policeman's dark glasses. There is an endless circularity between desire and the law, both of which, taken to an extreme, inspire terror (in Marion, in Lila).

Here, I cannot resist associating more or less freely. When Lila enters the cellar she sees, from behind, a woman seated. In the foreground to the right, in the upper part of the frame, there is an electric lightbulb so alive, so enormous, and disposed in such a manner that it seemed to me—at first sight and at each successive viewing, despite critical distance—to simulate a spherical screen, casting a blinding light onto the brick wall across from Mrs. Bates. The mother occupies, in this virtual image, the place of the spectator, thus evoking the real spectator, and even more so his mirror image (the fetish inhabited by the death wish) when she looks at him directly during the next two close-up shots. This is particularly true the second time, when Lila's terror causes her to knock against the lightbulb, making it swing back and forth. The vacillation in the lighting thus produced is repeated and amplified later (when Norman bursts in, unmasked and overcome by Sam): the skull seems to be animated by this vibration—this play of lights and shadows that also designates the cinema itself.

Following this, representation dissolves into the very image of the law (a metaphorical reappearance of the policeman): a general shot of the courthouse introduces the psychiatrist's speech.

3. That everything in *Psycho* seems immediately doubled must be seen as the effect—with repercussions in concentric waves down to the micro-systematic level of the smallest signifying units—of the two main rhetorical axes that organize the film, namely, its ternary composition and its two screenplays. Other of Hitchcock's films also manifest, by their very structure, the specific pressure of the doubling process that underlies all his films: *Shadow of a Doubt*, with the determining superimposition of the uncle's and niece's names (Charlie); *Strangers on a Train*, with the exchange of murders; *Vertigo*, with the mirror effect of the double heroine (Madeleine-Judy). However, this doubling process is, so to speak, exacerbated in *Psycho* by the crisscross effects of substitution, division, and echo among characters. The first couple, Sam and Marion, engenders the second, Norman and Marion: Norman has thus taken the place of Sam. Yet he has actually, diegetically speaking, taken the place of Marion, given the mirror dialectic between the sexes and their psychic structurations. Lila's appearance at the beginning of the second movement causes this network of transformations to double back on itself: she represents the return of the indispensable heroine, Marion's reappearance (like Judy's in *Vertigo*) in the form of her sister. Thus, the film could be said to be organized in yet another

way with respect to woman's body-look, because of the long sequence taking Lila from the motel to the cellar where she discovers—with an absolute horror that obviously recalls that of Marion in the shower—the stuffed body of the mother. Thus the diegetic couple disjoined at the end of the first segment is reconstituted as a shadow: Sam and Lila, pretending to be married—as Sam and Marion were intended to be—approach the motel where Marion first met Norman on the path that was supposed to lead her to Sam. The function of this shadow-couple reveals in an exemplary way, through repetition and mimed (undermined) resolution, the deep structural subversion of sameness that is here carried out.

4. To conclude, we might point out the constellation of signifiers that disseminate and recenter the differential doubling between men and women to which the fiction is continually and completely subjected:

—*Norman-Marion:* Christian names in mirror relation to one another, interchangeable but for a single phoneme (Marion was chosen instead of the Mary of Bloch's novel).

—*Nor-man:* he who is neither woman . . . nor man, since he can be one in the place of the other, or rather one and the other, one within the other.

—*Marie Samuels:* the name used by Marion to sign the motel register, derived from Sam's first name.

—*Phoenix* (superimposed on the first shot to situate the action): again, a bird; the bird that dies only in order to be transformed into another (as is here the case, through murder, of one character, one sex, one story). In fact, there is a double metamorphosis: a diegetic one (Marion becoming Norman) and a formative one (Norman becoming a living bird-mother) which renders possible the former.

—*Crane:* Marion's last name; once again a bird's name. It marks her body with the signifier that appears, to Norman, as a lack or an excess. But the word "crane" also means something else: the machine that embodies above all others, in the image-taking apparatus, the omniscient power of the look, what might be called the bird's-eye view. This is to say, once again but here with an element of humor, that the camera becomes one with woman's body, and that in this sense it is itself the fetish, adopting the forms of the bird and of Norman-the mother, going through the whole circuit of the fiction, only to be immediately acknowledged as the enunciating index, at the level of the apparatus that makes fiction possible.

Whence, indissolubly, here, it can be said of film and cinema, that they are the very institution of perversion.

1979
TRANSLATED BY NANCY HUSTON

The numbers of the following sixty-six frame enlargements, unlike those for other illustrations in the book, do not correspond to a linear succession of shots. They indicate only the order for reading. But of course certain shots may follow one another, and several frame enlargements may illustrate a single shot.

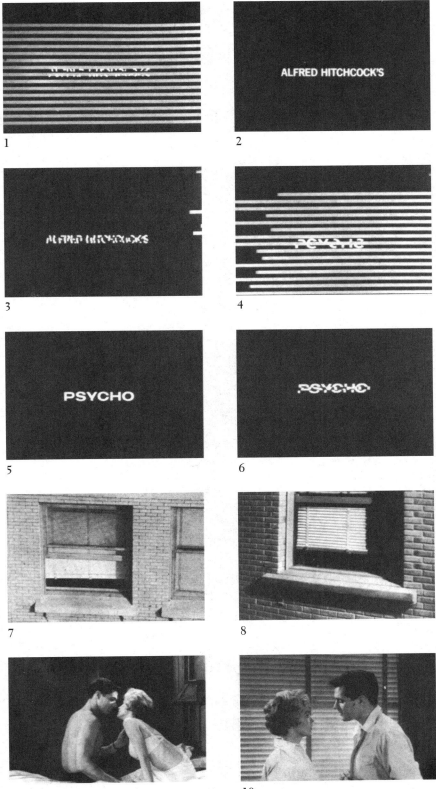

11

12

13

14

15

16

17

18

19

20

21

22

23

24

25

26

27

28

29

30

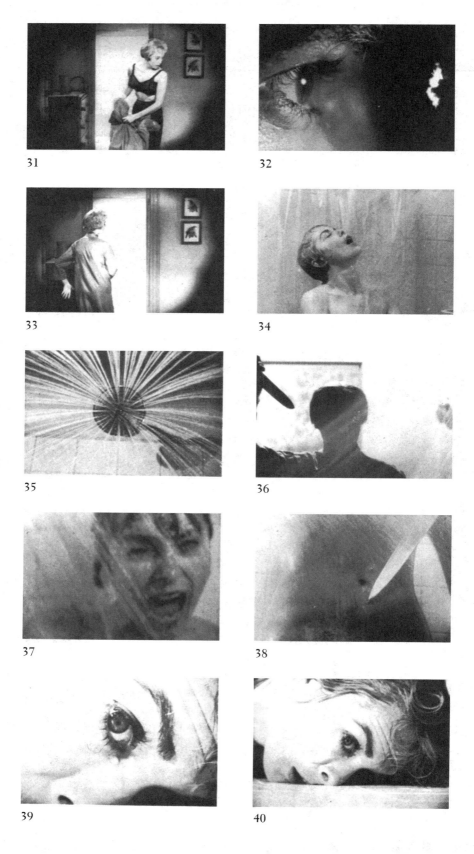

31

32

33

34

35

36

37

38

39

40

41

42

43

44

45

46

47

48

49

50

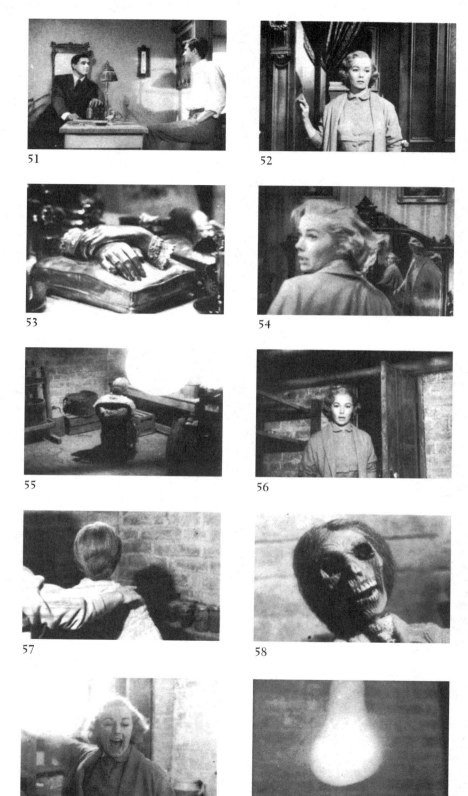

51

52

53

54

55

56

57

58

59

60

61

62

63

64

65

66

8. To Alternate/To Narrate
🔳 (on *The Lonedale Operator*)

Here we shall see how the systematicity at the heart of American high classicism is elaborated, proceeding from the reduction of a fundamental form of cinematographic discourse: *alternation.*

I shall not pause to define either the nature or the multiple determinations of a formal principle whose first general formulation—before returning to it more fully—I have already outlined.[1] This will emerge, as in most of my earlier analyses, from a step-by-step textual analysis whose systematic organization is largely regulated by it (even if the organization cannot be reduced simply to this), through the effects of repetition and almost deliberate abstraction that often characterize primitive works.

In order to follow this process, which sets out to reconstruct (because it is short) an entire film (*The Lonedale Operator,* D. W. Griffith),[2] it will be necessary to try to imagine the deployment of this principle of alternation, its extension, its dispersion, and its diversification, from shot to shot, from segment to segment: in short its mise-en-abîme (its mise-en-volume) in certain films by Hitchcock or Lang, Mann or Curtiz, Wyler or Thorpe. We must see it where it is at work—orchestrated, orchestrating all levels—in the classical cinema.

We must bear in mind that in *The Lonedale Operator:*

—all the shots are fixed; thus the description will specify, when necessary, only the movement of the characters and the objects inside the frame of the frame enlargements reproduced here;

—the shots are always strictly regulated by the immediate needs of the story and its dramatization, which alone determine the sometimes noticeable variations in the length of the shots; and

—there are no intertitles, at least not in the copy to which I had access.

Finally, it would be well to remember that although this exemplarily simple film brings into play textual operations of a certain degree of complexity, we are not concerned here with an analysis as such—that is, with an underlying logic that would be enlightened by a commentary. Rather, I see the following as an ordered description, whose repetition seeks to tease out additional knowledge, on a par with knowledge acquired directly.

He/She/He/She, she and he. At the beginning of the narrative, we have the diegetic couple, the mainstay of the story. The couple is the site of the first alternation, placing the film under the sign of the changing form that will be its governing

principle. This first alternation clearly is made
in order to be broken, and then to reunite (shot
4) its two terms—the man and the woman, the
train engineer and the telegraph operator—
in the same frame. The movement of the hero,
which brings about, from shot 1 to shot 3, a
slight variation in his body (from medium long
shot to medium shot) inside an identically arranged frame, produces this break in alternation by making the first term penetrate the
frame that until then had been given over to
the second. After this, from shot 4 to shot 7, the
action continues by repeated shots of the couple, in which, according to the purest romantic code, the ardent tenderness of the hero and
the affectionate reserve of the heroine are as-
serted. We see that the movements of the characters play, in a graduated way, on an opposition
between near and far (though in order to show
this one would need many more frame enlargements—one always needs too many): the characters leave the field of vision on the right in
shot 4 (following a placing similar to that in
shot 3) and are framed more and more closely
before disappearing, only to appear again in
shot 5 far back on the right and framed exactly
as they were at the end of shot 4. This operation is more or less repeated in shot 6 (except
that the trajectory is inverted: this time the
couple arrives on the left of the frame), helping to build the systematicity of the narrative.
This is sometimes done, as here, in a pure and
insistent way: in these less complex films, filmic

writing seems ceaselessly to put to work, as though for their own sake, the potentialities of cinematographic language.

6–9, 9–13. A sequence of frames that the narrative lays out in order to take them
up again later, according to an invariable succession, which will gain strength by
repetition. The separation in shot 7 prepares the way for the second alternation that
arises from it between shots 9 and 10: she/he again. But this time it is with the effect
of a liaison implied by the exchange of looks, wich makes of shot 10 a semi-implicit
subjective shot. A specifically cinematographic code (that of point of view) obliquely
takes up the diegetic alternation and incorporates itself into it: their superimposition (which could be layered with other specific codes and has already half done
so by the shifts in framing) is the body of the fiction itself.

This alternation continues: shot 11 effects a return to the first term; the alternation develops in this way right up to shot 13. And it is only interrupted to make way

for a new alternation, apparently less rigid, but no less distinct, which contributes to establishing a larg-er scale for the alternating distribution of the unfolding action.

Another office, in another station. Another train (for a moment we might even think it is the same train we saw leaving in shot 10; but when it stops in shot 15 after a lengthy forward climb, some passengers get off and others board, whereas the train operated by the hero consists of only a single locomotive). Another action: a man with a satchel enters an office, stops near a cashier who hides two bags of money in it, then goes out again by the same door on the left, onto the platform, where he holds out the satchel to a second man who is leaning out of the train we have just seen pulling into the station (15), and which we see leaving again at the end of this very lengthy shot (31 seconds).

This time the alternation is by groups of shots (thirteen shots, from 1 to 13, then two, 14–15, then X number of shots, according to the way one decides to divide up the rest of the action); that is to say, the alternation of actions is connected in a fairly linked continuity of units corresponding to segments or supra-segments, and no longer just from shot to shot. In this sense we can speak of a superior level of alternation since, at least in the first of its terms, it integrates earlier alternations; but it is superior in extent, not in nature: it is always the same process operating between the various spaces, whether close up or further away.

We return now to the office of the telegraph operator. Here there is a closer framing, a medium shot (16), then a medium long shot (17), returning to the earlier framing (9, 11, 13). These two frames (16, 17) thus sketch out an internal alternation within the alternation of the action, which models itself on the latter and develops on its own. We should note that, as with other configurations, this alternation cannot be resolved by the fusion of its two

6

7

8

9

10

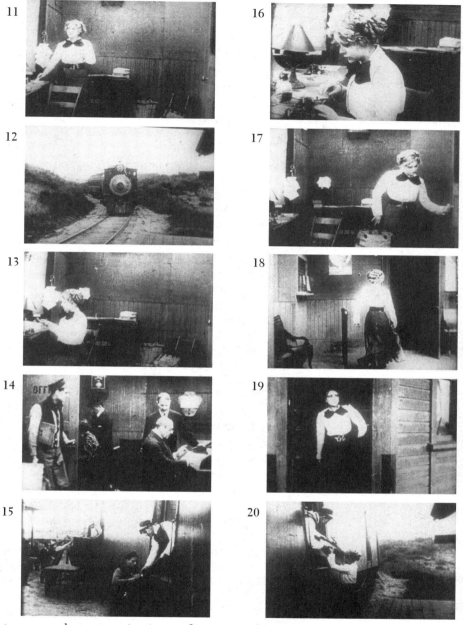

terms: no shot can maintain two framings at the same time (except by the perfect superimposition of the two shots), to mingle, for example, the subject and the object of its vision. Thus, one might classify the alternations according to this first criterion, which doubles back on itself by considering the specificity or the nonspecificity of the codes put into play.

So we have four shots (16–19) of the telegraph operator. After a glance out the window—analogous to the glance that determined the earlier alternation with the first train—she gets up and goes out of her office in shot 17 (bear in mind that

the shots remain invariably fixed), and retraces her steps exactly, in the opposite direction, from the walk that she accomplished from shots 7 to 9, in an e-quivalent number of shots. These shifts in the fiction are the result of the effects of repetition that carry the story: there is no longer anyone in the office in shot 18, and it is in shot 19 that we see her reappear alone in the doorway, the same spot where, in shot 9, she was saying goodbye to her lover.

In shot 20 the second train—from the other station—arrives, continuing this alternation of actions between the two stations—when it enters the first station, in the frame in which, on two occasions, the motifs of the action have already been inscribed. This alternation, initiated in shot 17 by the look of the telegraph operator (which recalls the farewell to the first train), materializes between shots 19 and 20; but it disappears in the latter part of the very shot that constitutes its second term: there the telegraph operator receives the bags of money from the person who himself had received them in shot 15 (by a left-right inversion in the arrangement of the characters, determined by that of the trains and the platforms), and she hides them in her own satchel. By a very subtle arrangement, the framing of shot 20, which reiterates that of shot 10 (departure of the first train), also repeats very nearly (with more or less floor or roof showing) the framing of shot 6 in which the couple were crossing the tracks, thus further accentuating the effect of inversion between the series that leads the young woman from the platform to her office (6–9) and that which leads her from her office to the platform (17–20). This micro-condensation of the textual system integrates into one of its units components of several earlier units and thus constructs itself by means of displaced similarities that constitute its repeated difference.

20–21. These shots contain a new motif, a third term: the robbers who appear from between the rails, under the train car, and cross

the field from left to right in shot 20. They open an alternation (20/21/22: she-he/robbers/she-he) which, as with that of the two stations, will arrange itself, at first according to groups of shots (she/22–25/robbers/26–27). It should be noticed that:

—shots 23–25 reiterate, in the strict succession of their three settings, the first entrance and the exit of shots 7–9 and 17–19;

—shot 27, of the robbers, repeats the framing of their appearance in shot 20, which combined the terms of the previous alternation (the telegraph operator/the train from the other station), thus imbricating, through both obvious and subtle interlocking, the two alternating movements, before the second systematizes itself through a relationship determined from shot to shot.

28–42. This time it is not her lover but the robbers whom the operator sees, or rather senses at the end of shot 28, which reiterates exactly shots 9, 11, and 13, even to the position of the chair. The alternation from shot to shot will be broken four times in different ways, without, however, interrupting itself, thus showing that it is the same serial movement, varied according to the dictates of the diegesis, following from shots 20–21, between the two robbers and the operator:

a. 32–34. From the second office to the exit door, three shots of the telegraph operator are repeated 7–9, 17–19, and 23–25.

b. In shot 34, alternation is not established from shot to shot but by means of the door that the operator closes and that serves as a shutter, thus dividing into 34a/34b the very shot in which the robbers appear. (This well-known framing, succeeding that of the window—29 and 31—will from then on be given over to the robbers until shot 70). This example shows very well that diegetic alternation (to show this *or* that in order to show this *and* that) merely coincides, through a kind of massive coding, with the limits of the shot; but it shows too that it spills over continually, either, as here, by dividing the shot within itself, or as shown

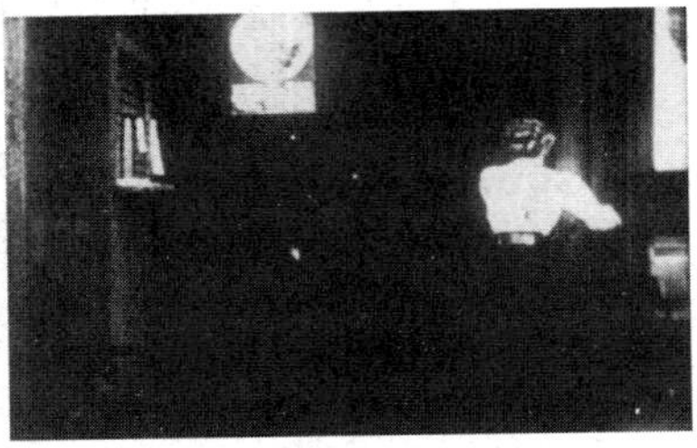

33

38

34a

39

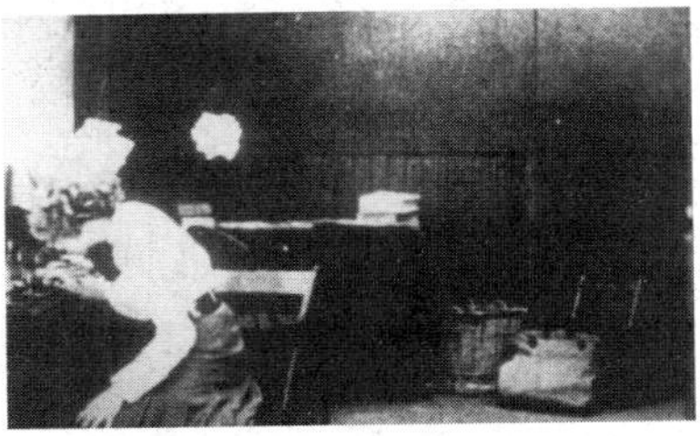

34b

40

35

41

36

42

37

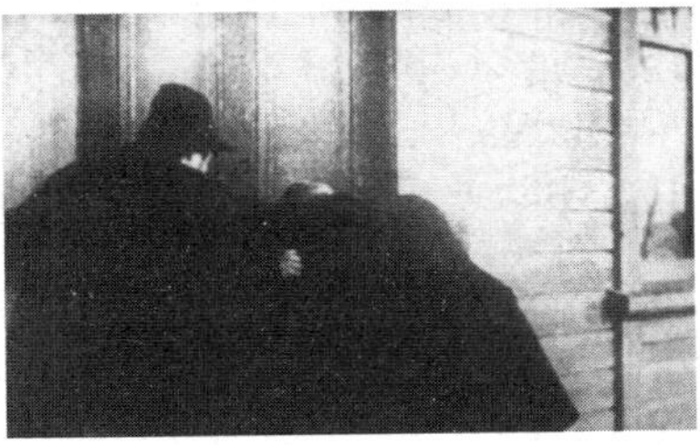

43

elsewhere by continuing through diverse re-groupings of shots, in an ongoing variation of a single principle.

c. The same again, for shots 37–38 and 40–41.

d. It should be noted how the movement of the operator is accomplished this time:

—shot 34, the third instance of her movement, from her desk to the door, becomes the first instance of a reverse movement, from the door to the desk, for the duration of a half-shot, which serves the theatrical dictates of the action;

—the second shot showing movement (first office) is, in contrast, repeated twice, conforming to the build-up of suspense, of which alternation—by the internal breaking up of motifs—is one of the major instruments (35 and 37: she closes the door, then runs across the room).

40–41. From the medium long shot to the medium shot: this placing reverses shots 16–17, again for the benefit of the suspense and the future alternation that serves it, through identical framings and positions but according to a strict logic that assigns the medium shot to the telegraphic activity.

With shots 42 and 43 a three-term alternation is set up, which will continue further, almost to the end of the film, more or less hiding itself behind the two-term alternations that it forms and the alternations within each of these terms. The heroine, the other operator, and the robbers form a movement that immediately focuses on the orderly exchange of the two telegraph operators at their desks, arranged as mirror opposites, as were the trains on the platforms of the two stations (42–52). A long and exemplary series finds its meaning only in the principle that carries it and is varied within it, even if the principle is triumphant. The second telegraph operator takes the place of the second station; he is the second term representing a distance to be covered; he is the other of a same term of which the heroine is the center, to which all disjunction will return.

In an apparently third station, shot 55 allows us again to meet the hero (from now on doubled by a second engineer), whom the male telegraph operator alerts.

(A third station: the economy of the sets that is evident in the entire film seems to prove that if this new station shot were meant to designate the second station, it would have been more or less similar to shot 15. But all the elements regrouped on the left of the frame are different and seem intended to mark that difference, despite a similarity due to the identity of the camera angles.)

The alternation, which is continued in the action, immediately reinscribes its third term (the robbers, 56); thus, by a return to the operator (57) it plays for a moment on what could be called at this stage of the narrative its second and third terms (the other station—itself divisible into its motifs, locations, and characters—and the robbers) placed first of all in their relationship with the first term (the heroine).

There is a continuous variation of the diegesis: the fainting of the young woman in shot 54 provides the fiction with one of the oppositions that it relishes when it reinstates (57/58/59) the alternation between the two telegraph operators: by calling out, the heroine wakes up the sleeping man in shots 45 and 47, whereas his call in turn cannot, in shot 58, revive the unconscious heroine, whose awakening is delayed until ten shots later, purely for the sake of the drama.

The repetition of shot 55 in shot 60 defers the shot-by-shot alternation with the heroine, whose sleep is used by the diegesis to put to work its other terms. The motifs of the second term, converging in shot 60 (the other station: the operator, the engineer[s]) divide up at first in order to weave together the motif of an internal alternation, almost immediately interrupted (60/61/62), since its only function is to formalize, according to a principle both permanent and variable, an acceleration of the

fiction. It is based on two frames, one of which will disappear; the other will regulate the development of the alternations to come: (a) a wide frame, which regroups the whole of the action: the station platform and the other telegraph operator who holds out the message and a gun to the engineer, who runs toward his locomotive; (b) a closer frame: the engineer in his locomotive, which is starting off (with the second engineer, who enters and leaves the field of vision [61]). (a') the same wide frame: the train leaving, facing the screen, and the telegraph operator on the platform (a title added to modern copies justly notes that the engineer runs away from the viewer in shot 60 in order to board his locomotive, which in shot 62 is seen from the opposite direction, turned toward us).

Next, a new alternation is set up, between the second term, made up from now on of the train (64–65, 68) and the third term, the robbers (63–66).

The second term immediately reproduces in this new alternation an arrangement sketched out in the shots that make the transition between the telegraph operator's office and the train (59–62). There is a division, this time, between a shot of the train advancing toward us frontally and leaving on the right of frame (64), and a medium close-up of the engineer (65). Two things are worth noting:

—Shot 65 strictly repeats shot 61 (except for the variable presence of the second engineer and the unavoidable differences linked to the realism of the representation); it thus presumes the ordered progression of the narrative, with differences having been settled by the insistent repetitions.

—In the alternate weaving together of the three terms, shots 61 and 65 open up a potential sub-alternation: this can remain either at the elementary, embryonic stage; develop by the return of one or the other of its two elements; or reabsorb itself by limiting itself to a single element so as to fuse more rigorously with the shot-by-shot development of the gen-

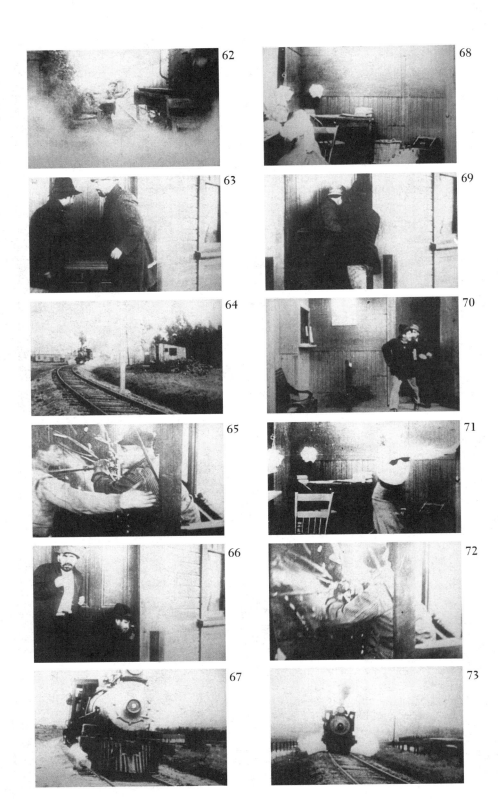

eral alternation. This is the case with shot 67, in which the train appears alone, before the narrative finally comes back to its first term: the female telegraph operator, who regains consciousness.

But there is also the balance of spatio-temporal masses: shot 64, followed by a shot of the engineers, shows the train only on a very short stretch of its journey (it enters from the back and advances to mid-frame); shot 67, which alone maintains the second term, positions the train at a distance and makes it come right up to us and exit on the right of the frame, leaving the field empty. But this balance is also an imbalance: shot 73, which precedes this time a shot of the engineers, noticeably repeats the course of shot 67. The narrative is thus built up by slightly displaced analogies, an accumulation of small differences.

68–71. She/the robbers. This time the shot doubles back on this pairing (69–70), following the latter's movements until they finally succeed in opening the door and entering the first office, thus repeating, through fragments ordered according to the dramatization of the diegesis, the path that has already been completed five times (in both directions) by the heroine.

Until shots 70–71, the alternation was modulated by the prevalent repetitions of the two terms, taken in turn from the three possible relationships (she/telegraph operator or she/train, she/robbers, robbers/telegraph operator or robbers/train). The alternating backtracking that operates on the heroine, opposing her successively to each of the other two terms (train/she: 67/68; thief/she: 69–70/71), while at the same time tightening the alternation a/b/a' between the young woman and the robbers (68/69–70/71), is resolved in favor of a regulated alternation with three terms, which we can write variously: robbers/she/train or she/train/robbers, up to shot 83.

This arrangement in no way hinders the divided arrangement of the second term, which is reaffirmed in shots 72–73, but in-

versely: the shot of the engineer this time preceding that of the train, which is contrary to shots 64–65.

76/77–80/81. Here the arrangement is the same, the only notable variations being: the countryside crossed by the train that is still coming toward us and the path it makes. In shots 77 and 81, instead of arriving from a little closer than in the preceding frames and going out of frame, the train arrives in shot 77 for the first time on the left.

82–85. Alternation is again crystallized in two of the terms, only to disappear in shot 85 when the robbers, after breaking down the door, finally enter the office of the telegraph operator and take their place with her in this frame, which had been devoted to her since shot 9.

It is thus a two-term alternation that now continues between the telegraph operator/robbers, on the one hand, and the train on the other.

Three variations operate on the second term. First, there is a new inversion of the elements, since the train again precedes the detailed shot of the engineers, as it did in shots 64–65. Then the potential alternation between the two elements develops by a return of the first element, the train, which structures shots 86/87/88 according to the scheme a/b/a'. Last, the detailed shot changes (87)—this time no longer showing the engineer in close-up on his locomotive (with the intermittent appearance of the second engineer), but the back of the locomotive, with each of the two men at his post, and a background of sky.

Shots 90–91 repeat this sequence. But the medium close-up of the engineer is substituted for a shot of the back of the locomotive: reiterating shots 64–65, where the same interior shot followed that of the train, and preceded it in the micro-series 71–72, 76–77, 80–81. Moreover, this internal alternation of the second term, which continues with the final arrival of the train in shot 92, is thwarted in

this very shot where the two men jump from the train to hurry toward the telegraph operator's office.

It should be added that in shot 90, where the train enters the setting of the first station (leaving aside shot 92, where it stops), the train covers only a fragment of its course, no longer

leaving the field of vision as, till then, only shot 64 had made it do: this is thus a way of distinguishing this from other instances of the train's arrival and departure.

Finally, shots 90 and 92 complete a paradigm: that of train arrivals and departures, which structure the entire film, according to a logic in which symmetry gives rise to dissym-

metry and so assures the development of the narrative.

Thus, on the one hand, there are two stations, B and C, from which two departures take place. On the other hand, there is station A, where the narrative begins and ends and where, according to an arrangement of interlocking cross-referencing and alternation,

there are two departures and two arrivals: almost at the beginning of the film, there is the departure of the first train, operated by the lover; and there is the almost consecutive arrival and departure of the second train, with an ellipsis of the entire journey; and finally, there is the arrival, at the end, of the last train,

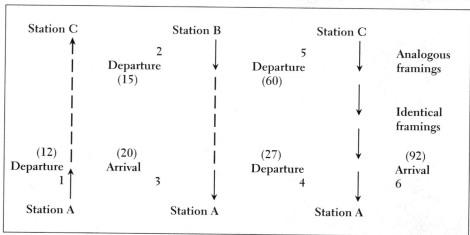

whose journey covers the final third of the film. This third train is, of course, the first, or is presented as such: at first by its engineer, then, as we have seen, because at its departure from station A, this train consists only of a locomotive, in contrast to the second train, which apparently includes two cars.

A relationship of symmetry-dissymmetry is thus set up between the two trains: the first, which will become the third; and the second, of which we also see only two departures and one arrival, according to an arrangement in which the second is inscribed within the journeys of the first like a double motif by which the architecture of suspense is structured and refined. We can also appreciate the neat systematicity of the framing: *analogous*, it could be said, in stations B and C because the train pulls into the station in the same way and is filmed from the same angle (left-right), in spite of the shift in setting and the distribution of the trains' bulk in the frames; *identical* (and inverted, with respect to the camera angle: right-left) in station A, where there are the same frames (with very slight internal variations) and the same distribution of mass in frames devoted to the two departures and the two arrivals.

92–95. The movement that leads the hero from the station platform to the telegraph operator's office reiterates with precision the path she takes at his side, then alone, in shots 6–9, and that she repeats in the opposite direction when she receives the satchel after the arrival of the second train; later it will again be traversed, in more or less fragmented or divided fashion, by the heroine and the robbers.

In one leap, true to the progression of the action, the hero re-enacts the course followed in the initially calm period of the unfolding drama. He thus puts an end to the alternation of the three terms (already reduced to two terms since shot 85, and heavily concentrated on the second term since shots 92–93), by bursting into the field of vision reserved until then

96

for the first term, then for its conjunction with the third. Thus, the terms of the narrative become combined, and they resolve the division posed by the narrative's premises: the diegetic couple, scarcely formed (4–7), apparently only separates in order to meet again, to strengthen its image by the test of a dramatized separa- 97a tion whose internal form is alternation, orchestrated at multiple levels in order to serve the principle that carries the narrative, by repetition, toward its resolution.

Shot 96 refines this final movement by means of an ultimate alternation: a close-up of the object with which the heroine held the two robbers in check, placed between the two 97b shots that reunite the five protagonists (95 and 97). Hermeneutic resolution. The unseen, or the badly seen object appears in its true colors: a monkey wrench instead of a revolver. There is a rhyming effect, too, with the revolver held by the young man, which re-establishes the distribution of objects according to sex.

But this close-up, the only one in the film, also acknowledges an added meaning, stemming from the rhymed difference that it inscribes between the man and the woman: it unites the couple, as if over and above the action that re-forms it, by isolating fragments of their bodies, which suddenly seem to be made, despite the contrast in the clothes (smooth white of the blouse, black and white stripes of the shirt), of a continuous material: the subject of the story can be read in the meaning of the principle that governs it.

N.B. Another print has since revealed to me another ending (quite simply, ten to twenty seconds were cut from the copy on which I worked), which completes the perfection of the system. Same shot, same frame: the two robbers leave, followed by the second engineer; the hero and the heroine embrace. The kiss that was gently refused in shot 4 is accepted in the final shot. Repetition-resolution. The conjunction of the couple, of the two terms posed by the opening alternation, constitutes the happy ending of the narrative.

1980

TRANSLATED BY INGE PRUKS;

REVISED BY ROXANNE LAPIDUS IN 1999

NOTES

[Editor's note: The notes have been updated from the original French book. Wherever possible, English translations of French citations have been added.]

A Bit of History

1. Michel Foucault, *Les mots et les choses* (Paris: Gallimard, 1966), pp. 314ff. Translated as *The Order of Things* (New York: Pantheon, 1971), pp. 303ff.

2. Raymond Bellour, "Sur Fritz Lang," translated as "On Fritz Lang," *Substance* 9 (1974): 25–34.

3. *Revue d'esthétique* 2 (1966).

4. Eric Rohmer, *Cahiers du cinéma* 63 (October 1956): 39.

5. François Truffaut, "Un trousseau de fausses clefs," *Cahiers du cinéma* 39 (October 1954): 49–50. Translated by Aruna Vasuder as "Skeleton Keys," *Film Culture* 32 (Spring 1964); gloss of the number "two," pp. 65–66. Reprinted in *Cahiers du Cinéma in English* 2 (1966).

6. Jean Mitry, *S. M. Eisenstein* (Paris: Editions Universitaires, 1955).

7. Here I do not use "fragment" in the sense Eisenstein gives it (= shot) but rather to denote a portion of indeterminate length set apart from the filmic chain, which does not correspond in any way to one of the segmental types in *la grande syntagmatique*. See *Essais sur la signification au cinéma* (Paris: Editions Klincksieck, 1971); translated by Michael Taylor as *Film Language: A Semiotics of the Cinema*, 2nd ed. (Chicago: University of Chicago Press, 1991).

8. To evaluate the changes and the progress made in film analysis, theory of cinema, and the *auteur* approach in the last fifteen years, one only has to compare Mitry's book to the more recent work of Jacques Aumont, *Montage Eisenstein* (Paris: Editions Albatros, 1979); translated by Lee Hildreth, Constance Penley, and Andrew Ross as *Montage Eisenstein* (Bloomington: Indiana University Press, 1987). In an effort to circumscribe the meaning of the concept of "montage" and the role it plays in Eisenstein's films and written work, Aumont devotes himself to true textual analyses of fragments of *The General Line* [*The Old and the New*] and *Ivan the Terrible* that are both implied by the development of his project and rigorously self-determined by the extension of their internal logic.

9. Christian Metz, "Le signifiant imaginaire," *Communications* 23 (1975): 37. Translated by Ben Brewster as "The Imaginary Signifier," in *The Imaginary Signifier* (Bloomington: Indiana University Press, 1982).

10. I say "at that time," even though we are talking about something that has never stopped and no doubt will never stop, unless there are formidable transformations in the practical (and mental) administration of the cinema-object (film libraries with immediately consultable videos, etc.). But, "at that time," this discourse of error reigned alone as the discourse of truth.

11. Jean Mitry, *Tout Chaplin* (Paris: Seghers, 1972), pp. 340–45.

12. "For the fluid camera, the lateral reframings of the deep-focus shots, Renoir here substitutes a pictorial stability in which the scenes are framed only once. There is not a single pan or dolly shot in the entire film." See André Bazin, *Jean Renoir* (Paris: Champ Libre, 1971), p. 112. Translated by William H. Simon as *Jean Renoir* (New York: Dell, 1974).

13. For more on this phenomenon, see my "Le monde et la distance," *Dictionnaire du*

cinéma (Paris: Editions Universitaires, 1966), p. 51 [reprinted in *L'analyse du film*, pp. 45–55].

14. Truffaut, "Skeleton Keys," p. 66.

15. Jean-Luc Godard, "Parlons de Pierrot," *Cahiers du cinéma* 171 (October 1965). Translated by Tom Milne as "Let's Talk about Pierrot," in *Godard on Godard*, ed. Tom Milne (New York: Viking Press, 1972), pp. 215–34. Cited by Thierry Kuntzel in "Savoir, pouvoir, voir," *Ça cinéma* 7–8 (1975): 85. Translated by Nancy Huston as "Sight, Insight, and Power," *Camera Obscura* 6 (1980): 91–110.

16. The articles published by Noël Burch from 1967 to 1968 in *Cahiers du cinéma* are collected in *Praxis du cinéma* (Paris: Gallimard, 1969). Translated by Helen R. Lane as *Theory of Film Practice* (Princeton: Princeton University Press, 1981). Those of Marie-Claire Ropars, published in *Esprit* from 1959 to 1970, are collected in *L'écran de la mémoire* (Paris: Seuil, 1971).

17. Eric Rohmer's fine book, *L'organisation de l'espace dans le Faust de Murnau* (Paris:10/18, 1977), offers a striking illustration of the effect produced by rupture and continuity together. While his assumptions have not changed since his articles in *La revue du cinéma*, *Cahiers du cinéma*, and his essay on Hitchcock, one can see what a leap this book is in its very meticulous work on the material composition of the image. In giving more depth to these assumptions, which are resolutely idealist at heart, this work also changes its point of application by conferring a sort of internal autonomy on the positivity of analyses. One finds oneself wondering what Bazin's work in this direction would have been had he lived.

18. Lotte Eisner, in particular, "Notes sur le style de Fritz Lang," *La revue du cinéma* 5 (February 1947), and "Aperçus sur le costume dans les films allemands," *La revue du cinéma* 19–20 (Fall 1949).

19. Lotte Eisner, *L'écran démoniaque* (Paris: André Bonne, 1952). Translated by Roger Greaves as *The Haunted Screen* (Berkeley: University of California Press, 1969). A second French edition was published in Paris by Le Terrain Vague in 1966.

20. Lotte Eisner, *F. W. Murnau* (Paris: Le Terrain Vague, 1966). Translated as *Murnau*, rev. and enl. ed. (Berkeley: University of California Press, 1973).

21. Lotte Eisner, *Fritz Lang*, trans. Gertrude Mander, ed. David Robinson (London: Secker and Warburg, 1976).

22. On *Murnau* and the second edition of *L'écran démoniaque*, see my essay "Siegfried et les ambiguités," *Critique* 238 (March 1967).

23. See, for example, *L'univers filmique*, a collective work edited by Etienne Souriau (Paris: Flammarion, 1953), in which Anne Souriau offers some remarks on the symbolism of colors in Michael Curtiz's *Robin Hood* in her article "Fonctions filmiques des costumes et des décors," pp. 95–96.

24. Roland Barthes, "Le problème de la signification au cinéma," *Revue internationale de filmologie* 10.32–33 (January–June 1960); "La recherche des unités traumatiques dans l'information visuelle," *Revue internationale de filmologie* 10.34 (July–September 1960). Interviews with Michel Delahaye and Jacques Rivette, *Cahiers du cinéma* 147 (September 1963); translated by Annwyl Williams as "Towards a Semiotics of Cinema: Roland Barthes in Interview with Michel Delahaye, Jacques Rivette," *Cahiers du cinéma: The 1960s*, ed. Jim Hillier (Cambridge, Mass.: Harvard University Press, 1986); with Philippe Pilard and Michel Tardy, *Image et son* 175 (July 1964).

25. "A critic wanting to treat the cinema as a language, putting aside the metaphorical inflation of the term, would therefore need to begin by working out whether in the filmic continuum there are elements which are not analogical, or whose analogical character has been deformed, transposed or codified; elements which are structured in such a way that they can be treated as fragments of language. These are practical research problems which have not yet been explored and which could be: you would need to begin by running experi-

mental tests of some kind, and after that you could see whether it's possible to establish a semantics, or even a partial semantics, of film (a partial semantics is surely what it would be). It would be a case of applying structuralist methods and isolating filmic elements, of seeing how they are understood, which signifieds they correspond to in this or that instance and, by varying them, of seeing at what point a variation in the signifier entails a variation in the signified. Linguistic units, in the proper sense, would then have been isolated, and from these you could construct the 'classes,' systems and declensions." See *Cahiers du cinéma* 147 (September 1963). See also *Cahiers du cinéma: The 1960s*, pp. 277–78.

"Do we have to reconstitute the system of dialogue on one side and the system of images on the other, then try to establish a system that extends to cover these subsidiary systems? Or do we have to enter the ensemble of messages with a gestaltist view to establish its original units? This question is hardly a settled one." See *Image et son* 175 (July 1964): 43.

26. "*Tu n'as rien vu à Hiroshima.*" *Un grand film*, Hiroshima mon amour, analysis by a group of scholars under the direction of Raymond Raver (Brussels: Université Libre de Bruxelles and Editions de l'Institut de Sociologie, 1962).

27. A few years later an offshoot of this genre will give rise to one of the first great filmic analyses: that of Stanley Kubrick's *2001: A Space Odyssey*, "essai d'analyse d'un mythe cinématographique," by two ethnologists, Jean Monod and Jean-Paul Dumont, in the vein of Claude Lévi-Strauss's work on myths in *Le foetus astral* (Paris: Christian Bourgois, 1970). Excerpts (pp. 1–38, 149–64) translated by Susan Thomas as "Beyond the Infinite: A Structural Analysis of *2001: A Space Odyssey*," *Quarterly Review of Film Studies* 3.3 (1978): 297–316.

28. Raver, "*Tu n'a rien vu à Hiroshima*," p. 17.

29. Michel Marie, "Description/analyse," *Ça cinéma* 7–8 (May 1975): 129–55.

30. Reprinted in Metz, *Essais*, pp. 39–93. Translated as "The Cinema: Language or Language System?" *Film Language*, pp. 31–91.

31. Raymond Bellour, "Pour une stylistique du film," *Revue d'esthétique* 19.2 (April–June 1966).

32. Christian Metz, *Langage et cinéma*, 2nd ed. (Paris: Editions Albatros, 1972). Translated by Donna Jean Umiker-Sebeok as *Language and Cinema* (The Hague: Mouton, 1974).

33. Thierry Kuntzel, "Le travail du film," *Communications* 19 (1972); translated by Larry Crawford, Kimball Lockhart, and Claudia Tysdal as "The Film-Work," *enclitic* 2.1 (Spring 1978). "Le travail du film 2," *Communications* 23 (1975): 136–89; translated by Nancy Huston as "The Film-Work 2," *Camera Obscura* 5 (Spring 1980): 7–69.

34. Christian Metz, "L'analyse syntagmatique de la bande-images" (in collaboration with Michèle Lacoste), *Image et son* 201 (January 1967); reprinted in *Essais*. Translated as "Syntagmatic Analysis of the Image Track," in *Film Language*, pp. 149–82.

35. It is this mode of operation that, following Metz's example, Adriano Aprà and Luigi Martelli will immediately try to put into play in their "Premesse sintagmatiche ad un analise di *Viaggio in Italia*," *Cinema e Film* 1–2 (Spring 1967), in enlarging the register of segmentation and thus proceeding toward an attempt at a global evaluation of Rossellini's film. See also "To Segment/To Analyze," chapter 5 in this volume, note 8.

36. Stephen Heath, "Narrative Space," *Screen* 17.3 (Fall 1976): 68–112.

37. Raymond Bellour, "Le monde et la distance," *Dictionnaire du cinéma* (Paris: Editions Universitaires, 1966) [reprinted in *L'analyse du film*].

38. [Editor's note]: On this point, see "System of a Fragment," chapter 2 in this volume.

39. Mallarmé to Valéry, when giving him *Un coup de dés*: "Don't you find it to be an act of madness?" Paul Valéry, "*Un coup de dés*," *Variété* II (Paris: Gallimard, 1930), p. 180.

40. Christian Metz, *Essais sur la signification au cinéma* II (Paris: Klincksieck, 1973). The ideas in the 1968 article can be found in chapter 2 of *Film Language*.

41. On the articulation between the semiology of cinema and filmic analysis in this first period, see my interview with Christian Metz, "Entretien sur la sémiologie du cinéma,"

Semiotica 4.5 (1971); reprinted in *Essais II* and in Raymond Bellour, *Le livre des autres* (Paris: 10/18, U.G.E., 1978).

42. Metz, *The Imaginary Signifier,* pp. 1–87.

43. Metz, translated by Celia Britton and Annwyl Williams as "Metaphor/Metonymy, or the Imaginary Referent," in *The Imaginary Signifier,* pp. 149–314.

44. Roger Odin, *Dix années d'analyses textuelles des films: Bibliographie analytique* (Lyon: Travaux du Centre de Recherches Linguistiques et Sémiotiques de Lyon 3, 1977).

45. Jacques Aumont and Michel Marie, *L'analyse des films* (Paris: Nathan, 1988).

46. [Editor's note]: See *Henri Michaux ou une mesure de l'être* (Paris: Gallimard, 1965), expanded edition, *Henri Michaux* (Paris: Folio Essais, 1986). See also the editions of Charlotte Brontë and Patrick Branwell Brontë, *Ecrits de jeunesse* (Paris: Pauvert, 1972); and of Emily Brontë, *Wuthering Heights* (Paris: Pauvert, 1972). See as well *Mademoiselle Guillotine: Caglistro, Dumas, Oedipe et la Révolution Française* (Paris: La Différance, 1989); special issue of *L'arc* on Alexandre Dumas 71 (1978).

47. See my study "Un jour, la castration," *L'arc* 71 (1978), special issue on Alexandre Dumas.

48. On the status of these operations, I would like to reprint on my own account—with every allowance made, and with the necessary omissions—the response given me by Lévi-Strauss during an interview in which I questioned him on the exact nature of the analytic operations of the *Mythologiques* and the eventual possibilities for a logico-mathematical formalization: "To establish transformational relations among myths, I perform a certain number of operations without knowing in reality what they are. I would very much like someone more competent than I in logic, someone with time to spare, to apply himself or herself to my work to try to determine the nature of these operations in an effort to classify them. I don't in fact know if they are all different from each other and therefore very numerous or if instead they are always the same and thus boil down to a small number of recurrent operations used as needed. If these operations are extremely numerous and if, in the end, there are as many operations as there are interpretations, they come down to a simple description—the material has merely been described in a language different from that in which it was formulated at the outset and no possibility for a logical treatment remains. On the other hand, if these operations are relatively less numerous than the cases in which they are used, we could say that we are faced with a logic defined by a set of rules and ask ourselves all sorts of problematic questions: Are these operations hierarchized? Does the use of an operation at a given moment entail the use of another operation at another moment? Can the recurrent rules of such a grammar be defined?" From "Entretien avec Claude Lévi-Strauss" in *Lévi-Strauss* (Paris: Gallimard, 1979), pp. 180–81.

49. *Le cinéma américain, analyses de films,* ed. Raymond Bellour (Paris: Flammarion, 1980).

50. See my "Entretien avec Claude Lévi-Strauss," p. 183.

51. Claude Bailblé, Michel Marie, Marie-Claire Ropars, *Muriel* (Paris: Galilée, 1974), pp. 195–263.

52. Marie-Claire Ropars, Pierre Sorlin, *Octobre, écriture et idéologie* (Paris: Editions Albatros, 1976), pp. 27–66.

53. Noël Burch, *To the Distant Observer* (Berkeley: University of California Press, 1979).

54. Pierre Sorlin, *Sociologie et cinéma* (Paris: Aubier, 1977).

55. Thierry Kuntzel, "Le défilement," *Revue d'esthétique,* special issue, *Cinéma: Théorie, lectures* (1971): 10. Translated by Bertrand Augst as "Le Défilement: A View in Close-up," *Camera Obscura* 2 (Fall 1977): 59.

56. "This other film . . . a film free from temporal constraints, where all the elements would be present at the same time . . . constantly referring to each other: intersecting, overlapping, regrouping in configurations 'never' seen or heard in the order of unreeling [du

défilement]." See Thierry Kuntzel, "Notes on the Filmic Apparatus," *Quarterly Review of Film Studies* 1.3 (August 1976): 27. The essay was never published in French.

57. See Kuntzel's discussion of Peter Foldes's *Appétit d'oiseau* in "Le défilement: A View in Close-up."

58. Bernhard Lindemann, *Experimental Film als Metafilm* (Hildesheim: Olms Verlag, 1977).

59. From the classical to the avant-garde film, within each of these overly broad categories and along the curve that ideally leads from one to the other, we of course find only cases of the sort that each demand an appropriate strategy. For example, the group (Dominique Chateau, François Jost, Olivier Veillon, André Gardies) that have been working for several years on the films of Alain Robbe-Grillet find themselves confronted with the problem of representational seriality determined by the global function of a "dysnarration." See *Cinémas de la modernité: Films, théories*, Colloque de Cerisy Conference Proceedings, ed. Dominique Chateau, André Gardies, François Jost (Paris: Klincksieck, 1981). Dominique Chateau and François Jost, *Nouveau cinéma, nouvelle sémiologie: Essai d'analyse des films d'Alain Robbe-Grillet* (Paris: Union Génerale d'Editions, 1979).

60. See my article "Images sur l'image," *Nouvelle revue française* 157 (January 1966).

61. The work group "Atelier Critique" was formed in 1976 under the auspices of the *Institut National de l'Audiovisuel* and the direction of Thierry Kuntzel. It is oriented in part toward analytic productions of this order, from the starting point of a group reflection on the relations between the different arts and the audiovisual.

For his own part, Noël Burch made a film in 1980 on the genealogy of cinematic language: *Correction Please or How to Get Into Pictures*, produced by The Arts Council of Great Britain.

62. *Artsept* 1, 2, 3 (Lyon 1963).

1. The Unattainable Text

1. Roland Barthes, "De l'oeuvre au texte," *Revue d'esthetique* 3 (1971). Translated by Richard Howard as "From Work to Text," in *Roland Barthes: The Rustle of Language* (Berkeley: University of California Press, 1989).

2. "The text participates in its way in a social utopia; before History (supposing that History does not choose barbarism), the Text fulfills if not the transparency of social relations, at least the transparency of language relations: it is the space in which no language prevails over any other, where the languages circulate (retaining the *circular* meaning of the word). . . . A theory of the Text cannot be satisfied with a meta-linguistic exposition; the destruction of meta-language, or at least (for it may be necessary to resort to it provisionally) calling it into question, is part of the theory itself: discourse on the Text should itself be only text, research, textual activity, since the Text is that *social* space which leaves no language safe, outside, and no subject of the speech-act in a situation of judge, master, analyst, confessor, decoder: the theory of the Text can coincide only with a practice of writing" (Barthes, "From Work to Text," p. 64).

2. System of a Fragment

*This essay is the only one whose title I have changed from the original ("*Les Oiseaux*: Analyse d'une séquence" [*The Birds*: Analysis of a Sequence]). For one thing, I did not want to repeat the word "analysis." For another, I wanted to retrospectively situate in a more exact fashion the status of the piece of film analyzed (on the term "fragment," see the introduction to this volume, "A Bit of History," note 6). I have not, on the other hand, with respect to this any more than to any other chapter, changed anything in the text: one can find in the "Preliminaries" section a trace of my earlier doubts about the designation of this fragment.

Then again, I have already mentioned in the introduction that Ben Brewster, my English translator, and Phil Hardy, the editor of a collection on Alfred Hitchcock from the British Film Institute, had pointed out some factual errors; I thank them for their vigilance. They made me aware of a certain number of variations between my shot breakdown (based on the final shot breakdown of the distribution company) and their own observations on the viewing table, which I have since been able to verify. These differences bear essentially on some shots that I described as static and that they showed to have more or less pronounced camera movements. This has very little effect on the overall interpretation, except for one point where it would have facilitated my argument. There are several cases that represent more a matter of reframing than of camera movement proper (it is a difficult distinction that any precise analysis needs to account for, even if this is perhaps one of the limits of analysis).

I have, of course, reestablished the exact script, corrected the chart of shot descriptions, and modified the text where it was only a matter of perfunctory remarks. The shot size descriptions are taken from the original Universal Studios shooting script given to me by François Truffaut. [Editor's note: All dialogue has been checked against the film for the English book.] For the rest, I have preferred to add explanatory notes rather than to rework, for minimal benefits, a text that was tightly wrought. Nonetheless, I found it worthwhile to note the extent to which film commentary is based on paradoxical attention, always haunted by the possibility of error.

1. [Translator's note]: The word "désir" here as elsewhere in the text translates Freud's "Wunsch." Hence, in English it should be given as "wish." However the different connotations acquired by the word in French translation force me to translate it as "desire." Other Freudian terms used by Bellour have been translated by their standard English equivalents, except for "denegation," Freud's "Verneinung," usually translated into English as "negation"; I have translated it as "denegation" because of the special use made of the term by Lacan, on whom Bellour is drawing.

2. On the ambiguities of the definition of the shot, see Jean Mitry, *Esthetique et psychologie du cinéma*, I: *Les structures* (Paris: Editions Universitaires, 1963), pp. 149–65; translated by Christopher King from the abridged edition (1990) as *The Aesthetics and Psychology of the Cinema* (Bloomington: Indiana University Press, 1997), pp. 59–72. And see Raymond Bellour, "Pour une stylistique du film," *Revue d'esthetique* 19.2 (April–June 1966), pp. 161–78. See especially p. 168.

3. Metz, *Essais*, pp. 125–33, 146 [*Film Language*, pp. 119–37].

4. In fact shot 33 is not strictly a static one, since a very short pan leads us from Melanie's hand to the lovebirds' cage. This may slightly affect the purity of the demonstration; yet here again we should be clear that oppositions are not absolute but rather established from term to term: the shot moves infinitely less than those that surround it, and the maintenance of the alternation is highly connoted in spite of that movement.

5. Let me correct straightaway an error whose consequences certainly did not facilitate this analysis and that affects both the division into series and many of my comments. Shot 24, which reveals the dock at the Brenners' house, is indisputably a forward traveling shot and not a static shot. Rather than beginning the series A2 at shot 24 to retain a clear opposition between a series of static shots and a series of moving shots (at the risk of creating a contrast with A4, whose folding onto A2 is strict, even to the number of shots), we should register here an asymmetry between A1 and A5, the effect of which becomes productive only much later at shot 73. (See note 13 below.) Whatever it is, it is finally a matter of analytic strategies and not anything that affects the work of the system, its "truth," even if one can imaginarily reestablish it by rereading some of the discrepancies.

Two very slight corrections should be made to the description of series A1 and A5. Shots

20 and 44 are not truly static. In both shots the camera briefly follows Mitch's movement from left to right to reframe him, thus establishing a differentiated mini-symmetry in these two series of static shots.

6. This is also true for groups A2 and A4, admittedly in spite of an inversion in the direction of the movement, backwards in one case, forwards in the other, which thus shows Melanie from the front and from the back in turn, so that her look is directed to her right in the first case and to her left in the second, over her shoulder. The inversion subtly marks the difference in the heart of a similarity, and thus serves to announce the ever present possibility of asymmetry even in the strictest symmetry.

7. It should be noted that this final rupture is established by the same criterion as the rupture that introduced B3 in shot 60. Mitch leaves the screen to the right in shot 71, in a car this time, as he left shot 59 to the right, running toward the car. The rupture is just as delicate: in the first case it divides the double smile of Melanie and Mitch, in the second, the series of close-ups of Melanie (70–76).

8. It is easy to see how much this claim, and those that follow, are reinforced by the fact that shots 69 and 71, especially the latter, are moving rather than static, as I first thought: series B3 is thus found to rhyme all the more with series A5–B1 and with series A2 and A4, which underline Melanie's advance with camera movement—without this removing, of course, any of the relief obtained from the opposition static in the shot/movement within the shot. This return to the alternation static/movement at the end of a series provides, on the other hand, a transition to shots 72–75—the period of the arrival.

9. The preciseness of the opposition is such that one could specify it even more. The boat moves more in shots 60–62, when Melanie leaves, than in the following series; these two shots alternate with shots 61–63, where Mitch's movement is more accentuated, in particular through the pan in shot 63. One can see here, in the example of this detail, how the oppositions are marked more by the maintenance of a relation than by fixed terms.

10. This dissymmetry was caused by a first rupture, not emphasized earlier (for the sake of not overly complicating the analysis at the start), between series A2 and A4.

11. With the exception, let us recall, of shots 60 and 62 (see note 9 above).

12. In fact there are at least two other fishermen who, in shot 5, watch Melanie moving onto the pier before she talks to the one who rents her the boat. Announcing the latter's interrogation, and on the other hand referring to the fisherman at the end so as to balance the symmetry fisherman/Mitch, they give this micro-structure, so to speak, its full complement of elements.

13. Let us not forget in what follows that shot 24, as mentioned in note 5 above, is a moving and not a fixed shot; this undoubtedly changes the order of reasons, but only to make them more manifest insofar as the symmetry between shots 74 and 73, which is obvious at the level of the plot, is reinforced in the form and the image and facilitates the operations of synthesis between series A1, A2, A4, A5 and shots 72–75.

14. It has been rightly pointed out to me that Melanie does not see the gull and therefore does not show any terror but has the same vague expression we have already seen her with twice at the beginning of the film, with men: Mitch and the occupant of the apartment across from his. Here, as other similar attempts since have proved to me, it is necessary to complicate the analysis between the alternation seeing/seen and the alternation seeing/unseen, which simultaneously prolongs it and sidesteps it, in short, takes its place. Even more stress would thus have to be put on the misrecognition of desire, hence its displacement, and the transition to the symbolic. On the other hand, this non-vision from 76–77 allows the direct articulation of these two shots with center A, even before this is made possible by shots 81–82 (identical with respect to the fragmentation of Melanie's body, opposed with respect to her vision).

15. Here shot 63 had to carry too much weight in the condensation operation, but the movements in shots 69 and 71 (see note 8 above) make it more manifest.

16. Let us note that this movement already shows a difference from that found in the series that surrounds it or in the shots at the very center, from the movement in shot 34: here the camera lies in wait for Melanie, and its movement controls the movement of the actor more than the actor controls it.

17. On this topic, see note 4 above on shot 33.

18. See note 14 above.

3. The Obvious and the Code

1. Bellour and Metz, "Entretien sur la sémiologie du cinéma," p. 10. For more detailed discussion, see Metz, *Essais II,* pp. 130–31.

2. [Editor's note]: See chapter 5, "To Segment/To Analyze," in this volume.

3. On this point, see the valuable distinctions established by Metz in "Ponctuations et démarcations dans le film de diégèse," *Essais II,* especially pp. 126–29. At the time, I had not clearly seen that the three criteria proposed by Metz in this article as instruments of delimitation for the autonomous segment (i.e., a change in syntagmatic type, in punctuation, in diegetic unity) in fact aim primarily at strictly specifying what I call textual unity here. The reason for this, it seems to me, is that in numerous cases the third criterion—strong but imprecise—must be the object of divisions inherent in its very definition, in order to respond to the complexity of textual arrangements. I address this problem in "To Segment/To Analyze." In fact, this segment of *The Big Sleep* unites all three of Metz's criteria of demarcation and corresponds, in part from this very fact, to the notion of minimal segmental unity as I have described it in my analysis of *Gigi* (even though, in a sense, the segmentation never stops performing a textual mise-en-abîme in relation to itself).

4. Metz, "Ponctuations et démarcations," *Essais II,* pp. 120–21.

5. Jacques Rivette, "Genie de Howard Hawks," *Cahiers du cinéma* 23 (May 1953): 16; translated by Russell Campbell and Marvin Pister as "The Genius of Howard Hawks," adapted from a translation by Adrian Brine in *Cahiers du cinéma: The 1950s,* ed. Jim Hillier (Cambridge, Mass.: Harvard University Press, 1985), pp. 126–31.

6. On this opposition between specific and non-specific codes and the correlative ideas cinema/film, see Metz's book *Langage et cinéma* (*Language and Cinema*). Following on Metz (see particularly pp. 169–80 in the French version, pp. 224–40 in the English), one might bring in here the notion of degree of specificity to establish a gradation between the specific codes: only the static/moving code is specific in an absolute way here. The pictorial arts have variations in scale and in angle, although within a radically different extension of the notion of a work or of textual closure. Film contains them within itself (except a film made up of a single shot filmed from a fixed camera position and without internal variation among the subjects filmed, in other words, almost a non-film), whereas it requires several paintings, etchings, or photographs to constitute an equivalent variability. It is in this sense that the frame, while it is the smallest unit into which the filmic chain can be broken down, cannot be retained as a pertinent unit for the theory of cinema and film analysis except at the cost of prior loss of the notion of specificity.

7. Note here the difficulty sometimes encountered in making clear distinctions. At a viewing, even a viewing slowed down by a projector that allows for reduction in speed, shot 11 appears to be silent, following a cut on Marlowe's admission, "I guess I am in love with you." On the viewing table, on the other hand, the "you" seems fairly clearly to straddle the two shots. This effect is certainly not negligible since it was intended in the editing and it accentuates the motivational relation in the succession of the two shots. It suggests once again the need to question the theoretical status of all that is only clearly apparent on the level of the frame.

8. A distinction needs to be made here between these two methods of balance, which correspond to each other and support each other, both equally aimed at giving the illusion of naturalness by the regulated control of artifice. While both are *codified*, to the degree demanded by the need to produce the illusion, only the first is *coded*, that is, capable of formulation into relatively strict systematic relationships. This is why the playing of the actors or the arrangements of tones in the image, which express themselves in the first case in terms of gestural dynamics and in the second in terms of intensity of light, resist analysis, which inversely finds its chosen ground in the coded or codable elements (to stress clearly its character as a construction). It should be added that what falls to a greater extent into the codified in one instance may in another instance fall to a greater extent into the coded: for example, the arrangement of lighting and certain features of the actors playing in certain German Expressionist films.

Thierry Kuntzel rightly pointed out to me that in this analysis I had underestimated the possibility of a codic differentiation at the level of the lighting. He had been struck by the fact that the light is diffused in a way that is both more intense and more enveloping on Vivian's face. This is true, even if the frame enlargements only half show it. Hence, the possibility, in my table, of a seventh column (g), giving a + to the close-ups of Vivian. This is surely a redoubling of the emphasis on the idealization of the woman, articulated in this, in the codes, in the changes in the camera angles, by presence or absence in dialogue and image, and in relation to the avowal of love and to the action.

4. Symbolic Blockage

1. Jean Domarchi and Jean Douchet, "Entretien avec Alfred Hitchcock," *Cahiers du cinéma* 102 (December 1959): 24.

2. See Jacques Lacan, *Ecrits* (Paris: Seuil, 1966). Translated by Alan Sheridan as *Ecrits* (New York: W. W. Norton, 1977). In particular, see "Of a Question Preliminary to All Possible Treatment of Psychosis." See as well Guy Rosolato, *Essais sur le symbolique* (Paris: N.R.F., 1970), especially "Du Père" and "Trois générations d'hommes dans le mythe religieux et la généalogie."

3. "Story" *(histoire)* and "narrative" *(récit)* are used here in the sense given them by Gérard Genette in *Figures III* (Paris: Seuil, 1972), p. 72.

4. See note 2 above.

5. "This term, borrowed from English, suggests a bit more than does '*rétorsion*' or '*représailles*'; it evokes the *lex talionis* ("fear of retaliation") that presides over the fantasmatic fears described by Melanie Klein and the English school" (Rosolato, *Essais*, p. 69).

6. François Truffaut, *Le cinéma selon Alfred Hitchcock* (Paris: Laffont, 1966), p. 77. Translated as *Hitchcock* (New York: Simon and Schuster, 1984), p. 107.

7. Lacan, *Ecrits*, p. 782.

8. Lacan, *Ecrits*, p. 785.

9. "Are the 'names of history' derivatives of the name of the father, and are the races, cultures, and continents substitutes for daddy-mommy, dependent on the Oedipal genealogy? Is history's signifier the dead father?" Gilles Deleuze and Félix Guattari, *L'Anti-Œdipe* (Paris: Minuit, 1972), p. 106. Translated by Robert Hurley, Mark Seem, and Helen R. Lane as *Anti-Oedipus* (Minneapolis: University of Minnesota Press, 1983), p. 89.

10. "Medusa's Head" in *The Standard Edition of the Complete Psychological Works of Sigmund Freud*, vol. 18 (London: Hogarth, 1955), pp. 273–74.

11. Peter Bogdanovich, *The Cinema of Alfred Hitchcock* (New York: Museum of Modern Art Library, 1963), p. 41; Truffaut, *Le cinéma selon Alfred Hitchcock*, pp. 102–73.

12. See Lacan, *Ecrits*, in particular "Seminar on 'The Purloined Letter.'" See also *Le mythe individuel du névrosé* (Paris: Centre de Documentation Universitaire, 1955); Gilles

Deleuze, *Logique du sens* (Paris: Minuit, 1969), pp. 264–72, translated as *The Logic of Sense* (New York: Columbia University Press, 1990), pp. 226–33; and idem, "A quoi reconnaît-on le structuralisme?" in *Histoire de la philosophie, le XXᵉ siècle* (Paris: Hachette-Littérature, 1973), pp. 326–30.

13. "I found I was faced with the old cliché situation: the man who is put on the spot, probably to be shot. Now, how is it usually done? A dark night at a narrow intersection of the city. The waiting victim stands in a pool of light under the street lamp. The cobbles are 'washed with the recent rains.' A close-up of a black cat slinking along against the wall of a house. A shot of a window, with a furtive face pulling back the curtain to look out. The slow approach of a black limousine, et cetera, et cetera. Now, what was the antithesis of a scene like this? No darkness, no pool of light, no mysterious figures in windows. Just nothing. Just bright sunshine and a blank, open countryside with barely a house or tree in which any lurking menaces could hide" (from Truffaut, *Hitchcock*, p. 256).

14. The letters *a* and *b* denote the two halves of the shot, its beginning and its end, symbolically defined by the first and last frames of each shot (in the print I worked on).

15. [Editor's note]: For the first English-language translation of "Symbolic Blockage" for this book, Ben Brewster made a new correlation between French terms for shot scale and their English equivalents in an attempt to establish some finer distinctions. The table below gives Bellour's terms, their translations in this essay (with abbreviations), and a rough definition. Because the shot scale descriptions in the other chapters are internally coherent and perfectly serviceable, no attempt has been made to go back and redo them to fit this later, more detailed system.

Plan général	Extreme long shot (ELS)	Character dwarfed in landscape
Demi-plan général	Very long shot (VLS)	Character half frame height
Plan moyen	Long shot (LS)	Character about frame height
Plan américain	Medium long shot (MLS)	Character framed from knees up
Plan rapproché	Medium shot (MS)	Character framed from waist up
Plan très rapproché	Medium close-up (MCU)	Character's head and shoulders
Gros plan	Close-up (CU)	Character's face alone
Très gros plan (insert)	Big close-up (BCU)	Less than the whole face

16. It is difficult to describe the framing of shot 73 exactly: a little wider than that of 72, if only to allow the conjunction with the airplane, but at the same time giving the movement of Thornhill's body (lying against the mound in 73b), an impression of proximity that connects it to shot 72.

17. John Buchan, *The Thirty-Nine Steps* (London: Blackwood, 1915), p. 106.

18. Truffaut, *Hitchcock*, p. 319.

19. In French, the "scénario-itinéraire" (Truffaut, *Hitchcock*, p. 145).

20. Truffaut, *Hitchcock*, p. 319.

21. Alfred Hitchcock quoted in Bogdanovich, *The Cinema of Alfred Hitchcock*, p. 41.

22. I did not realize how near the mark I was. Since writing this, I have learned from two anglophone students that this seemingly meaningless title is probably an echo of one of the most famous lines produced by Hamlet's feigned madness: "I am but mad north-north-west: when the wind is southerly, I know a hawk from a hand-saw!"; and subsequently I learned that this line was cited by Freud in *The Interpretation of Dreams* (*Standard Edition*, vol. 5, p. 444) as an illustration of the rationality of the unreason at stake in the dream work. A sign in support of everything that leads, in Freud as well as Ernest Jones, from Hamlet to Oedipus.

23. Truffaut, *Hitchcock*, p. 257.

24. *Cahiers du cinéma* 24.

25. Bogdanovich, *The Cinema of Alfred Hitchcock*, p. 41.

26. On the *dispositif*, see Jean-Louis Baudry, "Le dispositif," *Communication* 23 (1975),

special issue on cinema and psychoanalysis, ed. Raymond Bellour, Thierry Kuntzel, and Christian Metz; translated by Jean Andrews and Bertrand Augst as "The Apparatus," *Camera Obscura* 1 (Fall 1976). On the scopic drive and the primal scene, see Christian Metz, "The Imaginary Signifier." On their relation to the theater and to representation, see Thierry Kuntzel, "The Film-Work 2."

5. To Segment/To Analyze

1. Metz, "Cinéma: Langue ou langage?" *Essais,* pp. 39–93. Translated as "The Cinema: Language or Language System?" *Film Language,* pp. 31–91. See also, in *Essais II,* Bellour and Metz, "Entretien sur la sémiologie du cinéma," pp. 203–204.

2. Metz, *Essais,* pp. 134–35 [*Film Language,* pp. 134–35].

3. Metz, *Essais II,* "Entretien sur la sémiologie du cinéma," p. 206.

4. Metz, *Essais,* p. 164 [*Film Language,* p. 164, note].

5. "A purely logical entry which, by itself, does not take place in the film; . . . in this code of the large syntagmatic category, the distinctive units do not consist of filmic segments, but of sorts of abstract exponents each of which is attached to a filmic segment" (*Langage et cinéma,* p. 152; *Language and Cinema,* pp. 201–202). Compare also, "The autonomous segment is not a unit 'of the film,' but a unit of one of the systems of the film" (*Langage et cinéma,* p. 143 [*Language and Cinema,* p. 190, note 8]).

6. Metz, "Ponctuations et démarcations," *Essais II,* p. 129.

7. I have in mind here the works of Adriano Aprà and Luigi Martelli on *Viaggio in Italia,* "Premesse sintagmatiche ad un'analisi di *Viaggio in Italia,*" *Cinema e Film* 1–2 (Spring 1967); Jean-Claude Bernardet on the Brazilian film "São Paulo," sociedade anonima (see Metz, "A significaçào uo cinema," São Paolo, 1972); Jens Toft on *Battleship Potemkin* ("Christian Metz og Eisenstein," *Exil* 7.1 [October 1973]); Geneviève Jacquinot on the didactic film (*Image et pédagogie* [Paris: P.U.F., 1977]; Francis Ramirez and Christian Rollot on the films of the modern French comedy school; and the more partial utilizations of the grande syntagmatique by Roger Odin on a part of Grémillon's *Gardiens de phare:* "Sémiologie et analyse de film: lecture de codes," *Travaux de linguistique* 11 (Editions de l'Université de Saint-Etienne, 1972); John Ellis on *Passport to Pimlico:* "Made in Ealing," *Screen* 16.1 (1975); and Stephen Heath, "Film and System: Terms of Analysis" on *Touch of Evil* in *Screen* 16.1 (1975).

8. This is the case in my own work. See, in this volume, chapter 2, "System of a Fragment" and chapter 3, "The Obvious and the Code" (even if, in the second case, the appropriateness of the criteria of the grande syntagmatique posed no problem since it was so clearly a "scene"). See also Kuntzel, "The Film-Work."

9. For example, Kari Hanet, "The Narrative Text of *Shock Corridor,*" *Screen* 15.4 (1974/75), and Kuntzel, "The Film-Work 2."

10. Monod and Dumont, *Foetus astral.*

11. The editors of *Cahiers du cinéma* 223 (August–September 1970). Translated by Helen Lackner and Diana Matias as "John Ford's *Young Mr. Lincoln,*" *Screen* 13.3 (Fall 1972).

12. Bailblé, Marie, and Ropars, *Muriel.*

13. See Heath, "Film and System."

14. "Symbolic Blockage" [see chapter 4 in this volume].

15. Note on the segmentation, p. 15. Stephen Heath's study is nevertheless the only one that clearly poses, particularly in its first parts, certain of the problems I have raised here with respect to the validity of the criteria for the application of the grande syntagmatique. And in a very precise way he also notes the codic-textual specificity that binds the segmental level to the question of alternation.

16. Roland Barthes, "Par ou commencer?" *Poetique* 1 (1970). Translated by Richard Howard as "Where to Begin," in *New Critical Essays* (New York: Hill and Wang, 1980).

17. Metz, *Essais*, p. 164 [*Film Language*, p. 164, note].

18. I have since recognized that my use of the word "alternation" mixes some configurations which, although they are determined by a unique principle (that one could call the *principle of alternation*), are nonetheless extremely differentiated in their nature and scope. Thus the relative enumerative vacuity of this paragraph, whose meaning would have rested on an internal evaluation of the different segments concerned and on the multiple levels in which the alternation is inscribed (demonstrating this functioning would involve, moreover, a considerable augmentation of the number of segments concerned: in the end, almost all, with the exception of the autonomous shots).

These marginal, self-critical and problematic remarks by Metz (see above, pp. 194–95) emphasize the determining importance of alternation, a basic structure in cinematographic language that inevitably intersects segmentation. I intend to return to this point in a future work. [Editor's note: That "future work" was "To Alternate/To Narrate," chapter 8 of this book. Another notable discussion of alternation is the section "Alterner" in "Le cinéma et . . . ," in *L'entre-images 2: Mots, images*. In this essay, Bellour analyzes the greater speed of alternation that is possible in video, here Jean-Luc Godard's *Puissance de la parole* (25", 1988). He also shows, once again, the degree to which alternation is founded on the difference between the sexes. "Le cinéma et . . ." was translated as "Cinema and . . . ," in *Semiotica* 112-1/2 (1996), special issue on Christian Metz, guest editor Lisa Block de Behar.

19. Only the punctuation mark, when it is demarcatory, constitutes a pertinence of the same order as the syntagmatic type, because it participates in a specific code (the straight cut is obviously part of that code when it can be substituted for the punctuation mark). See Metz, *Essais II*, pp. 122–24.

20. "It seeks not the shot, *but the sequence*, which is a permanent concern and problem: actions, epochs, landscapes, must be distributed and organized over the totality of the film: regroupings both superior to the shot (= unit of shooting) and inferior to the *work* (the maximal unit) must be established" (Metz, *Essais II*, pp. 120–21).

21. In their syntagmatic analysis of *Viaggio in Italia*, Adriano Aprà and Luigi Martelli have very carefully noted the need for complementary segmentations: one at the superior or "structural" level, constituting units that they call *ciné-périodo* (after the cine-phrase adopted by the Russian formalists); the other at the inferior level, called "grammatical" (through an odd abuse of words current for a few years in Italy). But in spite of everything they essentially retain Metz's autonomous segments and compromise their work of decomposition and preanalysis largely by the distinction they make between the grammatical and the structural, which avoids the fundamental problem of the single and plural (i.e., textual) articulation of the different levels of description possible.

22. Metz, *Film Language*, p. 181.

23. By "large film sections" I mean the higher units that correspond more or less to acts in a play or the parts, sections, etc., of a novel: they are diversely materialized, through time in a theatrical representation and through white spaces and titles in a written text. The classical film contains few of these sharp divisions, which it traditionally reinscribes in the apparently seamless continuity of the image-track. But they are not less significant for that, more or less, depending on the film: in many films, these large sections tend to overlap, through a sort of indecision, a floating, largely due to the linking effects proper to representational continuity; in other films, conversely, they markedly cut up the large successive moments of an action whose linearity is affected above all by the fundamental fact that every classic narrative constitutes, first and foremost, a volume.

This is the case in *Gigi*, where one can clearly distinguish five parts (entered in the far right of the table), which can be diegetically summarized as follows: A. Introduction: Gigi and Gaston, Gaston and Liane; B. Gaston and Liane: their relationship, their breakup; C. Gaston and Gigi: the beginnings of love; D. Gigi takes Liane's place; E. From mistress to wife.

In this scenario, segment 47 poses an unusual problem. In fact, it seems to be an epilogue, and the virtual time that separates it from the rest of the film tends to distinguish it from the rest. On the other hand, it is by no means a "large film section," superior to a group of segments. On the contrary, it is in fact a very short segment. This frequent example shows very well how, in any classifying operation, at a certain point criteria are too exclusive or distinctions become blurred. This is to the text's credit and is due to its nature as a mobile volume. In this case we must consider this epilogue as a separate part and as the end of the fifth part. In fact, the argument for including it there, despite insurmountable contradictions, is that it preserves the vibrant unity of narrative condensation between the first four sections and the fifth.

24. Metz, *Essais II*, p. 127.

25. And all the episodic sequences except segment 35, whose bastardized character I have underlined.

26. At this level, the specific pertinence established between the segments by the differences between the syntagmatic types is displaced in the form of an opposition between segment and sub-segment (with, as we have just seen, the intermediary case of sub-segments constituted by the episodes of episodic sequences).

27. With one exception, 43a. This clearly underlines the way that from the moment the breakdown becomes textual, it is constantly opening up depths. To avoid being inaccurate I did not wish to credit Gaston alone with segment 43, in which he brings Gigi and Mamita into one shot; on the other hand, in order to be exact, I ought to have divided sub-segment 43a again into two sub-segments, Gigi-Gaston and Gigi-Gaston-Mamita, which would be perfectly practicable for numerous other scenes.

28. This is quite striking for the set of segments that rest totally or in part on alternations of a more or less structuring kind at various levels. By definition, they impel more strongly than the rest toward an approximation that can only be broken down by a deeper sub-segmentation.

29. The first figures in the summary table along with the other operations, to show that what is involved is always only the same operation displaced. I have not included the second, more complex example that can be described by analysis alone.

30. Metz, *Essais*, pp. 138–40 [*Film Language*, pp. 137–40].

31. See note 18 above.

6. To Enunciate

1. Truffaut, *Hitchcock*. Throughout this essay, page numbers following quotations refer to this book.

2. For a much more phenomenological version of this preoccupation, see my "Le monde et la distance."

3. André Malraux, *Esquisse d'une psychologie du cinéma* (Paris: Gallimard, 1946).

4. Jacques Lacan, *Les quatre concepts fondamentaux de la psychanalyse* (Paris: Seuil, 1973), p. 107. Translated by Alan Sheridan as *The Four Fundamental Concepts of Psychoanalysis* (New York: W. W. Norton, 1978), p. 118.

5. For more information about the director's working methods, see, in the special issue on Hitchcock, "Hitchcock at Work," *Take One* 5.50 (May 1976).

6. [Editor's note]: For further discussions of this principle, see in this book chapter 2,

"System of a Fragment"; chapter 5, "To Segment/To Analyze"; and chapter 4, "Symbolic Blockage."

7. [Editor's note]: The effect of "symbolic blockage" is discussed fully in this book (see chapter 4).

8. [Translator's note]: There is a discrepancy between the text quoted by Bellour in French and the English translation. The French text reads: "Immédiatement, j'ai dit: 'je prends ça,' car je savais que la-dessus je pouvais naviguer" (Truffaut, *Hitchcock*, p. 209). The English translation does not suggest that he could take advantage of the script's weaknesses. The French version does imply very strongly that Hitchcock accepted the script based on the play because he could do something with the play *Dial M for Murder*, which was a big hit. This means that, unlike the other script he was working on at the time, which was called "The Bramble Bush," the play was better suited for what he wanted to do at that time.

9. On the Holy Trinity, and the exclusion of the Holy Virgin whose repressed representation is assumed by the Holy Spirit in the interplay of Oedipal events, see the remarkable analyses by Ernest Jones in *Essays of Applied Psychoanalysis* (London: International Psychoanalytical Press, 1923), in particular "The Madonna's Conception." It should be understood that its significance must be seen in the perspective of a history of representations, in which psychoanalysis provides only the principle of explanation (an interpretation) to the extent that it is also historically, epistemologically, explained and understood. On all these points, see my "Un jour, la castration."

10. For a discussion of this sequence from *The Birds*, see chapter 2 in this volume, "System of a Fragment."

7. Psychosis, Neurosis, Perversion

1. Truffaut, *Hitchcock*, p. 269. Throughout this essay, page numbers following quotations refer to this book.

2. On the relationship between the film and the original narrative, see James Naremore, *Filmguide to Psycho* (Bloomington: Indiana University Press, 1973), pp. 23–24, 33–34. I found in this short essay, after having written a first, summary version of the present essay ("Psycho," *Dossiers du cinéma*, *Films II* (Paris: Casterman, 1972), several observations along the same lines as my analysis.

Some of the elements organized around Marion during the first section of the narrative appear, in Bloch's novel, as mental flashbacks to scenes that comprise, in Hitchcock's film, the second section.

3. Syntagmatic change, punctuation, diegetic unity. See Metz, "Ponctuations et démarcations," pp. 126–28. On this point, see also my study of Minnelli's *Gigi*, in "To Segment/To Analyze" (chapter 5 in this volume).

4. Sheriff Chambers expresses this in two sentences, the second of which closes the scene on a note of horror: "Norman Bates's mother has been dead and buried in Greenlawn Cemetery for the past ten years." "Well, if that woman up there is Mrs. Bates, who's that woman buried out in Greenlawn Cemetery?"

5. Sigmund Freud, "Loss of Reality in Neurosis and Psychosis" (1904), *Standard Edition*, vol. 19, pp. 183–87.

6. Freud, "Loss of Reality in Neurosis and Psychosis," p. 183.

7. *Marion*: Oh, Sam, I hate having to be with you in a place like this.
    Sam: I've heard of married couples who deliberately spend an occasional night in a cheap hotel.
    Marion: Oh, when you're married you can do a lot of things deliberately.
    Sam: You sure talk like a girl who's been married.
    Marion: Sam, this is the last time.

Sam: Yeah? For what?

Marion: For this. For meeting you in secret—so we can be secretive. You come down here on business trips and we steal lunch hours and I wish you wouldn't even come. . . .

Sam: I sweat to pay off my father's debts and he's in his grave. I sweat to pay my ex-wife's alimony, and she's—living on the other side of the world somewhere!

Marion: I pay, too. They also pay who meet in hotel rooms.

Sam: A couple of years and *my* debts will be paid off and, if she ever remarries, the alimony stops.

Marion: I haven't even been married once yet!

Sam: Yeah, but when you do you'll swing!

Marion: Oh, Sam, let's get married!

8. It might be added, for the pleasure of the "intertext," that the amount of money stolen by Marion ($40,000) is the same as the amount spent by Mark, in *Marnie*, on the wedding ring he offers Marnie. Moreover, this money was intended by the millionaire—who shows it off to Marion—for the purchase of a house as a wedding gift to his daughter.

9. *Norman's version:* Father's death when he was five. Some years later, his mother falls madly in love with a man who encourages her to build the motel. When he dies, the mother goes crazy.

Sheriff's version (emergence of the mystery in the middle of the third movement): Norman poisons the lover. The mother, in turn, poisons herself.

Psychiatrist's version (solution of the mystery): Norman poisons the lover and his mother.

10. J. Laplanche and J. B. Pontalis, *The Language of Psycho-Analysis* (New York: W. W. Norton, 1973), p. 309.

11. Hitchcock: "It also allows the viewer to become a Peeping Tom" (see Truffaut, *Hitchcock*, p. 266).

12. No contradiction is implied by the fact that in *Rope* it is a man who is being killed. Men, too, are killed in Hitchcock's films—and often—in more or less direct or displaced reference to the murder of the father. In *Rope*, the object of the murder may also be referred, in a complementary manner, to the virtually manifest homosexuality of the two murderers.

13. See "Symbolic Blockage," chapter 4 in this volume.

14. See Naremore, *Filmguide to Psycho*, p. 66.

15. *Sam: Well*, we could laze around here a while longer.

Marion: Checking out time is three p.m. Motels of this sort are not interested in you when you come in, but when your time is up.

16. Jacqueline Rose, "Paranoia and the Film System," *Screen* 17.4 (Winter 1976/77). [reprinted in *Feminism and Film Theory*, ed. Constance Penley (New York: BFI and Routledge, 1988)].

17. For an historical perspective on the symbolic constitution of the male subject, see my essay "Un jour, la castration."

18. See in particular "Perversions sexuelles," *Encyclopédie médico-chirurgicale* (Paris, 1968) 37392 CIO: 8–9.

19. Lacan, *Four Fundamental Concepts.*

20. Luce Irigaray, "Misère de la psychanalyse," *Critique* 365 (October 1977): 900. See also her *Ce sexe qui n'en est pas un* (Paris: Minuit, 1977), p. 25; translated by Catherine Porter with Carolyn Burke as *This Sex Which Is Not One* (Ithaca, N.Y.: Cornell University Press, 1985), pp. 25–26.

21. Guy Rosolato: "This perversion is practiced exclusively by men" (*Encyclopédie médico-chirurgicale* 9).

22. I owe this to the friendship of Thierry Kuntzel.

23. On the eye-phallus relationship, see Lacan, *Four Fundamental Concepts*, pp. 101–104.

24. In this regard, *Marnie* deals with the reappropriation of the image, whereas *Psycho* deals with its destruction. See "Hitchcock, the Enunciator," chapter 6 in this volume.

25. Kuntzel, "The Film-Work" and "The Film-Work 2." See also "To Enunciate" [chapter 6] and similar themes in my essays "System of a Fragment" [chapter 2], "Symbolic Blockage" [chapter 4], and "To Segment/To Analyze" [chapter 5], all in this volume.

26. Metz, "The Imaginary Signifier," p. 63.

27. Roger Dadoun, in the few suggestive lines devoted to *Psycho* in "Le fétichisme dans le film d'horreur," *Objets du fétichisme*, special issue of *Nouvelle revue de psychanalyse* 2 (Fall 1970): 238.

8. To Alternate/To Narrate

1. In Bellour, "To Segment/To Analyze," chapter 5 in this volume; and in "Alternation, Enunciation, Hypnosis: An Interview with Raymond Bellour," by Janet Bergstrom, *Camera Obscura* 3–4 (1979): 71–103.

2. *The Lonedale Operator*, Biograph Company, 1911; 998 feet (16'30" at 16 frames/second); Actors: Blanche Sweet (Telegraph Operator), Frank Grandon (Engineer).

WORKS BY RAYMOND BELLOUR

Books

Alexandre Astruc. Paris: Seghers, 1963

Henri Michaux ou une mesure de l'être. Paris: Gallimard, 1966 (expanded edition, *Henri Michaux,* "Folio Essais," 1986)

Les rendez-vous de Copenhague, novel. Paris: Gallimard, 1966

Le livre des autres, essays and interviews. Paris: L'Herne, 1971

Le livre des autres, interviews. Paris: 10/18, U.G.E., 1978

L'analyse du film. Paris: Editions Albatros, 1979 (reissue, Paris: Calmann-Lévy, 1995)

Mademoiselle Guillotine. Paris: La Différence, 1989

L'entre-images: Photo, cinéma, vidéo. Paris: La Différence, 1990

Oubli, texts. Paris: La Différence, 1992

L'entre-images 2: Mots, images. Paris: P.O.L., 1999

Edited Volumes

Le Western. Paris: 10/18, U.G.E., 1966 (expanded edition, "Tel," Paris: Gallimard, 1993)

Henri Michaux. L'Herne, no. 8, 1966 (expanded edition, 1983)

Dictionnaire du cinéma. Paris: Editions Universitaires, 1966 (with Jean-Jacques Brochier)

Psychanalyse et cinéma. Communications, no. 23, 1975 (with Thierry Kuntzel and Christian Metz)

Lévi-Strauss. Paris: Gallimard, 1979 (with Catherine Clément)

Le cinéma américain: Analyses de film, two volumes. Paris: Flammarion, 1980

Vidéo, Communications, no. 48, 1988 (with Anne-Marie Duguet)

Cinéma et peinture: Approaches. Paris: Coliartco-PUF, 1990

Passages de l'image. Paris: Centre Georges-Pompidou, 1990 (with Catherine David and Christine van Assche)

Unspeakable Images, Camera Obscura, no. 24, 1991 (with Elisabeth Lyon)

Jean-Luc Godard: Son + Image. New York: MOMA, 1992 (with Mary Lea Bandy)

Critical Editions

Charlotte Brontë, Patrick Branwell Brontë, *Ecrits de jeunesse* (selected). Paris: Pauvert, 1972 (reissue, "Bouqins," Paris: Laffont, 1992)

Emily Brontë, *Wuthering Heights.* Paris: Pauvert, 1972; Hurlevent, "Folio." Paris: Gallimard, 1992

Alice James, *Journal et choix de lettres.* Paris: Café-Clima, 1984

Henri Michaux, *Oeuvres complètes,* "Bibliothéque de la Pléiade," volume 1. Paris: Gallimard, 1998 (with Ysé Tran)

—

INDEX

RAYMOND BELLOUR is Director of Research at the Centre National de la Recherche Scientifique. He is a scholar and writer whose work has been devoted to both literature—especially the Brontës, Dumas, and Michaux—and film—most notably *L'analyse du film,* first published in 1979, and several related collections including *Le cinéma américain* and *Le western.* Since the early eighties his work has concentrated on new media and the relation between words and images. This new focus has resulted in an exhibition, *Passages de l'image* (1989); books, *L'entre-images* (1990) and *L'entre-images 2* (1999); and a MOMA catalog, *Jean-Luc Godard: Son + Image* (1992). In 1991, with Serge Daney, he started the film journal *Trafic.*

CONSTANCE PENLEY is Professor and Chair of Film Studies at the University of California, Santa Barbara. A founding editor of the feminist media journal, *Camera Obscura,* she also edited the influential collection *Feminism and Film Theory.* Penley has written widely in the fields of media studies, cultural studies, and science studies. Her most recent books are *NASA/TREK: Popular Science and Sex in America* and *The Invisible Woman: Imaging Technologies, Gender, and Science,* edited with Paula Treichler and Lisa Cartwright.